# THE SOVIET UNION
## REVISED FOURTH EDITION

## VADIM MEDISH
The American University

PRENTICE HALL, Englewood Cliffs, New Jersey 07632

*Library of Congress Cataloging-in-Publication Data*
Medish, Vadim, [date]
  The Soviet Union / Vadim Medish.—Rev. 4th ed.
    p.  cm.
  Includes bibliographies and index.
  ISBN 0-13-818196-9
  1. Soviet Union.  I. Title
DK17.M4  1991
947—dc20                              90-7537
                                          CIP

Cover design: *Ben Santora*
Prepress buyer: *Debra Kesar*
Manufacturing buyer: *Mary Ann Gloriande*
Page layout: *Audrey Kopciak*

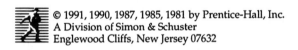
Printed in the United States of America
10  9  8  7  6  5  4  3  2  1

ISBN 0-13-818196-9

Prentice-Hall International (UK) Limited, *London*
Prentice-Hall of Australia Pty. Limited, *Sydney*
Prentice-Hall Canada Inc., *Toronto*
Prentice-Hall Hispanoamericana, S.A., *Mexico*
Prentice-Hall of India Private Limited, *New Delhi*
Prentice-Hall of Japan, Inc., *Tokyo*
Simon & Schuster Asia Pte. Ltd., *Singapore*
Editora Prentice-Hall do Brasil, Ltda., *Rio de Janeiro*

**TO RUTH**

# Contents

## CHAPTER THREE
## THE IDEOLOGY

## CHAPTER FOUR
## THE PARTY

## CHAPTER FIVE
## THE STATE

## CHAPTER SIX
## THE ECONOMY

## CHAPTER SEVEN
## SCIENCE AND TECHNOLOGY

## CHAPTER EIGHT
## THE EDUCATIONAL SYSTEM

## CHAPTER NINE
## THE MASS MEDIA

# Foreword

Only three decades ago, there was a dearth of published research on Russia. Today beginning students of Russia often have to cope with a reverse type of problem: deciding among numerous books on this subject readily available in stores and libraries. And yet, there continues to be a real need for good comprehensive texts on Russia, not just because of the constantly changing character of that huge country, but also because of some serious methodological problems involved in presenting a major foreign culture.

A natural tendency experienced by almost every student of a foreign language is to apply the familiar patterns of one's native tongue to the new verbal material at hand, which is an entirely different system of human communication. This so-called "negative transfer" can also be a serious impediment in understanding another culture as a whole. Moreover, a rational commitment to cultural relativity does not preclude a subliminal bias. One and the same nation may appear to outside observers, even the most scholarly writers, quite differently, depending on the prevailing opinions which are held of it at a given time.

In the case of Russian studies, this negative transfer is compounded by the fact that the Soviet Union claims and is perceived to be a challenge to the Western tradition. It may be said that, in a sense, all of our written research on Russia during the last seventy years has been done in the context of Lenin's famous definition of the meaning of the Soviet challenge: "Who will get whom." The ever-present challenge makes it difficult, if not outright impossible, not to take sides when discussing Russia.

As a byproduct of the Cold War, almost four decades of Russian studies were marked by still another peculiarity. Our books reflected an imbalance of emphasis on various aspects of the Soviet phenomenon: They stressed either that which was supposed to show the "clear and present danger" to the West or that which was believed to prove the existence of a "self-destruct mechanism" inherent in the Soviet system. As a result, the vast area of Soviet life that lies between the poles of strength and weakness received relatively little attention.

To be sure, many specialized studies of the selected aspects of the Soviet phenomenon are thorough, well documented, and detailed. But for a beginning reader on Russia they often present formidable problems. Firstly, there is the danger of following the example of the proverbial blind men who mistook parts of an elephant for the whole animal. Secondly, there is the problem of piecing together parts made on different scales, and even on improvising and filling in the missing components. On top of this, some of the best specialized studies utilize difficult technical terms perhaps unfamiliar to a general audience.

There are anthologies that try with varying degrees of success to present selected articles on different aspects as a comprehensive picture of the Soviet Union. Only a few of them, however, contain up-to-date information and well-selected topical discourses of even quality.

The most readable one-volume books on the Soviet Union as a whole are empirical accounts written by journalists. Based on first-hand information, personal impressions, and human interest stories, such books provide excellent background readings. Indeed, some of them offer a considerably more meaningful introduction to Soviet reality than can be expected of a typical tourist trip to the USSR. But all in all, such books are not designed for a systematic topical approach to the study of the USSR.

This revised fourth edition of *The Soviet Union*, like the earlier editions, is a book which tries, I think successfully, to combine the scholarly approach and objectivity with the realism of an eyewitness report. The result is a thorough and systematic survey of contemporary Russia, sufficiently detailed but not overburdened with theoretical arguments and value judgments. It is a welcome addition to the small number of comprehensive introductory texts currently available to beginning students of the Soviet Union.

*Victor Zorza*

# Preface

This new edition of *The Soviet Union*, resulting from the second major revision within the last three years, testifies to the rapidity of change in the Soviet Union and to the author's determination to provide the most up-to-date information on the subject. For several decades, it was more difficult to predict Russia's past, which was periodically rewritten to fit the fancies of Kremlin leaders, than to forecast the future of an allegedly perfect status quo over which they presided. Now, under Mikhail Gorbachev, whom *Time* has aptly called "an impresario of calculated disorder" (January 1, 1990), it is rather challenging to keep up with the ongoing changes and to make reliable predictions about the Soviet future.

Authors of many Western books about the Soviet Union, including this one, have been vindicated for having written what just a few years ago was denounced by Soviet critics as "libelous capitalist propaganda," but is now officially accepted as true. At the same time, many of us were humbled and embarrassed because our collective expertise had failed us in foreseeing the magnitude and depth of the changes to come under the new Soviet leader, Mikhail Gorbachev. Thanks to Gorbachev's policy of *glasnost* (openness), Soviet citizens now have easy access to factual information not only about their own country, much of which they have always known, but also about the United States—information that they would have liked to have known for years, but could not readily find. And thanks to an unprecedented fascination by the United States with watching Gorbachev and his *perestroika* (reforms), more Americans, historically disinterested in the Soviet Union, are now eager to take a good look at the country—not to be shocked, frightened, or reassured about the superiority of their own way of life, but to learn about a major foreign civilization that is likely to stay, evolve, and dominate many headlines in the years to come.

Hopefully, this book will serve this purpose, although admittedly it cannot be described as "the truth, the whole truth, and nothing but the truth" about the Soviet Union. Unfortunately, even with *glasnost*, it is not always possible to distinguish between facts and propaganda, to obtain all the facts, not to select among those that are available, or to completely abstain for making explicit or implicit value judgments and assumptions. It is also difficult to take an accurate aim (in a manner of speaking) at the Soviet Union which has become, under its new dynamic leader, a moving target. Aside from what he may still change, Gorbachev must be credited with introducing the element of the unpredictable into Soviet politics. Actually, the amount of revision found in this new edition of the text indicates that many changes have already occurred.

This book is intended to provide a comprehensive introduction to the contemporary Soviet Union. The main ideas behind the book may be summarized as follows: (1) to put between two covers up-to-date factual information about all important aspects of Soviet society, (2) to treat the subject matter in an objective and dispassionate manner, and (3) to present it in simple and plain language.

The text is divided into twelve chapters devoted to major components of the Soviet phenomenon. For easier reading and understanding, each chapter is subdivided into fifteen to twenty sections and is supplemented with graphs, tables, footnotes, and a brief glossary of special terms.

I am grateful to my many learned colleagues who were kind to share with me their comments and criticisms, including Paul Hamori of Ball State University; Harvey Fireside of Ithaca College; and Robert Horn of California State University. My special thanks go to my students whose enthusiasm and lively interest have been of tremendous help.

It is with great appreciation that I acknowledge valuable contributions made to this edition of the book by Edith Riker and Sylvia Pafenyk.

Much of the statistical data appearing in the book were derived from the following published Soviet sources:

*Narodnoye Khozyaistvo SSSR v 1988g (National Economy of the USSR in 1988)*. Statistika, Moscow, 1989.
*Narodnoye Khosyaistvo SSSR za 70 let* (National Economy of the USSR During 70 Years). Finansy i statistika, Moscow, 1987.
*Sovetski Soyuz (The Soviet Union)*, compiled by V. A. Golikov. Polizdat, Moscow, 1975.
*SSSR (The USSR)*, edited by A. M. Prokhorov. Sovetskaya Entsiklopediya, Moscow, 1979.
*SSSR v Tsifrakh v 1987g (The USSR in Numbers in 1987)*. Statistika, Moscow, 1988.
*USSR '89 Yearbook*. Moscow: Novosti Press Agency, 1989.

Throughout the text, tables compiled on the basis of these sources are identified as "Soviet statistics" or "Soviet data."

*Vadim Medish*

# 1

# THE LAND

## THE BIG COUNTRY

The Union of Soviet Socialist Republics (USSR) is by far the largest country in the world, occupying more than 8.6 million square miles (22.4 million km²) of continuous landmass. If all other countries were as large, only five more would have room on our planet. The USSR is more than twice the size of the United States, almost as big as the United States, Canada, and Mexico put together, bigger than all of South America, and only slightly smaller than the whole continent of Africa.

From east to west, the continental territory of the USSR stretches for nearly 6,800 miles (10,000 km) and encompasses eleven time zones. From north to south, it measures approximately 3,500 miles (5,000 km). In addition, the USSR possesses a number of large and small islands in the Arctic and Pacific Oceans. The perimeter of the continental USSR is close to 40,000 miles (60,000 km), of which two thirds comprise a long coastline, mainly in the north and east, and one third (approximately 13,000 miles) constitutes one of the longest land borders in the world, which is shared by twelve countries.

The USSR takes up almost one third of the territory of the so-called Old World—that is, the continents of Europe and Asia—and the northern shores of Africa. It occupies the eastern half of the European continent and almost the entire northern half of Asia. About 25 percent of the Soviet territory is in Europe, and the remaining 75 percent is in Asia. In Europe (in the west) the USSR borders on six countries (from north to south): Norway, Finland, Poland, Czechoslovakia, Hungary, and Romania. In Asia (in the south) its six immediate neighbors are (from west to east): Turkey, Iran, Afghanistan, China, Mongolia, and North Korea. Soviet-owned islands in the North Pacific are just a few miles away from islands belonging to Japan and the United States.

In addition to the Arctic and Pacific Oceans that half-encircle the country to the north and east, the USSR also has access to the Atlantic Ocean through the Black Sea (southwest) and the Baltic Sea (northwest).

During most of the eighteenth and nineteenth centuries, when the country was called the Russian Empire, it had overseas possessions that included all of Alaska and several small colonies in California. This "American connection" ended in 1867 with the purchase of Alaska by the United States.

## MAIN FEATURES

The Yenisei River, which flows south to north across Siberia, divide the USSR into its eastern and western halves, each distinctly different. The eastern half consists of highlands and mountains, including several active volcanoes. The western half is composed of two huge flatlands separated by the Ural Mountain Range. To the west of this divide lies the East European Plain and to the east is the Central Siberian Plateau, which is more elevated but just as flat.

The East European Plain, which occupies the entire European part of the country, is cut north to south by the valleys of several slow-flowing rivers. The largest of these rivers are (west to east): the Dnestr, the Dniepr, the Don, the Volga, and the Ural. The first two empty into the Black Sea and

**TABLE 1-1**    Area Occupied by Continents and Large Countries (in square km)

| | | | |
|---|---|---|---|
| USSR | 22,400,000 | Canada | 10,000,000 |
| Europe | 10,500,000 | China | 9,597,000 |
| Asia | 44,400,000 | United States | 9,363,000 |
| N. America* | 24,300,000 | Brazil | 8,512,000 |
| S. America | 17,800,000 | Australia | 7,687,000 |
| Australia† | 8,500,000 | India | 3,280,000 |
| World | 135,800,000 | | |

*Includes Central America

†includes Oceania

*Source:* Compiled from *Encyclopaedia Britannica* and converted to the metric system by author.

the third into the Sea of Azov (a part of the Black Sea). The last two empty into the Caspian Sea.

Siberia, the landmass that extends east from the Ural Mountains to the shores of the Pacific Ocean, also has several major river systems. The largest of these rivers—the Ob, Yenisei, and Lena—flow south to north and empty into the Arctic Ocean. Another great stream, the Amur River, flows east along the Sino-Soviet border and empties into the Pacific Ocean in the southeast corner of Siberia known as the Soviet Far East.

South of the Ural Mountains lies a large area occupied by arid steppes and deserts. It is called Soviet Central Asia.

In addition to the Urals and mountainous East Siberia, high mountain ranges are found along most of the USSR's southern border in Asia. From west to east, they are: the Caucasus (between the Black and Caspian Seas), Pamir, Tien Shan, and Altai. Much lower mountains are located on the Crimean Peninsula (Black Sea) and also on the USSR's border with Poland, Czechoslovakia, and Hungary in the west (Carpathian Mountains).

There are several large lakes in the USSR, including the largest (Caspian Sea)[1] and the deepest (Baikal)[2] lakes in the world. Among the many islands that belong to the USSR, the largest are Sakhalin (Pacific Ocean) and Novaya Zemlya (Arctic Ocean).

## NATURAL CONDITIONS

Given the vastness of the country, it is not surprising that its natural conditions, including the climate, are extremely diverse. In the northern parts of the country, especially east of the Ural Mountains, it is cold almost year round: During the long winter, the temperature drops to −94°F (−70°C); the summer is short and cool. In some places in the south the summer is quite long and very hot with temperatures reading 104°F (40°C) and higher. In these places the winter is short, and snow is virtually unknown.

Close to two thirds of the USSR, however, lies between these extremes and has a temperate climate with pronounced continental characteristics— that is, sharp differences between summer and winter temperatures. It is to the typically long winter that the USSR owes its not entirely justified reputation as a very cold country. Actually, most of the huge territory has a sufficiently warm summer, although the northern parts of the temperate zone may have a short one.

Approximately one third of the USSR's territory lies north of the temperate zone and indeed has a rigorous climate that makes normal human life quite difficult. A much smaller portion of the USSR's territory situated

---

[1]The Caspian Sea is not connected to any ocean and is, therefore, technically a lake.
[2]The Baikal Lake is more than 5,300 feet deep.

south of the temperate zone has a much warmer, and in a few places even subtropical, climate.

The general rigorousness of the climate in the USSR increases not only from south to north, but also from west to east. The latter trend applies equally to the continental character of the climate; the differences between summer and winter temperatures increase from west to east. The amounts of annual precipitation, on the other hand, decrease from west to east. As a result, the eastern parts of the European USSR and most of its Asian territory are colder and suffer from insufficient precipitation and, occasionally, from severe droughts. This capricious climate presents serious problems for agriculture.

In spite of the great variety of natural conditions, the USSR's territory shows certain clearly defined latitudinal patterns of climate, soil, and vegetation. These patterns, called "natural zones," are as follows (from north to south):

1. *Arctic desert* is a forbidding environment of ice and snow that characterizes the islands and coastline of the Arctic Ocean.
2. *Subarctic tundra*, a cold semidesert with vegetation (mostly moss and low shrubbery), stretches across the entire territory of the USSR in the north.
3. *Forest-tundra* is a transitional zone in which the tundra's features gradually yield to taller shrubs and coniferous trees.
4. *Taiga* is a thick coniferous forest that covers a huge wedge-shaped territory occupying a narrow northern part of the European USSR and most of Siberia.
5. *Mixed forest* forms a continuous belt along the southern limits of the taiga in both the European and Asian parts of the country.
6. *Broad-leaved forest* forms another huge wedge which is pointed toward the east and occupies much of the northern half of the European USSR.
7. *Forest-steppe*, another transitional zone, provides a gradual change from the tree-growing terrain to the grassland.
8. *Steppe*, as the grassland is usually called in Russia, occupies much of the southern half of the European USSR and extends to West Siberia.
9. *Semideserts* are arid steppes that stretch along the northern shores of the Caspian Sea and farther to the east.
10. *Deserts* are found mostly in Soviet Central Asia between the Caspian Sea and the Balkhash Lake.
11. *Humid subtropics* (Mediterranean type) are limited to relatively small areas in the Crimea and Transcaucasus.[3]

## NATURAL RESOURCES

The USSR is richly endowed with vast and diversified natural resources. This is especially true, as we shall see, of the Asian part of the country, which appears to have considerable deposits of almost all known, useful minerals. Siberia is also rich in timber and has great potential hydropower.

[3]Some of the oases in the south of Central Asia have a dry, subtropical climate.

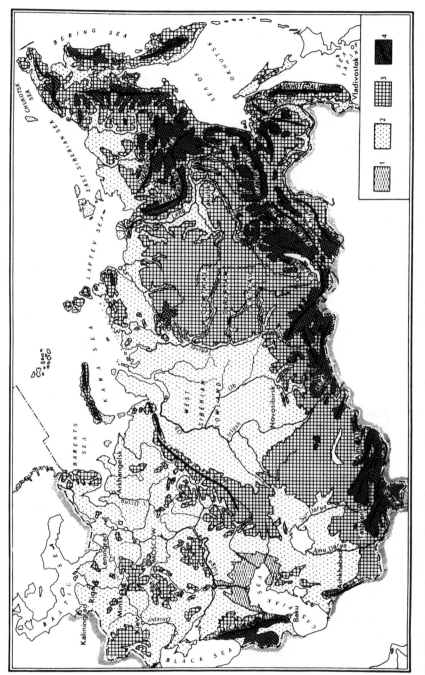

**FIGURE 1-1**  Relief map of USSR. (1) below sea level areas; (2) lowlands, plains; (3) elevations, highlands; (4) mountain ranges. Modified and updated reproduction from *Atlas* (Moscow: Administration of Geodesi and Cartography, 1975).

5

Perhaps somewhat ironically for a country of this size, land fit for cultivation is in relatively short supply in the USSR. Much of the land either lies in the high latitudes (too far north) or does not receive sufficient precipitation. Areas with the most fertile black soils (chernozems) suffer from a capricious climate, while the less fertile grey and yellow soils of arid areas require expensive artificial irrigation and fertilization. The total area fit for cultivation is variously estimated at between 10 and 20 percent of the USSR's territory. Much of it lies in the zone of high-risk agriculture.

The USSR's timber resources, on the other hand, are huge and estimated to account for a quarter of the world's forest area. The Siberian taiga supplies great quantities of high-quality timber for both domestic needs and export.

The known resources of mineral fuel are plentiful and varied. They include numerous oil-bearing areas, large deposits of black and brown coal, natural gas fields, shale, and peat. Conservative estimates put Soviet fuel resources at about one quarter of the world's reserves. In addition, the USSR has a considerable and as yet underdeveloped potential for hydropower provided by numerous rivers.

The USSR has virtually all types of metallic ores, which are extracted in various locations. Rich deposits of iron and manganese ores may exceed one half of the world's reserves. Nonferrous and rare metals, including gold and platinum, are found in different parts of the country, particularly in its Asian realm. An area in Siberia called Yakutiya even has diamonds. Other precious and semiprecious stones are found in the Ural Mountains.

A wide range of chemical raw materials, including large deposits of phosphate, potassium, sulfur, and salt, is being mined and extracted in various locations. Resources of such building materials as asbestos and limestone are also plentiful.

Although there is no such thing as unlimited natural resources, the Soviet Union comes close to being self-contained and secure for the foreseeable future in all its economic needs. Today the USSR leads the world in the production of many important raw materials and serves as their supplier to other countries.

Water resources are also large and fairly well distributed through the country, except for some arid areas in the south. Numerous large rivers are being used for production of electric power.

The main problems that the Soviet Union experiences with the exploitation of its vast natural resources are caused by the unfavorable location of the most promising deposits in remote regions that lack transportation networks and sufficient labor. Soviet officials estimate that the cost of oil coming from some of the newly discovered fields in Siberia will be much higher than the current average cost. Before too long, production costs of other minerals are also likely to reflect this special "cold tariff."

**TABLE 1–2**   USSR's Estimated Reserves of Natural Resources (In Percent of World's Reserves)

| Resource | Percent | Resource | Percent |
|---|---|---|---|
| Oil | 25 | Apatite | 30 |
| Gas | 65 | Copper ore | 15 |
| Coal | 55 | Peat | 65 |
| Iron ore | 43 | Nickel ore | 12 |
| Tin ore | 10 | Phosphate | 28 |
| Sulfur | 15 | Aluminiferous ore | 10 |

*Source:* Compiled by author from Soviet data.

Perhaps not surprisingly, other serious problems come about because the much-talked-about abundance of natural resources generates a feeling of false security. The Soviet press is full of complaints about wasteful use of nonrenewable minerals.

## PROTECTION OF ENVIRONMENT

The traditional perception of the Soviet Union's vastness as virtually limitless also tends to produce a feeling of complacency about the natural environment in general. As a result, many ambitious development projects have been carried out without much concern for environmental consequences. Here are some examples:

Extensive use of the Volga's water for irrigation and production of electric power has lowered the level of the Caspian Sea by more than 15 feet, triggering off an ecological chain reaction of serious proportions. Several varieties of fish are threatened with extinction.

Hydroelectric power stations, wood pulp mills, and chemical plants have polluted the Baikal Lake, which used to be famous for the purity of its deep water and its unique marine life.[4] The lake's delicate ecological balance appears to have been severely damaged.

Acid rains and industrial wastes have killed water life in the rivers and lakes around several large concentrations of industrial projects in the European part of the USSR. Until recently, many Soviet planners, concerned with transportation costs, promoted such a package approach to industrialization.

Reckless deforestation of large areas in central Russia has led to soil erosion that in many instances is beyond repair. The loss of valuable farmland in some areas has been substantial.

There have been several disasters involving Soviet nuclear facilities in the Urals and Ukraine resulting in human casualties and lasting damage to the envi-

[4]The lake is inhabited by more than 2,600 types of marine life, about 85 percent of which are unique—not found anywhere else in the world.

ronment. The worst disaster occurred near Kiev in Chernobyl in April 1986. A nuclear power plant barely escaped destruction during an earthquake in Armenia in December 1988.

The Sea of Azov, once a major resource for the fishing industry, is now practically dead because of water pollution and contamination. Several other large bodies of water, including the Aral Sea and the lakes Ladoga, Onega, and Balkhash, have been officially declared disaster zones. In about 100 industrial centers air and water quality rates are below acceptable standards.

Soviet authorities began to take serious protective measures against further damage to the environment only in the late 1970s. The new Soviet Constitution (1977) even includes the following proclamation (Article 67): Citizens of the USSR are obliged to protect nature and conserve its riches. Under Mikhail Gorbachev's policy of *glasnost*, numerous informal groups of concerned citizens have been actively campaigning against specific local cases of air and water pollution. Public pressure on a larger scale, involving the mass media, is credited with the abandonment of some ambitious schemes to change natural conditions, such as a project to use nuclear blasts to change the terrain and reverse the flow of several rivers in Siberia. The boastful motto, "To master and reform nature," has been replaced by frantic appeals to save and preserve what is still intact. Efforts to save nature are coordinated by a special, newly established state agency, called the Environmental Protection Committee.

However, by most accounts, there continues to be a gap between the proclaimed environmental concerns and the practice of rapid industrialization at almost any cost. Official Soviet sources admit that so far the improvement has been mostly in the methods used to mitigate or conceal environmental damage, rather than in the ways to prevent it from happening in the first place.

## TERRITORIAL GROWTH

Under different names, the USSR has been in existence for more than 1,100 years. Russian political history, which has sometimes been called "a tale of three cities," began with the establishment of Kievan Rus (862) along the midreaches of the Dniepr. For about 350 years, Kiev, Russia's first capital, presided over a loose coalition of small, semi-independent principalities scattered over a large territory lying between the Dniepr and Volga rivers. In the first half of the thirteenth century, most of these principalities were subjugated by the marauding Mongols. A small principality called Muscovite Rus replaced Kiev as the center of the surviving Russian political life. In the fourteenth century, Moscow became Russia's second capital.

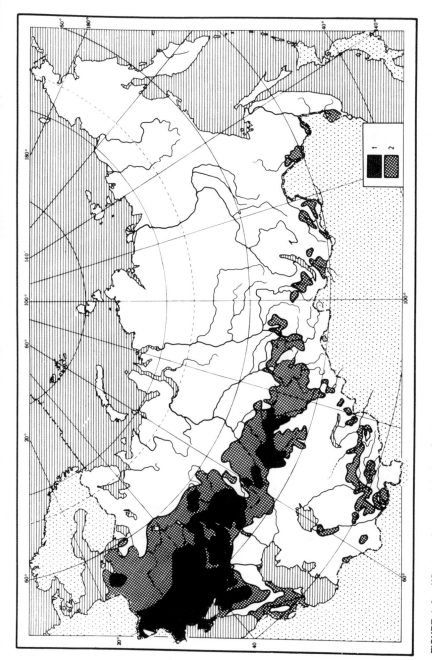

**FIGURE 1–2**  Wheat-growing areas: (1) wheat as the main crop; (2) wheat as a secondary crop. Modified and updated reproduction, from *Atlas* (Moscow: Administration of Geodesi and Cartography, 1975).

9

During the last hundred years of Mongolian domination, Muscovite princes managed to "gather Russian lands"[5] into a highly centralized auto-cratic state occupying the territory of present central Russia. In 1480, they formally ended their dependency on the Mongols. And in the middle of the sixteenth century, Muscovite Rus began its eastward territorial expansion by conquering two Mongolian (Tatar) states on the middle and lower Volga. Before the century was over, small bands of Russian frontier irregulars—the Cossacks—laid claim to much of Siberia. Later they not only reached the Pacific Ocean but also crossed to the New World and established Russian colonies in Alaska and California.

Russia's expansion in the west, which also began in the sixteenth century, was slower to gain momentum, mainly because it met with much greater resistance from such formidable European powers of the day as Poland and Sweden. But during the second half of the seventeenth century, Moscow extended its control over the territory of the former Kievan Rus, now called the Ukraine. At the turn of the next century, the seat of the Russian government was transferred from Moscow to a new city on the Baltic coast, as if to signal the westward direction of future territorial expansion. Thus began the story of Russia's third capital—St. Petersburg, today known as Leningrad. Soon thereafter, Russia was officially renamed the "Russian Empire."

During the eighteenth century, the Russian Empire grew in both the west and the south by annexing the Baltic lands, much of Poland, parts of the Transcaucasus, the Crimean Peninsula, and the northern shores of the

**TABLE 1–3**    Ten Longest Rivers (km)

| Ob | 5,410 | Kolyma | 2,513 |
| Amur | 4,416 | Ural | 2,428 |
| Lena | 4,400 | Dnieper | 2,201 |
| Yenesei | 4,092 | Indigirka | 1,997 |
| Volga | 3,531 | Don | 1,870 |

*Source:* Compiled by author from Soviet data.

**BOX 1–1**    *Soviet Underground Humor*

| Question: | Does the Soviet Union recognize international boundaries? |
| Answer: | Yes, but it should be remembered that Soviet friendship knows no boundaries. |
| Question: | With what countries does the Soviet Union border? |
| Answer: | With whatever countries it wishes to border. |

[5]The "gathering of Russian lands" was accomplished by Moscow rulers through a combination of diplomacy, force, bribery, and subversion.

**TABLE 1–4** Chronology of Territorial Changes

| | |
|---|---|
| 862 | First Russian state founded by Ryurik in Novgorod; capital is soon moved to Kiev; Kievan Rus becomes federation of feudal lands |
| 1220s–1240s | Kievan Rus conquered by Mongols (Tatars); rise of Moscow as new capital; Moscovite Rus forms centralized state by "gathering Russian lands"; Mongol occupation ends in 1480 |
| 1550s | Ivan the Terrible annexes Tatar states on Volga (Kazan and Astrakhan); Siberia annexed before end of sixteenth century; expansion in east |
| 1650s | Russia "reunited" with Ukraine; expansion in west |
| 1690s | Peter the Great gains access to Black Sea (Sea of Azov); expansion in south |
| 1700s | Russia gains access to Baltic Sea; expansion in northwest; Russian colonies in North America (Alaska and California) |
| 1700s (late) | Expansion in west (Poland) and southwest (Crimea, Bessarabia) |
| 1800s (early) | Annexation of Armenia, Georgia, and Finland |
| 1800s (late) | Conquest of central Caucasus, Central Asia, and Far East; Alaska sold to United States (1867) |
| 1905 | Japan takes southern half of Sakhalin |
| 1917–1920 | Some ethnic parts of Russian Empire gain independence: Baltic nations, Finland, Poland, Armenia, Georgia, Central Asia, and other territories; some of them recaptured during 1920s |
| 1939–1946 | USSR incorporates most of remaining "lost" territories and also some new ones: Tannu Tuva, East Prussia, Carpathian Ukraine, and North Bukovina |

*Source:* Compiled by author from Soviet sources.

**TABLE 1–5** Capitals of Russia-USSR

| | |
|---|---|
| Kiev | 9th–13th centuries |
| Moscow | 14th–17th centuries |
| St. Petersburg (Petrograd) | 1713–1917 |
| Moscow | 1918 to present* |

*During World War II, when the German armies approached Moscow, many government offices and foreign embassies were moved to Kuibyshev.

*Source:* Compiled by author from Soviet data.

Black Sea. The next century witnessed the annexation of Finland, the conquest of all of the Caucasus, and the occupation of Central Asia.[6] But in 1867, Russia gave up its overseas possessions (Alaska). In 1905, Russia lost to Japan the southern half of a large offshore island in the Pacific, Sakhalin.

The collapse of the Russian Empire in 1917 led at first to a substantial shrinkage of the territory controlled by Moscow, which once again became Russia's capital (1918). Most of the lost territory, however, was regained by the new Soviet regime, either in the course of the civil war (1918–1921) or at the very onset of World War II: eastern parts of Poland, Bessarabia, the Baltic

[6]The Russian Empire, and later the USSR, held territorial concessions in the northern provinces of China. Before World War I, Russia controlled two small districts, called Kars and Ardagan, which are now part of Turkey.

countries, and parts of Finland. During and immediately after World War II, the USSR reclaimed all of Sakhalin Island, annexed parts of eastern Asia (Tannu Tuva) and East Prussia, and obtained additional territorial concessions from Japan, Finland, Czechoslovakia, and Hungary.

The size or shape of the USSR's territory has not changed during the last four decades. But, as we shall soon see, some of the Soviet Union's borders, annexations, and territorial claims are being challenged.

## CENTRAL RUSSIA

The most important part of the huge country—the heart of its political, economic, and cultural life—is the landlocked area within a radius of from 200 to 250 miles around Moscow known as central Russia. A densely populated and economically developed area, it is covered by a thick network of railroads and highways. Besides Moscow, it contains several major urban communities: Kalinin, Rybinsk, Yaroslav, and Kostroma in the north and northwest; Vladimir, Ivanovo, Gorky, and Kazan in the east; Ryazan, Kuibyshev, and Saratov in the southeast; Tula, Voronezh, Kursk, and Kaluga in the south; and Smolensk in the west.

The physical features of central Russia are quite uniform and even monotonous: flat lowlands with occasional hilly areas. The typical landscape near Moscow is a large clearing rimmed by broad-leaved trees—oak, birch, maple, and lime—with an admixture of conifers (fir and pine). North of Moscow, forests are thicker and the proportion of coniferous trees is higher; the southern belt of central Russia lies in the forest-steppe zone characterized by larger open spaces. The climate of central Russia is moderately continental. In the northeast and east, the unofficial boundary of central Russia is the left bank of the Volga, one of the mightiest rivers in the world. The Volga and its major right-bank tributary, the Oka, are navigable about eight months a year. Several hydroelectric power stations on the upper and middle Volga provide some of the energy for local needs. Central Russia also has its own limited resources of mineral fuels: coal and peat. But the bulk of energy requirements is met by natural gas, oil, and coal brought from other parts of the USSR.

Because central Russia is both densely populated and highly industrialized, the quantities of imported fuels and raw materials are large. Its leading industry is engineering involving various kinds of machine-building projects—for automobiles, locomotives, machine tools, construction equipment, tractors, and other farming machines. Moscow and other cities have large textile, chemical, woodworking, and food-producing enterprises.

Central Russia's climatic conditions make it impossible for the local agricultural economy to satisfy the needs of the large and still-growing urban

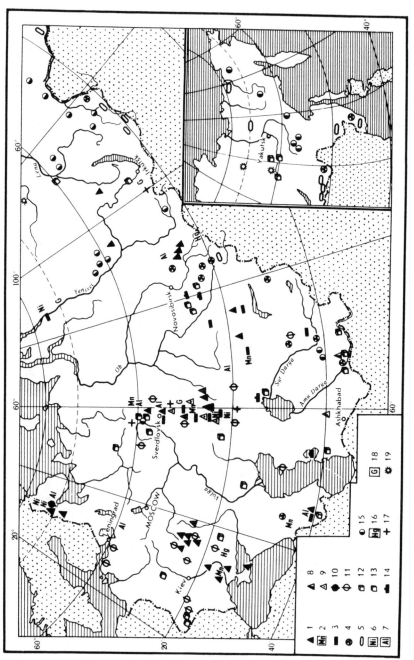

**FIGURE 1-3** Major mineral deposits: (1) iron; (2) manganese; (3) copper; (4) complex ores; (5) tin; (6) nickel; (7) aluminum; (8) sulphur; (9) pyrite; (10) apatite; (11) phosphorite; (12) salt; (13) potassium; (14) mirabilite; (15) gold; (16) mercury; (17) asbestos; (18) graphite; (19) diamonds. Modified and updated reproduction, from *Atlas* (Moscow: Administration of Geodesi and Cartography, 1975).

population. Just as in the case of raw materials and fuels, foodstuffs have to be brought in from elsewhere.

Moscow is by far the largest metropolis in the country. Together with its sprawling suburbs, Moscow provides homes for more than 12 million people. The 800-year-old city, which stands on the banks of the Moskva River (a tributary of the Oka which flows into the Volga), is a mixture of many architectural styles, ranging from ancient churches and palaces to modern skyscrapers. Its most famous landmark is the Kremlin[7]—the walled center of the city—which used to be a fortress and now serves as the seat of the Soviet government. Another famous attraction is Lenin's Tomb, which is located in Red Square on the northern side of the Kremlin.

## THE NORTHWEST

This part of the country lies west, northwest, and north of central Russia and consists of several distinctly different areas: Byelorussia, the Kaliningrad Region (formerly East Prussia), the Baltic lands, and a large territory that extends along the Soviet-Finnish border and includes the Kola Peninsula. Historically, this part has served as Russia's gateway to western Europe. Most of its major cities, which include Leningrad (formerly St. Petersburg),[8] are ports on the Baltic Sea, White Sea, and Barents Sea. Best known among them are Kaliningrad (formerly Königsberg), Riga, Tallin, Arkhangelsk, and

**TABLE 1–6**   Twenty Largest Soviet Cities (Population in Millions, 1989)

| City | Population | City | Population |
|------|-----------|------|-----------|
| Moscow | 9.0 | Sverdlovsk | 1.22 |
| Leningrad | 5.1 | Dnepropetrovsk | 1.12 |
| Kiev | 2.6 | Tbilisi | 1.10 |
| Tashkent | 2.1 | Odessa | 1.08 |
| Baku | 1.8 | Chelyabinsk | 1.05 |
| Kharkov | 1.6 | Donetsk | 1.03 |
| Gorki | 1.5 | Yerevan | 1.03 |
| Novosibirsk | 1.4 | Omsk | 1.02 |
| Minsk | 1.30 | Perm | 1.01 |
| Kuibyshev | 1.24 | Kazan | 1.01 |

Note: Three more cities have population in excess of 1,000,000 each; 60 cities—500,000 or more; 300 cities—100,000 or more. There are more than 2,000 cities and towns in the country.
*Source:* Compiled by author from Soviet statistics.

[7]The word "kremlin" means a citadel or burg. Besides Moscow, several other old Russian cities have kremlins.
[8]Leningrad was founded as St. Petersburg in 1703. In 1914 its name was "Russified" to Petrograd, and in 1924 it was changed to Leningrad (Lenin city).

Murmansk. Large inland urban centers include Minsk, Vilnius, Novgorod, and Petrozavodsk.

The physical environment varies greatly from one subarea to another, ranging from swampy forests in the southwest (Kaliningrad Region and Byelorussia) to the taiga and tundra in the north (Kola Peninsula). The southern half of the area, below Leningrad, is quite densely populated and has large tracts of arable land used primarily for growing potatoes, flax, and rye. Livestock breeding thrives not only in the south but also in the north, where the climate is too severe for farming. But because of the proximity of the Atlantic Ocean, the northwest as a whole has a relatively mild and very humid climate.

The area has many lakes and medium-sized rivers interconnected by an extensive system of canals. The rivers that flow through its northern part are used by the lumber industry. Timber is one of two important local natural resources. The other one is the huge deposits of apatite concentrate (a raw material for fertilizer) in the Kola Peninsula. Both the Baltic Sea and the seas of the Arctic Ocean are used for large-scale fishing industries.

But the main economic role played by the northwest is that of the second largest industrial base. Especially important are the machine-building, shipbuilding, and instrument-manufacturing industries. Other local industries include food processing and paper and lumber mills.

With a population of almost 5 million, Leningrad is the second largest Soviet city. It was founded at the beginning of the eighteenth century by Peter the Great as a symbolic "window on Europe" and Russia's new capital. In 1917, the capital of old Russia became, in the words of the official Soviet history, the "cradle of the Revolution." Built in the marshy delta of the Neva River and overlooking the Finnish Gulf of the Baltic Sea, Leningrad ranks among the most beautiful cities of Europe. Many of its palaces and public buildings were designed by world-famous architects. Leningrad is also the largest Soviet seaport and a major industrial center.

**TABLE 1–7**  Summer and Winter Temperatures

| City | Mean Temperature in the Warmest Month (C) | Mean Temperature in the Coldest Month (C) |
|---|---|---|
| Moscow | +18° | −11° |
| Kiev | +19° | −13° |
| Tashkent | +27° | −1° |
| Vladivostok | +21° | −14° |
| Yakutsk | +19° | −44° |
| *For comparison:* | | |
| New York | +23° | −1° |

Source: V. Pokshishevsky, *Geography of the Soviet Union* (Moscow: Progress Publishers, 1974), pp. 14–15.

**TABLE 1–8**  Five Largest Lakes (sg km)

| | |
|---|---|
| Caspian Sea | 371,000 |
| Aral Sea | 66,500 |
| Baikal | 31,500 |
| Ladoga | 18,400 |
| Balkhash | 18,200 |

*Source:* Compiled by author from Soviet data.

## THE SOUTHWEST

South and southwest of central Russia lies a vast lowland that extends to the shores of the Black Sea and to the eastern slopes of the Carpathian Mountains. Its perimeter coincides with the boundaries of the Ukraine, except that in the southwest it includes Moldavia. The largest city in this part of the country is Kiev, the ancient capital of Russia and the third most populous metropolis of the present USSR. Some of the other large cities are important ports on the Black Sea: Odessa, Kherson, Nikolaev, and Sevastopol. Major urban centers situated inland include Kharkov, Lvov, Dniepropetrovsk, Zaporozhe, Kishinev, and Semfiropol.

Much of the Ukraine (south of Kiev) and Moldavia is a fertile grassland—the steppe, which has traditionally served as the most important single "breadbasket" for the entire country. The climate is mild and generally conducive to agriculture, although some areas suffer from periodic droughts. The main crops are wheat and sunflowers. In the south, especially in the mountainous Crimea, the amount of solar radiation is quite sufficient for grape growing (vineyards). The Black Sea (including its northeast inlet called the Azov Sea) is used for commercial fishing. The Crimean Peninsula is a major summer resort area containing many health spas, rest homes, and other tourist facilities. Here the climate resembles that of the Mediterranean.

The southwest is endowed with a wealth of natural resources: coal, iron ore, oil, and many others. Conveniently located and well-developed mining and extracting industries provide a basis for large-scale metallurgical and machine-building engineering. Several Black Sea ports have shipbuilding facilities. One of the biggest hydroelectric power stations in the USSR is located in the middle reaches of the Dniepr River.

The Dniepr River, the Black Sea, and the Azov Sea play an important role as waterways for moving freight and passengers. This region also has an extensive network of railroads and a limited number of modern highways.

Standing on the banks of a mighty river, Kiev is a sprawling modern metropolis with a population in excess of 2 million. It is also one of the oldest cities in the country; some of its historical monuments, such as Sophia Cathedral, date back to the beginning of the eleventh century. Another famous monument is the statue of St. Vladimir, the Kievan ruler credited with the conversion of his subjects to Christianity in the year 988. Surrounding Kiev are major engineering, textile, chemical, and light industries.

## SOUTHEAST (EUROPE) AND THE CAUCASUS

This area, situated south and southeast of central Russia, consists of two distinctly different parts: (1) a vast steppe that lies between the lower reaches of the Don and Ural rivers and is bordered in the south by the Caucasian Mountains and the Caspian Sea, and (2) the Caucasus, a mountainous land situated between the Black and Caspian Seas. Among its large urban centers are: Rostov, Volgograd (formerly Stalingrad), Astrakhan, Krasnodar, Stavropol, and Grozny in the north; and Baku, Yerevan, and Tbilisi in the south (Transcaucasus).

The eastern half of the steppe here is, if anything, even more fertile and favorable to agriculture than is the Ukraine. This area chiefly produces wheat and rice. But further east, in the lowland[9] that lies along the northern shores of the Caspian Sea, the steppe becomes arid and even turns into a semidesert, unsuitable for farming. The climate of the steppe zone is mild and sufficiently humid in the west but colder, drier, and more continental in the east.

The Caucasus consists of several ranges of high mountains,[10] flat highlands, and deep valleys. Because of the difference in altitudes, the Caucasus has a great variety of natural conditions, including those of the humid subtropics (Lenkoran). Accordingly, rural economic activities range from sheep herding to tea and tobacco farming. Several ports on both the Black and Caspian seas are fishing industry centers.

The southwest, especially the Caucasus, is rich in mineral deposits. Oil is extracted around Baku and in several other locations in the Caucasus. There are also considerable deposits of various metallic ores, including the precious metals in the Caucasian Mountains. Engineering industries, on the other hand, are concentrated primarily in the two large cities in the north, Rostov and Volgograd, which are in exceptionally advantageous locations in regard to the flow of essential raw materials and the availability of energy and labor.

The Caucasus is the USSR's passage to the Middle East. Three overland routes—two railroad lines and a highway—connect Russia proper with the Transcaucasus—that is, the lands of Georgia, Armenia, and Azerbaijan bordering on Turkey and Iran. These two countries are also easily accessible from Soviet ports on the Black and Caspian Seas.

Thanks to their pleasant climatic conditions, many localities in the Caucasus are competing with the Crimea as the favorite places for summer

[9]The lowland north of the Caspian Sea is considerably below sea level.
[10]The highest peaks in the Caucasus are Elbrus (5,642 m) and Kazbek (5,033 m).

vacations. Prominent among them is a Black Sea coast area around the resort town called Sochi.

## THE URALS

To the north of the Caspian Sea, the dividing line between Europe and Asia is assumed to go along the Emba and Manych rivers and the Ural Mountains. The Urals are a very important crossroads between central Russia in the west, Siberia in the east, and Soviet Central Asia in the south. Large cities, all of which are major industrial centers, include: Sverdlovsk, Perm, Chelyabinsk, Magnitogorsk, Orenburg, and Ufa.

The Urals, a land of foothills and old, low-rising[11] mountains, are a natural treasury filled with some 150 different mineral ores. Because of millennia of erosion, many mineral deposits are unusually close to the surface or even exposed, making mining easy. As a result, the Urals have been for a long time both Russia's traditional source of raw materials and its workshop. In addition to mining, the region's principal industrial efforts are ferrous and nonferrous metallurgy, chemical production, and various kinds of engineering. The Urals' energy sources include rich oil and coal deposits, as well as a large hydroelectric power station that stands on the Kama River, a left-hand tributary of the Volga. In the northern Urals are located several large pulp and paper mills that utilize local supplies of timber.

The Kama River serves as the main water route connecting the Urals with central Russia. Other transportation routes are provided by numerous railroad lines that run both east to west and north to south.

The climatic and natural conditions of the Urals are quite similar to those of central Russia, but the continental features of the climate are more pronounced. Most of the area lies in the forest zone, which gradually changes

**TABLE 1–9**  Major Parts of the USSR

| Part | Area in % | Population in % |
|---|---|---|
| Central Russia | 7 | 20 |
| Northwest | 7 | 15 |
| Southwest | 4 | 20 |
| Southeast | 7 | 15 |
| Urals | 5 | 5 |
| Central Asia | 10 | 14 |
| Siberia | 50 | 8 |
| Far East | 5 | 2 |
| Far North | 5 | 1 |
| | 100% | 100% |

Source: Compiled by author from Soviet data.

[11]The Ural Mountains seldom rise above 1,000 m.

into a dry steppe to the south of the mountain range. Agriculture plays a negligible part in the Urals' economy, which is sometimes called the "black-smithy" of the USSR to emphasize its main occupation.

## CENTRAL ASIA

To the east of the Caspian Sea, the territory of the USSR forms a huge bulge that protrudes some 900 miles to the south and measures about 1,200 miles across. This area is called Soviet Central Asia. In the south it borders on Iran, Afghanistan, and China. The main urban centers of Central Asia are Tashkent, Frunze, Alma-Ata, Karaganda, and Ashkhabad.

The natural environment of Central Asia offers a most striking contrast with that of European Russia. It comes in several patterns that blend into each other as one moves from north to south: the arid steppes, semideserts, deserts with scattered large and small oases, and high, steep mountains covered with snow and ice.[12] From north to south, the climate ranges from moderate to subtropical while remaining very dry and continental. As a result, most of Central Asia's agriculture depends on artificial irrigation. The traditional agricultural production consists of cotton, rice, and fruits. Livestock breeding is of significant importance. During the last quarter of a century, the northern steppe belt has been developed into a major wheat-growing area.

Central Asia is also an important source of minerals: oil, natural gas, coal, copper, gold, fluorite, and sulphur. Special efforts are currently underway to develop engineering and manufacturing industries in the fast-growing urban centers. The cities usually stand in large oases, the most famous of which are the Tashkent Oasis and the Ferghana Valley—sites of ancient civilizations.

One serious problem that hinders the economic development of Central Asia is a relative dearth of modern transportation routes—railroads and highways. This problem is compounded by the fact that the vast countryside almost completely lacks major waterways. There are several quite large lakes and rivers and many mountain streams in Central Asia, but they are not well suited for regular navigation, either because of their location or because of shallow waters, marshy banks, and frequently changing riverbeds in sandy soils.

The largest lakes are: the Aral Sea, Balkhash, Issyk-Kul, and Kara Kul. The two major rivers that empty into the Aral Sea are called Amu-Darya and Syr-Darya. And, of course, the eastern shore of the Caspian Sea—the largest lake in the world—is an important part of Central Asia that provides access to the Caucasus, southwest Russia, and Iran.

---

[12]The high mountains in Central Asia are the Tien Shan and Pamirs (Roof of the World).

## SIBERIA

The name "Siberia" applies to an enormously large piece of real estate that occupies approximately one third of Asia: Siberia extends from the Urals to the Pacific Ocean and from the boundary of Central Asia and the state borders between the USSR and Mongolia and China to the Arctic Ocean. For the purpose of our discussion, we treat the southeast corner of Siberia—the Far East—separately. But even this contracted version of Siberia is larger than the entire rest of the USSR. It is also larger than all of the United States, including Alaska and Hawaii.

In the world at large, Siberia symbolizes an enormous prison under cold, open skies. Soviet propaganda refers to it as the "giant construction site of the USSR." The impartial historical record shows that both these images have been based on fact. Contemporary Siberia, however, tends to become progressively less the former and more the latter.

Despite its huge size, the physical features of Siberia are quite similar: a belt of tundra in the north along the long Arctic Ocean coastline, a somewhat narrower strip of steppe in the south, and a wide area in the middle completely covered by taiga—thick evergreen forest. Western Siberia, the territory west of the Yenisei River and Lake Baikal, is a flat lowland. Eastern Siberia, the area on the other side of these divides, has a mountainous terrain that consists of flat highlands, mountain ranges, and active volcanoes. Eastern Siberia has the most severe climatic conditions: low temperatures, inadequate humidity, and extreme continental characteristics.[13] Siberian rivers—the Ob, Yenisei, and Lena—are among the world's longest.

The economic development of Siberia has not proceeded very far. The cold and inhospitable subcontinent has few roads and a relatively small

**BOX 1–2**    *The Feeling of the Vastness of the Soviet Union is Conveyed by the Opening Lines of "The Song of the Native Land," One of the Most Popular Patriotic Songs:*

---

Vast is my native country.
She has many lakes, seas, and rivers.
I do not know any other such land
In which man can breathe so freely.

From Moscow to the very borders,
From the southern mountains to the northern seas
Man walks like the landlord
Of his immensely big country.

Original lyrics by V. Lebedyev-Kumach; translated by author.

---

[13]The area around the town of Verkhoyansk in East Siberia is the coldest spot in the northern hemisphere (Pole of Cold).

population. Only one major railroad line, the Trans-Siberian Railway, crosses from east to west. Most of the current economic activities are concentrated along this line and its branches. Siberia's largest cities are: Novosibirsk, Irkutsk, Ulan-Ude, Omsk, Chita, Krasnoyarsk. These cities are centers of fast-growing mining, extracting, and engineering industries.

There is much evidence that Siberia is extraordinarily rich in minerals. Still-incomplete geological surveys have revealed vast deposits of coal, oil, natural gas, iron ore, and nonferrous metals (copper, zinc, lead, aluminum, gold, nickel, and the like). The Siberian taiga offers an almost unlimited supply of timber. And the big rivers have a great potential for producing hydroelectric power. But the exploitation of all these natural resources is just beginning.

The steppe zone of Siberia has a limited capacity for farming and livestock breeding. The taiga is used for the professional hunting of furred animals. Numerous rivers and lakes, including the unusually picturesque Lake Baikal, provide excellent opportunities for fishing.

## THE FAR EAST

The southeast corner of Siberia is usually called the Far East. This area, especially its maritime part, is in many respects distinctly different from the rest of Siberia. The climate here is humid and relatively mild. The Far East has several large cities: Blagoveshchensk, Khabarovsk, Nikolaev, Komsomolsk, Vladivostok, and others. Sakhalin Island and other offshore islands are part of this area.

Historically, the Far East has served as Russia's main outpost on the Pacific Ocean, and later, as the terminal of the long Trans-Siberian Railway as well. Thanks to favorable natural conditions and economic opportunities, this part of the country has had no trouble attracting sufficient numbers of settlers from European Russia. Its remoteness—Vladivostok is more than 5,000 miles from Moscow—has stimulated the development of a self-contained economy that encompasses agricultural production (wheat, rice, soy beans), timber-felling and woodworking, fishing and fish processing, and mining and engineering. Several of the seaports—Vladivostok, Nakhodka, Sovetskaya Gavan—have large shipbuilding yards. Locally obtainable natural resources include various kinds of coal, metallic ores, and oil.

The Amur River provides an important link between different parts of the Far East. Railroads and highways are relatively few in number, although new ones are currently under construction. This includes a major project called the Baikal-Amur Mainline, which, when completed, will greatly add to the capacity of the railroad network of the Far East. Together with the rest of the Asian part of the USSR, the Far East is undergoing massive economic development.

## THE FAR NORTH

The maritime territory stretching along the Arctic and north Pacific coastline, from the Kola Peninsula in the west to the Kamchatka Peninsula in the east, and numerous offshore islands are referred to as the Far (or Extreme) North. The southern boundary of the Far North roughly corresponds to the Arctic Circle, and thus includes several places already mentioned, such as Murmansk. This is so because the term actually defines a legal-administrative status rather than a geographic subdivision. People who live and work in the territory designated as the Far North receive special pay differentials and fringe benefits in recognition of the rigors of its Arctic climate.

The Far North is indeed poorly suited for human habitation, and it is also quite costly for almost any kind of economic activity. Local sources of food, limited to fishing, hunting, and reindeer breeding, are inadequate. Very few railroads and highways reach that far north, and waterways are open to navigation only four months a year. The long-distance airlift for common freight is expensive. Construction of buildings and roads is handicapped by permafrost. But still, the Far North is slowly gaining population and developing its two main industries: (1) processing and shipping, via the

BOX 1–3  *Surviving in the Far North*

Some Soviet architects suggest that towns in the Far North should be either completely or partially sheltered by a glass roof. Such projects are particularly appealing for territories where natural conditions are most severe. When building Mirny, the diamond capital of Yakutiya, the designers took the experience of Norilsk into account, but in projecting the second diamond capital, the town of Aikhal, which stands much further north, serious thought had to be given to the problem of safeguarding its inhabitants from fierce frosts and blizzards. The draft plan of Aikhal, in accordance with which all vital communications inside the town will be sheltered by a roof, is viewed as an interesting experiment in the Soviet Union. In general, however, the majority of hygienists, architects, geographers and other Soviet specialists participating in the development of the Far North are inclined to believe that such a "hothouse" life should be organized only in rare cases, for it would not be conducive to rearing healthy generations well adapted to the life in the Far North. In areas where the climate is somewhat milder, the optimum solution of the problem of steady peopling would probably be a combination of sanitation and prophylactic measures, on the one hand, and correct planning of towns with the view to weakening the influence of the severe climate, on the other. This combination would make the inhabitants physically fit. This, of course, does not preclude the construction of roofed galleries linking houses with kindergartens, creches, shops and so forth, depending on local conditions and the severity of the climate.

Quoted from V. Pokshishevsky, *Geography of the Soviet Union* (Moscow: Progress Publishers, 1974), p. 276.

Northern Sea Route, raw materials, mostly timber that is rafted down the rivers from inland; and (2) mining rare earth metals.

There are several large urban communities in the Far North: Murmansk (population 350,000), Norilsk (population 180,000), Yakutsk, Magadan, Igarka, and others. The majority of them are ports on the Northern Sea Route, which provides navigation between Europe and Asia via the Arctic Ocean several months a year. Murmansk, which is an ice-free port because of the proximity of the north Atlantic current, also has large fishing-industry facilities.

## GEOGRAPHY AND HISTORY

Geography has been called the "matrix of history."[14] It is indeed easy to see how Russia's geography has influenced the course of its history. To begin with, Russia's original location on the East European Plain contributed directly to many of its important historic events. Being relatively close to Byzantium, for example, influenced Russia's choice of Eastern (Greek) Orthodoxy as its state religion (988). Two and a half centuries later, because of its location, Russia fell prey to the Mongol invasion and remained for several centuries almost completely isolated from Europe, which was then going through the Renaissance and Reformation. A result of this isolation was Russia's lagging behind Europe in technology and industrialization.

The lack of natural barriers, such as high mountains or large bodies of water, around the original territories of Kievan and Muscovite Rus was responsible for both the scourge of foreign invasions and the drive for territorial expansion, justified by a need to find "secure borders." Large-scale invasions of Russia have been a frequent occurrence in its history. Many of them penetrated deeply, and some were also followed by long periods of occupation. For example, at the beginning of the sixteenth century, Moscow was occupied for three years by a Polish army. In 1709, the Russians, led by Peter the Great, defeated an invading Swedish army near the city of Poltava in the Ukraine. In 1812, Napoleon took and plundered Moscow. During World War II, the Germans occupied and devastated much of European USSR, coming within sight of Moscow, Leningrad, the Volga, and the main range of the Caucasian Mountains.

As we have seen, when not being invaded, Russia itself was often invading neighboring countries, annexing them, building an empire, and pursuing territorial expansion in the quest for greater physical security. A variation of the "national security" or "national interests" theme applied to geography found its reflection in Russia's determined efforts to gain access to ice-free seaports.

[14]See, for example, Will Durant's *The Story of Civilization* (New York: Simon & Schuster, 1968).

**TABLE 1–10** Major Foreign Invasions

| | |
|---|---|
| The Mongol occupation ("Yoke") | 13th–15th centuries, 250 years |
| The German intrusions into Northwest Russia | 1280s |
| The Polish occupation of Moscow in "Times of Trouble" | 1600s |
| The Swedish invasion | 1709 |
| The Napoleon occupation of Moscow | 1812 |
| The German invasion in World War I | 1914–1918 |
| The foreign intervention in Russia's civil war | 1918–1921 |
| The German (Nazi) occupation during World War II | 1941–1944 |

*Source:* Compiled by author from Soviet data.

When Russia was being invaded by foreign armies, its climate often served it well as a powerful ally. But in times of peace the severity and capriciousness of the climate have instead been a source of constant economic headaches.

Having grown very large, Russia solved some problems but also created others. For instance, in defensive wars Russia often successfully traded space for time. The possession of so much real estate made Russia the world's richest country in natural resources. But the enormous distances inherent in Russia's geography have also been the source of serious and costly logistical and environmental protection problems. The sheer enormity of the Russian Empire (and its successor, the USSR) has most definitely contributed to its perception as potential menace by other nations.

Paradoxically, limitless spaces assured their early inhabitants of seemingly complete freedom of movement, making the need for personal (civil) freedom seem much less important. But the openness of the land with the attendant threat of foreign invasion actually precluded much freedom of mobility and accentuated the need for security through conformity at the expense of personal freedom.

Russia's climate and other natural conditions have determined the distribution of its population and its economic activities. This was especially true in the past when Russia was a predominantly agricultural country, but it is still valid today. As we shall see, the physical environment influences and sometimes controls and restricts life in the USSR. It has been said that every nation is, to a degree, a captive of its own history. But history is, in turn, a captive of its geography. Nonetheless, the contemporary Soviet Union is gradually escaping from the hold of Old Russia's history and is overcoming some of the limitations of its geographic environment.

## GEOGRAPHY AND CULTURE

As an ingredient constantly present in the historical process, geography has made a deep imprint on Russia's culture. Describing the intimate relation-

BOX 1–4   *Geography and State Security*

Before WWII and until very recently, all maps published in the USSR were purposely inaccurate in order to hide "state secrets" and "confuse potential invaders." This admission was made by Moscow's chief cartographer, V. Yaschenko in an interview with the Soviet government newspaper *Izvestia* (September 1, 1988), where he stated: "People could not recognize their Motherland on the map. Tourists tried in vain to figure out where they were."

Source: Compiled by author from Soviet data.

ship that existed between the early inhabitants of Russia and their natural surroundings, the famous Russian historian Vasili Klyuchevsky wrote:

> ...the forest, steppe and river are what may be called the basic elements of Russian nature in terms of their historical significance. Each of them separately played an active and unique part in the formation of the life and ideas of the Russian man.[15]

As we shall see, not all of the old ideas have survived the millennium of Russian history culminating in the 1917 Revolution. And still fewer are operative in the contemporary USSR, which proclaims itself a completely new, Socialist civilization. Owing to urbanization and industrialization, only a relatively small portion of the Soviet people, the peasants, continues to live so close to nature. On the other hand, the most important physical aspects of the world's largest country remain the same: its location on the globe, its vast spaces and distances, and its climatic conditions.

The Soviet Union is a new power with old geography. Consequently, at least some of the idiosyncrasies produced by these aspects remain intact. For example, it is fairly obvious that Soviet leaders, conditioned by their sense of history, attach great importance to controlling space, even though modern weapons systems have largely changed the traditional notion of physical security. In the recent past, this has affected Soviet policy toward the neighboring countries habitually viewed as Russia's first line of defense. Currently, the same reasoning may be underlying Moscow's determination to cling at any cost to its vast territorial possessions.

Here we should be careful not to make too much of history by viewing it as some sort of programming that once and for all determines the destiny of a nation. Russian history, especially its more dynamic Soviet phase, definitely involves both continuity and change—much change, as long as change is not defined solely by the acquisition of Western characteristics. Gorbachev's dynamic administration appears to place a very heavy empha-

---

[15]Vasili Klyuchevsky (1841–1911) is regarded as the most important native scholar of Russian history. The passage is from his *Sochineniya* [Works] (Moscow: Politizdat, 1956), vol. 1, p. 60.

**BOX 1–5**   *Geography and Politics*

Many cities in the Soviet Union have been at different names known by different names. The changes of names usuall have to do with politics.
Here are a few examples:

Leningrad(since 1924)-Petrograd(1914–1924)-St. Petersburg (1703–1914)

Volgograd (since 1961)-Stalingrad (1925–1961)-Tsaritsyn(1589–1925)

Naberezhnye chelny (since 1986)-Brezhnev (1982–1986)-Naberezhnye chelny (1934–1982)

Source: Compiled by author from Soviet data.

ses on change. If this trend continues, it may signify a turning point in Soviet history.

In the following chapters we discuss several geopolitical factors that influence Soviet domestic and foreign policies. However, one—perhaps the most unique—peculiarity of Russian geopolitical thinking should be mentioned briefly here: It is best known as the Slavophile-Westerner dispute, which was fully formulated and fervently pursued during the second half of the nineteenth century. But the controversy itself has not been limited either to that term or to that time. It has to do with Russia's vastness and its geographic position between Europe and Asia. The Slavophiles (and their predecessors and successors, known by various names) considered Russia to be a subcontinent and civilization by itself, unlike anything else in the world. From this it followed that Russia should preserve and emphasize its uniqueness and pursue its own special destiny. The Westerners (and their variations under other names) argued that Russia was merely a large backyard of Europe and a backward part of Western civilization. Their prescription for Russia's ills was "Europeanization"—that is, changes that would remake Russia in Europe's image.

This national superiority-inferiority complex, which is also part of the contemporary Soviet scene, has its roots in Russia's geography. In a more general sense, geography is the stage on which Russia's entire historical drama has been played. We proceed with our review of the current act of this drama by getting acquainted with its actors—the peoples of the USSR.

### GLOSSARY

**Chernozem:**  rich, black soil.
**Geopolitical:**  pertaining to the interplay of geographic, economic, and political factors.
**Glasnost:**  openness, publicity, freedom of expression.
**Kremlin:**  citadel, burg, or fortress.

**Slavophile:**  "one who loves Slavs"; A Russian who believes in the uniqueness and superiority of Russia's culture.
**Steppe:**  grassland or prairie.
**Taiga:**  evergreen forest in the North.
**Tundra:**  subarctic marshland or semidesert.
**Westerner:**  one who believes that Russia should imitate and follow the West (Europe).

## RECOMMENDED READINGS

LYDOLPH, PAUL E., *Geography of the USSR*. Elkhart Lake, WI: Misty Valley Publishing, 1979.
POKSHISHEVSKY, V., *Geography of the Soviet Union*. Moscow: Progress Publishers, 1974.
SHABAD, THEODORE, *Geography of the USSR: A Regional Survey*. New York: Praeger, 1951.

CHAPTER

# 2

# THE PEOPLE

## DEMOGRAPHY

The Soviet Union has a population of almost 290 million (1990), which constitutes approximately 6 percent of the world's population. It is the third largest nation in the world, far behind China and India, but almost 20 percent more populous than the next nation in line, the United States. In relation to its land area, economic ambitions, and potential resource base, the Soviet Union is a relatively underpopulated country: a situation that is not likely to change much in the foreseeable future. During the first half of this century, the rate of natural growth was high, but the net gain was drastically reduced by heavy losses sustained in the two world wars, civil strife, and related, human-caused calamities. For example, in World War II alone the Soviet Union lost more than 20 million people. During the last two decades, the annual rate of population growth has been approximately 0.7–1.0 percent and is expected to decrease before the end of the century. Some Soviet demographers are now predicting a zero population growth for the nation in the near future. Although this decline, due to a decreasing number of births, is comparable to similar trends experienced by urbanized Western nations, it also shows a failure of Soviet "pronatal" policies. These policies are based on the theory that under Socialism (and Communism) the population growth would progressively increase despite urbanization.

The process of urbanization has been advancing quite rapidly in the Soviet Union—for example, the share of the urban population has risen from less than 20 percent in 1917 to about 66 percent today. The growing urban population is concentrated mostly (almost 66 percent) in large cities, more than twenty of which have more than a million inhabitants each, and these cities continue to expand in spite of various administrative restrictions designed to prevent the influx of new residents. The development of large cities (100,000 or more residents) rather than small urban communities shattered another, much older, Marxist population theory concerning the future of industrial society under Socialism.

Compared with the declining rural population, the growing urban population tends to form smaller, two-generation families, with fewer children. The urban population is also younger than the rural population. But, as a whole, the population of the Soviet Union is aging, owing to the combination of the declining birthrate and a longer life expectancy, which currently stands at about seventy years. The life expectancy for Soviet women exceeds that of men. Women also outnumber men by more than 15 million, or 5 percent, as a lingering reminder of the heavy loss of young men during World War II.

Of certain political significance is that about 94 percent of all Soviet citizens alive today were born after the 1917 Revolution, and a majority of them belongs to the second and third postrevolution generations. In other words, they are true products of the Soviet system.

With the decline of the rural population and the lifting of travel restrictions, migratory tendencies within the country have increased. The percentage of people living in the same place from birth is about 55 and declining. More people are on the move every year (about 11 million in 1988), and the distance of their moves is growing. The main direction of this

**TABLE 2–1**   Population of Russia-USSR (In Millions)*

| Year | | Year | |
|------|------|------|------|
| 1500s | 6.5 | 1914 | 178.0 |
| 1600 | 7.0 | 1922 | 136.0 |
| 1646 | 7.0 | 1940 census | 194.1 |
| 1678 | 10.5 | 1959 census | 208.8 |
| 1719 | 15.5 | 1970 census | 241.7 |
| 1795 | 37.2 | 1974 census | 250.9 |
| 1858 | 74.0 | 1979 census | 262.4 |
| 1897 census | 128.0 | 1989 census | 286.7 |

*Estimates unless otherwise indicated.

Source: Compiled by author from Soviet statistics.

migration is eastward, from the European parts of the country to the vast spaces of Asia, which are still sparsely populated and underdeveloped. At present, more than 33 percent of the population, as compared to only 18 percent before World War II, lives east of the Ural Mountains. Next to urbanization, migration to Siberia, Central Asia, and the Far East is the most important demographic shift, and it is strongly encouraged by the government.

Emigration from and immigration to the Soviet Union are rather insignificant in the overall population picture. During the 1960s and 1970s, no more than 300,000 people were issued exit visas for emigration, and these were primarily Soviet Jews.[1] During the same period, a somewhat smaller number of Turkic refugees from China is believed to have been allowed to cross the border into Soviet Central Asia. In the early 1980s, emigration sharply declined and then picked up with the advent of the Gorbachev era (1985). In 1989 about 100,000 persons left the USSR.

A strict border security makes illegal emigration or immigration virtually impossible. Aside from diplomats and students, very few foreigners live in the USSR as permanent residents or long-time visitors.

## ETHNIC DIVERSITY

The absence of foreigners does not, however, mean that the Soviet population is homogeneous. On the contrary, the Soviet nation is composed of some 100 large and small ethnic groups with their own distinct cultural heritages.[2] Most of them are native to that part of the world. Many, but not all, ethnic groups have their own territories within the USSR. These territories are designated, in descending order of importance, as "union republics," "autonomous republics," "autonomous regions," and "autonomous areas." The ethnic Russians, or the Great Russians, constitute by far the largest of these groups, but even they total only about one half of the entire population. Only every second person in the Soviet Union is Russian. Besides the Russians, there are twenty-one other major ethnic groups numbering more than 1 million members each.

Currently, the Soviet Union is composed of fifteen union (component) republics, including the huge Russian Soviet Federative Socialist Republic (RSFSR). The other fourteen union republics are the historical homelands of large ethnic minorities and range widely in the size of their territories and populations. Called Soviet Socialist Republics (SSRs), they are, in alphabet-

---

[1] Also included in this number were Germans (20,000–25,000) and Armenians (15,000).

[2] In 1926, Soviet demographers identified 190 ethnic groups. In 1939, this number was reduced to 62, but then increased in 1959 to 109. In 1979, the number of ethnic groups was once again decreased to 92. In 1989, the number was raised again. The changes have not been explained.

ical order: the Armenian SSR, Azerbaijan SSR, Byelorussian SSR, Estonian SSR, Georgian SSR, Latvian SSR, Lithuanian SSR, Kazakh SSR, Kirghiz SSR, Moldavian SSR, Tajik SSR, Turkmen SSR, Ukrainian SSR, and Uzbek SSR. The Soviet Constitution (Article 70) claims that these republics are sovereign states joined together in a voluntary union from which they have the right to secede (Article 72). To be able to exercise this alleged right, they must border on a foreign nation or have an outlet to an open sea. Accordingly, the fourteen non-Russian union republics form an outer belt around the RSFSR in the west and, in part, in the south.

Most of the national territories of lesser rank—autonomous republics, autonomous regions, and autonomous areas—are located within the borders of the huge RSFSR, which occupies close to 76 percent of the entire land area of the USSR. Because even on paper these territories have no right to secede, they do not need outside borders, and many of them are situated deep inside the Soviet heartland. Some of the smaller national territories are located

**TABLE 2–2**  Large Ethnic Groups and Their Territories (1979 Census)

| Ethnic Group | Population in Millions | Union Republics | Autonomous Republics | Autonomous Regions | Autonomous Areas |
|---|---|---|---|---|---|
| 1. Russians | 137.4 | X | — | — | — |
| 2. Ukrainians | 42.3 | X | — | — | — |
| 3. Uzbecks | 12.5 | X | — | — | — |
| 4. Byelorussians | 9.5 | X | — | — | — |
| 5. Kazakhs | 6.6 | X | — | — | — |
| 6. Tatars | 6.4 | — | X | — | — |
| 7. Azerbaijans | 5.5 | X | — | — | — |
| 8. Armenians | 4.2 | X | — | — | — |
| 9. Georgians | 3.6 | X | — | — | — |
| 10. Moldavians | 3. | X | — | — | — |
| 11. Tajiks | 2.9 | X | — | — | — |
| 12. Lithuanians | 2.9 | X | — | — | — |
| 13. Turkmens | 2. | X | — | — | — |
| 14. Germans | 1.9 | — | — | — | — |
| 15. Kirghiz | 1.9 | X | — | — | — |
| 16. Jews | 1.8 | — | — | X | — |
| 17. Chuvash | 1.8 | — | X | — | — |
| 18. Latvians | 1.4 | X | — | — | — |
| 19. Bashkirs | 1.4 | — | X | — | — |
| 20. Mordva | 1.2 | — | X | — | — |
| 21. Poles | 1.2 | — | — | — | — |
| 22. Estonians | 1. | X | — | — | — |
| Totals | 252.4 | 15 | 4 | 1 | 0 |

Notes: 1. A group of closely related peoples of Daghestan (Caucasus) totaled 1.7 million.

2. Together, all ethnic minorities, large and small, totaled about 133 million or 48 percent of the total population.

3. The Russians, numbering about 137 million, accounted for the remaining 52 percent.

Source: Compiled by author from Soviet statistics.

**TABLE 2–3**    Population of Union Republics (1989 Census)

| | Millions | % (USSR = 100) | Increase Over 1979 |
|---|---|---|---|
| Russian Federation (RSFSR) | 147.4 | 51.3 | 107% |
| Ukrainian SSR | 51.7 | 18.0 | 104 |
| Byelorussian SSR | 10.2 | 3.6 | 107 |
| Uzbek SSR | 19.9 | 7.0 | 129 |
| Kazakh SSR | 16.5 | 5.6 | 113 |
| Georgian SSR | 5.4 | 2.0 | 109 |
| Azerbaijan SSR | 7.0 | 2.4 | 117 |
| Lithuanian SSR | 3.7 | 1.3 | 109 |
| Moldavian SSR | 4.3 | 1.5 | 110 |
| Latvian SSR | 2.7 | 0.9 | 106 |
| Kirghiz SSR | 4.3 | 1.5 | 122 |
| Tajik SSR | 5.1 | 1.8 | 134 |
| Armenian SSR | 3.3 | 1.2 | 108 |
| Turkmen SSR | 3.5 | 1.3 | 128 |
| Estonian SSR | 1.6 | 0.6 | 107 |

*Source:* Compiled by author from Soviet statistics.

within the borders of other union republics: Azerbaijan SSR, Georgian SSR, Tajik SSR, and Uzbek SSR. The remaining union republics have no smaller national territories within their borders.

At present, there are twenty autonomous republics (ASSRs),[3] eight autonomous regions (ARs), and ten autonomous areas (AAs) in the Soviet Union. Together with the union republics, this comes to fifty-three national territories, which is only about one half of the officially recognized ethnic groups. However, with two notable exceptions, which we will discuss later, ethnic groups who do not have their own territories are quite small: The total number of members of all "homeless" ethnic groups amounts to less than 3 percent of the USSR's population. A few closely related minorities share the same territories; other minorities have more than one national territory, presumably because of their geographic dislocation.[4]

The number of smaller ethnic groups is gradually decreasing owing to consolidation and assimilation. Assimilation is also affecting larger minorities. These processes, combined with growing disparities among rates of natural growth for different ethnic groups, result in continuous changes in the proportional national composition of the population—changes that may

[3] ASSR stands for "Autonomous Soviet Socialist Republic."

[4] There are two shared autonomous republics—the Chechen-Ingush ASSR and the Kabardin-Balkar ASSR—and one shared autonomous region—the Karachai-Cherkassian AR. All of them are in the RSFSR. An ethnic group called the Ossetians has an autonomous republic within the RSFSR (the North Ossetian ASSR) and an autonomous region within the Georgian SSR (the South Ossetian AR). Some autonomous areas are also shared by closely related minorities. In addition to their union republic, Armenians have two autonomous territories in the Azerbaijan SSR: the Nagorno-Karabakh Autonomous Region and the Nakhichivan Autonomous Republic.

have significant effects on the future of the USSR as a whole. The main trend here is clear: The population is becoming more Asian.

## HISTORY OF THE UNION

Almost without exception, the ethnic groups currently living in the Soviet Union were "captive nations" of the Russian Empire before the 1917 Revolution. Immediately after the revolution, the new regime issued a ringing "Declaration of the Rights of the Peoples of Russia," promising all minorities the right of self-determination and political independence by secession. A number of minorities, in fact, managed to establish their own national governments. In the course of the civil war, however, Moscow restored its control over much of the territory and population of the defunct empire.[5] Until the end of 1922, while the Soviet leaders sought to reconcile the theoretical principles of Marxist internationalism with the "national interests" of Communist Russia, a maze of haphazardly composed local agreements, treaties, and the like, regulated relations between the central government and the national minorities. A special ministry was set up to deal with the national minorities' problems. The central part of the old Russian Empire was now formally called the Russian Soviet Federative Socialist Republic (RSFSR). The RSFSR was joined by a number of separate treaties with those outer ethnic lands that had been occupied by the Red Army: the Ukraine, Byelorussia, Central Asia, Armenia, Georgia, Azerbaijan, and the Far East (predominantly Russian).

In 1922, after some disagreement among the Kremlin leaders,[6] the Union of Soviet Socialist Republics (USSR) was officially established as a "voluntary union" of four component republics: the Russian Federation (enlarged to include Central Asia and the Far East), the Ukraine, Byelorussia, and the Transcaucasian Federation (composed of Armenia, Azerbaijan, and Georgia). In 1924, the number of component republics was increased to six with the creation of the Turkmen SSR and the Uzbek SSR, which, until then, had had the status of autonomous republics within the RSFSR. In 1929, the southern part of the Uzbek SSR was renamed Tajik SSR and added to the union as its seventh member. In 1936, two more union republics were created out of parts of the RSFSR in Central Asia: the Kazakh SSR and the Kirghiz SSR. At the same time, the Transcaucasian Federation was abolished and its three components—Armenia, Azerbaijan, and Georgia—were made union

---

[5]Finland, Poland, and the Baltic republics—Estonia, Latvia, and Lithuania—escaped this fate. For the Baltic republics, however, this was a short-lived independence that ended in 1940.

[6]The disagreement, which involved Lenin and Stalin, was mostly a matter of semantics. Stalin proposed that the country retain its original new name, the RSFSR (Russian Federation), and admit outlying ethnic lands as autonomous units. But Lenin wanted to create a new "supernational" entity—the Soviet Union—arguing that Stalin's idea would look too much like the old Russian Empire. Lenin's opinion prevailed.

republics, thus increasing the total number to eleven. The criteria for the status of union republic were made public: (1) the titular nationality must number 1 million or more; (2) it must also comprise a majority of the population in a given territory; and (3) this territory must have sufficient economic potential and border on a foreign country or have access to an open sea. As we shall see, these criteria have not been strictly observed.

In 1940, the number of the union republics rose to sixteen when the actual territory of USSR expanded. First, in March of that year, the Karelian Autonomous Republic of the RSFSR, located on the border with Finland, was promoted to the rank of a union republic under the name "Karelo-Finnish SSR." The new SSR incorporated some of the territory annexed by the Soviet Union from Finland as a result of the Russo-Finnish War (1939–1940). Because the combined number of all Karelians and Finns in the USSR was less than 200,000, the creation of this union republic was obviously a purely political ploy, designed to intimidate Finland. The move was in direct violation of the criteria for union republics. Early in August 1940, Rumania was forced to yield to the Soviet Union a disputed territory, Bessarabia, along its eastern border. This was then combined with a part of the Ukraine, designated formerly as the Moldavian ASSR, to form the thirteenth union republic under the name "Moldavian SSR." Later in August 1940, three formerly independent Baltic countries—Estonia, Latvia, and Lithuania—were annexed by the Soviet Union and designated union republics. According to the official Soviet version of history, the peoples of these countries, which formerly belonged to the Russian Empire, asked to join the USSR. For the next sixteen years, the composition of the USSR did not change. In 1956, in an unprecedented move, the Karelo-Finnish SSR was demoted to its former status and resumed its original name: the Karelian Autonomous Soviet Socialist Republic within the RSFSR. In 1957, the word "Mongolian" was dropped from the name of the Buryat-Mongolian ASSR.

**BOX 2-1**    *The Declaration of Rights of the Peoples of Russia*

The October Revolution of the workers and peasants began under the general banner of liberation.

The *peasants* are being liberated from the power of the landlords, for landed proprietorship no longer exists—it has been abolished. The *soldiers and sailors* are being liberated from the power of despotic generals, for the generals will henceforth be elected and be subject to recall. The *workers* are being liberated from the caprice and despotism of the capitalists, for henceforth workers' control over the mills and factories will be established. Everything that is living and virile is being liberated from the detested fetters.

There remain only the *nations of Russia*, which have suffered and are suffering from oppression and depotism, and whose liberation must be begun immediately and accomplished decisively and for all time.

In the era of czarism the nations of Russia were systematically incited one against another. The results of this policy are well known: massacres and pogroms on the one hand, and the enslavement of the nations on the other.

This shameful policy of incitement has ended, and there must be no return to it. Henceforth, it must be replaced by a policy of *voluntary and honest* alliance between the nations of Russia.

In the period of imperialism, after the February Revolution, when the power passed into the hands of the Cadet* bourgeoisie, the unconcealed policy of incitement gave place to a policy of cowardly distrust of the nations of Russia, a policy of pinpricks and provocation, concealed by verbal proclamations of the "freedom" and "equality" of the nations. The results of this policy are well known: intensification of national enmity and undermining of mutual confidence.

This unworthy policy of lying and distrust, of pinpricks and provocation, must be ended. It must henceforth be replaced by a frank and honest policy that will lead to *complete mutual confidence* among the nations of Russia.

It is only by such confidence that an honest and durable alliance between the nations of Russia can be secured.

It is only by such an alliance that the workers and peasants of the nations of Russia can be welded together into a single revolutionary force capable of withstanding all attempts of the imperialist, annexationist bourgeoisie.

It was on these grounds that in June 1917 the First Congress of Soviets proclaimed the right of the nations of Russia to freedom of self-determination.

In October 1917 the Second Congress of Soviets endorsed this inalienable right of the nations of Russia in a more decided and definite form.

In pursuance of the will of these congresses, the Council of People's Commissars† has decided to base its activities with regard to the nationalities of Russia on the following principles:

1. The equality and sovereignty of the nations of Russia.
2. The right of the nations of Russia to freedom of self-determination, including the right to secede and form independent states.
3. Abolition of all national and national-religious privileges and restrictions whatsoever.
4. Freedom of development for the national minorities and ethnographic groups inhabiting the territory of Russia.

The specific decrees necessitated by this will be drawn up immediately after a Commission on Nationalities Affairs has been formed. In the name of the Russian Republic, Joseph Djugashvili-Stalin, People's Commissar for the Affairs of Nationalities, V. Ulyanov (Lenin), Chairman of the Council of People's Commissars, November 2, 1917. Pravda (November 3, 1917), p. 1.

*Constitutional Democrats, the party of the big Russian bourgeoisie that existed from 1905 to 1917.
†Originally, Soviet ministers were called "people's commissars."
Dates given according to the old ("Julian") calendar correspond to November 15 and 16 of the new standard ("Gregorian") calendar to which Russia changed in 1918.

**TABLE 2–4**  Ethnic Territories

| | | |
|---|---|---|
| Union republics (SSR) | 15 | (including RSFSR) |
| Autonomous republics (ASSR) | 20 | (within union republics) |
| Autonomous regions (AR) | 8 | (within union republics) |
| Autonomous Areas (AA) | 10 | (within union republics) |
| Total | 53 | |

These territories belong to the ethnic groups comprising approximately 97 percent of the USSR's population.

*Source:* Compiled by author from Soviet data.

Since then, the number of union republics in the Soviet Union has remained at fifteen, and during the last three decades there have been no more changes in numbers, ranks, or names of lesser national territories. So far, the Gorbachev regime has resisted pressure from the ethnic minorities to redress boundaries and change the nationality map.[7] Since 1988, the Baltic republics have been vigorously campaigning for complete independence. Other ethnic republics—Armenia, Azerbaijan, Georgia, and Moldavia—have periodically made similar demands.

## NATIONALITY MAP

Between 1918 and 1958 there were many changes in the nationality map of the country, involving not only semantics of titles but also actual mass resettlements of entire peoples. The most traumatic mass shifts of minorities occurred during World War II when several nationalities were accused of pro-Nazi sympathies and were forcibly moved from their homes in the Crimea, North Caucasus, and Volga regions to distant Siberia and Central Asia. Several million people—men, women, and children—were deported in a most cruel manner, and four national territories ceased to exist: the Crimean Tatar ASSR, Kalmyk ASSR, Chechen-Ingush ASSR, and Volga German ASSR. In addition, the Kabardin-Balkar ASSR was demoted to the rank of autonomous region, cut in size and deprived of 40 percent of its inhabitants (Balkars), who were deported. The same fate befell several other smaller minorities that had no territories of their own.[8]

In 1957, twelve years after the end of World War II, most, but not all, of these minorities were "rehabilitated," and their surviving members were allowed to return from exile. Two of the abolished national territories, the Chechen-Ingush ASSR and Kabardin-Balkar ASSR, regained their original

---

[7]The most dramatic drive for changing borders and transferring jurisdiction centers around an Armenian enclave, the Nogorno-Karabakh Autonomous Region, in the Azerbaijan SSR. Armenians there and in Armenia staged mass demonstrations and vigorously campaigned for unification of the region with the Armenian SSR. Nationalists in the Abkhazian ASSR are demanding that their autonomous republic be removed from the jurisdiction of Georgia.

[8]The mass deportations of whole minorities took place between 1941 and 1945. The following nationalities were deported: Volga Germans, Crimean Tatars, Chechens, Ingushi, Kalmyks, Balkars, Bulgarians, Greeks, Turks, and Kurds.

**TABLE 2–5** Union Republics

| Order in which they are Listed in the Soviet Constitution, Article 71 | Russian Alphabet | Date of Founding | Seniority of Membership | Size of Population | Size of Titular Group | Size of Territory |
|---|---|---|---|---|---|---|
| 1. RSFSR (Russia) | 10 | 1 | 1–3 | 1 | 1 | 1 |
| 2. Ukrainian SSR | 14 | 2 | 1–3 | 2 | 2 | 3 |
| 3. Byelorussian SSR | 3 | 3 | 1–3 | 5 | 4 | 6 |
| 4. Uzbek SSR | 13 | 7–8 | 4–5 | 3 | 3 | 5 |
| 5. Kazakh SSR | 5 | 10–11 | 7–11 | 4 | 5 | 2 |
| 6. Georgian SSR | 4 | 6 | 7–11 | 7 | 8 | 9 |
| 7. Azerbaijan SSR | 1 | 4 | 7–11 | 6 | 6 | 10 |
| 8. Lithuanian SSR | 8 | 12–14 | 13 | 11 | 10 | 11 |
| 9. Moldavian SSR | 9 | 15 | 12 | 8 | 9 | 14 |
| 10. Latvian SSR | 7 | 12–14 | 14 | 14 | 14 | 12 |
| 11. Kirghiz SSR | 6 | 10 | 7–11 | 10 | 13 | 7 |
| 12. Tajik SSR | 11 | 9 | 6 | 9 | 11 | 8 |
| 13. Armenian SSR | 2 | 5 | 7–11 | 12 | 7 | 15 |
| 14. Turkmen SSR | 12 | 7–8 | 4–5 | 13 | 12 | 4 |
| 15. Estonian SSR | 15 | 12–14 | 15 | 15 | 15 | 13 |

*Notes:* 1. Another "founding member" of the USSR was the Transcaucasian Federative Socialist Republic, which was composed of Armenia, Azerbaijan, and Georgia.
2. The sizes of titular groups, populations, and territories of union republics have fluctuated.
*Source:* Compiled by author from Soviet data.

status. The Kalmyk territory was at first restored only to an autonomous region, but a year later (1958) it was returned to its original rank of an ASSR. For the Volga Germans, the official "rehabilitation" did not come until 1964, and the Crimean Tatars had to wait their turn until 1967. Moreover, neither the Germans nor the Tatars have been restored to their historic national homes of several centuries. Today, they are still "lost nations" without their own territories. This anomaly is justified by Soviet authorities on the uncertain grounds that "Socialist lands" already exist that belong to the same nationalities. The "Socialist land" of the Soviet Germans, who number almost 2 million, is the German Democratic Republic (East Germany). The problem is that the Soviet Germans are not free to emigrate there. The already-existing national territory of the Tatars is the Tatar ASSR, situated in the mid-Volga valley, which, evidently, holds little attraction for the former natives of sunny Crimea. In 1988, the USSR Supreme Soviet turned down what was labeled "the last appeal" of Crimean Tatar activists for the restoration of their national territory.

Another large ethnic group that, like the Germans, has no national territory of its own, is the Poles. Some of the Soviet Poles who had been born in Poland were given a limited time in 1948 to reclaim their Polish citizenship and to be repatriated to Poland. But more than a million Poles who remained in the Soviet Union do not have the right to emigrate or to have their own national territory.

The case of the Jewish minority presents a different kind of anomaly. Since 1934, there has been a third-rank national Jewish territory in the Soviet Union, called the Jewish Autonomous Region (or Birobidzhan). However, it is located in the Soviet Far East on the border with China, many thousands of miles from the traditional centers of Jewish life in the urban communities of European Russia. It is hardly surprising, therefore, that less than 10 percent of the territory's 200,000 residents are Jewish, and that the other 1.6 million Jews live elsewhere in the Soviet Union.

In a curious way, the inconsistent and unequal treatment of Soviet minorities as groups is reflected in the realm of international politics. As a result of a Soviet-American compromise, two union republics, the Ukrainian SSR and the Byelorussian SSR, are full members of the United Nations, in addition to the USSR as a whole. This gives the Soviet Union a total of three votes in the U.N. Because the selection of the three Soviet delegations was entirely the Kremlin's decision, the omission of the largest component republic, the Russian Federation (RSFSR), in favor of an all-union representation is significant. It is actually a tacit admission that the dominant Russian majority considers the Soviet Union as a whole to be its domain.[9] Except for

[9]Initially, Moscow demanded sixteen votes in the United Nations on the grounds that each of the sixteen component republics comprising the USSR (in 1945) was a sovereign political state.

**TABLE 2–6**   Union Republics and Their Capitals*

| | |
|---|---|
| 1. Russian Federation: Moscow† | 9. Moldavian SSR: Kishinev |
| 2. Ukrainian SSR: Kiev | 10. Latvian SSR: Riga |
| 3. Byelorussian SSR: Minsk | 11. Kirghiz SSR: Frunze |
| 4. Uzbek SSR: Tashkent | 12. Tajik SSR: Dushanbe |
| 5. Kazakh SSR: Alma-Ata | 13. Armenian SSR: Yerevan |
| 6. Georgian SSR: Tbilisi | 14. Turkmen SSR: Ashkhabad |
| 7. Azerbaijan SSR: Baku | 15. Estonia SSR: Tallinn |
| 8. Lithuanian SSR: Vilnius | |

*This is the official order in which the union republics are listed in the Soviet Constitution, Article 71 (See Table 2–5).

†Moscow is the capital of both the Russian Federation (RSFSR) and the Soviet Union as a whole (USSR).

*Source:* Compiled by author from Soviet data.

official occasions, the names "Russia" and "Soviet Union" are used interchangeably by practically all ethnic Russians and many non-Russians.

But under Gorbachev's more liberal political climate and openness many formerly suppressed nationality problems have surfaced. Nationalist movements in the Baltic republics have mounted powerful campaigns for independence. Moscow's authority has been repeatedly put to test by bloody clashes, mass demonstrations, and strikes in Armenia, Azerbaijan, Moldavia, Georgia, and Central Asia. As a result, today there is much more realism and less bragging about the state of ethnic relations in the Soviet Union. In the immediate future, neither suppression nor satisfaction of many ethnic demands looks easy, and to find acceptable compromises promises to be very challenging at best. Demands of ethnic separatists for territorial secession, on the one hand, and Gorbachev's vague promises of a looser federation replacing the current structure, on the other hand, most likely foretell a protracted and difficult impasse.

## ETHNIC AUTONOMY

The maintenance of ethnic languages and cultures is governed by a special formula, "National in form, Socialist in content," which is supposed to reconcile the ethnic diversity of the Soviet Union with the political uniformity demanded by its leadership. On a personal level, this formula requires that the ethnic background, or nationality, be entered in all important records and documents issued to every Soviet citizen. The documents must identify him or her as a Russian, Ukrainian, Tatar, Jew, or whatever. When applied to entire national minorities, the formula both encourages and limits permitted manifestations of ethnic cultures. As a rule, the degree of cultural autonomy given to a minority depends on the rank of its national territory, from union republics down. In many non-Russian parts of the country, those designated as ethnic territories, vernacular languages are used by the local

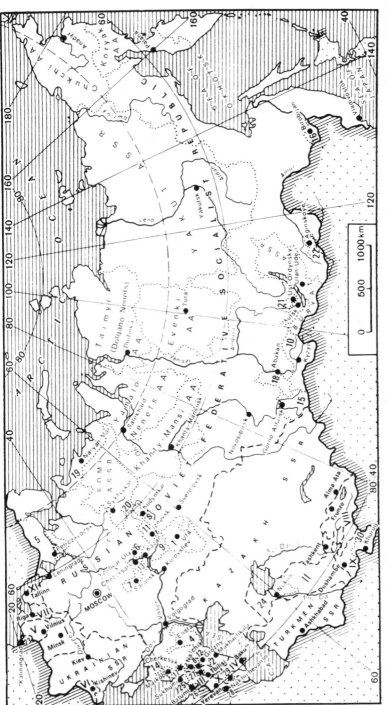

FIGURE 2–1. Map of the USSR. Russian Soviet Federative Socialist Republic (RSFSR): (1) Bashkir Autonomous Soviet Socialist Republic; (2) Daghestan ASSR; (3) Kabardin-Balkar (ASSR); (4) Kalmyk ASSR; (5) Karelian ASSR; (6) Mari ASSR; (7) Mordovian ASSR; (8) North Ossetian ASSR (cap. Ordzhonikidze); (9) Tatar ASSR; (10) Tuva ASSR; (11) Udmurt ASSR; (12) Chechen-Ingush ASSR; (13) Chuvash ASSR; (14) Adygei Autonomous Region; (15) Gorno-Altai Autonomous Region; (16) Jewish Autonomous Region; (17) Karachai-Circassian Autonomous Region; (18) Khakass Autonomous Region; (19) Nenets Autonomous Area; (20) Komi-Permyak Autonomous Area; (21) Ust-Ordynsk Burat Autonomous Area; (22) Aginski Buryat Autonomous Area; (23) Kaliningrad Region. I. Byelorussian Soviet Socialist Republic. II. Uzbek SSR; (24) Kara-Kalpak ASSR. III. Georgian SSR; (25) Abkhasian ASSR; (26) Adzhar ASSR; (27) South Ossetian Autonomous Region (cap. Tskhinvali). IV. Azerbaijan SSR; (28) Nakhichevan ASSR; (29) Nagorno-Karabakh Autonomous Region (cap. Stepanakert). V. Lithuanian SSR. VI. Moldavian SSR. VII. Latvian SSR. VIII. Kirghiz SSR. IX. Tajik SSR; (30) Gorno-Badakhshan Autonomous Region. X. Armenian SSR. XI. Estonian SSR.

press, radio and television, administrative offices, and schools, colleges, and universities. In such areas, especially in the union republics, ethnic names, attire, and the arts are very much in evidence. Minorities without territories of their own are at a great disadvantage in trying to preserve their cultural heritages under this formula.

Historically, changes in the official distinction between "form" and "content" have been even more important than the ranking of minorities. The first ten to fifteen years of the Soviet era were most liberal in this respect. During that time, "National in form" was extended to such things as ethnic military units and determined efforts on the part of minorities to rid their languages and cultures from Russian influence.[10] Members of ethnic minorities, many of whom had joined the revolutionary movement to fight the national oppression of the old regime, held key positions both in local administrations and in Moscow. Russian nationalism was kept in check by strictly enforced laws that equated it to counterrevolution. Commitment to the equality of all nationalities and the "principles of proletarian internationalism" was held as the basis of Soviet nationality policy. Then, in the mid-1930s, the situation dramatically changed: Russian nationalism openly became part of the official ideology; most of the first-generation Soviet leaders, including many non-Russians, were purged; and even the slightest manifestations of local ethnic feelings began to be treated as high treason. As we have seen, in the 1940s, extreme forms of national discrimination were used against not only individuals but also entire peoples. During the late 1940s and early 1950s, formerly encouraged "proletarian internationalism" was labeled "rootless cosmopolitanism," punishable as a grave offense against the national security of the USSR. This new cliché was used very frequently as a pretext for anti-Semitic actions of the regime both at home and abroad. Extreme forms of Russian nationalism were officially encouraged to the point that even the traditional Communist anthem, the "Internationale," was replaced. The opening lines of the new anthem stressed Russian nationalism:

> The unbreakable union
> Of the free republics
> Has been welded together forever
> By great Russia.

In the mid-1950s, the pendulum of Soviet nationality policy shifted again, this time to reemphasize local ethnic autonomy. Once again it became important for local bosses in national territories to have appropriate ethnic names and for all kinds of central political bodies to have proportional contingents of non-Russian members. Various ethnic theatrical companies began touring the country and even made frequent trips abroad. Yet, there

---

[10]There were also ethnic military units (divisions) during WWII.

**TABLE 2–7**  Autonomous Republics (Union Republics To Which They Belong)*

| | |
|---|---|
| 1. Abkhasian ASSR (Georgian SSR) | 11. Karelian ASSR (RSFSR) |
| 2. Adzhar (Georgian SSR) | 12. Komi ASSR (RSFSR) |
| 3. Bashkir ASSR (RSFSR) | 13. Mari ASSR (RSFSR) |
| 4. Buryat ASSR (RSFSR) | 14. Mordovian ASSR (RSFSR) |
| 5. Chechen-Ingush ASSR (RSFSR) | 15. Nakhichevan ASSR (Azerbaijan SSR) |
| 6. Chuvash ASSR (RFSFR) | 16. North Ossetian ASSR (RSFSR) |
| 7. Dagestan ASSR (RSFSR) | 17. Tatar ASSR (RSFSR) |
| 8. Kabardin-Balkar ASSR (RSFSR) | 18. Tuva ASSR (RSFSR) |
| 9. Kalmyk ASSR (RSFSR) | 19. Udmurt ASSR (RSFSR) |
| 10. Kara-Kalpak ASSR (Uzbek SSR) | 20. Yakut ASSR (RSFSR) |

*The Soviet Constitution, Article 85, lists autonomous republics in the Russian alphabetical order. Some ASSRs occupy larger areas and have larger populations than do the union republics. Of twenty ASSRs, sixteen are in the RSFSR.

*Source:* Compiled by author from Soviet data.

seemed to be a hollow ring to this renewed emphasis on "National in form," symbolized by the fact that although the lyrics of the new Soviet anthem were no longer heard on public occasions, the music remained the same. In 1977 after a two-decade ban, the lyrics of the national anthem exalting Russia were fully restored, thus signifying another shift in the nationality policy: away from the Soviet version of "affirmative action" for ethnic minorities and toward Russification, though not as extreme as it was under Stalin. As we see in the following chapters, this change is reflected in the ethnic composition of the current Kremlin leadership. Even though the ratio of ethnic Russians in the USSR's total population is declining, their representation in the highest political bodies of the country remains very high. This trend has continued after Gorbachev's rise to power in 1985.

## RUSSIFICATION

To be sure, throughout much of its history, Russia has functioned as a "melting-pot" for various ethnic minorities with whom it came into contact. Among the early converts to the Russian language and culture were some of Russia's Scandinavian conquerers and Mongolian overlords. In turn, subjugated minorities whose lands had been annexed by the expanding Russian Empire and European immigrants who had been attracted by economic and professional opportunities accepted Russification. Assimilation was the price that ambitious members of the minorities had to pay in order to join the mainstream of Russian life in regard to schools, careers, legal rights, and social prestige. At times, open coercion was used to expedite assimilation of selected minority groups, and various forms of ethnic discrimination were employed on a regular basis.

As a group, the Russians have shown a remarkable capacity to absorb large numbers of converts of both European and Asian stock, becoming, in the process, a thoroughly mixed ethnic entity. Names of converts to Russian culture can be found in every chapter of its history and in every field of endeavor: political, artistic, military, scientific, and so forth. Some of the converts appeared to be more "Russian" than the native Russians themselves.

The 1917 Revolution put a temporary halt to forced Russification, but it also encouraged deethnization of radical minority leaders in the name of "proletarian internationalism." The renewed emphasis on Russian nationalism that began during the 1930s has continued with some fluctuations ever since, once again creating a climate conducive to Russification.

Because for seventy years the Soviet Union was a highly centralized political and economic unit, it would be difficult to overestimate the tremendous pressures felt by Soviet ethnic minorities. On several past occasions Old Russia's "melting pot" turned into a modern "pressure cooker." Especially vulnerable to Russification are members of ethnic minorities who live outside their national territories or who have no territories of their own.

The latter category includes the German, Jewish (discounting Birobidzhan), and Polish minorities, which are classified in recent Soviet publications as "immigrant peoples," nonnative to the Soviet Union. This classification is both ironic and ominous: ironic because members of these minorities are not free to leave the Soviet Union, and ominous because, having been so labeled, they risk being viewed by others as second-class citizens. At the very least, this is an obvious effort to encourage assimilation—that is, complete Russification. Implied here is also a hint that the so-called Jewish Autonomous Region (Birobidzhan) may soon be abolished. For many years it has been little more than an embarrassing relic of a Soviet nationality policy failure.

A powerful instrument of assimilation is the Russian language, which is taught as a second language in practically all ethnic schools. It is also the only language used in the Soviet armed forces. The process of assimilation, or Russification, is intensified by such current demographic trends as urbanization, shifts of population within the Soviet Union, and, in particular, the continuing influx of Russians into ethnic territories. In non-Russian union republics, the ratio of Russians to the total population ranges from 2 percent (Armenian SSR) to more than 40 percent (Kazakh SSR), and Russians outnumber the natives in most of the lesser national territories within the RSFSR. Some nationalistic groups in the Baltic republics have demanded legal restrictions against the continuing influx of the nonnative migrants into the region.

According to Soviet statistics, a growing number of ethnically mixed marriages occurs within the country every year. In mixed marriages involv-

**BOX 2–2**   *Residence Restrictions in USSR*

During much of the postrevolution era, Soviet citizens could not move and choose freely where to live in their own country. Even today special permits are required to obtain housing and work in Moscow and in several other large cities. Foreigners living in the USSR are also subject to various travel and residence restrictions.

Compiled by author from Soviet data.

ing a Russian partner, the children, who can choose between either nationality of their parents, usually consider themselves Russian. More and more, members of the minorities who do not live in their own territories accept Russian as their native tongue, because only the Russian language (and culture) is "exportable" from one region to another inside the Soviet Union. Significantly, members of the growing Soviet ruling elite look at the Russian language and culture as symbols of the privileged status, regardless of their formal ethnic backgrounds or professed linguistic preferences. Ultimately, this tendency threatens to deprive national minorities of their natural leaders, and thus to undermine group efforts to resist mass assimilation.[11]

The coefficient of Russification, which is constantly increasing, most likely compensates for the fact that the natural growth rate of the ethnic Russians is lower than that of the combined national minorities. For example, Soviet census statistics show that a growing number of non-Russians—members of various Soviet minorities—claim Russian as their native tongue. Many people in this category (estimated at 20 million) no longer even speak ethnic languages. As groups, minorities without their own territories are most susceptible to becoming "Russophonic," which often leads to complete Russification. The ethnic (non-Russian) identity of many Soviet citizens—the so-called line five in their personal documents—is becoming an empty shell. Until a few years ago, this was particularly true about members of the ruling elite. But Gorbachev's liberalization has produced an ethnic backlash against Russification.

## ETHNIC CONVERGENCE

The official Soviet position rejects the notion that ethnic minorities are being assimilated into the dominant Russian group. Admitting that the formula, "National in form, Socialist in content," is considered a temporary compromise, Soviet leaders maintain that all national differences in the USSR are

[11]The incidence of ethnically mixed marriages is especially high in urban areas. In 1986 it exceeded 33 percent (one third) of all new marriages. In one out of every six families husbands and wives are of different nationalities. Estimated 90 million (almost 30 percent) of all Soviet citizens live outside their ethnic homelands.

being gradually eliminated in order to create a truly homogenized single "Soviet nation." In theory, this means an eventual "deethnization" of everybody, including the Russians. Ethnic characteristics and peculiarities are expected to be replaced and superseded by the Communist ideology, thus causing the Soviet people to break away from their national traditions and to feel and think alike as equal members of a supernational society.

But the theory appears to be only remotely connected with the realities of the contemporary Soviet Union, in which the Russians continue to play a dominant role. It seems much more probable that the net result of the ongoing demographic engineering will be a further Russification of ethnic minorities, and the promised classless society, if it is ever achieved, will be "Russian in form, Communist in content." In the meantime, during the transition to Communism, the difference between first-class and second-class Soviet citizens is likely to depend progressively more on the degree of conformity with both the "form" and the "content" of that optimal model. This will give the ethnic Russians a natural advantage over all the others and encourage them to assimilate faster. It should be noted that the advantage of being or becoming Russian applies primarily to political and professional career opportunities for individuals. In terms of relative standards of living, many ethnic groups compare favorably to the Russian majority, which includes the bulk of the poorest Soviet peasants.

To be sure, except for a few cases involving relatively small minorities that have found themselves engulfed by Russian settlers over several centuries, it is too early to speak of any wholesale national assimilation in the USSR. There are no published deadlines or timetables for total ethnic convergence, either. On the contrary, in numerical terms, the Soviet minorities are for the first time catching up with the Russians: the total number of non-Russians in the USSR's population is fast approaching 50 percent. The significance of these statistics should not be exaggerated, however, because the Soviet Union is anything but a "one-person, one-vote" democracy; nor are the Soviet minorities united among themselves. In fact, because of the lack of unity among them, it may be said that the Soviet minorities as a whole continue to comprise much less than the sum of their parts.[12]

The changing ratios within the USSR's population, favoring non-Russians and especially the traditionally Moslem minorities, are definitely of some concern to Soviet leaders. The same must be true about the ominous signs suggesting that the Soviet Union is heading toward an "ethnic explosion," resulting from the mounting separatist pressures. Barring a radical change of the status quo brought about by a major disaster, such as a military setback, or a political collapse, neither the quantity nor the quality of ethnic nationalism, however, presents an immediate danger for the integrity of the USSR.

[12]Should the ethnic Russians lose their status as a majority, it would not be the first time. During most of the last 100 years of the Russian Empire (1817–1917), the Russians comprised less than 50 percent of its population.

On the other hand, there cannot be any question that assimilation, or so-called ethnic convergence, meets with a considerable resistance that takes many different forms. In the ethnic union republics, the potential for resistance is stronger than elsewhere. This is especially true of the three clusters of union republics populated by the non-melting ethnic minorities whose cultures are distinctly different from that of the Russians—the Baltic countries, the Caucasian republics, and Central Asia. Pressure of Russification adds fuel to this smoldering fire. The dominant Russian group may be concerned about mass assimilation of minorities for a reason of its own: fear of losing its commanding position by becoming too large and diluted. The question "Who needs whom more?" is asked by both non-Russians and Russians.

At least for now, Gorbachev's more liberal approach to the nationality problem has lessened the threat of assimilation for even smaller ethnic groups. His regime has allowed a much larger degree of local autonomy as part of what is called "a return to the correct Leninist nationality policy."

## THE RUSSIANS

The historically dominant component of the Soviet nation consists of about 146 million Russians (or Great Russians)—that is, people who identify themselves as such in terms of both native tongue and ethnicity. This constitutes over one half of the USSR's total population. About 83 percent of the ethnic Russians live in the Russian Soviet Federative Socialist Republic (RSFSR), which occupies three fourths of the entire Soviet Union. The rest of the Russians, about 25 million, make their homes, and usually occupy positions of relative importance, in other union republics. Owing to many centuries of thorough mixing with other ethnic groups, the Russians have physical characteristics ranging from those of Nordic Europeans to those associated with Asia.

The political history of the Russian people began eleven centuries ago, when East Slavic tribes living along the Dniepr River and its tributaries formed a loose federation dominated by the principality of Kiev. The original name of the new nation was "Rus," which probably identified members of the ruling tribe or clan, possibly of Scandinavian roots. In 988, the Russians adopted Christianity from Byzantium, their neighbor in the south. During the first half of the thirteenth century, the Russian lands were overrun by hordes of Mongols (Tatars), and for the next 250 years the Russians were vassals of the vast Mongolian empire. It was a time of desperate struggle for survival, which is still remembered in Russian folklore: in ballads, songs, proverbs, and so on. The cause of national liberation was championed and skillfully organized by the principality of Moscow, which had succeeded Kiev as the center of Russian political and cultural life. Unlike its Kievan predecessor, Muscovite Russia was far removed and isolated from Europe.

In the second half of the sixteenth century, after having subjugated all other Russian principalities, Moscow began its eastward territorial expansion at the expense of neighboring lands and over great expanses roamed by small, primitive tribes. The former Mongolian masters of the Russians, from whom they had learned many social and political customs and who had settled along the Volga River, became their first victims. Moved by their quest for secure borders, adventure, economic considerations, political ambitions, and even messianic visions, the Russians continued their territorial expansion over vast spaces of northern Asia, meeting almost no resistance from small nomadic tribes of aborigines. By the end of the eighteenth century, Russian colonies were established in Alaska and California.

Ironically, as the Russian Empire grew, the lot of common Russians became worse. By the end of the sixteenth century, the majority of them were serfs: peasants tied to the land belonging to squires, the crown, or monasteries. This arrangement prevailed for several centuries, during which long periods of sullen acceptance of the socioeconomic status quo alternated with violent, spontaneous uprisings. Brief moments of social peace and national unity occurred only in the face of major foreign invasions.

The dynamic reign of Peter the Great (1689–1725) was aimed at making Russia a European power. It gave a strong impetus to its belated cultural renaissance, but at the same time added a cultural dimension to the socioeconomic gap between the ruling elite and the Russian masses.

The end of the Russian Empire was precipitated by military defeats in the Crimean War during the 1850s and in the Russo-Japanese War of 1904 to 1905. These ill-fated foreign policy ventures forced the government to make concessions: the formal abolition of serfdom in 1861 and the introduction of a limited parliamentary system in 1905. But these and similar countermeasures offered too little, too late. The opposite—too much, too soon—appeared to have been attempted by the "Provisional Government" that replaced the monarchy in February 1917, in the wake of Russia's military setbacks in World War I. This short-lived experiment with Western democracy was canceled by the celebrated October Revolution ushering in, in Lenin's words, a "new era in the world's history" in which Russia was to play a leading role.

For the last six decades, the Russians, who have retained their status as the dominant ethnic group, have been playing, willingly or otherwise, an increasingly important role in the destiny of the world. Just how much the Russians have changed since the revolution is a moot question. They have definitely been affected by Communism more than any other nation, but at the same time they also have "Russified" Communism.

The special "big brother" role of the ethnic Russians is indicated in many different ways. Their component territory—the RSFSR—has a distinctly unique status among the union republics: It is disproportionally large and has a complex federate structure. At the same time, the RSFSR deliberately lacks some of the trappings of the other union republics, such as a separate capital, as if to symbolize the fact that it is not just a part, but the central core of the Soviet Union.

## OTHER SLAVS

Besides the ethnic Russians, two other large groups of East Slavs live in the Soviet Union: the Ukrainians, who number more than 43 million, and the Byelorussians, who number close to 10 million. In addition, smaller contingents of West Slavs (Poles, Czechs, and Slovaks) and South Slavs (Bulgarians, Serbs, and Croats) exist within the Soviet population.

Ethnically and linguistically, the Ukrainians and the Byelorussians are closely related to the Russians. With them they share common ancestors and a cultural heritage including Orthodox Christianity. The three peoples began as one but later became separated after the Mongolian onslaught in the first half of the thirteenth century. The Ukrainians, the second largest Soviet nationality, are the direct descendants of the civilization that developed a millennium ago in the Dniepr basin around Kiev. For several centuries afterwards they managed, without ever achieving a formal statehood, to maintain a precarious existence between the two growing powers: Muscovite Russia in the east and Poland in the west. Only in the middle of the seventeenth century, when a choice between the two powerful neighbors became inevitable, did the Ukrainians "reunite" with the Russians, first as autonomous vassals, and later as a mere province (called "Little Russia") of the Russian Empire. More than two centuries of relentless efforts to eradicate Ukrainian nationalism followed. This, however, did not prevent the Ukrainians from trying to regain their independence from Russia immediately after the fall of the czarist regime in 1917. It was a short-lived attempt: In the course of the civil war the new Moscow rulers succeeded in extending their control over much of the Ukraine. At the same time, the western parts of the Ukraine were incorporated into the newly established states of Poland and Czechoslovakia. They were annexed by the Soviet Union in 1939 and 1945, respectively. In 1940 the USSR also annexed a small region of Romania (Bukovina) populated by the Ukrainians.

At present, approximately 85 percent of Soviet Ukrainians live in the Ukrainian Soviet Socialist Republic, where their proportion to the total population is about 74 percent. More than 3.5 million Ukrainians live in the RSFSR, and next to the Russians the Ukrainians are the most numerous nonnative residents in the other union republics. Mixed marriages between Ukrainians and Russians are quite common, and several million Ukrainians claim Russian as their native tongue. During the Soviet era, many persons of Ukrainian origin have served on the highest party and government councils in Moscow. On the other hand, there have also been frequent manifestations of Ukrainian nationalism directed against the Russians.

The less numerous Byelorussians (close to 10 million) compose the fourth largest Soviet nationality (after the Russians, Ukrainians, and Uzbeks). Throughout its history, this smallest of the three East Slavic groups was too weak to prevent domination by Lithuania, Poland, or Russia. As a result, the Byelorussians never had a chance to taste real national independence. Perhaps because of this they have appeared less resentful of their status within the Russian Empire and the Soviet Union. Most of Byelorussia (the name means "White Russia") has been under Russian control for more than 200 years. But a small part of it, called "West Byelorussia," belonged to Poland between World War I and World War II. In 1939, it was annexed by the Soviet Union.

About 83 percent of the Soviet Byelorussians live in the Byelorussian Soviet Socialist Republic, and account for almost 80 percent of its population. The Byelorussians, especially those who live outside their own republic (more than 1.6 million), seem to assimilate more easily into Russian culture than members of any other large minority. Several thoroughly Russified Byelorussians have achieved high positions in Moscow.

The Soviet Union received a majority of its fourth largest Slavic group, the Poles, through the annexation of former Polish territories in 1939. During the nearly 150 years of Russian imperial rule over most of Poland before 1917, other Poles settled in various parts of the Soviet Union as migrants or deportees. Deprived of its own national territory, the bulk of the Polish minority appears to consist of thoroughly Russified persons and mixed families in which one spouse is Polish.

Other West and South Slavs constitute small minorities that reside primarily in the western regions of the Ukraine. Like the Poles, they have practically no cultural life of their own.

All Slavs combined account for almost three fourths of the total population. But their proportion is declining in favor of non-Slavic (and non-European) inhabitants of the Soviet Union (Table 2–8).

**TABLE 2–8**    Slavic Component of USSR Population (In Percentages)

|  | 1959 | 1970 | 1979 |
|---|---|---|---|
| Russians | 54.7 | 53.4 | 52.4 |
| Ukrainians | 17.8 | 16.9 | 16.2 |
| Byelorussians | 3.8 | 3.7 | 3.6 |
| Other Slavs | .8 | .8 | .7 |
|  | 77.1 | 74.8 | 72.9 |

Source: Compiled by author from Soviet data.

## BALTIC NATIONS

The three Baltic nations are Estonia, Latvia, and Lithuania. Although ethnically only the last two are related, all three of these relatively small nations share both a common geography and a unique experience among Soviet minorities of having been free and independent for more than twenty years between World War I and World War II. Together, they number more than 5 million, or 2 percent of the USSR's total population.

The Estonians, who number only slightly less than 1 million, are the smallest nationality with a union republic. Almost all Estonians live in the Estonian Soviet Socialist Republic constituting about 60 percent of its population. Linguistically, the Estonians belong to the Uralic family, which is represented in Europe by two other major languages: Hungarian and Finnish. From the twelfth century until the middle of the sixteenth century, Estonia (Estland) was under German domination. Then, for the next 250 years, it fell alternately under the control of Poland, Denmark, and Sweden. In 1711 Estonia, a Swedish province at the time, was annexed by Russia. It became independent in 1918, but was annexed by the USSR in 1940.

The Latvians (Letts) have a similar history, except that in the twelfth century they enjoyed a brief period of national independence before being subjugated by the Germans. Latvia became part of the Russian Empire at the end of the eighteenth century, seceded in 1918, and was recaptured in 1940. There are almost 1.5 million Latvians in the Soviet Union today, about 95 percent of whom live in the Latvian Soviet Socialist Republic, making up approximately 50 percent of its population. The Latvian and Lithuanian languages belong to the same Baltic branch of the Indo-European linguistic family.

The Lithuanians, who number more than 2.9 million, are the most numerous of the three Baltic peoples. Most of them live in Lithuania, where their share of the total population is about 75 percent. Unlike its two Baltic neighbors, Lithuania has not only a long history of independence but also memories of political and military superiority. The Grand Duchy of Lithuania, having existed as an independent state from the beginning of the thirteenth century to the second half of the sixteenth century, formed a binational state with Poland in 1569. This union lasted until the end of the

TABLE 2–9    Autonomous Regions (Union Republics to Which they Belong)*

| | |
|---|---|
| 1. Adygei AR (RSFSR) | 5. Karachai-Circassian AR (RSFSR) |
| 2. Gorno-Altai AR (RSFSR) | 6. Khakass AR (RSFSR) |
| 3. Gorno-Badakhshan (Tajik SSR) | 7. Nagorno-Karabakh (Azerbaijan SSR) |
| 4. Jewish AR (RSFSR) | 8. South Ossetian AR (Georgian SSR) |

*The Soviet Constitution (Article 87) lists the autonomous regions in the Russian alphabetical order.
Source: Compiled by author from Soviet data.

**TABLE 2–10**  Autonomous Areas*

| | | | |
|---|---|---|---|
| 1. | Aginski-Buryat AA | 6. | Koryak AA |
| 2. | Chukot AA | 7. | Nenets AA |
| 3. | Evenki AA | 8. | Taimyr AA |
| 4. | Khanty-Mansi AA | 9. | Ust-Ordynsk AA |
| 5. | Komi-Permyak AA | 10. | Yamal-Nenets AA |

*All ten autonomous areas are in the RSFSR. Their names are not mentioned in the Soviet Constitution.

Source: Compiled by author from Soviet data.

eighteenth century. Lithuania was annexed by Russia in 1814, became independent in 1918, and was annexed again in 1940.

Culturally, the three Baltic nations appear to be closer to Europe than to the rest of the Soviet Union. A Western traveler going to the Soviet Union via the Baltic republics is likely to feel less "cultural shock" on arriving in Tallinn (or Riga or Vilnius) than after leaving there and arriving in Moscow. The Baltic natives must also feel this way; as a result, few of them live in other parts of the Soviet Union. The traditional religions of the Baltic peoples are Catholicism and Protestantism (Lutheran). Because of their geographic location, the three small union republics are easily reached not only by radio signals but also by telecasts originating in the Scandinavian countries.

All this adds to the special position of the Baltic nations among the national minorities in the Soviet Union, even though they have been involuntary members of the USSR for over four decades. In fact, the annexation of Estonia, Latvia, and Lithuania by the Soviet Union in 1940 has never been officially recognized by the United States and several other Western countries. It is being openly denounced in the Baltic republics themselves, where nationalist feelings run very high. If orderly secession from the USSR should become possible, they would be the first to leave.

## NATIONS OF THE CAUCASUS

About 5 percent of the total population of the USSR is composed of the titular peoples of the three union republics in the Caucasus—Armenians, Azerbaijans (Azerbaijani), and Georgians. They are heirs to three distinctly different ancient civilizations.

There are more than 4.3 million Armenians in the Soviet Union, many of whom do not live in their historic mountainous homeland, called the Armenian Soviet Socialist Republic (or Armenia). With a population of about 3.4 million, slightly more than 10 percent of whom are non-Armenians, Armenia is the most homogeneous union republic. Linguistically, Armenians belong to the Indo-European family. Their traditional religion is a special branch of Christianity called the Gregorian Church, and their culture is almost 3,000 years old. The Armenians also have a long political tradition. The first independent Armenian state was established in the fourth century B.C. Beginning in the eighth century, after a long period of national independence, Armenia was conquered by a succession of invaders: the Arabs, Mongols, Turks, and others. In 1639, the country was divided between Turkey and Iran. In 1828, Iran was forced to yield its part of Armenia to Russia. A smaller part of Armenia remained under Turkish control. In the wake of the 1917 Revolution, the Armenians regained their independence in the Russian part of their homeland, but in 1920, Russian control was fully restored.

The Azerbaijans number approximately 7 million. About 90 percent of this number live in the Azerbaijan Soviet Socialist Republic (or Azerbaijan), where they account for about 78 percent of the population. Their traditional religion is Islam and their language belongs to the Turko-Mongolian family. Azerbaijan culture is more than 2,500 years old. As one of the important crossroads of the ancient world, the country suffered many conquests and invasions by the Macedonians, Romans, Mongols, Arabs, and others. But there were also periods of national independence as far back as the seventh century B.C. In modern times, the Azerbaijans found themselves constantly threatened by Iran, Turkey, and Russia. In the beginning of the nineteenth century, their land was divided between Iran and Russia. After the 1917 Revolution, Russia's part of Azerbaijan temporarily gained independence with some military help from Turkey and Britain. But by the early 1920s it was recaptured by the Russians. In the course of World War II, Soviet troops occupied the northern part of Iran populated by the Azerbaijans, setting the stage for an abortive attempt to "reunite" them with their fellow Azerbaijans in the Azerbaijan Soviet Socialist Republic.

A similar fate befell the third large minority of the Caucasus—the Georgians—whose native land is called the Georgian Soviet Socialist Republic (or Georgia). Georgia has a population of approximately 5 million, only about 3.3 million of whom are Georgians. About 300,000 Georgians live in other parts of the Soviet Union. Ethnically and linguistically, Georgians belong to the Caucasian family, which also includes many smaller nationalities who live in the northern Caucasus. The traditional religion of Georgia is a variation of Eastern Orthodox Christianity, closely related to that of Russia. The struggle for national independence began for the Georgians almost 2,500 years ago. Like the Armenians, time and again the Georgians found themselves hopelessly outnumbered by invading armies. After the sixteenth century, Georgian kings were forced to rely more and more on Russia's protection against Islamic Iran and Turkey. In 1801, Georgia was incorporated into the Russian Empire. For a few short years after the Revolution of 1917, the Georgians were independent once again.

Unlike Armenia, both Azerbaijan and Georgia contain smaller ethnic territories, autonomous republics and regions, within their borders.[13] Azerbaijan also has a large number of Russian settlers. In 1988, serious tensions developed between the Armenians and Azerbaijans.

## CENTRAL ASIAN REPUBLICS

The cluster of five[14] union republics in Central Asia is populated by peoples who have very much in common with each other. Their traditional religion is Islam, and, with the exception of the Tajiks, they are closely related as members of the Turko-Mongolian linguistic family. The Tajiks are of Iranian stock, making them members of the Indo-European family. The four major Turkic peoples are the Kazakhs, Kirghiz, Turkmens, and Uzbeks. There is some question concerning the real reasons for this division, which did not become final until the mid-1930s. Before then, the official Soviet nationalities policy for the area fluctuated between consolidation and further subdivision. Thus, for example, until 1925, the name Kirghiz was extended to all Kazakhs, and until 1936, the Turkmens were treated as a subgroup of the Uzbeks.

When this vast land of dry steppes, deserts, and high mountains was overrun by the Russians in the second half of the last century, the native peoples lived in a number of semifeudal states organized around oases in ancient cities built many centuries ago. These states were easily incorporated one by one into the Russian Empire as colonies under the name of "Russian Turkestan." For several years after the revolution the countryside remained in the hands of armed nationalists who, with some British aid, tried to prevent the return of Russian rule. The Tajiks had, by and large, a similar experience in their mountainous country situated on the border with both Afghanistan and China.

The largest of the titular nationalities is the Uzbek people, who number more than 14 million. The Kazakhs number about 7.5 million, followed by the Tajiks (3.5 million), the Turkmens (2.5 million), and the Kirghiz (2.3 million). Together, this comes to about 30 million people who live mostly in their native lands bordering on Iran, Afghanistan, and the Sinkiang Province of China. It is a strictly political border because these peoples are very closely related—linguistically, ethnically, and culturally—to their neighbors outside the Soviet Union.

---

[13]The Georgian SSR contains the Abkhasian and Adzhar ASSRs and the South Ossetian AR (region). The Azerbaijan SSR includes the Nakhichevan ASSR and the Nagorno-Karabakh AR (region).

[14]Since the northwestern part of the Kazakh SSR is actually in Europe (west of the Ural Mountains), the republic is sometimes excluded from the concept of "Central Asia."

The Kazakh SSR is the largest ethnic union republic in area, and the Uzbek SSR is the second largest ethnic union republic in population. The population of all Central Asia exceeds 40 million, or about 15 percent of the total population of the Soviet Union. However, less than two thirds of Central Asia's population is composed of the titular nations and related smaller minorities. In fact, in two of the republics—Kazakh and Kirghiz SSRs—members of the titular nationalities make up about one third and less than one half of the total populations, respectively. This means that the legal status of these republics may be in jeopardy. If the influx of nonnatives (Russians, Ukrainians, and the like) continues, the Central Asian peoples may soon be in the minority in their own lands, even though their birthrates are among the highest in the Soviet Union, as a kind of biological self-defense, giving this region the nickname "baby factory."

## OTHER MINORITIES

Among the remaining minorities numbering 1 million or more, only one has a union republic—namely, Moldavia. Most of the Moldavian people (about 3 million) live in the Moldavian Soviet Socialist Republic, situated in the southwest corner of the Soviet Union on the border with Romania. The republic has a population of more than 4 million, about 64 percent of whom are Moldavians. It is the most rural of all union republics. Linguistically, the Moldavians are related to the Romanians. The two dialects of the same language belong to the Romance branch of the Indo-European family. Much of present Moldavia was originally incorporated into the Russian Empire at the turn of the eighteenth century, but between 1917 and 1940, its western half (Bessarabia) was part of Romania. The traditional religion of the Moldavians is Eastern Orthodox, which they share with all their neighbors, including the Romanians. In fact, the division between the Moldavians and Romanians appears to be based primarily on political grounds. Since 1988, there have been serious ethnic disturbances in Kishinev and other Moldavian cities.

The seven large minorities without their own union republics include the four already mentioned peoples:

1. The Germans, most of whom immigrated to Russia during the eighteenth century. Many of them live in Central Asia and Siberia where they were forcibly moved during World War II.
2. The Jews, who are found primarily in urban centers of the European Soviet Union. Their ancestors populated the parts of Poland and Lithuania that were annexed by Russia at the end of the eighteenth century. Because of their determined efforts to leave the USSR or to assimilate to escape anti-Semitism, the number of Jews has been steadily declining.

**TABLE 2–11** Urban and Rural Populations (In Millions)

| Year | Total | Urban | Rural | % of Urbanization |
|------|-------|-------|-------|-------------------|
| 1913 | 159.2 | 28.5  | 131.7 | 18 |
| 1940 | 194.1 | 63.1  | 131.0 | 33 |
| 1959 | 208.8 | 100.0 | 108.8 | 48 |
| 1970 | 241.7 | 136.0 | 105.7 | 56 |
| 1979 | 262.4 | 163.6 | 98.8  | 62 |
| 1989 | 286.7 | 188.8 | 97.9  | 66 |

*Source:* Compiled by author from Soviet statistics.

3. The Poles, many of whom live in the Ukraine and Byelorussia, which formerly belonged to Poland.
4. The Tatars, who are located mostly in regions along the Volga.

The three other large minorities are the Chuvash, Mordva, and Bashkirs. The Chuvash and Bashkirs are closely related to the Tatars. The Mordva (Mordvins) belong to the Uralic family. These people, and smaller minorities closely related to them, live primarily along the midreaches of the Volga, where they, as well as the Tatars, have their own autonomous republics that border on each other.

The northern and central parts of the Caucasus, which are incorporated into the RSFSR, are populated by more than thirty smaller ethnic groups. A majority of them belongs to the Caucasian linguistic family, but some are of Turko-Mongolian and Indo-European stock. Almost all of them, however, share the same Islamic religion and many common mountaineer customs. Most of this area was annexed by Russia as a result of a slow and bloody conquest that lasted for almost the entire nineteenth century.

The largest closely related linguistic group in the northern and central Caucasus are the Daghestan languages, spoken by more than 1.7 million mountaineers who are divided into ten major subgroups and numerous tribes. Some of them have their own ASSRs and ARs.

The south of the European USSR is populated, among other nationalities, by more than 200,000 Gypsies.

A substantial group of small minorities inhabit the far northern regions of the European RSFSR, Siberia, and the Soviet Far East. Many of them are distant relatives of the American Indians.[15] The already mentioned Kalmyks, who live along the lower reaches of the Volga, are the only people in Europe whose traditional religion is Buddhism. They are of Mongolian stock, which is represented also by other minorities living along the long Soviet border with China and Mongolia.

[15]These minorities are called the "Peoples of the North." They number more than 160,000, are divided into about twenty distinct nationalities, and share ten autonomous areas (Table 2–11).

## LANGUAGES

Although theoretically the languages of the fifteen union republics enjoy an equal status, for all practical purposes, Russian is the official language of the Soviet Union. It is spoken as a native tongue by about 60 percent of the population and used as a second language by the majority of the rest.

Aside from being the main communication medium, Russian is the language of a great literature and a rich culture that have dominated the life of the entire country for hundreds of years. Russian evolved as a distinct language between the thirteenth and fifteenth centuries after the conquest of the East Slavs by the Mongolian invaders. As their literary language, the East Slavs, and later the Russians, used Old Bulgarian (Church Slavonic), along with its writing system, called "Cyrillics," which was created by Greek missionaries in the ninth century and then brought to Russia together with Christianity. During the early period of its development, Russian received an influx of Tatar words. Later, at the turn of the eighteenth century, Peter the Great's efforts to westernize Russia resulted in the borrowing of many technical terms from English, Dutch, and German. At the same time, a new Russian alphabet was devised on the basis of the Cyrillics, to simplify the writing system and bring it closer to the spoken language.

The next hundred years (the eighteenth century) witnessed the impact of the French language, which eventually became the second language of the Russian nobility. As a result, many French words became part of the Russian vocabulary. The modern Russian language was fully developed and established during the first half of the nineteenth century. Much credit for this is given to the most admired Russian poet of all times, Alexander Pushkin (1799–1837). The Revolution of 1917 brought about minor modifications of the alphabet and a wave of new sociopolitical words ("sovietisms") and scientific and technical terms, usually based on Latin and Greek roots.

Slight dialectical differences exist between Russian spoken in various parts of the big country, but they are rapidly disappearing under the impact of education and the mass media. Russian is the language of the Soviet government and the Soviet Armed Forces.

Closely related to Russian are the two other East Slavic languages, Ukrainian and Byelorussian. Native speakers of these three languages understand one another. Other Slavic languages spoken in the Soviet Union include Polish, Bulgarian, Serbo-Croatian, Slovak, and Czech.

The Slavic languages belong to the Indo-European linguistic family, which is represented in the USSR by several other groups of languages and separate tongues: the Germanic languages (German and Yiddish), the Romance languages (Moldavian), the Baltic languages (Latvian and Lithuanian), Armenian, Tajik, and others. In numbers of speakers, the Indo-European family is by far the largest. Another large group of languages, the Turko-Mongolian family, is represented by such languages as Kazakh,

**BOX 2–3** *Language Policy Under Mikhail Gorbachev*

The most important principle of our multinational state is the free development and equal use by all Soviet citizens of their mother tongues, and the learning of Russian, which has been voluntarily adopted by Soviet people as a means of communication between nations. Every condition should be provided for national-Russian bilingualism to develop harmoniously and naturally, with an eye to the specific features of every region, and without formalism; more concern should be shown for the active functioning of national languages in various spheres of political, public and cultural life; the study of the language of the republic by citizens of other nationalities residing in it, above all by children and young people, should be encouraged. All this should not be contraposed to the democratic principle of free choice of the language of instruction.

Resolutions of the 19th All-Union CPSU Conference, July 1, 1988.

Kirghiz, Uzbek, Turkmen, and Azerbaijani. The Uralic family includes Estonian, Karelian, and several other tongues. The Caucasian family consists of more than thirty tongues, including the Georgian language. The last official census (1979) identified more than 100 different languages native to the Soviet Union. Some of them are spoken by only several hundred people, members of almost extinct Siberian tribes. In addition to Russian, Ukrainian, and Byelorussian, approximately eighty large and small languages use Cyrillic writing systems. In only three union republics—Estonia, Latvia, and Lithuania—do the languages of the titular nationalities use Latin letter alphabets. (Nationalist groups in Moldavia are pressuring local authorities for a complete change to the Latin alphabet.) The Armenians and the Georgians have ancient writing systems of their own. The Yiddish language is written with Hebrew letters, bringing the number of alphabets in official use to five.

   The linguistic diversity is the most visible manifestation of the heterogeneous character of the population of the Soviet Union. It is, in fact, a source of major problems and worries for Soviet leaders, who emphasize the unity and uniformity prescribed by their ideology. The only realistic solution appears to be a gradual conversion to Russian as the main language (regardless of how this process is accomplished).

   The long-range linguistic strategy envisages three overlapping phases: (1) promoting Russian as a compulsory second language; (2) encouraging bilingualism; and (3) substituting Russian for ethnic languages. At present about 65 percent of the total non-Russian population speaks Russian fluently, more than 50 percent of the non-Russians are bilingual, and close to 25 percent of them consider Russian to be their native tongue. In addition, the Russian vocabulary is growing at a much faster rate than the vocabularies of other languages of the USSR.

Until recently, these indicators were steadily rising. But under *glasnost* many national minorities began to assert their constitutional right to a wider use of native tongues, and in some ethnic republics legislatures have challenged the coequal status of the Russian language. However, it does not seem likely that the advanced process of linguistic Russification will be reversed or even slowed down for very long.

## GLOSSARY

**Bilingualism:** complete mastery of two languages.
**Demography:** branch of science dealing with population problems; data pertaining to population trends.
**Heterogeneous:** of a different, diversified nature; consisting of different nationalities.
**Homogeneous:** of one kind; of one nationality.
**Perestroika:** major reforms, restructuring initiated by M. Gorbachev.
**Pronatal:** encouraging large families, population growth.
**Russification:** assimilation into Russian culture.

## RECOMMENDED READINGS

ALLWORTH, EDWARD, *Soviet Nationality Problems*. New York: Columbia University Press, 1971.
AZRAEL, JEREMY R. (ed.), *Soviet Nationality Policies and Practices*. New York: Praeger, 1978.
CONQUEST, ROBERT, *The Last Empire: Nationality and the Soviet Future*. Stanford, CA: Hoover Institution Press, 1986.

CHAPTER

# 3

# THE IDEOLOGY

## MARXISM-LENINISM

The Soviet Union has an official ideology called Marxism-Leninism. It consists of the original writings of Karl Marx (1818–1883) and his closest associate, Friedrich Engels (1820–1895). Numerous additions and modifications were contributed later by Vladimir Lenin (1870–1924) and other Russian Marxists. Marxism-Leninism claims to be the only true scientific body of knowledge able to explain the human universe and the past and present, and thereby lead people to a better future. Frequent references to Marxism-Leninism permeate all aspects of Soviet life. On every level of education Soviet students must take courses dealing with various parts of the ideology's history, theory, and application. More than 50,000 specially trained, full-time instructors, researchers, writers, and commentators are needed for this enormous propaganda operation, which is aided by the modern mass media. Top ideologists are among the most important and privileged Soviet citizens. The words "science" and "scientific" are generously used in countless multilingual Soviet publications devoted to Marxism-Leninism.

Marx believed that his chief accomplishment was the application of the latest scientific methods to a systematic study of the human condition. He strove to provide a comprehensive explanation of the mechanism of human history in the same way that his contemporary Charles Darwin strove to explain the evolution of the species. Marx maintained that his findings could be used in political, economic, and social engineering to expedite the inevitable (in his opinion) advent of a Communist era. This was to begin in the most developed industrial nations and then spread throughout the rest of the world. In Marx's opinion, the backward czarist empire was completely unsuited for this role. Ironically, Russia, on the verge of economic collapse and military defeat in 1917, was the first country to apply Marx's ideas on a large scale. Since that time, the USSR has served as the main repository of Marx's legacy.

**BOX 3–1**    *Excerpt from the Communist Manifesto, Written and Published by Marx and Engels in December 1848*

A spectre is haunting Europe—the spectre of Communism. All the Powers of old Europe have entered into a holy alliance to exorcize this spectre: Pope and Czar, Metternich and Guizot, French Radicals and German police-spies.

Where is the party in opposition that has not been decried as Communistic by its opponents in power? Where the Opposition that has not hurled back the branding reproach of Communism, against the more advanced opposition parties, as well as against its reactionary adversaries?

Two things result from this fact.

I. Communism is already acknowledged by all European Powers to be itself a Power.

II. It is high time that Communists should openly, in the face of the whole world, publish their views, their aims, their tendencies, and meet this nursery tale of the Spectre of Communism with a Manifesto of the party itself.

Quoted in Sidney Hook, *Marx and the Marxists* (New York: D. Van Nostrand, 1955), p. 133.

The Soviet ideologists maintain that all important decisions must be made on the basis of a "creative interpretation of Marxism-Leninism." The USSR proudly calls itself a goal-oriented society possessing the scientific know-how to achieve a single lofty objective: a classless Communist society in which there will be no want, inequality, or oppression of any kind. In theory, Soviet citizens do not perform their jobs simply to make a living for themselves and their families but to contribute all they can to the building of the new society. During the last seventy years, millions of them have made, or were forced to make, great sacrifices for this cause.

Although it denies the existence of God, Marxist-Leninist ideology is a surrogate state religion of the USSR. As we shall see, it determines the economic development, social composition, and political nature of Soviet society, as well as the personal duties and rights of Soviet citizens. Soviet leaders who rule in the name of this "infallible" creed contend that they

**FIGURE 3–1**
Karl Marx (1818–1883), founder of the modern Communist ideology that bears his name.

speak for the future of humankind and that ultimately Communism will prevail throughout the world. They claim to understand the "objective laws of history" that Marx is credited with discovering and affirm that they act accordingly.

The impact and appeal of Marxism-Leninism are not limited to the Soviet Union: China and several other nations, containing almost one third of the world's population, have Marxist regimes, and more than 100 Communist parties[1] are seeking power in countries of Europe, Africa, Asia, and the Americas. Most, but not all, owe varying degrees of allegiance to the Soviet Union, which they consider to be their ideological leader. This makes the Soviet Union much more than a traditional nation-state or even an empire: It is the recognized headquarters of a worldwide cause.

## MARX'S AND ENGELS'S LEGACY

Marx derived his system of ideas, values, and beliefs from three sources: (1) German philosophy; (2) French Socialist theories; and (3) English political economy. While a student of various universities in his native Germany, he became greatly influenced by the German philosophers Hegel and

[1]In some countries, Communist parties are called "Workers" or "Marxist" parties.

Feuerbach.[2] From the former, Marx took the concept of dialectics, and from the latter, a materialistic world outlook. He used these to develop a comprehensive explanation of the world and human society. His familiarity with the ideas of Utopian Socialists came later, when he lived as a young radical journalist in France and Belgium. According to his followers, Marx succeeded in transforming the Utopians' dream of an ideal human society into a modern science that both proved the historic inevitability of such a society and showed how this process could be accelerated. Much later in life, while living as an exile in London, he developed a deep interest in economics and thoroughly studied the works of Ricardo and Adam Smith. During this period he wrote his most important single work, *Capital* (in German, *Das Kapital*), which offers an original critique of the early (the mid-nineteenth century) phase of capitalism in Europe. The first and most significant volume of *Capital* was written by Marx alone in 1867. The second and third volumes were edited and published by Engels several years after Marx's death in 1883. Together and individually, they also wrote several other scholarly works.

Marx and Engels also played leading roles in the early efforts to establish international cooperation among various radical groups in Europe. Throughout their lives, they were concerned for the underdogs of the day— the industrial workers, or "the proletarians" as they preferred to call them. This concern was well founded: Factory hands were paid starvation wages, working conditions were appalling, labor laws did not exist, and there was no job security of any kind. Marx did not believe that these conditions that existed in continental western Europe could be improved simply through political reforms. Only violent revolutions, in his opinion, could free the workers from the heavy chains of unbridled exploitation. Many critics of Marx are quick to point out that time has proved the error of this theory, as well as other pessimistic predictions about the evolution and reform of capitalism. However, it is important to keep in mind that had it not been for Marx's ideas and the threat of their realization, a very different situation might exist today. For more than a century, the entire world has felt Marx's influence. He has generated an international movement of unprecedented proportions, which is still growing. The movement that bears his name has not, so far, produced "Socialism with a human face," but it may have inadvertently contributed to the emergence of more humane forms of capitalism.

Because Marx conceived his ideas at different points in his long, creative life, it is not surprising to find inconsistencies and even contradictions among them. To ensure a fair evaluation, his ideas must be considered in the

---

[2]Georg Hegel (1770–1831). Hegel's "dialectics" theory posited that in our thinking we proceed toward truth through three progressively higher stages. Unlike Marx, Hegel never applied this theory to physical phenomena and social development. Ludwig Feuerbach (1804–1872) was a disciple of Hegel, whose world outlook changed from an idealistic to a materialistic one.

overall context and judged in terms of their place and time, an approach that has not often been taken by either Marx's friends or his foes. In fact, a disagreement among his disciples over the most accurate interpretation of his writings began immediately after his death. At present this disagreement continues. Because so many explanations have been offered, it is necessary to distinguish between Marx's and Engels's own writings and interpretations of these writings by such diverse groups of followers as extreme Marxist terrorists and moderate Social Democrats. Here, we examine the official Soviet interpretation that divides Marx's and Engels's legacy into three parts: philosophy, political economy, and "scientific Socialism."

## MARXIST PHILOSOPHY

Marxist philosophy—the theoretical foundation of Marxism-Leninism—consists of two parts: "dialectical materialism," which is concerned with the physical world, and "historical materialism," which deals with social phenomena. This philosophy as a whole not only explains the human world, but also shows how it can be changed. In Marx's own words: "The philosophers have only interpreted the world, in various ways; the point, however, is to change it."[3]

Dialectical materialism gives a total view of the physical world. According to this theory, matter is the sole basis of the universe, in which there is no God. Matter is also the sole objective source of all human knowledge. Everything in this world is made of matter and, therefore, is interconnected. The unity of the world, however, does not prevent it from being in a constant state of flux and change occurring in space and time. The world, therefore, is simultaneously the unity and the struggle of opposites. This is the essence of the dialectical process and may be summarized by this equation: Thesis clashes with antithesis to produce synthesis. Because this synthesis in turn becomes a new thesis on a higher level, the dialectical process of the "negation of negation" never ends. In addition to this "quantitative" kind of change, the dialectical process includes an abrupt "qualitative change." In fact, at certain points of accumulation, all quantitative changes are dialectically transformed into qualitative changes. For example, when water is heated, its temperature rises. This is conceived of as a quantitative change. Then, when the temperature has reached the boiling point, the water turns into steam. This represents a qualitative change.

Because people are an integral part of this material world, it follows that the same "laws" have underlaid their behavior throughout history. According to this aspect of Marxist philosophy, which is called historical materialism, people's consciousness is merely a reflection of the material world around them, and material production is the root of their social life.

[3]K. Marx and F. Engels, *Selected Works* (Moscow: Progress Publishers, 1968), vol. 1, p. 15.

People are seen first as socioeconomic beings. The mode of material production and the ensuing production relations form the "base" of every human society. The base determines and influences everything else that belongs to a given society: politics, religion, philosophy, norms of behavior, and spiritual values. This is called the "superstructure." Changes in the base lead to changes in entire societies. Just as in the physical world, the accumulation of quantitative changes results in qualitative changes—for example, revolutions. When analyzed dialectically, the unity and diversity of historical process show that the mainspring of history is class struggle. The spiral course of history (that is, its natural evolution) moves from a preclass society (family, clan, and tribe), to a class society (slave, feudal, and capitalist), and eventually to a classless, or Communist, society. Communism is preceded by a transitional phase called Socialism.

**BOX 3–2**  *Marx on the Nature of Money*

> The need for money is therefore the true need produced by the modern economic system [capitalism] and it is the only need which the latter produces. The *quantity* of money becomes to an ever greater degree its sole *effective* attribute: just as it reduces everything to its abstract form, so it reduces itself in the course of its own movement to something merely *quantitative*. *Excess* and *intemperance* come to be its true norm. Subjectively, this is even partly manifested in that the extension of products and needs falls into *contriving* and ever-*calculating* subservience to inhuman, refined, unnatural and *imaginary* appetites. Private property does not know how to change crude need into *human* need. Its *idealism* is *fantasy, caprice* and *whim;* and no eunuch flatters his despot more basely or uses more despicable means to stimulate his dulled capacity for pleasure in order to sneak a favour for himself than does the industrial eunuch—the producer—in order to sneak for himself a few pennies—in order to charm the golden birds out of the pockets of his Christianly beloved neighbours. He puts himself at the service of the other's most depraved fancies, plays the pimp between him and his need, excites in him morbid appetites, lies in wait for each of his weaknesses—all so that he can then demand the cash for this service of love.
>
> Karl Marx, "Economic and Philosophic Manuscripts of 1844" in Robert C. Tucker, *The Marx-Engel Reader* (New York W.W. Norton, 1978), pp. 93, 94.

Marx believed that he had scientifically proved the inevitable replacement of capitalism by Socialism (and eventually Communism). As used by Marx, the word "inevitable" refers to general trends of history, stemming from its economic development. Marxists put great faith in the inevitability of history; at the same time, planning, organization, political action, and revolutionary zeal have always been essential ingredients of their ideology.

Thus, we see that Marxism combines these two seemingly opposite notions: a belief in economic determination of history and a demand for volitional interference in history. In practice this means that there is no need to take unnecessary risks in promoting Communist takeovers, but at the same time, it is the "historic duty" of all Communists to speed up the process as much as possible. Every new situation in the world must be carefully considered in order to determine whether it represents a risk or an opportunity. In this way, Marxist philosophy is used as a self-fulfilling prophecy of action or as a built-in excuse for inaction.

## POLITICAL ECONOMY

In the introduction to *Capital*, Marx writes: "The ultimate objective of my work is to discover the economic law of the development of contemporary society."[4] His analysis begins with a definition of the two aspects of a commodity: its consumer value and its exchange value. Because all commodities are products of labor, their value is measured by the "socionecessary" time required for their production. Marx then proceeds to discuss the nature and functions of money. According to him, money becomes capital when the formula of the commodity production—that is, commodity-money-commodity—is replaced by the formula governing purchase for resale for profit—namely, money-commodity-money. Marx calls the new monetary profit made in this transaction "surplus value." The supplier of capital, the capitalist, looks for a commodity that could yield the highest surplus value. This commodity is labor power, and it is the only thing that the formally free workers, the proletariat, can offer for sale. Labor power, like no other commodity, makes the capital grow rapidly by producing surplus value.

Marx distinguishes two kinds of surplus value derived from labor power: the absolute surplus value, which depends on the length of the workday (workweek, or whatever), and the relative surplus value, which is determined by labor productivity. Capitalists strive to maximize their profits by finding ways to increase both kinds of surplus value. They do this by intensifying the exploitation of their workers, replacing them with machines, introducing better technical and managerial methods, enlarging production, and eliminating competition. This inevitably leads to unemployment, overproduction, the emergence of monopolies, and eventually to an economic crisis.

Capitalism, according to Marx, is self-destructive and cannot change its own nature. Capitalist development cannot occur without periodic economic crises, alternating with wars that make further expansion possible. In the end, the internal contradictions of capitalism can no longer be controlled, the proletariat rises, the "expropriators are expropriated," and all means of production become nationalized. This, Marx argues, is both historically

[4]K. Marx and F. Engels, *Selected Works* (Moscow: Progress Publishers, 1968), vol. 1, p. 15.

inevitable and morally just. Because surplus value is the sole source of profit, rent, and interest, all manufactured goods should rightly belong to their producers—the workers.

Marx extends his critique of capitalism to deal with the agricultural situation of his day. There he finds the progressive impoverishment and decline of small farmers who are forced either to become hired hands on large farms or to join the pool of cheap industrial labor. He contends that in the long run the development of agriculture under capitalism will lead to the same disastrous results as those met by industry. "Moreover," writes Marx in *Capital*, "any progress in the capitalist agriculture is not only a progress in the art of robbing the workers but also in the art of robbing the land."[5]

Seeing no possibility for economic justice under capitalism, Marx confidently predicts its inevitable replacement by a new form of society based on the collective ownership of all means of production. The change is to occur first in the most developed industrial countries. Using his firsthand knowledge of nineteenth-century continental western Europe, Marx maintains that the old order of things has to be destroyed by violent revolution. However, he does concede that in political democracies such as Britain and the United States a peaceful transition to Socialism is also possible.

## SCIENTIFIC SOCIALISM

Marx was so preoccupied with the study of capitalism that he wrote little about Socialism. His collaborator, Engels, however, devoted several articles to this subject. Marx fully shared Engels's ideas. According to the latter scholar, there are two phases, or stages, of Socialism: the lower and the higher. The lower stage immediately follows the collapse of capitalism. It is this stage that is called Socialism in a narrower sense, as in the Soviet Union today. Under Socialism, many features of the old capitalistic way of life, including some of its contradictions, continue to exist. The new Socialist state makes every effort to eliminate gradually the remnants of capitalism from the lives and the minds of the people. Members of the new society are rewarded according to the principle: "From each according to his ability, to each according to his work." This means that there is still no economic equality.

Engels uses the term "dictatorship of the proletariat" to describe the new form of government under Socialism. Because the assumption is that Socialism would be established in a highly industrialized country, the dictatorship of the proletariat alludes to a majority rule, but without any safeguards to protect the minority of the former capitalists, peasants, and the like that remain. Engels believed that the government machine would quickly become obsolete: "The first action carried out by the state really on behalf of

[5]K. Marx and F. Engels, *Selected Works* (Moscow: Progress Publishers, 1968), vol. 2, p. 47.

**FIGURE 3–2**
Friedrich Engels (1820–1895), a close associate and friend of Karl Marx.

the entire society—the expropriation of the means of production for the benefit of the entire society—will be, at the same time, its last independent action. The state will not be 'abolished,' it will wither away." According to Engels, under Socialism, small peasants would voluntarily give up their private businesses and form cooperative farms.

As envisaged by Engels, the higher stage, called "Communism," represents the ideal form of human society, in which there are no classes. The distribution of material goods and services under Communism is based on the principle: "From each according to his ability, to each according to his needs." This, of course, presupposes a very high level of economic development and an equally high level of social consciousness. Under Communism, the state in its traditional form no longer exists. Society consists of free associations (communes) of hard-working, unselfish, and considerate people. Differences between urban and rural life, physical and mental work, levels of education, nationalities, and so on, disappear. All people are completely equal in every respect. All citizens are able to develop their personalities fully and harmoniously. Marx called this future society the "kingdom of freedom," in comparison with the "kingdom of necessity," in which people have lived since time immemorial. Because human requirements never stop expanding, progress in science, technology, education, and such must continue accordingly. But Marx, who at times tended to be melodramatic, believed it would be a new kind of progress: "Human progress ceases to resemble that hideous pagan idol, who would not drink the nectar but from the skulls of the slain."[6]

The Soviet Union maintains that it has achieved Socialism and is currently building the higher stage, called Communism. Neither of these claims would be valid in terms of Marx's original ideas; however, these ideas have been thoroughly modified by Lenin and other Soviet Marxists to fit Russia's special conditions.

## LENIN'S CONTRIBUTIONS

When Marxist ideas were first introduced to Russia at the end of the last century, they were grafted to, and did not replace, the existing body of revolutionary thought and tradition. The founder of Russian Marxism was Georgi Plekhanov (1856–1918), a convert from the so-called Populist Movement. The radical wing of this movement, called the People's Will, was responsible for the murder of Alexander II in 1881, in a futile effort to promote spontaneous peasants' Socialism in Russia. In 1883, Plekhanov and a handful of other moderate populists embraced Marxism as an alternative to revolutionary terror, which had failed to produce expected results. From the security of political exile in Switzerland, they began to preach Marxism to their former comrades in Russia, urging them to give up terrorist tactics doomed to failure and concentrate instead on the political education of the industrial workers. According to Plekhanov's interpretation of Marxism, Russia was simply not ready for a Socialist revolution; an opinion expressed earlier by Marx himself.[7] Plekhanov believed Russia had to go through a capitalist phase first.

During the next two decades, under Plekhanov's guidance from abroad, scattered Marxist groups, consisting almost exclusively of young intellectuals, formed inside Russia. The moderates among them, nicknamed "Legal Marxists," had no trouble airing Marxist ideas on the pages of censored publications,[8] while their more radical comrades, called "Revolutionary Marxists," sought to organize Marxist study groups among industrial workers. Among the latter was a young lawyer, Vladimir Ulyanov, better known to history by his pseudonym, Lenin. A rare combination of skillful conspirator, brilliant organizer, and scholarly writer, Lenin from the very beginning was concerned with ways to adapt Marxism to Russia's

[6]K. Marx and F. Engels, *On Colonialism* (Moscow: Progress Publishers, 1968), p. 87.

[7]To be sure, Marx was not always consistent in his evaluation of Russia's chances for a successful revolution. In a letter to a Russian revolutionary (1881) he stated his belief that Russia may succeed in achieving "agrarian Socialism" and bypass capitalism.

[8]The original text of *Capital* was written and published (1867) in German. Its first translation was into Russian. The Russian version was legally published in Russia in 1872.

**FIGURE 3–3**
Georgi Plekhanov (1856–1918), founder
of Russian Marxism.

conditions. His revision of Marxism greatly contributed to an irreconcilable
split among the "Revolutionary Marxists" in 1903. Fourteen years later,
Lenin and his followers rose to power in Russia while their opponents sank
into obscurity. The difference in personality of each group's leaders, along
with such factors as old-fashioned, non-Marxist chance, were responsible for
the dramatic outcome. However, the most important single reason for
Lenin's success was his readiness to change Marxism to fit Russia, while his
rivals chose to wait until Russia changed to fit Marxism.

Lenin's major revisions of Marxism were in the following areas:

1. He insisted upon a paramilitary structure and discipline in the Russian Marxist
   party, in sharp contrast to the existing Marxist parties in Europe. His argument,
   in essence, was that in a nondemocratic country a Marxist party built on
   democratic principles was doomed to failure.
2. He promoted an alliance between the numerically weak class of Russian
   industrial workers (proletarians) and the poorer majority of the peasants.
   According to Lenin (but in opposition to Marx), the peasantry consisted of three
   subgroups: the rich, the middle, and the poor.
3. He justified a "proletarian revolution" in backward Russia in terms of the
   weakest-link-in-the-chain theory. According to this theory, the national capitalistic establishments of Marx's time had merged into a worldwide imperial-
   istic system that could be most readily broken up in its weakest member
   country.

In light of these important revisions, the addition of Lenin's name to that of
Marx in the official title of Soviet ideology appears to be well justified. In

terms of Marxist dialectics, Marxism-Leninism was the synthesis of Marx's thesis and Lenin's antithesis that had developed already before the 1917 Revolution. After 1917, this process continued to gain momentum under Lenin and his successors.

**BOX 3–3**   *Lenin's Major Contributions to Marxism (Books and Articles)*

1. *What the "Friends of the People" Are and How They Fight the Social-Democrats* (1884). Criticism of the Populists (Agrarian Socialists) for their reliance on individual leaders rather than on "the masses."
2. *Development of Capitalism in Russia* (1899). A historic survey of the early phase of Russia's industrialization.
3. *What Is to Be Done?* (1902). Criticism of liberal tendencies within the Marxist movement. Proposals for party structure and organization.
4. *One Step Forward, Two Steps Backward* (1904). A detailed blueprint for the development of the party organization as the "leader of the proletariat."
5. *Two Tactics of Social-Democracy in the Democratic Revolution* (1905). A detailed analysis of the leading role of the party representing the "hegemony of the proletariat."
6. *Materialism and Empiric-Criticism* (1909). An analysis of changing world conditions in light of the Marxist ideology.
7. *The Military Progress of the Revolution* (1916). An outline for an armed takeover in case of a "revolutionary situation."
8. *Philosophical Notebooks* (1916). Comments, reflections, and ideas concerning various aspects of Marxist ideology and its application to modern times.
9. *Imperialism, the Highest Stage of Capitalism* (1916). An analysis of the new economic and political relations between the major world powers that led to World War I.
10. *Left-Wing Communism: An Infantile Disorder* (1920). Criticism of excessive zeal, lack of discipline, and inability to accept temporary compromises.

A prolific writer, Lenin wrote many other articles, essays, and speeches. His complete works have been translated into many languages.

Compiled by author.

## SOCIALISM IN ONE COUNTRY

The ideological baggage with which Lenin and his supporters came to power in Russia in 1917 contained only a sketchy theoretical outline of a future classless society. They soon discovered that these ideas could not be used as a manual for managing a huge multinational empire in a state of turmoil.

**FIGURE 3-4**
Vladimir (Ulyanov) Lenin (1870–1924),
leader of the 1917 Revolution and founder
of the USSR.

Pinning their hopes on a chain-reaction effect that would produce similar revolutions in Europe, the Soviet leaders at first did not undertake systematic efforts to figure out how to apply the Marxist ideology to the immediate situation in Russia. In fact, Russia was seen by them merely as a base or a steppingstone for achieving the world revolution.

By the early 1920s it became clear to Lenin that the revolutionary upheaval in Europe had spent itself without producing any lasting effects. This meant that the "great experiment" would have to be limited, at least for the time being, to Russia. The immediate result was Lenin's New Economic Policy (NEP), designed to restore the Russian economy to its pre-revolution production level.[9] Next came Joseph Stalin's (1879–1953) "building Socialism in one country" by means of five-year plans, collectivization, and mass terror.

Different in many aspects, these two periods had one important common denominator—a realization by Lenin and Stalin that the regime could survive only by transcending theoretical clouds and recognizing the realities of the time and place in which it existed. This did not mean that the Communist ideology was forsaken, as was reported by many foreign visitors

[9]There were also other reasons for Lenin's decision to call for a temporary retreat. Important among them was the peasants' resistance to "War Communism" (discussed in Chapter 6).

**BOX 3–4**   *Marx on the Transition from Capitalism to Communism*

Between capitalist and Communist societies lies the period of the revolutionary transition of the one into the other. Corresponding to this is also a political transition period in which the state can be nothing but the revolutionary dictatorship of the proletariat.

Quoted in *Marx, Engels, Lenin* [anthology] (Moscow: Novosti Press, 1976), p. 82.

to the Soviet Union during those years, but rather that it had to be further "Russified"—that is, synthesized with the heritage of a millennium of Russian history. On the eve of World War II, this process of "uniting the opposites" rapidly gained momentum, giving a new impetus to premature obituaries in the West about the alleged death of the Communist ideology in Russia. Actually, the infusion of Russian national traditions considerably strengthened the appeal of ideological propaganda by providing it with roots firmly set in the native soil. By the end of the war these roots included such ideas as Russia's historical quest for secure borders, Ivan the Terrible's rationale for absolute autocracy and the annexation of non-Russian lands,

**FIGURE 3–5**
Joseph Stalin (Iosif Dzhugashvili) (1879–1953), Lenin's successor as the leader of the USSR.

Peter the Great's urge to modernize the country at any cost, and a vague but persistent notion of Moscow's being "the third Rome."[10]

The history of Russia and the history of Marxism were reinterpreted and rewritten as two variations of uninterrupted progress and advancement toward the same goal. Ironically, much of the "dialectical mixing" of Marxism with Russian nationalism was done by the non-Russian Stalin, who by that time had replaced Lenin as the high priest of ideology. During the last two decades of his long tenure, the official name of the ideology was Marxism-Leninism-Stalinism. (In fact, this term is still in use in China and Albania.) However, in actuality, Stalin's theoretical contributions were few and of little importance. They are either completely ignored or treated as erroneous in the Soviet Union today. On the other hand, Stalin's efforts to further the "Russification" of Marxism have survived the so-called de-Stalinization campaign that was undertaken by his heirs in the late 1950s. In Gorbachev's USSR today, Marxism-Leninism, its internationalistic claims abroad notwithstanding, continues to have a strong Russian nationalistic appeal.

## DE-STALINIZATION

This strange word came into existence in 1956 when Nikita Khrushchev (1894–1971) mounted an attack against his former boss, Stalin, who had died three years earlier. The immediate reason for Khrushchev's dramatic move concerned the power struggle among Stalin's heirs. But, according to Khrushchev, his approach was also the best way to bring about badly needed rationalization and modernization of the entire Soviet system.

Although the de-Stalinization campaign was carefully orchestrated and directed from above, it involved a certain degree of risk, because any criticism of Stalin was bound to reflect on various aspects of the Communist ideology as a whole, to raise embarrassing questions, and to establish a potentially dangerous precedent for further denunciations. Initially, there were indeed signs of strain and confusion in the Soviet Union, as well as in other Communist countries and parties. In the West the news of de-Staliniza-tion produced an avalanche of predictions about the "beginning of the end," the "point of no return," "run-away liberalization," and, of course, "ideolog-ical bankruptcy." But, on balance, the calculated risk of the new Kremlin leader appears to have paid generous dividends. In spite of some lingering opposition and dissent among intellectuals at home and in "fraternal" Marxist parties abroad, the Kremlin leadership under Khrushchev has re-tained its commanding position in the realm of Communist ideology.[11]

[10]The notion of Moscow's being "the third Rome" dates back to the end of the fifteenth century, when Moscow declared itself heir to Byzantium ("the second Rome") as the center of Eastern (Orthodox) Christianity.

[11]De-Stalinization was a major contributing factor to the split between the USSR and China (PRC) in the early 1960s.

**FIGURE 3–6**
Nikita Khrushchev (1894–1971), leader of the USSR from 1953 to 1964. In 1956 he initiated the de-Stalinization campaign.

**BOX 3–5**    *Soviet Underground Humor*

---

If Marx's version of Socialism is indeed scientific, why was it not tested first on rats or guinea pigs?

---

In the late 1950s and early 1960s, several new ideological premises were introduced to fit the post-Stalin self-image of the Soviet regime: (1) Marxism-Leninism is a creative and flexible guide, not a static dogma; (2) the infallibility of this ideology does not prevent its top enforcers from making occasional mistakes; (3) the Soviet Union has advanced from being a dictatorship of the proletariat to being, at a higher stage, a "state of the whole people"; (4) relations between foreign Communist parties and Moscow should allow for a degree of autonomy; and (5) international relations should be based on the principle of "peaceful coexistence."

Domestically, the revision of Marxism-Leninism produced a welcome relief from the rigor and excesses of the preceding decades. In the realm of international politics it amounted to a declaration of the new Soviet leaders' determination to avoid major conflicts with the West. The purpose of these

**BOX 3–6**  *Excerpt from Nikita Khrushchev's "Secret" Speech at the Twentieth Party Congress in 1956*

Facts prove that many abuses were made on Stalin's orders without reckoning with any norms of Party and Soviet legality. Stalin was a very distrustful man, sickly suspicious; we knew this from our work with him. He could look at a man and say: "Why are your eyes so shifty today," or "Why are you turning so much today and avoiding to look me directly in the eyes?" The sickly suspicion created in him a general distrust even toward eminent Party workers whom he had known for years. Everywhere and in everything he saw "enemies," "two-facers," and "spies."

Possessing unlimited power, he indulged in great willfulness and choked a person morally and physically. A situation was created where one could not express one's own will.

Quoted in Nikita Khrushchev, *Khrushchev Remembers* (Boston: Little, Brown, 1970), p. 585.

changes, however, was not to lead the Soviet Union into a merger with Western democracies, as some foreign observers had speculated at the time. On the contrary, from an ideological point of view, the USSR was supposed to be moving faster than ever before toward full Communism.

During the Khrushchev decade (1953–1964), which was characterized by a mood of boundless optimism, it was often implied that a Communist society would be reached as early as the 1980s. But under Khrushchev's somber successors the prognoses become considerably more restrained and ambiguous.

## STAGNATION

The removal of Khrushchev from power in 1964 did not, however, alter the basic ideological premise that the Soviet Union must continue "building Communism." In 1977, the new Soviet constitution appeared to add emphasis to this premise by describing the effort to build Communism as an "all-out" one. But, in reality, for almost two decades under Leonid Brezhnev (1964–1982) there was more continuity and stagnation than change and progress in the Soviet way of life. The whole period now is condemned for its demoralizing effect on the Soviet people, and is described as a "pre-crisis situation."

Under Brezhnev, the process of de-Stalinization was effectively held in check and even reversed on several issues in order to achieve a balanced, official view of the Stalin era. This official view was approximately as follows: By pursuing the guidelines set by Lenin and remaining faithful to

**FIGURE 3–7**
Leonid Brezhnev (1906–1982), leader of
the USSR from 1964 to 1982.

the basic tenets of Marxism-Leninism, the Soviet nation was able to make swift progress toward achieving Socialism by the mid-1930s. Unfortunately, the "cult of Stalin's personality," which grew steadily worse during the late 1930s and 1940s, caused certain ideological errors, which resulted in temporary setbacks for the Communist cause. However, soon after Stalin's death all the wrongs of his era were corrected, and the Soviet nation, having come to terms with its past, is now moving full speed toward a bright future.

In the meantime, the progress toward Communism was measured primarily in terms of expanding the economic "base," as was done in the past when the USSR was building Socialism. This meant that the development of heavy industries continued to be given priority over the production of consumer goods. And as long as this prevailed, there could not be an abundance of material goods, which is the main prerequisite for the change of distribution promised under Communism: "From each according to his ability, to each according to his needs." The brief reign of Yuri Andropov (1982–1984) amounted to a weak attempt to move forward, and that of Konstantin Chernenko (1984–1985), to an equally uncertain effort to go backward on the question of further de-Stalinization.

## PERESTROIKA

Since the beginning of the Gorbachev administration in March 1985, different ideological formulas have been in use: "perfecting Socialism," "purifying Socialism," and "realizing the full potential of Socialism." These and similar euphemisms are supposed to convey a perceived urgent need for radical changes of socioeconomic conditions in the USSR, while at the same time to instill confidence that the country is now on the right course toward its bright Communistic future. Various programmatic statements by Gorbachev and his associates imply, rather than explicitly promise, that the massive campaign of reforms known as *perestroika* (restructuring) will produce revolutionary "qualitative" changes by the year 2000, though even then the ultimate goal—Communism—will still remain far away.

In fact, Soviet ideologists now openly admit that under the best circumstances it would take many additional years and efforts to completely overcome the "contradiction between supply and demand," which simply means chronical shortages of consumer goods and services. Other kinds of perceived inequities must also be gradually eliminated [the difference between high and low salaries and wages, the unequal quality of urban and rural life, different levels of education, and the divisiveness of ethnic cultures.] Crucially important is the problem of creating a new "Communist mentality" and a new "Communist morality" completely free of such human failings as greed, envy, vanity, and selfishness. At this time, there is little evidence that much headway is being made in changing this important area of the "superstructure."

In general, by Western standards, the Soviet Union continues to be a country of modest means, inferior goods, limited food supplies, and inadequate personal services. Average Soviet citizens live regimented lives with few opportunities for personal fulfillment. They are neither free nor equal in terms of the income and care that they receive from the state. Moreover, Soviet society is plagued by conditions that are supposed to be incompatible with true Communism, or even Socialism—for example, alcoholism, poor workmanship, deterioration of family relations, common crime, corruption, and other "remnants of the cursed past." So far, Gorbachev's *perestroika* has not brought Soviet society closer to the blissful state—that is, the "kingdom of freedom" as promised by Marx—which takes "from each according to his ability," and gives "to each according to his needs."

But *perestroika* does call for most profound and comprehensive reforms. Its ideological foundation is Gorbachev's professed belief that Socialism, as defined by Marxism-Leninism, is compatable with and would be cured of its ills by a much greater degree of individual freedom and political democracy. This promised humanization of the ideology is hailed as a long-overdue return to the "Leninist norms," and it is accompanied by a second—and much more thorough—round of de-Stalinization. Included among the many posthumously rehabilitated victims of Stalin's terror are the leaders of the so-called Rightist Opposition who had believed it possible to reconcile individual and collective interests under Socialism. Their belief, of course, bears a striking resemblence to Gorbachev's own ideas. Stalin's "cult of personality" and Brezhnev's "pre-crisis situation" are now treated as tragic departures from the "Leninist path," resulting in the erosion of ideological values. According to this explanation, the ideology was virtually hijacked by individuals who were unscrupulous, cynical, and corrupted by their lust for power and greed for material possessions.

**BOX 3–7**   *Soviet Underground Humor*

> Gorbachev's name is actually an acronym which means (in Russian): *Gotov Otmenit Resheniya Brezhneva, Andropova, Chernenko, Esli Vyzhivu.* (Ready [to] Abolish [the] Decisions [of] Brezhnev, Andropov [and] Chernenko if [I] Survive.)

What is not explained is how the "objective laws of history," which Karl Marx claimed he had discovered, could have allowed such aberrations to occur in the first place and to continue for so many years. By condemning more than a half of the Soviet era, the Gorbachev regime comes dangerously close to admitting that Marxism-Leninism has been refuted by the reality of life.

Almost as vulnerable from an ideological point of view is Gorbachev's position on some key economic issues, which could be interpreted as the abandonment of Socialist principles. Should his political luck change or should his *perestroika* fail to deliver on its many promises, Gorbachev may find himself accused of a "rightist deviation" which could conceivably lead to an impeachment (Soviet style). If the past is a guide to the future, despite the often-repeated incantations that *perestroika* is irreversible and that it has no rational alternative, the fortunes of both Gorbachev and his reforms are not necessarily secure. In fact, *perestroika* is proclaimed to embody an ongoing dialectical struggle between the old and the new, or the conservative and the progressive. Calling it a struggle implies that the outcome of *perestroika* is far from certain.

**BOX 3–8**   *An Old Russian Proverb*

> It is easier to make a pot of fish soup from a bowl with live fish than to make a bowl of live fish from a pot of fish soup.

## GLASNOST

The aspect of Soviet life, which has been affected most by *perestroika* so far is freedom of expression. This is Gorbachev's famous *glasnost*, meaning "openness" and "frankness." To Gorbachev and his allies in the Kremlin, *glasnost* is not just a public relations gimmick, as has been suggested in the West, but an important tool for the promotion of their far-reaching reforms. It also serves as an insurance for personal safety against the risk of being ousted from power by a secret conspiracy similar to the one that toppled Nikita Khrushchev in 1964. But *glasnost* is, in turn, a calculated risk because it speaks openly about the rather dismal conditions in the Soviet Union, which present a dramatic contrast to the Utopian society envisaged by Karl Marx. *Glasnost* has already completely destroyed the image of "substitute reality" which was created over several decades by the ideological propaganda machine intending to paternalistically shield Soviet citizens from the unpleasant facts of life.

**BOX 3–9**  *Perestroika and Socialism*

> The purpose of restructuring or perestroika is fully to reveal the humanitarian nature and constructive vigour of socialism. Attainment of this objective is inseparable from promotion of democracy and openness, from self-management of the people, a radical economic reform, moral cleansing of society, and from discovery of the creative potentialities inherent in the free and all-round development of the person.
>
> Theses of the CPSU Central Committee for the 19th All-Union Party Conference May 23, 1988.

Before the advent of *glasnost*, Soviet propaganda was based on the positive approach. Its messages, always expressed in optimistic tones, appealed to progressive and constructive human aspirations. Flattery and praises of the reader, listener, or viewer were extensively used as psychological rewards. The Soviet people were constantly exalted for being the most conscientious and progressive society in the world, thanks to their trust in the Marxist-Leninist ideology. Propaganda signals that could trigger negative emotions, such as fear, anger, and hatred, were carefully rationed to provide the needed contrast, without endangering the prevailing mood of optimism. The idea was to make average Soviet citizens believe that their society was superior to all others. Not everyone was taken in by this propaganda image. Among the better educated and informed, skeptical and even cynical attitudes were not uncommon. However, very few people dared to reveal such feelings publicly for fear of losing their privileges and being punished. This was especially true of members of the Communist Party, who were expected to show total commitment to Marxism-Leninism, regardless of personal doubts.

With the help of implied threats of punishment, the Soviet propaganda machine could be manipulated at will to produce a variety of conditioned reflexes and desired emotional responses, including expressions of "Soviet patriotism," "revolutionary solidarity," and "class indignation." It could also be used to muster "enthusiastic support" for any Soviet action or policy abroad, ranging from détente with the United States to armed intervention in a foreign country such as Afghanistan. By means of Marxist dialectics, abrupt changes in both domestic and foreign policies were explained and rationalized as logical and "historically justifiable."

*Glasnost* changed all this: Emphasis in Soviet propaganda has abruptly shifted from the positive to the negative, subjecting Soviet citizens to a shock treatment consisting of bad news, exposes, criticisms, and painful revelations. It is comparable, perhaps, to suddenly turning off anesthesia during surgery. But *glasnost*, while earning Gorbachev high marks for openness, has so far failed to produce an upsurge of enthusiasm in the masses who have grown apathetic and leary of promises. Ironically, just a few years ago, the main mission of the same propaganda machine (which now serves *glasnost*) was to make the Soviet people passive, indifferent, and apolitical instead of infecting them with new revolutionary ideas. This used to be accomplished by endlessly repeating Marxist-Leninist generalities and platitudes which was believed to be sufficient guarantee against the formation of potentially dangerous vacuums in the minds of Soviet citizens—vacuums that could be filled with outside ideas.

It is obvious that Gorbachev's *glasnost* is designed to make the ideology fit reality, rather than the other way around, as was attempted for such a long time in the past. But is *glasnost* turning skeptics into believers? Is it reforming cynics? Is it replacing indifference with the enthusiasm needed to carry out *perestroika*? Or has the Soviet propaganda machine been compromised beyond repair, like the credibility of the boy who cried wolf once too often? It will probably take several more years before these questions can be answered with certainty. But remember that Gorbachev has always maintained that his reforms will take years to be fully executed and to take root.

## POLITICAL OPPOSITION

A virtual ideological monopoly of Marxism-Leninism during most of the Soviet era has been a major factor contributing to its success in the USSR. At various times during the civil war large parts of the country were controlled by the fiercely anti-Communist "White Movement," which received considerable support from France, Great Britain, the United States, and several other foreign countries. During World War II, there was some anti-Soviet political activity in the parts of the Soviet Union under German occupation. But neither Lenin nor Stalin was willing to tolerate ideological opposition in any area under Soviet authority.

In 1956, the sudden changes resulting from the de-Stalinization campaign produced in Moscow and in other major centers several small groups of intellectuals openly opposed to some or all aspects of the Soviet political system and ideology. Harassed by the authorities, deprived of basic human rights, barred from the public media, these people have fought a protracted battle with the establishment. Many of them were charged with "anti-Soviet agitation," arrested, declared insane, or exiled. Still, their voices had never been completely silenced, and they continued for almost three decades to defy the regime at an even greater personal risk. The ideas generated by the dissidents during the pre-Gorbachev years fall into three general categories:

1. A liberal and pro-Western ideology whose best known spokesperson was Academician Andrei Sakharov.[12] This viewpoint emphasized the need for political democracy, legal justice, fair play, and rationality.
2. A much more conservative political philosophy with strong Russian national-istic and religious overtones. Its most celebrated proponent has been Alexander Solzhenitsyn.[13]
3. A "true" Marxist alternative that was usually identified with the Medvedev brothers, who sought to purify and democratize the existing system.[14]

It is difficult to measure how much impact these ideas have had on people in the Soviet Union, where the number of known dissidents had always remained quite small. But it is reasonable to assume that these brave people have made a significant contribution to the change of political climate which began in the mid 1980s.

A new kind of "left" opposition emerged in 1987 when Boris Yeltsin, a former candidate-member of the Politburo began to openly protest the slow pace of *perestroika*. By 1989, he became a "populist" leader pushing for more radical and speedy reforms.

In the wake of *perestroika*, some more moderate dissidents, including recently freed political prisoners, have been co-opted by Gorbachev's liber-

[12]Andrei Sakharov is a prominent Soviet scientist, member of the USSR Academy of Sciences, and receiver of many official honors. In the early 1960s, he began to take active part in political dissent. A laureate of the Nobel Peace Prize, he had lived for several years in internal exile before Gorbachev allowed him to return to Moscow in 1986. He died in 1989.

[13]Alexander Solzhenitsyn was expelled from the Soviet Union in 1974. He now resides in the United States.

[14]The twin brothers, Roy and Zhores Medvedev, are sons of a prominent Soviet Communist who perished in one of Stalin's purges. Roy lives in the USSR, and his brother lives in England. In 1989, Roy was reinstated in the Communist Party and elected to the new legislature.

alization campaign. Those more radical continue sporadically to stage public protests and street demonstrations, probing the limits of *glasnost*. There have even been attempts to launch "left" and "right" nationwide opposition parties and run independent candidates for elected government offices, but so far none of these efforts have been very successful.

## RELIGION AND ATHEISM

Although Marxism-Leninism is openly and militantly atheistic, the Soviet Constitution (Article 52) guarantees "freedom of religious worship"; it also speaks of "freedom of antireligious propaganda." By omission, freedom of religious propaganda is denied. This enables Soviet authorities to declare any openly religious activity illegal on the grounds that it may have a propagandistic effect in violation of the law safeguarding separation of school and church.[15]

Religion may be practiced only privately, either in one's home or in officially recognized churches, which are controlled by a special state organ called the "Council for the Affairs of Religious Cults." The USSR has fewer than 20,000 such houses of worship, belonging to some forty different denominations and serving an estimated 50 million parishioners, approximately 20 percent of the population. Most parishioners are elderly people, and their number is said to be diminishing. Religious organizations are allowed to train ministers only as replacements for those who retire or die. In fact, every effort is made to reduce the number of functioning churches, mosques, synagogues, and other temples. Many former houses of worship have been either destroyed or turned into historical or antireligious museums. Restricted editions of religious literature published by licensed churches are not intended for general distribution.

There is no religious instruction in public schools, though classes in "Sunday" schools are now permitted. The Soviet educational system and mass media treat religious beliefs as superstitions and lingering remnants of a dark past in the minds of backward people. Organized religions, which Marx called "opiate of the masses," are denounced as instruments of counterrevolution. On a personal level, this means that individuals who do not conceal their religious beliefs are looked upon either as victims, if they are poorly educated or very young, or as accomplices of an "un-Soviet" organization. To be religious and work for the atheistic Soviet state is perhaps comparable to belonging to the American Communist Party while holding

[15]The RSFSR Criminal Code (Article 142) provides punishments by fine and/or imprisonment for violation of the separation of school and church. But the Gorbachev regime has promised to allow some religious education in the near future.

**TABLE 3–1**    USSR Population According to Religious Background (estimates in millions and percentages)

|  | Millions | % |
| --- | --- | --- |
| Christian | 215.0 | 77.0 |
|   Eastern Orthodox | 206.8 | 74.0 |
|   Western (RC and Prot) | 5.1 | 1.9 |
|   Armenian Church | 3.1 | 1.1 |
| Moslem | 62.1 | 22.1 |
| Jewish | 1.8 | 0.6 |
| Buddhist | 0.6 | 0.2 |
| Other | 0.5 | 0.2 |

Source: Compiled by author from Soviet data.

a civil service job. The difference is that in the USSR there are no private employers, and almost everyone has to work for the state.

In spite of its avowed hostility to religion in general, the Soviet regime exhibits favoritism toward organized religions that can be controlled in their entirety. Faiths and denominations with centers of gravity outside the Soviet Union—Catholicism, Protestantism, Judaism, and Islam—are viewed with much more suspicion and mistrust than such "domestic" religions as Russian Orthodoxy, Georgian Orthodoxy, and, to a lesser degree, Armenian Christianity. Perhaps as a result of Soviet pro-Arab foreign policy, Islam is treated more leniently than other "outside" religions. But by far the largest and most important denomination is the Russian Orthodox Church, which controls between one third and one half of the functioning parishes and is allowed to maintain several monasteries, nunneries, and seminaries. On the occasion of the Millenium of Russian Christianity (988–1988), Gorbachev promised to liberalize Soviet policy toward the church and religion. Several historic buildings were returned to the Russian Orthodox Church, which was also given permission to build a commemorative temple in Moscow and to reopen some old churches. In 1989, three top clerics were elected to the newly established USSR Congress of People's Deputies.

But, as before, religion is acceptable only as a cultural relic or a personal idiosyncrasy, but not as a competing ideology. From an ideological point of view, all religions are equally bad because they are what Marxism-Leninism calls "false ideologies," which mislead and deceive the masses as to the real meaning of human life and history. Therefore, there cannot be, in the long run, a peaceful coexistence between Communist ideology and religion. The "all-out building of Communism" calls for intensified efforts to eradicate religious faith by means of atheistic propaganda as well as by administrative measures. So far, these efforts appear to be effectively discouraging younger

BOX 3–10   *Excerpt From a Recent Soviet Textbook on Marxism-Leninism*

Marxism-Leninism is a fully integrated theory consisting of three component parts: philosophy, political economy and the theory of scientific communism. These three components have an inseparable inner connection. The philosophy of Marxism-Leninism—dialectical and historical materialism—is the general theoretical basis of all Marxist-Leninist teaching.

The integrity, the wholeness, the irrefutable logic and consistency of Marxism-Leninism, which are acknowledged even by its opponents, have been achieved by the application of the unified philosophical dialectical-materialist world outlook and method. Marxism-Leninism cannot properly be understood without its philosophical basis.

The philosophy of Marxism-Leninism is a result and the highest stage of the development of world philosophical thought. It has assimilated all that was best and most progressive in the centuries of development of philosophy. At the same time its emergence signified a qualitative leap, a revolutionary upheaval in philosophy. Evolved by Marx and Engels as the world outlook of a new revolutionary class—the working class—whose mission is to overthrow the rule of the bourgeoisie, abolish capitalism and build the new communist society, which will be the most advanced and just society the world has ever seen. Marxist philosophy is called upon not only to give a strictly scientific explanation of the world, but also to serve as the theoretical instrument for its transformation.

*The Foundations of Marxist-Leninist Philosophy* (Moscow: Progress Publishers, 1974), p. 15.

generations from embracing religion. There is, however, strong evidence of a real religious revival in the USSR.

All churches, clergy, and religious groups are required to be registered with the authorities. Any association with an "underground"—that is, non-registered—religious activity is punishable as a criminal offense.

## NATIONALISM AND PATRIOTISM

Compared with religion or political dissent, the nationalistic feelings of some of the non-Russian minorities is of greater concern to Soviet leaders. As demonstrated by many examples in recent history, Marxism-Leninism does not make people immune to nationalism. In contrast to purely political ideas or religion, which appeal mainly to small groups of sophisticated Soviet intellectuals or the elderly, respectively, nationalistic feelings can be readily shared by a larger number of persons belonging to different social and educational strata. In 1988, this was dramatized when hundreds of thousands of Armenians and Azerbaijans took part in mass demonstrations, protest rallies, and strikes in a dispute over the jurisdiction of the Nagorno-Karabakh region. Even when manifestations of anti-Russian nationalism are limited to local issues and, therefore, attract less public attention abroad, allowing the Soviet regime to be more oppressive without much fear of exposure, nationalistic aspirations could represent the most serious single challenge to the monopoly of Communist ideology in the Soviet Union. As we have seen, ethnic diversity is an important exception to the forced uniformity in Soviet society.

Although it is difficult to gauge the intensity and perseverance of nationalism among various minorities, it is in the three Baltic union republics—Estonia, Latvia, and Lithuania—and in western parts of the Ukraine that large numbers of natives continue to show visible signs of an uncompromising desire for a break from the Soviet Union. Equally strong and no less ambitious demands for complete national independence have recently surfaced in Armenia and Georgia. Peoples of Soviet Central Asia are showing a growing resentment toward the rising flood of migrants from the European parts of the Soviet Union. In 1986, there were violent demonstrations in Alma-Ata in a vain attempt by the natives to block a Russian from taking over as the new party boss of Kazakhstan. For several decades, a small but determined group of exiled Tatars have been unsuccessfully pressing for the right to return to their historic homeland, the Crimea. A different kind of national aspiration, a desire to reunite with compatriots outside the USSR, is being openly displayed by large numbers of Armenians, Germans, and Jews.

As was noted in the previous chapter, the most numerous among the emigrants have been the Jews. Because leaving the "Socialist Motherland" is all but equated with desertion, many Soviet Jews are caught in a vicious circle of cause and effect: Their emigration causes anti-Semitic feelings, and vice versa. Although anti-Semitism is officially condemned, Moscow's openly anti-Zionist policy definitely contributes to it.[16]

Great Russian nationalism is kept in check because, in extreme forms, it could lead to serious problems for the regime based on "proletarian internationalism." Perhaps a more immediate fallout from too much open Russian nationalism would be its catalytic effect on non-Russian minorities. But, in controlled doses, Russian nationalism, as well as interethnic antagonisms, can be used effectively against selected non-Russian minorities. For this reason, the Gorbachev regime shows a degree of tolerance and treats with kid gloves an unofficial organization of the extreme Russian nationalists, called "Pamyat" (Memory) and similar groups.

The Soviet attitude toward nationalism vividly illustrates the dialectical relativity of Marxist values: The same nationalistic aspirations are viewed

[16]In April 1983, a number of officially prominent Soviet Jews founded an "Anti-Zionist Committee" to combat "Zionist propaganda coming from abroad."

**BOX 3–11**    *Gorbachev on Socialism*

> Those who hope that we will turn off from the socialist path are heading for a
> bitter disappointment. Our entire program of *perestroika*—as a whole and in its
> individual components—is fully based on the principle: more Socialism, more
> democracy.
>
> Gorbachev, M. S. *Perestroika i Novoye Myshlenie* ("Perestroika and the New Thinking")
> (Moscow: Political Literature Publishing, 1987), p. 32.

as positive and progressive under capitalism, but as negative and reactionary
under Socialism.

In its concentrated efforts to defuse minorities and nationalism, and to
create a more homogeneous Soviet nation, the regime relies on an official
version of supernationalism called "Soviet patriotism." Based primarily on
the tragic and proud memories of World War II, Soviet patriotism seeks to
supersede and replace local nationalistic feelings. The war, referred to as the
"Great Patriotic War," is depicted as the supreme trial by fire and sword for
all Soviet nationalities. Young people are urged to act worthy of their
predecessors' sacrifices and to follow their heroic example: to form a multiethnic association united by a common love for the Soviet Motherland and
fighting under the banner of Marxism-Leninism.

For more than four decades, carefully selected and sometimes doctored
accounts from the war saga have been enshrined in school textbooks, mass
media coverage, fiction and nonfiction books, countless monuments, and
elaborate rituals. New patriotic customs and traditions are being invented.
For example, all over the Soviet Union, newlywed couples are now encouraged to place flowers at a local monument to the Unknown Soldier immediately after their official marriage ceremonies. Soviet propaganda also
presents current Soviet achievements in space exploration, scientific discovery, economic development, and so forth, in a manner designed to instill
pride in the hearts of all Soviet citizens regardless of their ethnic belonging.

Campaigns to promote Soviet patriotism seem to be meeting with some
success. However, it is reasonable to assume that the danger of anti-Russian
nationalism and ethnic antagonisms in the Soviet Union will persist as long
as the minorities manage to preserve their separate identities. As was said
before, in case of a major political crisis, military defeat or another national
catastrophe it is even possible to envisage the breakup of the Soviet Union
into a patchwork of ethnic minorities.

Gorbachev and his reform administration must be painfully aware of
and alarmed by what, during the last several years, has often been referred
to (even by the Soviet Union media) as ethnic crisis situations. Gorbachev is

**BOX 3–12**   *A "Balanced" Official View of Stalin*

One of the most widely used almanac-calendars in Soviet homes for 1989 (Political Publishing Houses, 13,000,000 copies) offered a brief biography of Joseph Stalin on the occasion of the 110th anniversary of his birth (December 21). After paying him homage as a leader and listing all his party and government positions, it stated:

"The most important phase of Stalin's leadership is tied to the period of radical social changes in the country and the formulation of the strategy and tactics for the initial stage of building Socialism. The novelty and complexity of problems on hand in those years revealed the extremely controversial nature of Stalin as politician. He strayed more and more away from the Leninist norms and principles of the party and state life. In practice, this led to the emergence of a cult of personality, grave violations of legality, and mass repressions. It took great efforts and a long time to overcome the consequences of the cult of personality in accordance with the decisions of the Twentieth Party Congress. The ongoing systematic democratization of the life of Soviet society, which was initiated by the April Plenum of the Central Committee (1985), is intended to put an end forever to manifestations of this dangerous social disease and to open up completely the potential for realization of the advantages of the Socialist system."

faced with a difficult dilemma: His *perestroika* threatens to reverse the formula, "National in form, Socialist in content," by encouraging nationalistic aspirations while reducing the "Socialist content" to a mere tokenism. So far, various high level conferences devoted to this quandary, including a special meeting of the Central Committee of the Communist Party, have not arrived at effective solutions.

Officially, the surge of ethnic unrest is explained as a necessary price for the less restrictive political climate. It is optimistically predicted that, before long, interethnic relations will find a new equilibrium.

## IDEOLOGY AND LEADERS

The relationship of the ideology to the decision-making process in the Kremlin has been the subject of much controversy in the West. The top Soviet leaders who make all important decisions have been considered narrow fanatics or unlimited opportunists, dogmatic believers or complete cynics, or international conspirators or steadfast Russian nationalists. Actually, all of these seemingly conflicting observations are substantially correct. Their diversity stems from the fact that Marxism-Leninism consists of many different components. Depending on the circumstances, the emphasis may shift from one component to another, but the sum total remains the same. Shifts in emphasis determine the choice of different tactics. However, the ultimate ideological goal—to usher in a new Communist era for humankind—remains unchanged.

In the Soviet Union, Marxist ideology is officially treated with an almost religious fervor and, at the same time, is given the status of a true science. It is credited with the following virtues: As a system of beliefs, the ideology provides a common denominator for people of diversified backgrounds and renders a sense of community interests. As a frame of reference, it helps to relate new situations to past experiences, thus creating a feeling of continuity. As a code of signals, it ensures desirable responses and behavior. And as a statement of purpose, it elicits commitment and gives the satisfaction of accomplishment.

None of these claims is without foundation. However, just as important (but not celebrated by Soviet propaganda) is another function of Marxism-Leninism: The ideology supplies Soviet leaders with ready-made excuses for their failures (although such failures are seldom even acknowledged). Any failure can be either blamed on "objective forces of history" or justified as a tactical retreat. By the same "dialectic" logic, poor judgments and improper decisions are classified as deviations from ideological tenets.

The constant dependence on the ideology is also a source of some problems for the Soviet policymakers. Perhaps the most serious of them is the hazard of becoming victims of their own ideological propaganda. Although Marxism-Leninism is referred to as a science, a wide discrepancy persists between objective reality and perceived reality as seen through ideologically colored glasses. In certain areas, such as the national economy, opportunities for improvement and progress have been forfeited for purely ideological reasons. At least in the past, ideological obstacles and constraints sometimes interfered with common sense, and thus caused problems even in everyday life.

There is a persistent tendency in the West, dominated by modern secular humanism, to underestimate the power of Soviet ideology. On balance, however, it is quite clear that the ideology of Marxism-Leninism has been a great asset to the group of people of humble beginnings and apparently average intelligence who run the largest country in the world and have far-reaching designs for the future. For over seventy years, this ideology was the sole source of legitimacy for the Soviet regime at home and an important tool of its policy abroad. It is no wonder, therefore, that Marxism-Leninism is one legacy from the discredited recent past that Gorbachev is determined to salvage. He claims, somewhat illogically, that the ideology has inspired all his reforms, but, at the same time, promises to remove from it the dead wood of obsolete concepts.

BOX 3–13   *Gorbachev's Homage to Lenin*

> We have learned and are learning from Lenin to creatively approach the theory and practice of the Socialist construction. We are arming ourselves with his scientific methods, and mastering [his] art to concretely analyze concrete situations.
>
> Gorbachev, M. S. *Perestroika i Novoye Myshlenie* ("Perestroika and the New Thinking") (Moscow: Political Literature Publishing, 1987), p. 41.

## DOGMA OR DOCTRINE

Officially, Marxism-Leninism is always called a "creative doctrine," "living theory," or "guide for action," but never a dogma. Early in his revolutionary career Lenin said: "We do not regard Marx's theory as something completed and inviolable; on the contrary, we are convinced that it has only laid the foundation stone of the science which Socialists must develop in all directions if they wish to keep pace with life."[17] This admonition to keep the ideology alive by constantly modifying, revising, and expanding it to include further evidence of its validity has been followed by Lenin's heirs, although some of them at times have favored a more conservative approach to their "gospel." Occasional charges that Marxism-Leninism has been allowed to calcify do not seem to be based on fact. On the other hand, since all the basic principles of the ideology remain intact, it is probably just as wrong to speak of its complete degeneration or transformation beyond recognition. After all, the history of modern civilization has numerous examples of concepts and beliefs that have retained their fundamental meaning over long periods of time while undergoing evolutionary changes. Most of our surviving religions are in this category of old sets of values adapted to new conditions. This is what Gorbachev is trying to do with the legacy of Marxism-Leninism to justify his *perestroika*, which is, in a manner of speaking, comparable to the Reformation of Christianity. Or, perhaps a better analogy would be President Franklin D. Roosevelt's New Deal, which obviously was meant not to destroy democracy and capitalism in America, but rather to make them more vital.

Another often repeated assertion about Marxism-Leninism should be mentioned here even at the risk of sounding a bit ludicrous. Many Western observers have expressed surprise that the Marxist-Leninist ideology does not readily show in the appearance and everyday behavior of its supposed followers—the Soviet Communist officials. Some of them have found it almost insulting that these people, who claim to adhere to the Communist ideology, look and act in personal situations so much like "everybody else."

[17]V. I. Lenin, *Sobranie sochinenii* [Collected Works] (Moscow: Politizdat, 1961), vol. 4, pp. 211–212.

Could it be that they really have no ideology? This is a reasonable assumption. But it is not reasonable to expect to find visual proof of ideological beliefs in the believers' faces, in their personal behavior, or even in their utterances, particularly in conversations with nonbelievers.

As it applies to the Soviet Union, the word "ideology" is not analogous to the exhibitionist fanaticism characteristic of some religious cults and creeds. The contemporary Soviet functionaries and bureaucrats indeed do not resemble the daredevils whom John Reed[18] saw scaling the high iron grills around the Winter Palace on the first of the "ten days that shook the world" in 1917. But it does not necessarily follow from this indisputable fact that ideological zeal and faith have been lost. A more likely explanation of the change would be to compare it to what happened to Christianity after the new faith had triumphed and moved from the catacombs to cathedrals and palaces.

In the Soviet Union, the Marxist-Leninist ideology has been for a long time institutionalized in a most elaborate and thorough way that could vie with any known established religious faith. Organization has replaced spontaneity. Even the overdramatized assault on the Winter Palace was actually an operation carefully planned by Lenin and his followers, rather than just a spontaneous burst of ideological fanaticism. The Communist faith in the Soviet Union is embodied in a complex organization. In the next chapter we examine the structure and operation of this organization: a secular state church built on the words of Marx, Engels, Lenin, and their disciples.

## GLOSSARY

Atheism:  denial of the existence of God.
Communism:  classless society based on complete socioeconomic equality and common ownership of means of production.
De-Stalinization:  posthumous criticism of Stalin and some of his policies.
Dialectical Materialism:  materialistic explanation of the universe.
Dialectics:  process of constant and interrelated changes through synthesis of opposites.
Doctrine:  theory, hypothesis.
Dogma:  established and unchangeable principles.
Historical Materialism:  economic explanation of human history.
Philosophy:  efforts to understand and explain the universe and human experience.
Populists (narodniki):  non-Marxist Socialist revolutionaries (in Russia).
Proletarian Internationalism:  global aspirations of Marxism-Leninism.
Proletariat:  industrial workers (as a class).
Socialism:  transitional society based on collective ownership and striving for equality.
Stagnation:  definition of the Brezhnev era (1964–1982).

---

[18]The storming of the Winter Palace, seat of the Provisional Government, during the night on November 6 and 7, 1917, signaled the beginning of the Bolshevik Revolution. John Reed was an American journalist who wrote an eyewitness account of this event, entitled *The Ten Days that Shook the World*. The movie *Reds* is based on John Reed's life story.

## RECOMMENDED READINGS

COHEN, STEPHEN F., *Rethinking the Soviet Experience*. New York: Oxford University Press, 1989.
LEONARD, WOLFGANG, *Three Faces of Marxism*. New York: Holt, Rinehart & Winston, 1974.
TUCKER, ROBERT C., *The Marxian Revolutionary Idea*. New York: W. W. Norton, 1969.

CHAPTER

# 4

# THE PARTY

## HISTORIC PERSPECTIVE

The organization that claims the exclusive right to safeguard, develop, and interpret the ideology of Marxism-Leninism in the USSR is the Communist Party of the Soviet Union (CPSU). In the name of this ideology, the CPSU leads the nation toward the ultimate victory of Communism. The party exists because of the ideology; it is an ideological party.

The party traces its beginnings to a small group of Russian revolutionary exiles living in Switzerland who embraced Marxism in 1883. They were led by the former populist, Plekhanov. During the following decade, similar groups or "circles" consisting of young intellectuals sprang up inside Russia. The czarist police paid little attention to these early Marxists until the late 1890s, when some of them attempted to organize their activities on a larger scale by recruiting industrial workers and promoting strikes.

In 1895 and 1896, two young intellectuals, Lenin and Martov,[1] succeeded in forming the first citywide Marxist organization in Russia's capital, St. Petersburg (Leningrad). Their fellow Marxists in other large cities soon followed their example. In 1897, Jewish Marxists in Russia's western prov-

---

[1]Yuli (Tsenderbaum) Martov (1873–1923). Martov led the Menshevik opposition to Lenin at the Second Party Congress in 1903; expelled from Russia in 1921, he died in Berlin.

inces established a regional organization called the "Bund." Early in 1898, at a secret meeting in Minsk (Byelorussia), delegates from the Bund and other Marxist groups proclaimed the founding of the Russian Social Democratic Workers' Party (RSDWP), encompassing no more than 1,000 members. The meeting, attended by only nine delegates, became known as the First Party Congress.

The Second Party Congress conducted its business abroad, in Brussels and London, in the summer of 1903. From this emerged two competing Marxist groups: the Bolsheviks ("majorityites"), followers of Lenin, and the Mensheviks ("minorityites"), followers of Martov. The main difference between them was in the internal organization of their respective factions. In spite of their name, the Mensheviks, who strove to imitate the European Social Democratic parties, actually had stronger popular support and performed more effectively in the open political arena that existed in Russia for about twelve years following the abortive 1905 Revolution. The Bolsheviks, on the other hand, had a more capable underground, bound together by paramilitary discipline and proudly called a "party of a new kind" or "the Leninist Party." Formally, the two groups continued to regard themselves as factions of the same party, the RSDWP, making periodic appeals to each other for the restoration of party unity.

In the spring of 1917, after the fall of the czarist regime, the Bolsheviks under Lenin's leadership used every opportunity to arm themselves and form special assault units. In October, with the help of other radical revolutionary groups, they overthrew the Provisional Government and seized power. A few months later, they renamed themselves the Russian Communist Party (of Bolsheviks).

In the course of the civil strife that followed the October Revolution, all other political parties, including the Mensheviks, were banned, thus giving the relatively small band of Lenin's disciples a complete political monopoly.[2] But even then, and until Lenin's death in 1924, the party retained many of its original characteristics. It continued to function as an elite group of dedicated, professional revolutionaries, trained to manipulate, inspire, and lead the masses by personal example. From the end of 1917 to the beginning of 1924, the membership of the party increased by only 100,000—from 380,000 to 480,000—representing approximately one half of 1 percent of the adult population.

Under Stalin, the character of the party changed drastically. It was transformed into a huge bureaucratic machine with permanent offices on all administrative levels. By the early 1930s, after Stalin had consolidated his power, the party's membership already exceeded 3 million. During the mass purges of the mid- and late 1930s, this trend was temporarily reversed, but

[2]The word "party" implies division of the political spectrum of a given society into several parts. It is, therefore, a misnomer to use this term to refer to a sole political organization allowed to operate in the USSR—the CPSU.

**BOX 4–1**   *Definition of Democratic Centralism (The Soviet Constitution)*

> *Chapter 1, Article 3:* The Soviet state is organized and functions on the principle of democratic centralism, namely the electiveness of all bodies of state authority from the lowest to the highest, their accountability to the people, and the obligation of lower bodies to observe the decisions of higher ones. Democratic centralism combines central leadership with local initiative and creative activity and with the responsibility of each state body and official for the work entrusted to them.

on the eve of World War II the membership again began to rise. It reached almost 7 million at the time of Stalin's death in March 1953.

In 1952, the name of the party was changed to the Communist Party of the Soviet Union, omitting the word "Bolsheviks." Since Stalin's death, the party's membership has continued to grow very fast in proportion to the population. At the beginning of 1990, the membership totaled about 20 million, but there are indications that Gorbachev is actually planning to reduce the size of the party making it "leaner and meaner."

## DEMOCRATIC CENTRALISM

The CPSU has its own constitution, called the "Rules," which sets forth operational principles known as "democratic centralism." These principles are: (1) election of all executive party organs from the lowest to the highest; (2) unconditional subordination of all lower organs to those above them; (3) majority rule; and (4) periodic accountability. The second of these principles is of particular importance for understanding how the CPSU operates. The unconditional subordination prescribed by this principle effectively cancels the other three principles: Lower echelons of the party are given direct orders by their superiors as to whom to elect; a majority vote is produced on command from above; and accountability is demanded only of subordinates by their bosses. Gorbachev's *perestroika* is aimed at liberalizing the application of these harsh rules and giving democratic centralism a better public relations image. Open discussions and even heated debates of issues prior to their resolution are encouraged, and there is a discernible shift from discipline to ideology in conducting party affairs and managing personnel matters.

Conceived by Lenin, democratic centralism is the most significant feature of the CPSU and other Communist parties organized in its image. Democratic centralism is responsible for the party's functioning much like a military establishment. Orders go down the chain of command and are rigorously enforced. Discussions and debates at various party meetings remain strictly within the limits prescribed from above. Decisions are never

**BOX 4–2**   *Definition of the Party (The Soviet Constitution)*

*New Version:* The Communist Party of the Soviet Union, other political parties, trade unions, youth, social organizations, and mass movements participate in shaping the policies of the Soviet state and in running state and social affairs through their representatives elected to the Congress of People's Deputies as well as in other ways.

*Old Version:* The leading and guiding force of Soviet society and the nucleus of its political system, of all state organizations and public organizations, is the Communist Party of the Soviet Union. The CPSU exists for the people and serves the people.

   The Communist Party, armed witt Marxism-Leninism, determines the general perspectives of the development of society and the course of the domestic and foreign policy of the U.S.S.R., directs the great constructive work of the Soviet people, and imparts a planned, systematic and theoretically substantiated character to their struggle for the victory of communism.

   All party organizations shall function within the framework of the constitutions of the U.S.S.R.

questioned once they have been made. As a rule, elections to party organs are simply promotions of loyal subordinates by their superiors. In terms of the American experience, this mode of operation resembles that of a corporation that places loyalty and conformity above everything else. Because the CPSU is the only legal political party in the USSR, its members stand to lose all and gain nothing by going against the system. Transgressors are dealt with summarily and are given punishments ranging from reprimands and demotions to expulsion, similar to dishonorable discharge from the military.

   The ideology of Marxism-Leninism, in whose name the party exists, is expected to inspire and motivate every party member. But it is democratic centralism that ensures that all of them work together as parts of the party's machine, blindly obeying the party discipline and following the party line. Under democratic centralism no factions within the party are allowed.

   From a Western point of view, democratic centralism looks like an obvious contradiction in terms that makes a sham of due democratic process. But in the USSR, it is the governing principle for the operation of not only the Communist Party but also all government and public organizations—a fact that is duly recorded in the Soviet Constitution (Box 4–1).

   Under democratic centralism, party members are denied due process and may be expelled even without a formal hearing. Article 12 of the Rules, for example, states: "A party member bears a double responsibility to the state and to the party for the violation of Soviet laws. Persons who have committed indictable offenses are expelled from the CPSU." In other words, expulsion from the party precedes the verdict of the court. In this way the party preserves its propaganda image of purity, because it can claim that no party member has ever been convicted of any serious crime.

## PARTY MEMBERSHIP

With the aid of democratic centralism, the size and composition of the CPSU can easily be controlled by its leaders. For example, the succession of top leaders in the Kremlin is usually followed by a "flooding of the ranks" in order to weaken the position of the remaining stalwarts of the previous administration. More drastic methods include purges and mass expulsions. At times, concentrated efforts are made to recruit certain categories of new members deemed particularly desirable: various professions, ethnic minorities, age groups, and the like. Currently this applies to women, who are encouraged to join the heretofore predominantly male party, and to blue-collar workers, who are expected to constitute a majority in what is called the "workers' party."

Under normal conditions, the admission of new members occurs on a fairly selective basis. To be eligible for party membership, an applicant must be 18 or older, have a good personal record, and know the basics of Marxism-Leninism. Every applicant is required to secure written recommendations from several members who have belonged to the party for at least five years. The application is then considered at a meeting of the entire primary organization, with the applicant present and obliged to answer questions pertaining to his or her political beliefs, private life, personal ambitions, and familiarity with Marxism-Leninism. A favorable decision by the primary organization must be approved by the appropriate upper-level party office. During the first year, the new member, or "candidate," is on probation and may not vote. All members pay monthly dues that range from a token fee, required from students and pensioners (equivalent to ten cents per month), to 3 percent of their salary, required from high-ranking officials. Members are expected to attend periodic meetings of their primary organization, take an active part in various political campaigns, and set an example for non-members in work, study, and general conduct. Party members are also expected to do volunteer work in various community projects.

The standards for a member's behavior are expressed in the party's Rules, which demand the strictest adherence to party discipline. Any serious deviation from this militarylike discipline is considered insubordination and is dealt with in a most stringent manner, including expulsion from the party, which in Stalin's days called for immediate arrest, exile to Siberia, or worse. To be sure, after Stalin's death most of the victims who survived his arbitrary rule were released and in many cases reinstated as members of the party. At present, to be expelled from the party still means a kind of civil death: disruption of one's career, forced unemployment, and public disgrace.

It would be futile to try to estimate how many Soviet citizens join the party as a matter of convenience, rather than because of strict ideological conviction. In most cases both these motivations probably reinforce each other. Some individuals who join the party want to become political leaders and realize that this is the only way to power. Others who lack political aspirations seek membership in the party in order to further their careers, because the majority of responsible positions in the USSR are reserved for party members. Party membership provides educational, career, and other opportunities denied to nonmembers; however, it also carries very real additional burdens and even risks. For example, it is still remembered that Stalin's bloody purges hit the party the hardest and that during the initial phase of World War II the Nazis on frequent occasions executed card-carrying Communists they had captured. Party members accounted for approximately 15 percent of war casualties. Also, being a party member puts a certain distance between the individual and his or her fellow citizens. The CPSU, its size notwithstanding, is still a privileged minority group quite apart from the rest of the nation. All this means that the decision to join the party is often the most important step in the life of a Soviet citizen and is, therefore, taken very seriously.

**BOX 4–3**    *Excerpt from the Party's Rules*

---

Definition of the Party:

The Communist Party of the Soviet Union is the tried and tested combat vanguard of the Soviet people.

It unites, on a voluntary basis, the more progressive and politically more conscious part of the working class, collective peasantry and the intelligentsia of the USSR.

Definition of a Party member:

Membership in the CPSU is open to any citizen of the Soviet Union who recognizes the Party's Program and Rules, actively participates in the building of Communism, works in one of the Party's organizations, carries out the Party's decisions, and pays membership dues.

---

## PARTY COMPOSITION

In actuality, the CPSU is not a homogeneous body. The membership of the party consists of two subgroups, distinctly different in size and importance. The first subgroup has about 1 million members and includes party functionaries, or *apparatchiks*, who number approximately a quarter of a million. These are the executives of the party machine, and they are therefore the most politically powerful individuals in the Soviet Union. The rest of the subgroup is made up of at least three quarters of a million high-ranking party members, occupying important executive positions within the civil administration, the national economy, the armed forces, police, and so on, or holding politically sensitive jobs as diplomats, political officers, or journalists.

There is a distinct division between the party elite and the rank-and-file CPSU members who compose the bulk of its huge membership. To be sure, the second subgroup contains a number of politically ambitious individuals trying to move up to the first subgroup, but an overwhelming majority of rank-and-file members are people who love their professions or trades. Membership cards ensure them the best possible career opportunities in their chosen fields; their belonging to the party simultaneously gives credence to the claim of its democratic character. Some of them also sympathize with the cause. But many are merely make-believe Communists.

There are no reliable Soviet statistics on the social composition of the party. Every effort, including a substitution of social origin for actual occupation, is made to justify the official contention that the CPSU is and always has been a workers' party. However, it is estimated that blue-collar industrial workers constitute only about 30 percent of the overall membership. Peasants constitute less than 12 percent. The majority of members, more than 55 percent, are white-collar workers. Official Soviet statistics give a different picture, substituting background for occupation (see Table 4–1). Of course, the first subgroup of party executives and high-ranking party members employed outside the party machine consists exclusively of professional white-collar bureaucrats; all blue-collar workers and peasants belong to the second subgroup.

As a group, party members are better educated than the national average for their age brackets (see Table 4–1). This is especially true of those who belong to the first subgroup of top executives. Approximately one third of male college graduates and one half of female college graduates are members of the CPSU.

Consistent with the social composition of the party, average party members receive larger salaries than the population at large. The same is true about their fringe benefits which, in the case of high-ranking party members, include special discount stores, summer homes, foreign travel, chauffeur-driven limousines, and other creature comforts inaccessible to the ordinary Soviet citizen. The brief period following the revolution, when all party members regardless of their ranks and positions received the same modest

**TABLE 4–1**   CPSU Membership Education Level and Social Background (in Percentages)

| | | | |
|---|---|---|---|
| Below high school | 7.9 | Blue-collar | 45.0 |
| High school | 58.2 | Peasants | 11.8 |
| Higher education | 33.9 | White-collar | 43.2 |

*Source:* Compiled by author from Soviet data.

salaries (the so-called party maximum), is no longer even mentioned in official books on the history of the party.

The composition of the party according to sex does not conform to the official self-image of Soviet society: Women, who make up more than half the population, constitute about 30 percent of the card-carrying Communists. They, too, are found mostly in the second subgroup. Very few women have ever reached high executive positions in the party.

The overall membership of the CPSU generally reflects the multinational character of the Soviet Union. Some ethnic groups—including the Georgians, Jews, and Russians—have disproportionately high membership ratios. The ethnic Russians account for more than 60 percent of the membership, which is about 10 percent higher than their share of the population. Lower ratios for some of the component nationalities appear to be due mainly to various historical peculiarities, rather than to any kind of deliberate discrimination. Local party bosses (first secretaries) in union republics, autonomous republics, and autonomous regions and areas are almost always members of indigenous ethnic groups. On the national level, however, ethnic Russians serve in disproportionately large numbers on the highest councils of the party.

The CPSU age composition is approximately as follows: (1) below 30 years age group—17 percent; (2) 30 to 40 years group—28 percent; (3) 41–50 years group—26 percent; (4) 51–60 years group—16.5 percent; and (5) over 60 years group—12.5 percent. Representative age composition of the party as a whole tends to conceal the fact that the top echelons of its bureaucracy are dominated by older people. For example, in 1990 the median age for rank-and-file party members was about 40, but for the members of the Central Committee and its Politburo it was about 55 and 60, respectively. The membership of these two important bodies was at least 70 percent Russian. The membership of the Central Committee as a whole included less than 5 percent women. Only one of these women also served on the Politburo as a candidate-member.

By comparison, the leadership of the party was much younger and had higher ratios of non-Russian members under Lenin, Stalin, and Khrushchev. During the two decades of the Brezhnev era, the Party as a whole grew older very quickly. The trend continued under Andropov and Chernenko but at a slower pace. Currently, efforts are under way to recruit younger members.

## PARTY STRUCTURE

For more than seventy years, 1918–1990, the CPSU was officially the sole political party, assigned the dual role of "the guiding force of Soviet society" and "the nucleus of its political system, of all state organizations and public organizations" (see Box 4–2, p. 95). In 1990, the CPSU lost its legal monopoly, but not its actual power.

As the "guiding force," the party maintains a giant network of permanent offices on every level of the administrative-territorial structure: national, union republic, autonomous republic, province, region, city, district, and so forth. The party's permanent offices on various levels are called "committees." On the higher levels, from union republic up, they are referred to as "central committees"; on the lower levels, they are designated "local committees." The executive officers of these committees are called "secretaries." Every committee has a steering subcommittee called the "bureau." The average local party committee consists of several departments and sections in charge of various functions ranging from political indoctrination to agricultural production and from personnel allocation to sports and recreation. The committee's purpose is to monitor and direct official governmental authorities operating on the same level. Central committees have larger staffs and more complex structures. Through a hierarchy of approximately 4,600 such committees, the CPSU leadership guides and supervises the work of the entire country on a daily basis. In fact, the apparatus of the CPSU functions as a supergovernment.

A special pyramidal structure of permanent party offices exists in the Soviet Armed Forces and police. These offices, called "political sections," are attached to military units from the level of platoon and up and are staffed with professional party officials who also are commissioned officers (formerly known as commissars).

Most of the day-to-day hustle concerned with the operation of the huge party machine occurs on the district level. Urban and rural district party committees (and their counterparts in the armed forces) form the foundations of this machine.

As the "nucleus," the CPSU is officially present at every enterprise, office, college, farm, military unit, institution, and the like, that has three or more party members among its staff. These members are joined together in "primary party organizations" (formerly called "cells"). Currently, there are approximately 420,000 primary organizations throughout the Soviet Union. Every primary organization is headed by a secretary. Larger primary organizations with 150 members or more are often subdivided into "groups," and in addition to secretaries they have steering committees or "bureaus." Their secretaries are full-time party functionaries; the secretaries of smaller primary organizations combine part-time party duties with their regular work. Typically, the career of a professional party bureaucrat begins with the position of part-time or full-time secretary in a primary organization. The main function of the primary party organization is to provide internal leadership for every group of Soviet citizens performing a specific task. At the same time, primary organizations serve as a controlling mechanism that monitors and directs the lives and activities of rank-and-file party members on the grass-roots level. The work of primary organizations is in turn

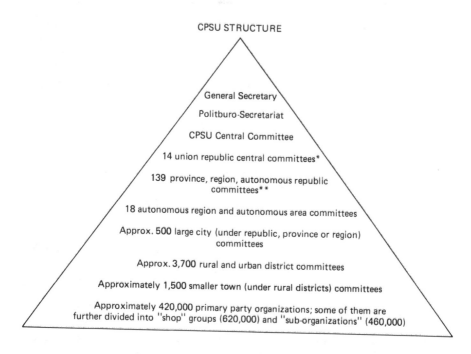

CPSU STRUCTURE

General Secretary

Politburo-Secretariat

CPSU Central Committee

14 union republic central committees*

139 province, region, autonomous republic committees**

18 autonomous region and autonomous area committees

Approx. 500 large city (under republic, province or region) committees

Approx. 3,700 rural and urban district committees

Approximately 1,500 smaller town (under rural districts) committees

Approximately 420,000 primary party organizations; some of them are further divided into "shop" groups (620,000) and "sub-organizations" (460,000)

*The Russian Federation (RSFSR) does not have a separate central committee. Its branch of the party comes directly under a special "bureau" of the CPSU Central Committee.
**Two large city committees (Moscow and Kiev) are equated with union republic central committees. Leningrad, however, does not have this special status.

**FIGURE 4–1.** CPSU Structure. *Source:* Compiled by author from Soviet data.

supervised by the appropriate permanent party offices, usually on a district (county, precinct) level.

The hierarchy of permanent offices (committees) and political sections, together with the network of primary organizations, constitutes the main body of the party machine. Major local components of the machine—party committees for the republics, provinces, regions, and large cities—are headed by several hundred of the most senior party executives. In addition, the CPSU has its own schools, publishing houses, printing shops, and other auxiliary enterprises. Next to the Soviet government, it is the largest employer in the USSR. The CPSU is supposed to be financially self-supporting. The bulk of its revenue comes from membership dues, and the remainder from various publishing ventures and other sources. In countless Soviet

**BOX 4–4**  *On Joining the Party*

> A person is being admitted to the party. It is an exiting and unique moment! This moment marks the most important step in the life of everyone who receives a party membership card. From now on, this life will follow specially strict laws—the laws of Lenin's party which demand much from all its members. Therefore, it is perfectly logical for comrades to ask: Are you ready to accept this new lofty responsibility?
>
> *Pravda* (Sept. 22, 1987), p. 1 [editorial].

novels, movies, stories, songs, and even operas, the Communist Party has been exalted as the most important, noble, and glorious organization in the world. Of course, this is not necessarily a true reflection of the popular opinion about the party.

As we have seen, the Soviet Constitution paid the CPSU the highest compliment by calling it "the guiding force." Now let us take a look at who guides the "guiding force" and how.

## PARTY CONGRESSES

The party's Rules define periodical national party congresses as the supreme councils of the CPSU, empowered to make the most crucial decisions, set long-range goals, and elect the top leaders. However, during the last half-century, party congresses have served mainly as public forums for speeches by the top leaders, rather than as decision-making bodies.

The most recent one, the Twenty-seventh Party Congress, took place in 1986. It had all the trappings of a well-orchestrated political show. The congress was attended by 5,000 delegates (one per 3,670 party members), including, of course, all top-level leaders. Among the delegates were 1,074 important party functionaries, 1,240 executive government officials, 147 distinguished scientists and scholars, 332 high-ranking military officers, and 279 noted writers and artists. The rest were rank-and-file party members from all parts of the Soviet Union who had been handpicked by their local party bosses and approved by Moscow. Special care was given to ensure equal representation based on sex, ethnic origin, and social status. Several hundred guests from sympathetic foreign Communist and Socialist parties also were invited.

In a sense, the congress served as the inauguration of the Gorbachev era. General Secretary Gorbachev delivered his "State of the Soviet Union Message," and Chairman of the Council of Ministers Nikolai Ryzhkov detailed a new five-year plan for the development of the national economy. Various delegates and foreign guests later took the floor to make brief

**TABLE 4–2**   Party Congress and Membership

| Designation | Year | Place | Number of Delegates | Party Membership* |
|---|---|---|---|---|
| 1st "Founding" | 1898 | Minsk | 9 | approx. 1,000 |
| 2nd | 1903 | Brussels/ London | 57 | approx. 4,000 |
| 3rd | 1905 | London | 38 | 8,400 |
| 4th "Unifying" | 1906 | Stockholm | 134 | 45,000 |
| 5th | 1907 | London | 342 | 46,000 |
| 6th | 1917 | Petrograd (Leningrad) | 267 | 250,000 |
| 7th "Extraordinary" | 1918 | Petrograd (Leningrad) | 104 | 390,000 |
| 8th | 1919 | Moscow | 403 | 350,000 |
| 9th | 1920 | Moscow | 716 | 611,978 |
| 10th | 1921 | Moscow | 990 | 732,521 |
| 11th | 1922 | Moscow | 687 | 528,354 |
| 12th | 1923 | Moscow | 825 | 499,100 |
| 13th | 1924 | Moscow | 1,164 | 472,000 |
| 14th | 1925 | Moscow | 1,306 | 801,804 |
| 15th | 1927 | Moscow | 1,669 | 1,212,505 |
| 16th | 1930 | Moscow | 2,159 | 1,677,910 |
| 17th "Of the Victors" | 1934 | Moscow | 1,961 | 2,701,608 |
| 18th | 1939 | Moscow | 2,035 | 2,306,973 |
| 19th | 1952 | Moscow | 1,359 | 6,707,539 |
| 20th | 1956 | Moscow | 1,430 | 7,137,521 |
| 21st "Special" | 1959 | Moscow | 1,367 | 8,239,131 |
| 22nd | 1961 | Moscow | 4,799 | 9,275,826 |
| 23rd | 1966 | Moscow | 4,942 | 12,357,308 |
| 24th | 1971 | Moscow | 4,949 | 14,372,563 |
| 25th | 1976 | Moscow | 4,998 | 15,694,000 |
| 26th | 1981 | Moscow | 5,002 | 17,000,000 |
| 27th | 1986 | Moscow | 5,000 | 18,300,000 |

*Beginning with 1920, the figures include newly admitted members on probation (candidate members). The current membership includes about 600,000 such candidate members. In 1918 the original names of the party—Russian Social Democratic Workers Party—was changed to Russian Communist Party (Bolshevik). In 1924 the word "Russian" was changed to "All Union." In 1952 the name was changed again to (current version): The Communist Party of the Soviet Union (CPSU).

*Source:* Compiled by the author from Soviet statistics.

speeches. But there was no real debate on the issues before the congress. In strict compliance with democratic centralism, the delegates unanimously ratified everything that their superiors presented. Later, in a closed session, the delegates cast their ballots approving a slate of new members of the party's Central Committee, which had been prepared beforehand. All those nominated were duly elected. There were no rejections, nominations from the floor, or write-ins. The congress completed its business in ten days, from February 25 to March 6.

The just-described procedures have been the same at most postrevolution congresses. To find even a semblance of free debate one has to go back almost sixty years to the Fifteenth (1927), Fourteenth (1925), or even Thirteenth (1924) Party Congresses. Campaigning, competing for votes, and running opposing slates of candidates had halted by the time of the Tenth Party Congress (1921) when it was decreed that all such manifestations of "bourgeois democracy" were incompatible with the principles of democratic centralism. Soon afterwards, the party congresses began to lose their importance as policy-making bodies; however, they continued to convene every year until 1925. During the next decade, the intervals between such meetings gradually extended to three or four years. And during the last twenty years of the Stalin era, there were only three congresses, with an interval of thirteen years between the last two (1939–1952). After Stalin's death, these meetings again became more frequent; the current edition of the party's Rules stipulates, in fact, that a congress must be held every five years.

The best remembered of the eight post-Stalin congresses is the Twentieth Party Congress which was held in February 1956. From the rostrum of its closed session, Nikita Khrushchev delivered his famous "secret" speech in which he denounced some of Stalin's most hideous crimes.[3]

Prior to the seizure of power by the Bolsheviks in October 1917, the party held six congresses. The first (the Founding) and the last (the Sixth) were held on Russian soil. The remaining four conducted their business abroad. It is rather ironic that "Lenin's Party" was actually founded in London where the famous Bolshevik-Menshevik split occurred at the Second Party Congress in 1903.

In Soviet historical texts party congresses are used as milestones for the periodization of the postrevolutionary era. Customarily, the mass media make frequent references to the proceedings and resolutions of the most recent congress, claiming that it provides guidance and inspiration for the entire Soviet nation. Currently, the Twenty-seventh Party Congress receives this kind of "hype-treatment" in the daily news coverage. The Twenty-eighth Party Congress, originally scheduled for 1991, will meet in 1990.

During the first two decades of the Soviet era, special "party conferences" were held between party congresses. Their main function was to review the progress made since the last congress and make recommendations for the next one. Gorbachev has renewed this practice after almost five decades, and the Nineteenth Party Conference, attended by about 5,000 delegates, was held in the summer of 1988. Celebrated as the most open and democratic forum of this size in almost sixty years, the conference was an important milestone in Gorbachev's *perestroika* campaign. It issued recommendations but made no personnel changes in the Politburo. Presumably,

---

[3]The full text of Khrushchev's speech has never been published in the Soviet Union. However, its contents are known from oral presentations at special meetings of primary party organizations.

FIGURE 4–2.    Artist's rendering of the clandestine meeting of the First Party Congress in Minsk in 1898. It was attended by only nine delegates.

such conferences will be held in the future at five-year intervals between congresses.

## CENTRAL COMMITTEE

Between congresses, the leadership of the party is vested in its Central Committee (CC), which is elected by the most recent congress and is accountable to the next congress. This institution is as old as the party itself. As early as 1898, the First Party Congress, attended by only nine delegates, elected a three-member "Central Committee."

The current Central Committee, elected in 1986, originally consisted of 307 full members and 170 nonvoting "candidate-members." The committee was predominantly composed of Russian male representatives of the party machine. In 1989 some 70 older members were retired. The average age of its remaining members is about 55. Among these members are the most important party and government officials.

The term of each member of the current Central Committee will expire in summer, 1990 when the next regular party congress is scheduled to meet and install a new Central Committee. Gorbachev wants it to have only about 200 members. The number of surviving incumbent members who will be retained depends on the changes that will occur on the highest level in the Kremlin. As a rule, the turnover among members of the Central Committee is quite rapid during periods of succession to power. This change slows down considerably when the leadership at the top remains the same.

The Central Committee membership has not changed much during the intervals between the four congresses—the Twenty-third, Twenty-fourth, Twenty-fifth, and Twenty-sixth—that occurred under Brezhnev. The same was true of the entire Lenin era and the latter part of Khrushchev's decade in power. Exceptions did transpire during the years of Stalin's purges, however, when continuity of the top leadership did not guarantee stability. At the height of Stalin's purges, more than 70 percent of Central Committee members installed by the Seventeenth Party Congress in 1934 did not survive until the Eighteenth Party Congress in 1939. The turnover between the last two congresses—the Twenty-sixth under Brezhnev and the Twenty-seventh under Gorbachev—was about 40 percent.

At the beginning of the Khrushchev era, attempts were made to devise a rotation system that would incorporate new members into the Central Committee. However, these efforts were successfully resisted by the Central Committee membership as a whole. After Khrushchev's ouster, all references to the need for periodic rejuvenation were deleted from party rules. No system of rotation is in operation at present, but Gorbachev appears determined to change this situation. By all indications, the Central Committee continues to play a significant role in setting long-range policies and goals. There is reason to believe that the Central Committee as a whole took an active part in all post-Stalin leadership crises—a role which it is also likely to play in the future.

The Central Committee meets in closed sessions at least twice a year. These full-committee sessions are called "plenums." (Under Gorbachev's plan the new Central Committee will be in permanent session.) To be a member of the Central Committee represents the ultimate success in terms of prestige, influence, material comforts, and career opportunities. Members and candidate-members of this exclusive political club constitute the upper crust of the Soviet elite. They can co-opt new members (as replacements), but they do not collectively run the numerous permanent offices of the Central Committee, nor are they in charge of the day-to-day operation of the party and the Soviet government. In the past, the Central Committee delegated its executive authority to a much smaller group of its own senior members, organized into two permanent subcommittees called the Politburo (Political Bureau) and the Secretariat. In a separate vote, the Central Committee also elected the General Secretary. In reality, the process was reversed. Acting in accordance with the principles of democratic centralism, these self-perpetuating bodies, the Politburo and the Secretariat, arranged the "election" of delegates to party congresses, determined the composition of the Central Committee "elected" by these delegates, and ultimately decided on any changes among their own memberships and on the position of the General

**FIGURE 4–3.** The opening session of the Twenty-fifth Party Congress, 1976. The slogan on the wall reads: "The party is the intellect, honor, and conscience of our epoch." It is attributed to Lenin, whose statue stands on the right.

Secretary. All this was usually endorsed later by the Central Committee without any debates.

The term "Central Committee" is also used to denote the highest party bureaucracy: a permanent office located in Moscow that functions as the supergovernment of the USSR. It is the "White House" of the Soviet power structure, whose supreme authority is unchecked by any legislative body or outside pressure group. As a bureaucracy (often called "Central Apparat"), the Central Committee used to work directly under the Politburo and Secretariat. It is discussed in more detail later.

The current Politburo and Secretariat were "elected" by the new Central Committee (the "board of directors") immediately after the Twenty-seventh Party Congress in 1986. Two other central organs of lesser prestige and importance were "elected" at the same time: the Party Control Commission and the Central Auditing Commission. These offices will be operative until the next congress meets in summer 1990, although some of their members have already been replaced, others may be replaced in the future, and some of the vacancies owing to deaths or removals may not be filled.

## POLITBURO AND SECRETARIAT

Technically, the terms the Politburo and the Secretariat denote standing subcommittees of the Central Committee.[4] By tradition, rather than by any set rule, their memberships overlapped and both bodies were chaired by the General Secretary. At the time when Gorbachev proposed to change the top party structure (February 1990), his "last" Politburo was composed of twelve full members and seven nonvoting candidate-members. The Secretariat also had twelve members, seven of whom served concurrently on the Politburo: six, including the General Secretary, as full members, and one as a candidate-member (Figure 4-4).

As a separate body, the Secretariat is in charge of all of the party's internal affairs: operation of party offices, personnel appointments, training, discipline, and so on. It controls the appointments to all important positions throughout the government and supervises activities for which the party's apparatus is directly responsible—for example, the development of Marxism-Leninism, ideological indoctrination, political propaganda, and ties with foreign Communist parties. In sum, the Secretariat is the general staff of the CPSU, which includes the numerous departments and sections needed to run this vast and complex organization. The members of the Secretariat—the Secretaries—are heads of its major subdivisions. They usually meet as a committee once a week.

1. General Secretary, Gorbachev chaired both councils.
2. Of the 11 other Secretaries, 6 were members and 1 was a candidate member of the Politburo.
3. Altogether, 24 persons served on the Politburo and Secretariat.

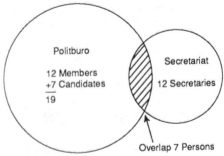

Politburo

12 Members
+7 Candidates
19

Secretariat

12 Secretaries

Overlap 7 Persons

**FIGURE 4-4.** Gorbachev's Politburo and Secretariat, February 1990.

[4]The Politburo was established in 1917, two weeks before the October Revolution. The Secretariat emerged as an important office in the early 1920s.

At that time, the Politburo was the highest decision-making body in the country. It met behind closed doors on a weekly basis, and its sessions often involved reports and presentations by various resource persons. For several years, the Soviet press had been publishing brief accounts of the meetings, but information concerning the operation of this highest political council was very scant. There were indications that its meetings were conducted informally; discussions were businesslike and frank; and arguments sometimes became extremely sharp. The Politburo was supposed to function as a committee of peers in which the presiding General Secretary had one vote, just as every other full member did. It is assumed that final decisions required a consensus and were made by a show of hands or a similar kind of open voting. Candidate-members did not vote.

In addition to the secretaries, the Politburo's membership usually included the senior members of the Soviet government: the prime minister, his main deputy, the minister of defense, the foreign minister, and the KGB chairman. Also included were the most important local party bosses. The members of both the Secretariat and the Politburo were always listed in alphabetical order. Only their presiding officer, the General Secretary, was listed before the others. Normally, new full members were selected from candidate-members, who in turn were promoted from the ranks of full members of the Central Committee. To become a full member of the Central Committee one usually had first to serve as a candidate-member. This has always been the beginning of the climb to the very top, which is usually quite slow and uncertain. In this context, the designation "candidate" does not necessarily mean probationary status. Instead, it may denote a permanent rank of indefinite tenure. On the other hand, individuals have sometimes become full members of the Central Committee or even the Politburo without having served as candidate-members. In 1971, for example, Gorbachev was made a full member of the Central Committee without having served first as a candidate-member. It was rumored at the time that this unusual promotion was arranged by Gorbachev's benefactor, Yuri Andropov. In 1985, General Secretary Gorbachev promoted two of his own alleged protégés, Ligachev and Ryzhkov, to full Politburo membership, so they too skipped the rank of candidate. In fact, most of the Gorbachev era's promotions to the full membership of the Politburo were done in this direct manner, bypassing the candidate-member status: for example, Zaikov (1986), Medvedev (1988), and Kryuchkov (1989). This presumably helped Gorbachev to speed up a generational change of the guard in the Kremlin.

During the last twenty-five years, the chances of becoming a new member—candidate or full—of the Politburo favored the male members of the Central Committee who were of Russian origin, worked in the party's bureaucracy, and were about 60 years old. Under Lenin, Stalin, and even Khrushchev the Politburo's membership was considerably younger and included proportionately more non-Russians: Jews, Georgians, and Armenians. For several years under Khrushchev, the Politburo had its first, and so far the only, female full member, Yekaterina Furtseva. Under Brezhnev, the all-male membership was much older than it is under Gorbachev. The average age of Gorbachev's "last" Politburo (1990) was about 62 for full members, 57 for candidate-members, and 60 for the entire group. Of the twelve full members, one was almost 70, eight were in their 60s, and three in their 50s. At 58, Gorbachev was the third youngest. Ages of the seven candidate-members ranged from 53 to 56 (see Table 4–3).

The predominance of professional party bureaucrats on the Politburo was always relatively the same. During the 1960s and 1970s, the turnover in the Politburo's membership was approximately one full member per year, but the rate accelerated in the early 1980s. With Gorbachev firmly in power, the turnover doubled.

Historically, most personnel changes on this level took place during the struggles for succession following the deaths of Lenin and Stalin. By the mid-1930s, more than one half of the original members of "Lenin's Politburo" had lost their positions and were about to lose their lives. It appears that a similar massacre was in the making a few months before Stalin's death.

**TABLE 4–3**   The Politburo of the CC of the CPSU, February 1990

| Full Members | | |
| --- | --- | --- |
| Mikhail Gorbachev | b. 1931, Russian | General Secretary, CC CPSU |
| Vladimir Ivashko | b. 1932, Ukrainian | First Secretary, Ukrainian SSR |
| Vladimir Kryuchkov | b. 1924, Russian | Chairman, KGB |
| Yegor Ligachev | b. 1920, Russian | Secretary, CC CPSU |
| Yuri Maslyukov | b. 1936, Russian | Chairman, Gosplan |
| Vadim Medvedev | b. 1929, Russian | Secretary, CC CPSU |
| Nikolai Ryzhkov | b. 1929, Russian | Premier, USSR |
| Eduard Shevardnadze | b. 1928, Georgian | Foreign Minister, USSR |
| Nikolai Slyunkov | b. 1929, Byelorussian | Secretary, CC CPSU |
| Vitali Vorotnikov | b. 1926, Russia | Chairman, RSFSR Supreme Soviet |
| Alexander Yakovlev | b. 1925, Russian | Secretary, CC CPSU |
| Lev Zaikov | b. 1923, Russian | Secretary, CC CPSU |

| Candidate-Members | | |
| --- | --- | --- |
| Alexandra Biryukova | b. 1929, Russian | Deputy Premier, USSR |
| Alexander Lukyanov | b. 1931, Russian | First Vice-Chairman, USSR Supreme Soviet |
| Yevgeni Primakov | b. 1929, Russian | Co-Chairman, USSR Supreme Soviet |
| Boris Pugo | b. 1926, Latvian | Chairman, CPS Review Commission |
| Georgi Razumovski | b. 1937, Russian | Secretary, CC CPSU |
| Alexander Vlasov | b. 1932, Russian | Premier, RSFSR |
| Dmitri Yazov | b. 1930 Russia | Defense Minister, USSR |

*Source:* Compiled by author from Soviet data.

**TABLE 4–4**　The Secretariat of the CC of the CPSU, February 1990

| Mikhail Gorbachev | b. 1931, Russian | General Secretary |
|---|---|---|
| Oleg Baklanov | b. 1935, Russian | Secretary for Foreign Communist Parties |
| Andrei Girenko | b. 1936, Ukrainian | Secretary for Transportation |
| Yegor Ligachev | b. 1936, Russian | Secretary for Agriculture |
| Yuri Manaenkov | b. 1936, Russian | Secretary for Labor |
| Vadim Medvedev | b. 1929, Russian | Secretary for Ideology |
| Georgi Razumovski | b. 1937, Russian | Secretary for Personnel |
| Nikolai Slyunkov | b. 1929, Byelorussian | Secretary for Socio-Economic Matters |
| Yegor Stroyev | b. 1937, Russian | Secretary for Industry |
| Gumer Usmanov | b. 1936, Tatar | Secretary for Nationalities |
| Alexander Yakovlev | b. 1925, Russian | Secretary for International Relations |
| Lev Zaikov | b. 1923, Russian | Secretary for Armaments |

*Source:* Compiled by author from Soviet data.

Stalin, in a sudden move, doubled the size of his Politburo, gave it a new name, the "Presidium," [5] and created a steering committee within it, called the Bureau. Immediately after his death, his heirs cut the size of the Presidium in half and abolished its steering committee. Several years later Khrushchev organized his own purge of the Politburo (Presidium), and he expelled more than 50 percent of its members. In 1966, the former name, Politburo, was restored. Despite these two mass upheavals, the degree of continuity among top leadership remained remarkably high: since its inception in 1917 and until 1990, fewer than 90 persons had served on the Politburo (Presidium) as full members.

The size and composition of the Politburo and the Secretariat were never specified in the Rules; moreover, the existence of candidate members of the Politburo was not even mentioned in this governing document.

The lopsided composition of the Politburo and the Secretariat in terms of age, gender, and ethnic background of their members is somewhat surprising, given Gorbachev's known concern for good public relations. The average age of the entire team was going down, but very slowly. There was only one woman, Alexandra Biryukova, on the team, serving as a candidate-member of the Politburo.

Perhaps most puzzling was Gorbachev's failure to put more non-Russians on his team. Of the twenty-four persons in the two highest and most visible councils of power, only six (25 percent) could claim ethnic backgrounds. This unprecedented Russian predominance probably compounded Gorbachev's problems with ethnic tensions. It may even suggest that during the 1980s Gorbachev was not actually in full control of top appointments in the Kremlin and it may explain why he ultimately decided to replace the Politburo with a thirty-member Presidium structured to preclude Russian domination (Table 4–5).

[5]The Presidium was formed by combining the Politburo and the Orgburo (Organizational Bureau), which had been another subcommittee of the Central Committee.

**TABLE 4–5**    Structure of the New Presidium, CC CPSU

---

The body consists of 30 members and is presided over by the Chairman of the CPSU.
Fifteen of the council's members are first secretaries of the Union republics, serving ex officio.
The other fifteen members are elected by the Central Committee. The Presidium meets
every week (just as did its predecessor, the Politburo).

---

*Source:* Compiled by author from Soviet data.

**BOX 4–5**   *Soviet Underground Humor*

Question:   Why is there only one party in the USSR?
Answer:     The country is too poor to support two such parties in the high
            style to which party members are accustomed.

## GENERAL SECRETARY

For more than sixty years the General Secretary was the highest party official
and consequently the most influential person in the country. In addition to
presiding over the Politburo and Secretariat, the General Secretary also
chaired meetings of the Central Committee and party congresses. Only six
men have held this position for significant lengths of time; Lenin was not
among them.

Lenin's official position from 1917 until his death in 1924 was head of
the Soviet government. He was, of course, also a member of the Politburo,
over which he presided as the acknowledged, but unofficial, supreme leader
of the party. The position of General Secretary was created in 1922. Apparently, it was meant to deal exclusively with the control and assignment of
top-level personnel. Upon Lenin's suggestion, the new position was given
to Stalin, then a member of the Politburo. One year later, in his "Testament,"
the mortally ill Lenin warned the party that, "As General Secretary, Comrade
Stalin has concentrated in his hands an enormous power."[6] Lenin's heirs
ignored the warning, and Stalin proceeded to acquire additional power,
mainly at the expense of the Politburo and the Central Committee—that is,
the people who had originally appointed him General Secretary.

By the mid-1930s, the title of General Secretary became tantamount to
that of supreme ruler and absolute dictator of the USSR. But in October 1952,
the title of General Secretary, which by that time was just one of the many
top positions amassed by Stalin, was changed to a more modest one—"First
Secretary." After Stalin's death in March 1953, the office was further down-

[6]B. Ponomarev (ed.), *Istoriya Kommunisticheskoi Partii Sovetskogo Soyuza* [History of the
Communist Party of the Soviet Union] (Moscow: Politizdat, 1976), p. 342.

graded and later even temporarily abolished. The sequence of events was as follows: Initially, Georgi Malenkov assumed both top positions vacated by Stalin and became head of the party and the Soviet government. After only one week, he relinquished the former title in an apparent attempt to fulfill the solemn promise of "collective leadership."

Six months later (September 1953), Nikita Khrushchev was publicly identified as the new First Secretary. The next decade witnessed sharp clashes between Khrushchev and other members of the Presidium (Politburo), who acted individually or in small groups. In the beginning, Khrushchev scored impressive victories by playing the Presidium (Politburo) and the Central Committee against each other. He denounced Stalin in a way that cast shadows on the senior members of the Presidium and finally purged most of them, including Malenkov, for their alleged participation in an "antiparty conspiracy." In 1958 Khrushchev managed to do what only Stalin had accomplished before him: He assumed and successfully held the dual post of head of the party and head of the government. However, six years later, in 1964, he was dethroned and disgraced by a combined effort of the Presidium and the Central Committee, which supposedly consisted entirely of his personal protégés. The top party and government positions were again split, with the former going to Leonid Brezhnev.

In 1966, the title was returned to the original, General Secretary, and the principle of collective leadership was declared to be the only correct, "Leninist" form of governance. Under this formula, the General Secretary was supposed to be no more than "the first among equals" in the ruling Politburo. Brezhnev's appointment to the largely ceremonial position of chief of state (Chairman of the Presidium of the Supreme Soviet) in 1977 did not change this and in all Soviet mass media, Brezhnev's title of General Secretary always preceded his title of chief of state, emphasizing the dominant role of the party. Assumption of the dual party-state leadership by Yuri Andropov and Konstantin Chernenko was treated in the same manner. After Mikhail Gorbachev succeeded Chernenko in 1985 as head of the party, it took

**TABLE 4–6**   Previous Heads of the Party

| Name | Years in Office | Born—Died | Ultimate Fate |
|------|-----------------|-----------|---------------|
| Vladimir Lenin | 1903–1924 | 1870–1924 | died in office |
| Iosif (Joseph) Stalin | 1924–1953* | 1879–1953 | died in office |
| Nikita Krushchev | 1953–1964 | 1894–1971 | forced to resign, died in disgrace |
| Leonid Brezhnev | 1964–1982 | 1906–1982 | died in office |
| Yuri Andropov | 1982–1984 | 1914–1984 | died in office |
| Konstantin Chernenko | 1984–1985 | 1911–1985 | died in office |

*Nominally, Stalin became head of the party—General Secretary—in 1922.
Source: Compiled by author from Soviet data.

him more than three years to follow the example of his three immediate predecessors and become also chief of state. In 1990, Gorbachev decided to drop the title General Secretary as an unwelcome legacy from the past, in favor of a new title—Chairman of the CPSU.

## PROBLEM OF SUCCESSION

The locus of power in the Soviet Union has been alternating between an individual leader and a small group of persons at the very top of the party's structure. During the entire course of Soviet history the struggle for supreme power has been limited to the highest level, and all successful and unsuccessful contenders alike were members of the Politburo.

The official Soviet version of history admits to only one long period of individual rule, euphemistically called the "cult of Stalin's personality" and condemned as a "deviation from the norm." The norm, according to this version, has been a "collective leadership"—that is, an oligarchy, represented by the Politburo (Presidium), ruling in consultation with the entire Central Committee. Actually, there were at least two more shorter periods of individual rule in Soviet history: the early years of Lenin's rule (prior to his illness), which was achieved because of the sheer dominance of his personality, and the late years of Khrushchev's solo showmanship, which led to his forced retirement. Moreover, the years immediately following the deaths of Lenin and Stalin were periods of collective struggle for power, rather than collective leadership. When we count and compare the years of group power and the rule by individual leaders, it turns out that collective leadership has not been the prevailing norm.

There is, however, no reason to assume that the Soviet power system is a captive of its own history and that it is, as such, incapable of change and reform. On the contrary, even the ouster of Khrushchev—as crude as it looked at the time to outside observers—actually marked an important departure from the previous pattern according to which the top leader died in office. Since there were no discernible signs of a succession struggle following Khrushchev's political demise, it appears likely that Brezhnev was a prevacancy choice. The same was probably true about Andropov, Chernenko, and Gorbachev. It is, in fact, reasonable to assume that the actual heir apparent is known in advance, as has been suggested by the rapidity and smoothness of these recent takeovers.

Our lack of knowledge about the succession process does not mean that there is no such mechanism and that power succession in the Kremlin is a free-for-all struggle. We never knew the actual ranking within the Politburo, which indicated the order of succession, but it was clear that during the entire post-Stalin era, eligibility for the top leader's position was limited to the persons with dual membership on the Politburo and Secretariat. The age factor did not seem to be one of the selection criteria.[7]

We can no longer assume that Gorbachev's term as top leader will last his lifetime, which was the case with all but one of his six predecessors; Lenin, Stalin, Brezhnev, Andropov, and Chernenko died in office. Only Khrushchev was forced to step down and retire. But now, according to a new rule introduced by Gorbachev himself, the tenure of the General Secretary is to be limited to two consecutive five-year terms. The new rule is supposed to take effect after the next party congress. This means that Gorbachev could stay in the top political office until, but not beyond, the end of the century. The same tenure limitation applies to all other members of the "collective leadership"—a concept which continues to be defined only in the most general terms, leaving it up to every new top leader to establish a pattern for sharing power and responsibilities.

It is not clear at this time whether under the new structure proposed by Gorbachev one of his vice chairmen of the CPSU, elected by the Central Committee, will be designated as heir apparent to the party throne. This would provide formal safeguards for orderly succession.

The lack of formal safeguards does not necessarily mean that the rule by committee is doomed to failure. In fact, it is reasonable to think that the memory of what Stalin did as a dictator and of what was done to Khrushchev when he tried to become one will further strengthen this alternative ensuring orderly succession to the top party post and limiting its power. Collective leadership, as the term is currently used in the Soviet Union, recognizes the leading role of the party head but limits his power by making it dependent on the collective will of the ruling elite. The Central Committee, under this formula, stands by as a power broker and referee in case of a serious disagreement between the top leader and the ruling elite or its majority. The party as a whole continues to make sure that no rival power structures develop anywhere in the Soviet Union. There are no indications that this status quo is likely to be changed in the foreseeable future.

Chiefly because the Politburo's affairs are still concealed under a veil of secrecy, there are never-ending rumors about power struggles in the Kremlin. Gorbachev's main rival is supposedly Yegor Ligachev, who was identified as Gorbachev's personal protege only a few years ago. Ligachev is seen as "conservative." Vadim Medvedev, Alexander Yakovlev, and Eduard Shevardnadze are believed to be "liberals." How much of this is real—as opposed to either idle speculation or political role playing—cannot be determined accurately. It is, however, quite evident that real differences

[7]At the time of the Revolution Lenin was 47. At the time of Lenin's death Stalin was 44. In 1953, when Stalin died, Khrushchev was 58. Brezhnev came to power at 58, Andropov at 68, and Chernenko at 72. Gorbachev became top leader at age 53.

of opinion among the ruling elite do exist. Unlike in the past, calculated information leaks are used, making them public, perhaps, to prove that democracy has now reached the very top of the party machine.[8]

## CENTRAL APPARAT

The "Central Apparat" name is given to a permanent executive office of the party that operates directly under the Politburo and is managed by the Secretariat. The Central Apparat carries out decisions made by the Politburo on behalf of the Central Committee. It is a large bureaucracy staffed with several hundred important officials aided by numerous support personnel, who include experts and consultants in different fields and on various matters. The jurisdiction and functions of the Central Apparat appear to be unlimited and all-inclusive, extending to every aspect of Soviet life. The most important single responsibility of the office is to appoint and control key personnel throughout the administrative structure: the Communist Party, the Soviet government, and even the trade unions. Called *nomenklatura* (nomenclature), this system of patronage is used to control key appoint-

**FIGURE 4–5.**
Yuri Andropov (1914–1984), leader of the USSR from 1982 to 1984.

[8]For example, sharp differences of opinion on important issues and personalities surrounded the February 1990 meeting of the Central Committe. It will be interesting to see who of the current members of the Politburo (February 1990) will be chosen to the new CC Presidium.

**FIGURE 4–6.**
Konstantin Chernenko (1911–1985), leader of the
USSR from 1984 to 1985.

ments in the entire country and its missions abroad. Starting with the CPSU
Central Committee, all party committees maintain rosters both of positions
considered politically important on their levels of operation and of people
eligible to fill them.

In the Party Rules (Article 35) this executive office of the Central
Committee is mandated to

> ...supervise the entire activity of the Party and local party organs; carry out the
> selection and distribution of leading cadres; direct the work of the central state
> and public organizations of the working people through the party groups in
> them; establish various organs, institutions and enterprises of the Party and
> supervise their activities; appoint editorial boards of the central newspapers
> and magazines that work under its control; and distribute funds of the party
> budget and control their expenditure.

The bureaucratic machinery that executes this broad mandate has
never been described in any detail in official Soviet literature. It seems that
the table of organization of the Central Apparat has undergone periodic
changes, presumably reflecting the personal preference of its top bosses, the
General Secretaries. Currently the main departments, called "commissions"
and headed by secretaries, are: (1) Ideology (Medvedev), (2) Socio-Economic
Matters (Slyunkov), (3) Personnel (Razumovsky), (4) International Affairs
(Yakovlev), (5) Agriculture (Ligachev). There is also a special department
called Bureau for the RSFSR (which does not have its own central commit-

**FIGURE 4–7.**
Mikhail Gorbachev (born 1931), leader of the USSR since 1985.

tee). Departments are subdivided into both territorial and functional sections. For example, the Personnel Department has separate sections responsible for all key appointments in party committees, government branches, or trade unions. The work of these sections is coordinated by other offices in charge of specific parts of the country. The same applies to the ideology department, which is responsible for research, training, and dissemination of propaganda.

The Central Apparat also exercises direct control over the Soviet Armed Forces through an extensive network of political officers attached to all military and police units. The department in charge of this activity is called the Chief Political Administration.

By the virtue of its position, which at least until now has actually been above Soviet law, the Central Apparat can occasionally perform official "miracles": shortcuts through bureaucratic red tape, reversals of administrative decisions, redresses of serious grievances, and corrections of various wrongs. Sending a complaint to the Central Apparat of the Central Committee is considered to be an act of the last resort. If it does not work, nothing else will. The office must handle a huge volume of correspondence that probably provides the top Soviet leaders with accurate information about the state of affairs in the country. The Central Apparat has its own investigative organ, the Party Control Commission, which checks on complaints, denunciations, and charges. The offices of the Central Committee are housed in a huge old building in downtown Moscow several blocks away from the Kremlin—the traditional symbol of Soviet power.

## PARTY REFORM

Like charity, to be believable Gorbachev's *perestroika* has to begin at home, that is, within the Communist Party itself. The ongoing party reforms, which have been mandated by the (All-Union) Party Conference in 1988 and the subsequent plenums of the Central Committee, can be summarized as follows:

1. Phasing out the practice of party's usurping or duplicating the duties of government and economic agencies. Guiding these agencies indirectly through party members who work in them.
2. Promoting free discussions and multicandidate elections by secret ballot on all levels of the party machine. Strengthening the degree of independence granted to primary party organizations.
3. Limiting all party functionaries' tenures, from bottom to top, to two five-year terms in office. Imposing age limits for mandatory retirement.
4. Purging the ranks of the party by removing "opportunists," corrupted officials, and "dead wood." Tightening up admission procedures for new members.
5. Liberalizing the party's press. Demanding more public accountability from party functionaries.
6. Deemphasizing the party's direct role in selecting and appointing executive officials (*nomenklatura*).
7. Reducing the size of personnel in all permanent party offices, from the Central Committee's apparatus down to rural and urban district committees.
8. Reducing the size of the Central Committee to about 200 members and making the Central Committee into a permanent (continually in session) body.
9. Replacing the Politburo with a thirty-member "Presidium" serving as a sub-committee of the Central Committee.
10. Changing the title of head of the party from "General Secretary" to "Chairman," to be elected by the Central Committee. Also elected by the Central Committee will be two deputy-chairmen.

Together, these and related reforms are supposed to change the image of the party, bringing it closer to Lenin's idea of a "vanguard," which leads by ideological persuasion rather than by administrative command.

What is not being changed is just as significant: party functionaries may continue to concurrently occupy government offices and no factionalism within the party is to be tolerated. This too is quite consistent with Lenin's party model and the principles of "democratic centralism."

Whatever else can be said about the party, as a group it is the most active and ambitious segment of the USSR's population. Some 20 million

**BOX 4–6**  *Gorbachev on Party and Perestroika*

---

It would seem that our current *perestroika* may be called a "revolution from above." It is true that *perestroika* was initiated by the Communist Party and is proceeding under its leadership.

Gorbachev, M.S., *Perestroika i Novoye Myshlinie* ("*Perestroika* and the New Thinking") (Moscow: Political Literature Publishing, 1987), pp. 53–54.

---

party members represent that "critical mass" that could make or break Gorbachev's perestroika campaign. It is of particular importance, therefore, how willingly and successfully the party reforms itself before undertaking to reform the rest of Soviet society. But if the expected show of unity by the Party is Gorbachev's brightest hope, his worst nightmare must be a prospect of a serious split in its ranks—something similar to what has happened in several East European countries.

## YOUTH ORGANIZATIONS

The overwhelming majority of new recruits to the party ranks (about 75 percent) comes from its own vast "pool" called Komsomol, which is an acronym for the Russian name, "Young Communist League." The league embraces about 37 million young people, from the ages of 14 to 28. During the last three or four years, the membership dropped by almost 10 percent due, presumably, to the lessening of pressure for conformity. Like the party after which it is modeled, the league has a nationwide network of primary organizations in schools, economic enterprises, offices, military units, and so forth. Every primary organization is headed by a secretary who is nominally elected by its members after having been approved by a party member serving as an adviser. There are close to 450,000 such primary organizations in the country. In addition, a hierarchy of the league's permanent offices, called committees, exists on every level of the administrative division, from counties to the nation's capital, where the league has its Central Committee. The executive officers of these committees—secretaries—are party members professionally trained to work with young adults. As a rule, high-ranking leaders of the league are members of the Central Committee of the CPSU. Many top Soviet leaders, including Gorbachev, began their careers in the Komsomol.

The professed mission of the league is "to bring up the growing generation in the spirit of Communism." To this end, the league not only maintains its presence in all educational institutions but is also heavily involved in publishing, radio, and television. For example, the league publishes more than 220 magazines and newspapers designed for young readers. The league also plays the role of "big brother" for millions of younger children enrolled in the Soviet equivalent of the scout organization, called the Pioneers and the Oktyabriata.[9] Since its founding in 1918, the league has been traditionally assigned to "sponsor" such mass campaigns as the construction of new factories, development of virgin lands, settling of remote regions, exceeding of production quotas, and the provision of help with harvesting.

Membership in the league entails privileges and duties that are modified versions of those that come with membership in the party: better opportunities for study, higher probability of admission to colleges, easier terms for continuation of postgraduate education, better chances for promotions, and the like. However, this also entails more taxing obligations related to various voluntary activities, fewer excuses for nonconformity, and many other demands and prohibitions imposed by Komsomol discipline. League members are expected to be politically active and well versed in Marxism-Leninism. Their "code of honor" demands proper behavior, vigilance, and, above all, loyalty to the cause.

In sum, the league prepares young people for membership in the party, and at the same time, provides a screening mechanism. Although it is easier for the members of Komsomol to become full-fledged Communists[10] not all of them reach the party. Admission to the league is relatively easy, and expulsion of errant members is used only as the last resort when other corrective efforts have failed. Unlike the party, the Young Communist League attracts approximately equal numbers of young men and women. The party always pays much attention to matters that concern the league, because it evidently believes that to win the younger generation means to win the future.

## PROPAGANDA AND AGITATION

As we shall discuss in the next chapter, most of the activities that the party supervises are carried out by specialized branches of the Soviet government. Because the party personifies the infallible ideological truth, the indirect method of governing through an intermediary—the government bureaucracy—helps to deflect criticism for failures and shortcomings from the party

---

[9]Pioneers are boys and girls, aged 10 to 15. Younger children, aged 5 to 9, are called *Oktyabriata* (Children of October). These two organizations enroll practically all school-age children.

[10]Komsomol members may be admitted to the party at age 18, and they need to have only two recommendations from party members and a character report from their local Komsomol committee. For others, the minimum age is 25, and they need recommendations from three party members.

and the ideology itself. However, for the development and dissemination of Communist ideology, the party prefers direct involvement, which underscores the importance attached to this aspect of Soviet life. For this purpose, the Central Committee runs an extensive research organization called the Institute of Marxism-Leninism. The institute has its headquarters in Moscow and branch offices in several other large cities. The main function of its staff of several thousand experts is to prepare articles and books for publication with the correct ideological interpretation of both current and historical events considered to be of special political interest.

One of the institute's more ambitious and seemingly unending projects is the writing of the history of the CPSU by a large team of senior historians, who are constantly required to "rewrite" the past in order to fit the changing needs of the present. For example, Nikita Khrushchev, who for a whole decade had epitomized the post-Stalin Soviet Union, became a virtual "nonperson" immediately after his forced retirement in 1964. As a result, laudatory mentions of him had to be purged from all books on the party's history. Prior to that, Khrushchev's denunciation of Stalin had caused a similar revision of texts on an even greater scale. With the advent of Gorbachev's *glasnost*, a new revision of the CPSU's history had to be undertaken. Its avowed purpose is to fill in so-called blank pages and come up with an objective presentation of the party's checkered past—a difficult task under the best of circumstances. Closely related to the Institute of Marxism-Leninism are several periodic publications of the Central Committee, including the most important Soviet daily, *Pravda* (Truth), and the main theoretical monthly called *Kommunist*, which we shall discuss later.

The institute employs a large number of instructors to deliver lectures at factories, on collective farms, in military units, and the like. Another important institution under the direct control of the Central Apparat is a school for professional propagandists. It is called the Academy of Social Sciences and is located in Moscow. Graduation from the academy is equivalent to graduation from college. Many other schools, research activities, and "think tanks" are also sponsored by the apparat of the Central Committee. In addition, special propaganda schools operate on various lower levels of the party's pyramid to provide training programs of different duration and intensity for both full-time and part-time students. Every permanent party office (committee) has professional propagandists on its staff. Special refresher courses and workshops, called Universities of Marxism-Leninism, are offered exclusively to local party executives.

In the Soviet Union, the term "propaganda" conveys the idea of continuous political indoctrination. The word "agitation," on the other hand, is used to mean intensive public campaigns of short duration designed to promote a specific political issue—for example, approval of a Politburo's decision, condemnation of Israel's intrusion into Lebanon, or support for

**BOX 4–7**   *The Moral Code of the Builders of Communism*

1. Devotion to the cause of Communism, love for the Socialist homeland (and) for the countries of Socialism;
2. Conscientious labor for the good of society; he who does not work, neither shall eat;
3. Concern of everyone for the preservation and growth of public property;
4. A high sense of public duty, intolerance toward infringements of public interests;
5. Collectivism and comradely mutual assistance: one for all, all for one;
6. Humane relations and mutual respect among people: one person to another person—friend, comrade, brother;
7. Honesty and truthfulness, moral purity, simplicity and modesty in public and personal life;
8. Mutual respect in family life, concern for the upbringing of children;
9. Intolerance toward injustice, parasitism, dishonesty, careerism (and) profiteering;
10. Friendship and brotherhood of all the peoples of the USSR, intolerance toward national and racial animosity;
11. Intolerance toward the enemies of Communism, the cause of peace, and the freedom of nations;
12. Fraternal solidarity with the working people of all countries, with all nations.

From a current Soviet political poster (until 1986, "The Moral Code" was included in the Party Rules and the Party Program).

nuclear disarmament. Propaganda and agitation go hand in hand: What one learns from propaganda one uses to react correctly to agitation. Both tactics are handled by the same section or branch of the Central Apparat, which is usually headed by a senior secretary.

## PARTY PROGRAM

The party has a long-range mission statement, called the Program, to which every member must swear his or her allegiance. The current Program is the fourth such document to be issued. The first Program was adopted at the Second Party Congress (1903), before Bolshevik-Menshevik differences split the party into two factions. Written chiefly by Lenin, it was a double-barreled statement that set forth "minimal" and "maximal" objectives for the Russian Marxists in their fight against the czarist regime. In 1919, at the Eighth Party Congress, Lenin introduced his second Program, which contained a detailed analysis of the world situation, confident predictions of the inevitable collapse of the "imperialist system," and a rather sketchy outline for the building of Socialism in Russia. The document remained operative for more than forty years.

At the Twentieth Party Congress (1956), Khrushchev declared that a new blueprint for the building of Communism was soon to be unveiled. Five years later, the Twenty-second Party Congress (1961), the last one to be orchestrated by Khrushchev, duly adopted a new document, entitled "The Program of the CPSU," which consisted of a preamble, with the usual rhetoric about Marxism-Leninism, and two main parts, with a detailed twenty-year plan to overtake America in economic development. Khrushchev's promise to surpass the United States by 1981 was a source of embarrassment for his more realistic successors, who knew that they could not live up to it. For a long time they seemed afraid that any attempt to change the text of the program would serve only to attract attention to this unwelcome bequest. Under Brezhnev their predictable answer to this dilemma was to soft-pedal the second part of the program, which was seldom even mentioned in political publications. Finally, the Twenty-sixth Party Congress (1981) faced the issue and appointed a commission, chaired by Chernenko, to draft a new programmatic statement. Three years later, after Chernenko had come to power, Pravda published the first outline of the draft. The following year, already under Gorbachev, the full text of the draft was made public, and party members were invited to offer comments and suggestions.

The fourth Program, adopted by the Twenty-seventh Party Congress and officially called "The Revised Third Edition," is much more pragmatic and general. The document, which consists of an introduction and four parts, contains no specific deadlines or quantitative indicators. Its introduction and first part trace the history of the CPSU all the way back to the Communist Manifesto. The conclusion is that "The entire course of world development confirms the Marxist-Leninist analysis of the character and main content of the present epoch." The second part talks about the gradual transition of the USSR from Socialism to Communism in terms of both economic growth and development of the "Communist morality," which is supposed to be collectivist, humanistic, and active. The third part defines the role of the CPSU in the international arena: a double (but "dialectically consistent") role of promoting and strengthening world peace, while at the same time supporting "the just struggle waged by the countries of Asia, Africa, and Latin America against imperialism." The Program predicts the demise of capitalism. The fourth part talks about the CPSU's "leading role" in Soviet society, and observes that this role "inevitably grows" as the country moves closer to Communism. Will this be toned down by the next party congress?

Just how important this document is, and what its relationship is to Soviet reality, is a moot question. The fact that the party Program had to be

**BOX 4–8**   *Soviet Underground Humor*

> Question:   What is the difference between a Christian and a Communist?
> Answer:    A Christian believes in life after death, and a Communist believes in rehabilitation after death.

rewritten and changed so many times casts doubt on its reliability. In the past, Soviet leaders' promises and predictions of what they would do often proved to be off the mark. But the newest version of the CPSU Program appears to be the most complete summary of ideas expounded by Gorbachev who, by all accounts, deserves to be taken seriously. Besides, the United States' own record of predicting what Soviets cannot or could not do is also dismal. It would seem, therefore, that further examination of the Soviet Union should include studying relevant passages from this document, provided we do so critically. For example, reading the following definition of the Soviet state found in the CPSU Program can clarify the party-government relationship, which is the subject of the next chapter:

> It is the main tool for perfecting Socialism in our country, while on the international scene it performs the functions of protecting Socialist gains, strengthening world Socialism, countering the aggressive policy of imperialist forces and developing peaceful cooperation with all nations.

## GLOSSARY

**Active:**  party active; leading party members.
**Agitation:**  public campaigns promoting specific political issues.
**Apparat (apparatus):**  central party machine.
**Apparatchik:**  party bureaucrat.
**Bolshevik (majorityite):**  follower of Lenin.
**Bureau:**  permanent steering committee of party organizations.
**Candidate-member:**  nonvoting (probational) member.
**Democratic Centralism:**  operational procedure requiring subordination.
**General Secretary:**  highest officer of the CPSU.
**Komsomol:**  Communist Youth League.
**Menshevik (minorityite):**  opponent of Lenin.
**Nomenklatura:**  rosters of political appointments.
**Oktyabriata:**  Soviet cub scouts and brownies.
**Pioneers:**  Soviet boy and girl scouts.
**Plenum:**  formal meeting of the Central Committee of the CPSU.
**Politburo (political bureau):**  ruling council of the CPSU.
**Primary organization:**  grass-roots level party structure.
**Secretariat:**  central personnel office of the CPSU.
**Secretary:**  party officer.

## RECOMMENDED READINGS

HILL, RONALD, and PETER FRANK, *The Soviet Communist Party*. Winchester, MA: Allen and Unwin, 1983.

RESHETAR, JOHN S., JR., *A Concise History of the Communist Party of the Soviet Union*. New York: Praeger, 1964.

SCHAPIRO, LEONARD, *The Communist Party of the Soviet Union*. New York: Random House, 1960.

# CHAPTER
# 5
# THE STATE

## POLITICAL THEORY

Marxism-Leninism defines the state as the organization of political power serving the interests of the ruling—economically dominant—class. The state, according to this definition, is the most important part of the "superstructure," which embraces all other political institutions, relations, and activities. As part of the superstructure, the state always strives to strengthen and preserve the economic base from which it is derived. In fact, to do so is the main function of the state.

From this it follows that (1) a capitalist state can never change its class nature and become representative of the entire society; (2) profound economic changes can occur only with equally drastic political changes; and (3) all capitalist states, regardless of their political institutions and formal rights and freedoms, are "dictatorships of the bourgeoisie."

In addition to the capitalist state, which Marx so thoroughly studied and criticized, Marxism-Leninism recognizes two other historical forms of the state: slave labor and feudal systems. It also envisages two future stages in the development of human society after the fall of capitalism: the Socialist state, representing a transitional stage, and the completely harmonious

**BOX 5–1**    *An Experiment With Free Elections*

The liberals who came to power in Russia in February 1917 called themselves the "Provisional Government" and proclaimed that the nation's political future must be decided by a democratically elected "Constituent Assembly." The election to the Constituent Assembly took place only at the end of November, some two weeks after the overthrow of the Provisional Government by the Bolsheviks. It was the first, and so far the only, nationwide multiparty election in Soviet Russia's history.

Approximately 36 million people (about 60 percent of the electorate) cast secret ballots for candidates of several parties. Fifty-four electoral districts (out of seventy-nine) reported these results:

| | | |
|---|---|---|
| Bolsheviks (Communists) | 9 million | 25 percent |
| Social Revolutionaries | 21 million | 61 percent |
| All other parties | 4.5 million | 14 percent |

After several delays, the Constituent Assembly met for its opening session on January 18, 1918. On the next day, January 19, the Constituent Assembly was officially prorogued by a governmental decree.

Compiled by author from Soviet data.

Communist society that would ultimately grow out of Socialism. According to Marx's closest collaborator, Friedrich Engels, who devoted considerably more time to this problem, during the Socialist (lower) stage, the state apparatus is supposed to have already begun to wither away. It then completely disappears under Communism, a classless and stateless society populated by truly free people living in self-governing communities.

To be sure, both Marx and Engels must have been thinking in terms of a worldwide phenomenon—that is, the achievement of Socialism and Communism throughout the entire world. It was left to Lenin and his heirs to work on the theory of first building Socialism and then Communism in one country or several, but not all, countries of the world. According to this theory, much of which Lenin developed on the eve of the 1917 Revolution, the destruction of the old capitalist state is followed by the establishment of a transitional state, termed the "dictatorship of the proletariat," in which the revolutionary mass organizations instrumental in the overthrow of capitalism become either a part of the state apparatus (for example, "soviets" in Russia), or are very closely associated with it (for example, labor unions in Russia). The Communist Party becomes the ruling party and the leader in the building of a Communist society. Unlike Marx and Engels, Lenin had no illusions concerning the need for political institutions under Socialism. In

Lenin's words: "We are not Utopians, and we do not indulge in 'dreams' about the best way to do away immediately with all administration and subordination. Those are anarchist dreams stemming from a lack of understanding of the tasks of the dictatorship of the proletariat...."[1]

For more than forty years, the Soviet Union was officially known as the dictatorship of the proletariat, which was proceeding with the tasks of building and consolidating Socialism. Then, in 1961, Khrushchev, in an effort to distinguish his own era from that of Stalin, announced that the dictatorship of the proletariat had been replaced by a higher political formation called "the state of the whole people." The 1977 Soviet Constitution (Article 1) defines this semantic addition to the Marxist-Leninist political theory as the expression of "the will and interests of the workers, peasants, and intelligentsia, the working people of all the nations and nationalities of the country." Actually, much the same language was used in the previous Soviet constitution to describe the dictatorship of the proletariat. The superiority of the Communist Party is further emphasized (Article 6). Only the preamble of the new constitution makes any reference to the eventual transformation of the centralized government into a "public, Communist self-government." Lenin's words about not being Utopian certainly apply to Gorbachev, whose concern with problems at hand has postponed, at least for the time being, discussions of the distant future.

## SOVIET CONSTITUTIONS

During much of its earlier history, Russia was an absolute monarchy in which the will of its "Lord's anointed" rulers was the supreme law. In October 1905, its last "anointed" ruler, Nicholas II, was forced to issue a manifesto granting limited freedoms and establishing a consultative parliament called the Duma. For the next twelve years, this vaguely worded document served as Russia's de facto constitution. In 1918, the Lenin government inaugurated a new constitution, the first Soviet Constitution, for the Russian Federation that for a time being was the only part of the defunct empire under its control. In 1924, the second Soviet Constitution was published on behalf of the newly founded Soviet Union (1922). This document was replaced by the third ("Stalin") Soviet Constitution in 1936, upon completion of "building Socialism in the USSR." By the same token, the adoption of the fourth Soviet Constitution in 1977 was supposed to signal the beginning of the new era of "all-out building Communism in the USSR."

Every time the national constitution was changed, constitutions of all existing union and autonomous republics were obliged to follow suit. These frequent and numerous changes in the basic laws did not, however, cause

[1]V. I. Lenin, *State and Revolution* (Moscow: Foreign Language Publishers, 1950), p. 27.

REBELS SEIZE 4 BUILDINGS IN PETROGRAD; ARMED BOLSHEVIKI BREAK UP PRELIMINARY PARLIAMENT

\*\*\*

RUSSIAN GOVERNMENT UPSET BY REVOLUTIONISTS, PREMIER FLEES; "REDS" TO ASK IMMEDIATE PEACE

Petrograd, Nov. 8. The Bolsheviki, headed by Nikolai Lenine,\* have overturned the Provisional Government. Petrograd is under their complete control.

Premier Kerenski has fled the capital. Several of his ministers have been placed under arrest, and the Winter Palace, seat of the government, has been seized by the rebels.

\*"Nikolai Lenine" was one of several pen names used by Lenin. In the West, Lenin was almost completely unknown.

any noticeable ramifications in the structure and operation of the Soviet system. The reason for this seeming paradox is that the Soviet constitutions are propagandistic self-images, like misleading advertisements with fine-print disclaimers and qualifications that cancel many important promises, rather than supreme legal instruments that are meant to be used. For example, in the current Soviet Constitution the long list of human rights and freedoms is preceded by the following restriction: "Enjoyment by citizens of their rights and freedoms must not be to the detriment of the interests of society or the state, or infringe on the rights of other citizens" (Article 39). Article 50, which guarantees freedom of speech, press, assembly, meetings, street processions, and demonstrations, opens with the following stipulation: "In accordance with the interests of the people and in order to strengthen and develop the Socialist system...." The right to belong to public and political organizations must be exercised "in accordance with the aims of building Communism" (Article 51).

In a more general way, the preamble to the current Soviet Constitution makes it clear that this "fundamental law" must function within the ideology of Marxism-Leninism, not vice versa. To paraphrase a well-known expression: At its very best the Soviet Union is governed not by men but by ideology. At no point in the past was the USSR really governed by written laws, including the constitution. But now there are efforts to move toward what Gorbachev calls a "Socialist rule-of-law state."

The Constitution is a lengthy document divided into nine parts with twenty-one chapters, containing more than 170 articles with declaratory pronouncements and technical specifications for various components of the Soviet system. New among the former category are statements on Soviet

BOX 5–3   *1988 Constitutional Amendments*

The amendments, which affect fifty-five articles or almost one third of the 1977 ("Brezhnev") Constitution, were adopted by the Supreme Soviet in December 1988. The text of the constitution, as amended, is included in the Appendix. Here is a brief summary of the changes:

1. Addition of a new top legislative layer, called "Congress of People's Deputies," on every administrative level. Definition of terms, duties, and responsibilities of these new legislative bodies.
2. Revision of the electoral system, including the eligibility of voters and candidates. Introduction of a new concept which makes certain public organizations into electorates.
3. Encouragement of multicandidate elections. Provisions for election campaign and nomination procedures.
4. New procedures for indirect elections of various soviets—members and chief officers—by the appropriate congresses of people's deputies.
5. Giving more power to the Supreme Soviet and its Chairman (head of state). Strengthening the authority of all soviets.
6. Redefining the relationship between soviets (legislative bodies) and their executive branches (governments).
7. Limiting the tenure of all officials, elected or appointed by congresses of people's deputies and soviets, to two five-year terms.
8. Introducing the concept of permanent (standing) legislative bodies (soviets) meeting seven to eight months a year and consisting of full-time members.
9. Creating a special committee to decide on the constitutionality of enacted legislation.
10. Redefinition of duties and rights of the Supreme Court of the USSR and of the Procurator General.
11. Changing rules for election of judges and people's assessors. Providing legal venues for complaints, petitions, appeals, and redresses.

foreign policy (Articles 28 to 30) and the aforementioned definition of the USSR as a "Socialist state of the whole people" (Article 1), thus replacing "dictatorship of the proletariat," which under Stalin became a synonym for mass terror. The most significant change in the structure of the Soviet government was the addition of a first vice chairman to the Presidium of the Supreme Soviet. This presumably took the burden of routine ceremonial tasks off the shoulders of the Presidium's chairman, thus allowing for the head of the Communist Party to be the chief of state at the same time.

Like its predecessors, the 1977 Soviet Constitution defines the USSR as a parliamentary republic. This means that the chief executive officer in the government is the prime minister (Chairman of the Council of Ministers), rather than the president (Chairman of the Supreme Soviet). In March 1990, Gorbachev changed to a presidential system similar to those in existence in France and the United States. Under the new system, all executive power will be concentrated in the hands of the chief of state called "President."

We should note that the Constitution makes no mention of the top party office, which for so many years served as a repository of real power.

The 1977 ("Brezhnev") Constitution has been already changed so much to accommodate the ongoing reforms that before long it will probably be replaced by a new charter more in line with Gorbachev's thinking.

## HISTORY OF SOVIETS

The official state apparatus is composed of elected bodies called the "Soviets of People's Deputies" (soviets). The 1977 Constitution (Article 2) states that the soviets constitute the "political foundation of the USSR" and control the activities of all other state organs. The word "soviet," which gives the name for the entire system, is Russian for "council." The prototype soviets first emerged during the 1905 abortive revolution as a "revolutionary government" in which Leon Trotsky played a leading role.[2] After the fall of the czarist regime in March 1917, the soviets were resurrected as a "second government." They were dominated by radicals who opposed the official and more moderate Provisional Government. At first, the Mensheviks and non-Marxist Socialists were in the majority in all soviets, but gradually the Bolsheviks began to gain control over the soviets in Russia's capital and other large cities. In July 1917, after some hesitation, Lenin decided to adopt the slogan, "All power to the soviets!" as one of the goals for his own revolution, which was still to come. In fact, the beginning of this revolution was timed to coincide with the opening of the Second All-Russian Congress of Soviets on November 7, 1917. It was this gathering of 649 representatives from soviets in various cities, rural areas, and military units that sanctioned, ex post facto, the seizure of power by armed Bolsheviks during the early hours of that day. The congress also established a new government headed by Lenin, the Soviet Government. Lenin returned the favor by declaring the soviets to be the only "instruments of the dictatorship of the proletariat" in Russia.

The number of soviets grew rapidly during the next few months. But this quantitative increase was accompanied by an important qualitative change: Most soviets lost their multiparty character and came under the

[2]Leon Trotsky (Lev Bronshtein, 1879–1940) was a major figure in the Russian Marxist movement. In 1917, as Lenin's chief collaborator, he played a key role in the October Revolution. In the power struggle that followed Lenin's death, Trotsky lost to Stalin; he was subsequently expelled from Russia in 1929 and murdered by an alleged Soviet agent in Mexico in 1940.

complete control of the Bolsheviks. The dictatorship of the proletariat was turning out to be the dictatorship of a single party.

However, in retrospect, it appears that for several years after the revolution the concepts of the "Soviet Power" and the "Communist Rule" were not considered one and the same, as they are today. Thus, for example, during the early 1920s, some of the numerous peasant uprisings against the new regime demanded "Soviets without Communists." The uprisings were crushed, and the process of strengthening the party's control over the soviets continued.

Under Lenin, this meant controlling the soviets from within, by placing party members on their executive committees. Under Stalin, another type of control was added by creating permanent party offices on every level of the administrative structure. At the same time, soviets representing people on the basis of their place of work or profession rather than on their place of residence were abolished. All soviets became territorial.

Another major change affected the system of electing members of various soviets. Before, only members of the lowest-level soviets were elected directly by the voters; members of higher-level soviets were elected representatives from levels immediately below. This system was replaced by a multiballot, direct election to the soviets on several levels. As a result, the personal contact between the voters and the candidates was lost. The same change in relations occurred between members of lower and higher soviets. Soviets began to be completely subordinated to party committees.

When a new constitution was inaugurated in 1936, proclaiming that soviets possessed all political power, there was talk both in the Soviet press and abroad of an imminent strengthening of the role of soviets. What actually happened was the opposite: During the remaining years of Stalin's rule, soviets were completely subordinated to the party machine. Reforms that took place after Stalin's death made the dual party-soviet system of governing more rational and effective, without, however, changing the basic superior-subordinate relationship between them. The new 1977 Soviet Constitution reiterated and strengthened this principle by granting a special "leading and guiding" role to the CPSU. In 1988, Gorbachev did make a determined effort to resurrect the administrative power of soviets and to delineate functions performed by the party and state agencies. This new division of labor is changing, but not eliminating the supreme role of the party.

## SOVIETS TODAY

Currently, more than 50,000 soviets in the USSR form a huge, pyramidal structure with several administrative levels. Those on lower levels, from village through region and province, are called "local soviets." Union republics and autonomous republics have unicameral, elected bodies designated "supreme soviets" (see Figure 5–1).

The equivalent of a permanent national parliament is known as the Supreme Soviet of the USSR. For more than fifty years, the Supreme Soviet was supposed to represent the "highest body of state authority," while in reality it was just a rubber stamp parliament deprived of any real power.

Republic-level and local soviets did not exercise much power either. In fact, they were dominated and bossed not only by corresponding branches of the party machine, but also by their own executive committees composed of *nomenklatura* appointees. These bureaucrats were responsible and responsive to their real "electorate," the Party, rather than to their fictitious parent legislatures.

In sharp contrast to past practices, the newly installed soviets, including the USSR Supreme Soviet, turned out to be very open, argumentative,

**FIGURE 5–1**  Soviet Government Structure (*Source:* Soviet statistics.)

| Levels | Legislative Bodies | Number | Executive Offices |
|---|---|---|---|
| 1 | Congress of People's Deputies | 1 | None |
| 2 | USSR Supreme Soviet, Presidium, Chairman | 1 | USSR Council of Ministers, Chairman (prime-minister) |
| 3 | Union republic supreme soviets, presidiums | 15 | Union republic councils of ministers |
| 4 | Autonomous republic supreme soviets, presidiums | 20 | Autonomous republic councils of ministers |
| 5 | Province and region soviets, presidiums | 119 | Province and region soviets' executive committees |
| 6 | Autonomous region and area soviets, presidiums | 18 | Autonomous region and area soviets' executive committees |
| 7 | Larger city soviets, presidiums | Approximately 500 | Larger city soviets' executive committees |
| 8 | District (rural or urban) soviets, presidiums | Approximately 3,700 | District soviets' executive committees |
| 9 | Smaller city soviets, presidiums | Approximately 1,500 | Smaller city soviets' executive committees |
| 10 | Village (and settlement) soviets | Approximately 42,000 | Village (and settlement) soviets' executive committees |

and, at times, even unruly forums. All of this seems to be encouraged by Gorbachev and members of his team, who must have decided that a real majority of even 51 percent is better than a phony majority of 99 percent.

Here is how the new system of the central government is structured and operated since its introduction, as part of Gorbachev's *perestroika*, in 1988:

1. *Elections:* Conducted every 5 years; minimum age to vote—18, to be elected—21 (18 for all elected offices other than the Congress.); high government officials, except the prime minister, are ineligible to be elected; candidates must abide by the USSR Constitution. To be elected a candidate must receive more than 50 percent of the vote, regardless of how many other candidates are in the running (even if he or she runs unopposed). Runoff elections are used to resolve no-wins or ties.

2. *Congress of People's Deputies:* 2,250 members, called "people's deputies," elected for five years as follows: 750—one from each of the 750 territorial electoral districts; 750—one from each of the 750 extra electoral districts in ethnic components (each union republic—32, each autonomous republic—11, each autonomous region—5, and each autonomous area—1); and 750—from "public organizations" (CPSU—100; trade unions—100; cooperatives—100; Komsomol—75; veterans—75; women's organizations—75; scientific-technical associations—75; professional unions—75; and other formal groups—75). CPD meets for a few days at least once a year (members keep their regular jobs); it elects the Supreme Soviet and its Chairman (Gorbachev changed the title to "President," who will be eventually elected by direct popular vote).

3. *Supreme Soviet:* 544 members (including the Chairman and the First Vice Chairman) serving in two coequal houses (called "Council of the Union" and "Council of Nationalities"), chaired by the Chairman (President) who is the chief of state; 20 percent of its members are rotated every year; Supreme Soviet appoints the Council of Ministers and its Chairman (prime-minister), Supreme Court, and Procurator General; the Supreme Soviet is in permanent session (7–8 months per year) and its members are full-time legislators.

4. *Executive and Judicial Branches:* The Council of Ministers consists of the Chairman (prime minister), several vice chairmen, and heads of about 60 major bureaucracies (ministries, state committees, et cetera). Members of the Supreme Court and the Procurator General are the highest legal officials in the country.

## SOVIET ELECTIONS

The word "democratic" has been used by the Soviet media to describe periodical elections of members of various legislative bodies. The constitution (Article 95) guarantees a "universal, equal, and direct suffrage by secret ballot" to all Soviet citizens who have reached age 18. Participation in elections is strongly encouraged, and in the past, turnouts of almost 100 percent were not unusual.

Almost as high was the percentage of votes customarily cast for the slate of the officially sponsored candidates who used to run unopposed.

**BOX 5–4** *Soviet Underground Humor*

Question: Is the Soviet Union a one-man, one-vote country?
Answer: Yes, it is. The one man is Gorbachev, and it is his one vote that counts.

Now, the election ballot contains several names for each open seat. The first election campaign for so-called people's deputies (March 1989) went something like this: During a period of about four months (December 1988–March 1989), various officially recognized organizations, associations, and groups nominated candidates agreeing to abide by the Soviet Constitution including its provisions concerning "the leading role of the Communist Party" (Article 6) and the pledge to uphold "Socialism" (Article 50). Nominations were followed by election campaigns and the actual voting took place on March 26, 1989. In a departure from the past, high-ranking government officials, with the exception of the Chairman of the USSR Council of Ministers (prime minister), were ineligible to run for the election to the new legislative bodies. This limitation did not, however, apply to top party officials, including the General Secretary.

For many years, it was not unusual for the results of the Soviet elections to show that close to 100 percent of the voters supported the single candidates nominated, thus demonstrating their complete loyalty to the party. In a sense, Soviet elected officials owed their positions to their electorates and served at their pleasure and mercy. Their real electorates, however, were not the voters but the appropriate party committees that made the risk-proof nominations. It was reasoned that a single ideology justified the existence of only one political party in the USSR, and this party nominated a single candidate for every elected office.

This is done quite differently now. For example, in 1989, two thirds of the new USSR Congress of People's Deputies were chosen in multicandidate, secret-ballot elections. Ballots with the names of several candidates were used in most (77 percent) of the 750 electoral districts representing the population at large, and in the 750 electoral districts allocated to the ethnic territories according to their rank. Runoff elections were used to decide cases where no candidate had won a majority. Very simple procedures were used to register voters and to nominate candidates. There were no primary elections nor opinion polls before or during the elections.

The remaining 750 members of the 2,250-seat USSR Congress of People's Deputies were elected from various organizations including: The Communist Party, Komsomol, trade unions, veterans' associations, and women's groups. Here, too, the selective process had all the trappings of democratic elections, though top party officials ran unopposed, practically assured of victory.

**BOX 5–5**  *New Executive Branch*

*President of the USSR*—elected for five years by a direct popular ballot*; must receive more than 50 percent of all votes and win at least eight union republics.
*Council of the Federation*—a panel appointed by the President to monitor, coordinate, and regulate interethnic relations.
*Presidential Council*—an advisory committee appointed by the President to help him with major domestic and foreign policy issues.
*Chairman, Council of Ministers of the USSR*—nominated by the President and confirmed by the Supreme Soviet; Chairman (prime minister) and all members of the Council (cabinet) serve at the President's pleasure.

Note: As a time-saving expediency, in March 1990 Mikhail Gorbachev was elected as the first President by the Congress of People's Deputies, rather than by popular ballot.
Source: compiled by author from Soviet data.

In May 1989, the USSR Congress of People's Deputies elected the new USSR Supreme Soviet—a permanent bichamber national parliament consisting, for the first time, of 542 full-time politicians. The USSR Congress of People's Deputies also elected Mikhail Gorbachev to be the Chairman and Anatoli Lukyanov to be the First Vice Chairman of the USSR Supreme Soviet. Under their chairmanship, the Supreme Soviet met in a joint session to elect several standing commissions (committees) and its steering committee, the Presidium. The Presidium consists of Gorbachev, Lukyanov, chairmen of the two houses, fifteen chairmen of the supreme soviets of the union republics who serve ex officio, and heads of the standing commissions.

## GOVERNMENT REFORM

Gorbachev's *perestroika*—a revolution from above and inside—includes a number of reforms designed to decentralize, liberalize, and streamline the huge Soviet political (government) establishment. Some of these reforms require changes in the USSR Constitution and the constitutions of the union and autonomous republics which are expected to be completed in 1990. The main political reforms may be summarized as follows:

1. All state organs are given more authority within their jurisdictions and more independence from the parallel party offices operating on the same administrative levels. Thus, after more than seventy years, the famous slogan, "All power to Soviets!" gets a new lease on life. Will it be more meaningful this time? The answer is a qualified yes: Soviets now have more independent responsibility for routine matters under their jurisdictions, but, in accordance with a new unwritten rule, the first secretaries of the corresponding party committees strive to serve concurrently as chairmen of these

**TABLE 5-1**   Chiefs of the Soviet State

| Name | Born–Died | Nationality | Years in Office | Ultimate Fate |
|---|---|---|---|---|
| Leo Kamenev (Rosenfeld) | 1883–1936 | Jewish | 1917 | Purged and executed |
| Yakov Sverdlov | 1885–1919 | Jewish | 1917–1919 | Died in office |
| Mikhail Kalinin | 1875–1946 | Russian | 1919–1946 | Died in office |
| Nikolai Shvernik | 1888–1968 | Ukrainian | 1946–1953 | Moved to another top post |
| Klementi Voroshilov | 1881–1969 | Russian | 1953–1960 | Purged and retired in disgrace |
| Leonid Brezhnev* | 1906–1982 | Russian | 1960–1964 | Moved to another top post |
| Anastas Mikoyan | 1895–1978 | Armenian | 1964–1965 | Retired with honors |
| Nikolai Podgorny | 1903–1983 | Ukrainian | 1965–1977 | Retired in disgrace |
| Leonid Brezhnev | 1906–1982 | Russian | 1977–1982 | Died in office |
| Yuri Andropov | 1914–1984 | Russian | 1983–1984 | Died in office |
| Konstantin Chernenko | 1911–1985 | Russian | 1984–1985 | Died in office |
| Andrei Gromyko | 1909– | Byelorussian | 1985–1988 | Retired with honors |
| Mikhail Gorbachev | 1931– | Russian | (Appointed October 1, 1988) | |

*Brezhnev was the first person to serve two separate tenures as chief of state.

*Source:* Compiled by author from Soviet data.

soviets. Thus the "leading role" of the Communist Party, though no longer unchallenged, continues to be a fact of Soviet politics.

2. By the same token, the long professed—but not really practiced—principle of federalism is now expressed in more concrete terms delimitating the central authority and defining the rights of the union and autonomous republics, other ethnic territories, and local governments. But the Soviet Union remains a highly authoritarian and centrally directed state.

3. The enormous bureaucratic machine, both at its center in Moscow and in the provinces, is being consolidated, reshuffled, and considerably reduced in size. Many government office employees (estimated at 18.5 million in 1988) are being transferred, relocated, and retrained—presumably to become more useful members of society. Somewhat ironically, Gorbachev is counting on many of these same party members for support of his *perestroika*.

4. A new large legislative body called "The USSR Congress of People's Deputies" has been created. It is elected for five years and meets once a year

to decide on most important political and socioeconomic issues facing the nation. Its 2,250 members represent not only national and administrative territories of the country, but also the principal components of its sociopolitical system: the Communist Party, Komsomol, trade unions, and some public organizations. This is a new concept.

5. The USSR Congress of People's Deputies elects (also for five years) a new USSR Supreme Soviet (which used to be elected directly by voters). The Supreme Soviet is a bicameral (two equal houses) assembly as it was before, but much smaller in size (271 in each house) and permanently in session (a standing legislative body). Up to 20 percent of its membership is rotated every year. It is headed by the Chairman (President) and the First Deputy (or Vice) Chairman (President), elected by the parent body, the USSR Congress of People's Deputies. The Supreme Soviet has a steering committee, called Presidium, which includes the heads of union republic supreme soviets (serving ex officio), and chairmen of standing commissions.

6. All elections now allow for multiple candidacies on the ballots. Thus, finally, one Soviet contradiction in terms—elections without choice—is beginning to fade away. This move speaks well of Gorbachev's common sense, though not necessarily of his commitment to the Western style political pluralism.

7. Hopefully, Gorbachev is not creating a new contradiction in terms with his promise to make the Soviet Union into a "Socialist state based on law." The main thrust of the current legal reform is to make the state—as it is represented by its various organizations, branches, and individual officials—responsible for its duties and liable for misdeeds. Litigations are becoming part of life, and ordinary Soviet citizens can now take their mighty superiors to court without fear of extralegal retaliation. Given their past experience, Soviet citizens are entitled to ask whether this is too good to be true.

8. On Gorbachev's initiative, the Soviet Union changed from a parliamentary to a presidential system of government (similar to the United States, and France). This means that Gorbachev's present government office is known as "President" and given much more executive power to make independent decisions, including a limited veto power over the legislation passed by the Supreme Soviet. The next time around, in 1994, the President will be elected by direct popular vote.

**TABLE 5–2**   Council of Nationalities of the Supreme Soviet

| | |
|---|---|
| 15 Union Republics, each 11 deputies | 165 |
| 20 Autonomous Republics, each 4 deputies | 80 |
| 8 Autonomous Regions, each 2 deputies | 16 |
| 10 Autonomous Areas, each 1 deputy | 10 |
| | 271 |

Source: Compiled by author from Soviet data.

**BOX 5–6**    *Anomalies of the New Election System*

---

The new system allows some people to have more votes than others. Every eligible citizen can vote for one people's deputy from the population at large and one more—representing a given union republic. But a person who lives in an autonomous republic, region, or area has an extra vote for a people's deputy from his or her ethnic subdivision. Members of certain, but not all, "public organizations," including the CPSU and Komsomol, can vote for representatives from one or even several such groups.

There are no published criteria for selecting eligible organizations and determining their quotas of deputies.

Compiled by author from Soviet data.

---

9. The USSR Constitution is being changed to provide a legal mechanism for secession of union republics. The proposed procedure calls for referenda, long "cool-off" periods, and legislative votes.

Other constitutional amendments are in various stages of preparation and discussion.

## SOVIET GOVERNMENT

The Soviet parliament, the Supreme Soviet of the USSR, which is elected by the newly created Congress of People's Deputies, makes periodic appointments to its executive arm, the Council of Ministers of the USSR. (Between 1917 and 1946, the ministers were known as "people's commissars"). The actual selection of members of government is done on the highest level of the party. The Council of Ministers consists of the chairman (prime minister), his deputies, and heads of various ministries, agencies, and boards. In addition, heads of the governments of the fifteen union republics, appointed by their respective supreme soviets, serve as voting, ex officio members of the council. With a membership of about 90, this is by far the largest cabinet in the world, administering and managing an enormously huge and complex nation. The council has a steering committee called the Presidium, which consists of the chairman (premier) and his deputies.

There are two types of ministries on this level in the USSR: the all-union ministries, which are in direct charge of activities within their purviews throughout the entire country, and the union-republic ministries, which operate through their proper counterparts on the republic level. Currently, there are more than thirty ministries altogether. The rationale behind the division into the two groups is not always clear. For example, the defense industry (armaments) is under a single all-union ministry, but defense itself is in the hands of a union-republic ministry in Moscow and fifteen identical ministries in the capitals of the union republics. There is an all-union Ministry of the Oil Industry and a union-republic Ministry of the Coal Industry. The Ministry of Foreign Trade has an all-union status, whereas the Ministry of Foreign Affairs is a union-republic institution.

About twenty permanent agencies and boards on the cabinet level are similarly divided into all-union and union-republic units. The best-known union-republic agency is the Committee of State Security, often referred to as the KGB, which are the initials of its Russian name. Until July 1978 the KGB was "attached to" the Council of Ministries, and its head was a nonvoting member of the cabinet, as if to convey the notion of its relative unimportance. Perhaps this was the initial intent of Khrushchev, who presided over the ouster of Lavrenti Beria in 1953.[3] The KGB's chief is usually included in the highest organ of the party, the Politburo. This distinction, as we already know, is reserved for only a few of the most important members of the governmental bureaucracy. After the KGB became a committee "of" the Council of Ministers, its head began to serve as a full (voting) member of the cabinet and also as member or candidate-member of the Politburo. In October 1988, Gorbachev appointed his own protégé to be the new head (chairman) of the KGB.[4]

The council is defined by the constitution as the "highest executive and administrative body of state authority of the USSR" (Article 128). Under its direct supervision are a number of lesser bureaucracies called "chief administrations" and "special committees," whose heads do not have the rank of cabinet members. All agencies of the council, large and small, perform one or more of the three main tasks with which the Soviet government is charged: (1) internal and external security; (2) economic development, production, and distribution; and (3) political (ideological) indoctrination and education. These are the three pillars on which the Soviet world rests.

In terms of the sheer size and scope of its operation, the Soviet government has few, if any, rivals. Moreover, the Soviet government not only regulates but actually manages, supervises, and completely controls every aspect of life. Instead of withering away, the state apparatus in the Soviet Union has been constantly expanding. Its administrative staff (not counting the party bureaucrats) numbers approximately 2 million officials. About one-third of these administrators holding more important jobs are so-called nomenclatured officials whose appointments come under the direct control of party committees.

---

[3]Lavrenti Beria (1899–1953) was a close associate of Stalin and the chief of the secret police during most of the Stalin era. Shortly after Stalin's death, Beria was ousted from his post and executed.

[4]The new Chairman of the KGB is a four-star general, Vladimir Kryuchkov, who is a member of the Politburo (1989).

Before Gorbachev's coming to power, the turnover among the top-level bureaucrats was quite slow. It was not unusual for cabinet ministers and other high government officials to stay in their jobs for many years. A forced exodus of top officials took place during the first three years of the new administration. Their replacements are serving five-year terms, which can be repeated only once.

## STATE SECURITY

Internal and external security has always been a top priority in the eyes of Soviet leaders, who perceive the human condition in terms of continuing conflict and struggle. To Lenin, the main question of the twentieth century was: "Who will get whom?" When his regime was but a few weeks old, Lenin ordered the creation of an extralegal agency designed to protect the revolution from internal resistance. This precursor of the KGB was called the Extraordinary Commission (known best by its Russian initials "Cheka") and was hailed as "the punishing sword of the revolution," merciless and deadly to all its enemies.

As measured by the growth of the "punishing sword," the number of enemies of the revolution increased progressively, as, indeed, Stalin argued in one of his written contributions to Marxism-Leninism.[5] Accordingly, during the last two decades of his life, the machine of political terror became an empire within an empire, ruled directly by Stalin and growing less dependent on the party. In fact, on a percentage basis, very few other groups in Soviet society suffered as many casualties from random arrests, brutal tortures, wanton killings, and slow death in slave labor camps as did the party.

It is not surprising, therefore, that after Stalin's death his heirs made a strong effort to restore the supremacy of the party. The most notorious police chiefs were summarily executed, independent police power was curbed, and the name of the somewhat emasculated organization was changed from that of a superministry to a committee—namely, the Committee of State Security, or the KGB. Since June 1982, the KGB has been chaired by a professional police officer. For the fourteen years prior to that time, the KGB was headed

**TABLE 5–3**   Composition of the USSR Supreme Soviet 1982/1989 (in %)

| | | | |
|---|---|---|---|
| Workers and peasants | 51/25 | Party members | 72/88 |
| Women | 31/16 | Non-Russians | 47/46 |
| Young people (under 30) | 21/22 | First-term deputies | 55/87 |

*Source:* Compiled by author from Soviet statistics.

[5]This paranoid notion was expounded by Stalin in his last published work, entitled *Problems of Socialism in the USSR* (1952).

by Yuri Andropov, who is credited with streamlining and modernizing its operation while at the same time improving its public image. The KGB has become a sophisticated instrument of control which no longer relies on brute force and terror.

Until the emergence of *glasnost*, the KGB as a topic was off limits to public discussion and criticism. Now some activities of its local branches are frequently described in the Soviet press in less than flattering terms. But most of what the KGB is doing remains shrouded in secrecy.

The KGB is believed to have a staff of approximately 50,000 career officers, plus a large number of secret informers.[6] Its main areas of responsibility include espionage and counterespionage, surveillance, investigation of activities deemed harmful to the regime, and protection of the top Soviet leaders. It is in charge of the uniformed border and coast guards. This roughly corresponds to the combined scope of activities performed by the CIA, FBI, NSA (National Security Agency), and U.S. Secret Service. The KGB also maintains offices at large enterprises and in the armed forces. On the grass-roots level of Soviet society, matters of internal security—watching and reporting politically undesirable activities—are entrusted to party activists, paid secret informers, and members of voluntary detachments of young vigilantes, called *druzhinniki* and supervised by the Young Communist League.

The KGB continued to have a free hand in the use of extralegal methods. There were, for example, many well-documented reports about Soviet dissenters' being confined to special psychiatric wards and subjected to compulsory "medical" treatment designed to break their willpower and to "brainwash" them. In all cases involving internal security the Soviet judicial system also appeared to be completely at the disposal of the KGB. Under Gorbachev, things have changed for the better and such flagrant abuses of the legal system have been curtailed.

In its domestic operations, the KGB is assisted by the union-republic Ministry of Internal Affairs (its initials in Russian are MVD), which is in charge of the regular uniformed police, prisons, and labor camps. Both the KGB and the MVD have branch offices on every level of the administrative structure. Officers of both organizations have military rank and are, almost without exception, members of the party.

A special section of the KGB that combines both security and espionage functions maintains a spy network abroad. Its agents are often camouflaged as Soviet diplomats, trade representatives, and journalists, a practice not uncommon in other intelligence services. Although its official history dates back only to 1917, the Russian tradition of having secret police with extrajudicial powers is much older. The first institutionalized security service, called *oprichnina*, came into existence during the time of Ivan the Terrible (1533–

---

[6]Some Western sources put the number of KGB's career officers at 100,000 or even 150,000.

**TABLE 5–4**  Heads of the Soviet Government (Prime Ministers)

| Name | Born–Died | Nationality | Years in Office | Ultimate Fate |
| --- | --- | --- | --- | --- |
| Vladimir Lenin (Ulyanov) | 1870–1924 | Russian | 1917–1924 | Died in office |
| Aleksei Rykov | 1881–1938 | Russian | 1924–1930 | Purged and executed |
| Viacheslav Molotov (Skriabin) | 1890–1986 | Russian | 1930–1941 | Demoted, retired in disgrace |
| Iosif (Joseph) Stalin (Djugashvili) | 1879–1953 | Georgian | 1941–1953 | Died in office |
| Georgi Malenkov | 1902– | Russian | 1953–1955 | Demoted, retired in disgrace |
| Nikolai Bulganin | 1905–1975 | Russian | 1955–1958 | Demoted, retired in disgrace |
| Nikita Khrushchev | 1894–1971 | Russian | 1958–1964 | Retired in disgrace |
| Aleksei Kosygin | 1904–1980 | Russian | 1964–1980 | Retired, died |
| Nikolai Tikhonov | 1905– | Russian | 1980–1985 | Retired |
| Nikolai Ryzhkov | 1929– | Russian | (Appointed September 26, 1985 |

*Source:* Compiled by author from Soviet data.

1584). Under different names, it has been an acknowledged part of Russian life ever since.

## SYSTEM OF JUSTICE

The all-union Supreme Soviet appoints the Procurator General of the USSR and the members of the Supreme Court to serve seven- and ten-year terms, respectively. Members of the court on all levels above district (town) are appointed by the appropriate soviets to five-year terms. The higher courts are concerned mainly with appeals, but on special occasions they are called upon to try particularly important criminal cases. Courts, including the Supreme Court of the USSR, do not decide on questions of the constitutionality of laws enacted by the legislative bodies, and legal precedents cannot be used as a basis for court decisions. In other words, the judicial branch does not make laws.

Most criminal and all civil cases are tried first before the district (town) court, called the "People's Court." It consists of three members: a professional jurist who serves as the presiding judge and two lay members called "people's assessors." All judges are elected by the appropriate soviets, and the people's assessors by a direct popular vote.

The judge, who must be 25 or older, is elected for ten years, and the assessors, whose minimum age is 21, are elected for five years of being on

**FIGURE 5–2**   A joint session of the two houses of the Supreme Soviet.

call. They are required to take a leave of absence from their regular jobs and to serve in court only about two weeks per year. Together, the three-member panel decides the question of guilt and agrees on the sentence. Appeals may be based on both procedural and substantive grounds, and sentences may be appealed to higher courts by either side. Criminal cases are prosecuted in the lower court by district (town) procurators, appointed by procurators on the next higher level. Every city and town has "collegiums" of jurists specializing in courtroom defense. The accused, or his or her family, selects a suitable defense lawyer for a standard, low fee or has one appointed by the court. Civil cases are tried by the same courts, and representation of either side by a lawyer is optional.

The Soviet judicial system does not provide for plea bargaining or court-granted immunity. Although the burden of proof is on the state, the defendant can be subjected to cross-examination by both sides. It is not an adversary system.

Courtroom proceedings are extremely informal, with all five officers of the court—the judge, two people's assessors, procurator, and defense attorney—taking turns asking questions and even offering comments. Dur-

**BOX 5–7**  *Courts and Justice*

---

From the *Soviet Constitution, Article 151:*
In the USSR justice is administered only by the courts.
In the USSR there are the following courts: the Supreme Court of the USSR, the Supreme Courts of the Union Republics, the Supreme Courts of the Autonomous Republics, Territorial, Regional, and city courts, courts of Autonomous Regions, courts of Autonomous Areas, district (city) people's courts, and military tribunals in the Armed Forces.

From the *Soviet Constitution, Article 155:*
Judges and people's assessors are independent and subject only to the law.

---

ing a typical trial, all technicalities are kept to a minimum, and there is no swearing in of witnesses. Soviet judges do not wear robes.

Although formal legality is not and never has been an important feature of the Soviet (or, for that matter, the Russian) way of life, the legal bureaucracy required to handle various governmental transactions is very big and includes a whole union-republic ministry, the Ministry of Justice, with offices on every upper level of the administration. Each of the union and autonomous republics has its own criminal, civil, and procedural codes, containing almost identical legal standards. But they are written in ethnic languages that are also used in local courts. Minor differences found in the laws of the ethnic republics pertain to such things as marriage ages and similar codified customs and traditions.

On the Soviet scale of values, the legal profession does not rate very high. With the noted exception of Mikhail Gorbachev, lawyers occupy a rather modest place in the professional composition of the ruling Soviet elite: They trail behind the favored economists and engineers in terms of prestige. This ranking is an accurate reflection of the entire Soviet system and its goals and priorities. In 1990, there were only about 30,000 defense lawyers in the USSR.

The Soviet judiciary system has its own extralegal extension, called "Comradely Courts," which is used for arbitration and adjudication of various forms of "antisocial" behavior: family fights, drunken quarrels, and so forth. It is within the power of these courts to reprimand, fine, and even evict or fire "undesirables." Run by activists with strong party connections, these courts have been employed on occasion against political nonconformists.

## SOVIET LAW

As a system of public order, Soviet law is a mixture of old and new concepts, values, and norms. Its roots go back to the legal system of the Russian

Empire, which was a variation of the so-called Roman Law[7] prevailing in continental Europe. But many specific laws reflect Marxist attitudes toward private property, labor, and other societal values. The most important distinction of Soviet law, however, is not its form or even its content, but the fact that it is clearly subordinated to ideology. Whenever ideology and law come into conflict, the latter must yield. And this happens quite often.

For example, according to the Soviet Constitution, judges must act independently and obey only the law (Article 155). However, according to the ideology of Marxism-Leninism, law and justice are not anterior or superior to politics, but rather are instruments for achieving political-ideological goals. As we have seen, the Communist Party claims the exclusive right to interpret ideology, formulate policies, and set political-ideological goals. Soviet law is just another instrument for building Communism. Because of this, the party exercises as much influence on Soviet justice as it does on all other areas of social and political life in the USSR. It would suffice to note that the majority of the officers of the courts, including defense lawyers, are members of the party, and as such, must adhere to the principle that law can be neither neutral nor objective. Procurators, who are supposed to ensure a strict adherence to the legal system, are, with few exceptions, members of the party. Therefore, constitutional assurances of their complete independence from any outside pressure do not sound very convincing. In fact, because of the sensitivity of their work, they cooperate closely not only with the appropriate party committees but also with local offices of the KGB in all situations involving security. This situation is slowly improving.

For over seven decades, the quality of Soviet justice has been quite uneven and inconsistent. During the period of War Communism (1918–1921), when written laws were almost nonexistent, it was "justice in accor-

**FIGURE 5-3**   USSR Supreme Court

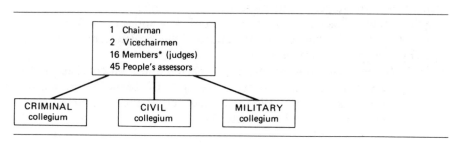

* Chairmen of the supreme courts of union republics (15)
are also considered members of the USSR Supreme Court.

[7]The term "Roman Law" is given to all European legal systems that are historically derived from legal theories and practices of the ancient Roman Empire.

**BOX 5–8**  *Soviet Underground Humor*

| | |
|---|---|
| Question: | Does the USSR Constitution guarantee freedom of demonstration? |
| Answer: | Yes, but it does not guarantee freedom *after* demonstration. |

dance with the revolutionary conscience" that led to the countless cases of punishment without crime. And for most of the Stalin era, punishment "by analogy" for acts not in violation of any written law became a widely used practice. Other systematic miscarriages of justice under Stalin included secret trials by police tribunals, sentencing in absentia, and the use of forced "confessions" as the basis for verdicts. Barbaric laws were enacted, such as the Law of August 7, 1932, which made the theft of a handful of grain from a state granary a capital offense punishable by death. As we have seen, during World War II entire ethnic minorities were rounded up and exiled to the Asian parts of the USSR. By most conservative estimates, several million people perished and many more spent long years in Stalin's infamous slave labor camps—the Gulag Archipelago.

Since Stalin's death in 1953, much of the abuse of justice for political reasons has been eliminated, laws have been rewritten, and procedural norms have been codified and strengthened, thereby putting the relationship between crime and punishment on a more rational basis. As a result, the number of political prisoners was drastically reduced, and Stalin's paranoid notion that the number of "enemies of revolution" is constantly growing was replaced by a much more rational and predictable use of terror on a "need-be" basis. In other words, its use was limited to situations in which the regime actually feels threatened. Even then the basic written laws and legal norms were usually observed, as long as they did not present a challenge to established ideological principles. Today the Soviet notion of "Socialist legality" comes close to the Western idea of "law and order." But until the beginning of the Gorbachev era, the abuse of the legal system for personal gain by corrupt officials was rampant.

If the new legal reforms are fully enacted and then consistently followed, the Soviet Union may, indeed, live up to Gorbachev's promise of a "socialist State based in law." We shall discuss crime and punishment in the Soviet Union in more detail in Chapter 11.

## MILITARY ESTABLISHMENT

The Soviet military establishment governing external security consists of several ministries and lesser agencies. Its main component is the union-republic Ministry of Defense, headed by a professional military officer. Usually the minister of defense is concurrently serving on the ruling Politburo, which has the ultimate responsibility in all military matters.

The all-union Ministry of the Defense Industry and Ministry of Medium Machine-Building (this is a euphemism for "nuclear armaments") also deal exclusively with military matters. Other ministries and agencies, including the KGB, devote a substantial portion of their efforts to the various needs of the military establishment, the maintenance and constant modernization of which is believed to cost much more than was officially admitted in the past. Gorbachev appears determined to make deep cuts in the military expenditures, which are very taxing on the Soviet economy.

The Soviet Armed Forces are organized into five services: the land forces (the army), the strategic rocket forces, the air defense forces, the air force, and the navy (which has its own aviation branch and a marine corps). Military personnel consists of career (and reserve) commissioned and noncommissioned officers, and drafted enlisted men, some of whom may also become noncommissioned officers. According to the Soviet Constitution, military service is universal and applies to both sexes (Article 63), but currently it is limited to only able-bodied young men.[8] A large public organization, called the Voluntary Society for Promotion of Army, Aviation, and Navy (its Russian abbreviation is DOSAAF), sponsors all kinds of military training for both men and women.

The special feature of the Soviet Armed Forces is the crucially important role played by the Communist Party in their organization and operation. Since the creation of a regular army in February 1918, the party has taken every precaution against the danger of a military conspiracy or takeover. At first, the new regime had no choice but to use the professional military officers whose loyalty was questionable. Acting on Trotsky's initiative, it instituted a system of political commissars recruited from the ranks of the party. These commissars were attached as equals to every commanding officer throughout the armed forces. From the standpoint of military efficiency, the officer-commissar split of responsibility made little sense, but politically it served its purpose well by preventing any major military mutiny prior to World War II.

The importance of political loyalty over professional competence was emphasized in a more dramatic way on the very eve of war, when Stalin began a bloody purge of his top military leaders. During the initial phase of the German-Soviet war, as a result of both bitter memories of Stalin's purges and military setbacks, many Soviet soldiers and officers defected. Later, some of these men were even used, quite unsuccessfully, by the Germans to set up a "Russian Liberation Army" under the command of a former Soviet general, Andrei Vlasov.

[8]College students are usually exempt from the draft but are required to take reserve officer training as part of their higher education. Women are accepted only on a voluntary basis for noncombat duties.

After the war, Stalin and, later, his heirs did their best to put the armed forces under even tighter control of the party. To get their point across, Stalin and Khrushchev used the same method: demotion of the most famous Soviet military leader, Marshal Georgi Zhukov. Stalin assigned Zhukov to an obscure post in the provinces; Khrushchev, who at first was forced to seek Zhukov's help in his bid for power in the Kremlin, later denounced the old war hero for his apparent efforts to lessen political controls over the armed forces. Zhukov was retired in disgrace.

Currently, the Communist Party's control over the Soviet Armed Forces takes the following forms

1.  The supreme military command is vested in the Defense Council chaired by the head of the party (in his capacity as chief of state).
2.  The minister of defense is a candidate-member of the Politburo.
3.  All large military units (military districts in time of peace) have special military councils, consisting of top party functionaries and overseeing the work of military headquarters.
4.  Every commanding officer has a professional commissar (now called "political officer") acting as his deputy in charge of ideological and political matters, including compulsory troop education.
5.  The overwhelming majority of career officers (practically all those of field rank and above) are members of the party.
6.  All military units have their own primary party and Komsomol organizations.

The official contention is that the Soviet military might is not designed to exceed the level necessary to defend the integrity of the USSR and to provide a deterrent to aggression. Given Russia's long history of being forced to combat foreign invasions, there is no doubt that the average Societ citizen does not question this reasoning. Such misadventures as the protracted involvement in Afghanistan and the use of troops against ethnic extremists are deemphasized or explained as abberations. Military personnel are usually held in high esteem by the population at large, but recently there have been protests against the military presence in the Baltic region and Caucasus. Gorbachev's pragmatism has affected the Soviet armed forces not only quantitatively, but also qualitatively: younger generals have taken over high commands, troop training has been improved, and equipment has been modernized. There is even some talk about switching from the traditional conscription system to a "smaller professional" army.

## TRADE UNIONS

The majority of other all-union and union-republic ministries, along with governmental agencies, deal with various aspects of the national economy, culture, and public health, all of which are discussed in later chapters. Later we also look at the ministries and agencies in charge of education and information mass media.

One more pyramidal structure of watchdog operations affects the lives of practically all working Soviet citizens, including many retirees. Officially classified as a nonpolitical mass organization, it is called, quite misleadingly, "trade unions." Actually it is a quasi-governmental bureaucracy, similar to the Civil Service Commission, and an auxiliary agency of the party. For a short time after the revolution, independent-minded labor unions, inherited from the Provisional Government, raised difficulties for the new regime by insisting on a political role for themselves and encouraging demands for the workers' direct control over nationalized enterprises. These ideas found their proponents even among Lenin's close associates, who became known as leaders of the so-called "workers' opposition" at the Ninth Party Congress in 1920. However, soon after, the central organs of the unions and their locals were reformed into subservient bureaucratic appendages of the official establishment. Under Lenin, the role of the unions was described as that of "schools of Communism." Under Stalin, they became known as "transmission belts" between the party and the masses.

The current official definition of trade unions refers to them as "vital instruments in building Communist society." As such, the unions concentrate their efforts on the fulfillment of production quotas, improvement of production quality, increase of labor productivity, and strengthening of labor discipline—all of which hardly fit the accepted idea of the function of organized labor. This apparent contradiction is justified on the grounds that because everything belongs to everybody in the USSR, the blue-collar and white-collar workers are actually self-employed. From this argument it also follows that as "shareholders" in enterprises where they work, Soviet citizens have no reason to strike, bargain, protest, or even petition for the improvement of working conditions. In the past, attempts to organize and stage strikes were brutally suppressed as "anti-Soviet activities." Under Gorbachev labor disputes and strikes have become very frequent, but they are not led by the official unions.

In a typical Soviet factory or shop, the union local's officials spend their time and energy pleading with the workers, urging them to work harder, reproaching and criticizing laggards, praising achievers, threatening, intimidating, and begging those who step out of line. They also have at their disposal such tangible fringe benefits as prepaid vacations in various resorts, tourist trips, and new housing, which they can use to reward, bribe, and tempt the employees to work harder. The locals accept grievances, but only on an individual basis.

In the wake of the Polish labor unrest of the early 1980s, an effort emerged to improve the public image of the Soviet trade unions. Their actual character and functions, however, have remained unchanged.

Trade union locals exist at all Soviet state enterprises employing twenty-five or more people. About 732,000 such locals, organized from the bottom up, by profession, embrace more than 140 million members, including some retirees. They are run by professional bosses who are elected and usually reelected in the usual Soviet way. Membership in trade unions is compulsory for holders of permanent jobs, and membership dues amount to about 1 percent of wages or salaries. Closely associated with trade unions are the unions of free professions: writers, artists, architects, journalists, moviemakers, and composers. These unions oversee the work and the behavior of approximately 100,000 members, and try to control their professional careers. Most union officials are party members.

## LOCAL GOVERNMENTS

During the first half of 1900, elections were held in all fifteen union republics and various local jurisdictions within their borders. The principle of multi-candidate ballots was followed in choosing, by popular vote, the new republic-level congresses of people's deputies. All these assemblies, acting as electoral colleges, proceeded then to elect from among their memberships permanent legislatures—the one-house supreme soviets. Local legislatures (soviets) were also elected in all urban and rural communities.

Supreme soviets of union and autonomous republics periodically appoint their own councils of ministers headed by chairmen. Of course, all this is done under the watchful eyes of the appropriate committees of the party. As a rule, members of local governments belong to the ethnic minorities indigenous to the republics. Many of them are also party members in good standing, but other belong to various ethnic groups, "fronts," and parties. The ministries that they manage are either branches of union-republic bureaucracies centered in Moscow or specialized agencies in charge of activities of local scope and significance. The latter agencies are called "republic ministries," and do not have counterparts in Moscow.

On the level of local soviets, permanent administrative organs are called "Executive Committees" (Excoms). Every local executive committee has a chairman, and on levels above that of village, deputy chairmen nominally elected by the soviet on whose behalf they administer. Depending on the level and size of the operation, an Excom's staff of administrative, professional, and technical employees may number a few people or several thousand assigned to different departments, divisions, sections, and so on. In a typical Soviet city, the local administration, called the Executive Committee of the City Soviet ("City Excom" for short), has a much greater range of responsibility than is carried out by the city hall of an American community of corresponding size. Because there are few private businesses in the USSR, the local government takes care of such services as public transportation, utilities, much retail trade, schools, funeral homes, barber shops, restaurants, hotels, newspapers, housing, and many others.

Large cities often serve as capitals of component republics and, at the same time, as administrative centers of other territorial divisions. For example, in addition to being the capital of the USSR and the largest city in the country, Moscow is the capital of the RSFSR (Russian Soviet Federative Socialist Republic) and the administrative center of the Moscow Region. Moscow is subdivided into 30 boroughs called "urban districts" which have their own soviets with excoms, chairmen, and staffs. Thus, in Moscow there are four levels of local administration: union republic, region, city, and urban district. This is also true of several other large cities; even many smaller cities have two or three layers of local government.

As we already know, the multiethnic USSR consists of fifteen union republics, several of which contain lesser ethnic territories within their borders: twenty autonomous republics, eight regions, and ten areas. The larger union republics are also divided into purely administrative units called provinces and regions. Currently, there are six administrative provinces and 113 administrative regions in the USSR. A province (*krai*) may include both autonomous regions and autonomous areas within its borders. A region (*oblast*) may contain only autonomous areas and is, therefore, one notch below a province in prestige and importance, except for such key regions as those of Moscow and Leningrad.

There are more than 2,000 cities and towns. The larger cities are subdivided into about 660 "urban districts" (boroughs), administered by separate district soviets. The countryside is subdivided into approximately 3,225 counties called "rural districts," which also have their own soviets. On the very bottom of the pyramid are more than 42,000 village soviets.

The chain of command descends from the union-republic level to that of autonomous republic, province, region, or large city; from there to a smaller city, town, autonomous region, autonomous area, or rural district level; and then to the level of city district or village. The same principle of democratic centralism—that is, complete subordination of the lower levels to the higher levels—which governs the operation of the party underlies the functioning of the system of soviets. In the past, local governments had no "state's rights" or any other form of administrative autonomy. The only concession that was made to local interests was the use of ethnic languages in governmental offices of non-Russian union and autonomous republics and autonomous regions and areas. It is quite different now: union republics and lesser ethnic territories exercise real home rule, while all other local authorities have been given some degree of autonomy.

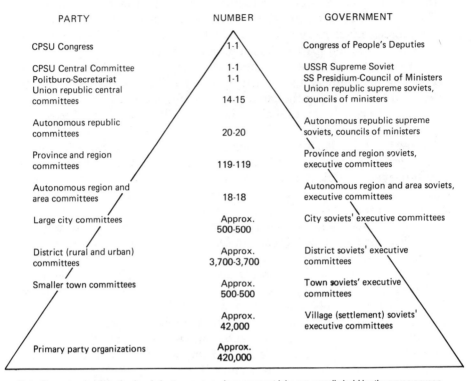

| PARTY | NUMBER | GOVERNMENT |
|---|---|---|
| CPSU Congress | 1-1 | Congress of People's Deputies |
| CPSU Central Committee | 1-1 | USSR Supreme Soviet |
| Politburo-Secretariat | 1-1 | SS Presidium-Council of Ministers |
| Union republic central committees | 14-15 | Union republic supreme soviets, councils of ministers |
| Autonomous republic committees | 20-20 | Autonomous republic supreme soviets, councils of ministers |
| Province and region committees | 119-119 | Province and region soviets, executive committees |
| Autonomous region and area committees | 18-18 | Autonomous region and area soviets, executive committees |
| Large city committees | Approx. 500-500 | City soviets' executive committees |
| District (rural and urban) committees | Approx. 3,700-3,700 | District soviets' executive committees |
| Smaller town committees | Approx. 500-500 | Town soviets' executive committees |
| | Approx. 42,000 | Village (settlement) soviets' executive committees |
| Primary party organizations | Approx. 420,000 | |

*Note:* On each administrative level, the top party and government jobs are usually held by the same person.

**FIGURE 5–4**    Party and Government Parallel Structure    *Source:* Compiled by author from Soviet statistics.

## QUALITY OF GOVERNMENT

The ultimate test of any political system is its ability to endure. The Soviet system has been in operation for more than sixty years, including prolonged periods of severe trials and tribulations. Not even during the disastrous initial phase of World War II was it in serious danger of collapse. Judged on the basis of its historical record, the Soviet government must be given high marks for survival, an unqualified accomplishment that it shares with relatively few political regimes of the contemporary world. Now, the entire system is undergoing another difficult test presented by a combination of ethnic riots and demands, acts of civic disobedience, a rising incidence of crime, and economic setbacks.

On the other hand, the quality of the Soviet government's performance is less impressive and very uneven, reflecting ideological priorities. As a result, the Soviet government functions relatively well in such areas of its vast responsibility as national security, the military establishment, and scientific research and development. It has earned high marks in public education and health care. But in public administration and services, it is notoriously inefficient and insensitive to basic human needs. Ugly bureaucratic behavior of big and small civil servants is the norm rather than the exception, and the average Soviet citizen has only limited opportunities for redress of his or her grievances. Various kinds of corruption thrive in this climate, in which big and small bureaucrats can often abuse their power with relative impunity. Gorbachev's administration has a long way to go in its efforts to completely remedy this situation.

All this, however, does not mean that a majority of Soviet people feels alienated from the government. The main reason for this seeming paradox is the fact that practically everyone in the USSR not only works for the government, but also receives from it his or her food, clothing, education, transportation, housing, medical care, and just about everything else that keeps soul and body together. This total dependency on the government, which lasts literally from cradle to grave, makes the overwhelming majority of the people much more willing to accept as inevitable all kinds of shortcomings and malfunctions in its day-to-day operation. Such acceptance may be compared with the way one usually tolerates weather and eventually gets used to adverse climates, even making a virtue of necessity. To paraphrase an old cliché, the Soviet people have a government which they do not necessarily deserve or like but which they nevertheless accept as a perfectly natural and permanent condition.

Note, however, that thanks to *glasnost*, contested elections, and independent opinion polls, the Soviet people's attitudes toward their government are changing. For the same reasons, the Soviet government is becoming more responsive and responsible to its people. There are now fledging political lobbies, recognized interest groups, and similar citizens' organizations in the USSR that can exercise pressure. In the past, the only boss of the Soviet government was the Communist Party, but now the same people who were previously believed incapable of governing themselves because their "conscience lags behind the changing sociopolitical reality" are being urged to get involved.

A successful government career still depends on one's good standing in the Communist Party. All other things being equal, personal and family connections can be of considerable advantage. The overwhelming majority of positions does not require passing civil service examinations or tests. The initial hiring is usually done on the basis of rather informal interviews with applicants. Official preference is afforded only to veterans. As part of a vigorous campaign against inefficiency, many people have been forced to retire from even fairly high executive positions. During his first five years in power, Gorbachev replaced almost 95 percent of the old—and in most cases elderly—holders of the top executive positions, including ministers and heads of agencies.

## PARTY-GOVERNMENT RELATIONSHIP

The relationship between the party and the government could be compared with the relationship between the owner and the hired managers of private enterprise, provided that most of the managers are also members of the owner's family. In fact, well over 50 percent of the members of various legislative bodies and practically all important officers of the executive branch belong to the party. The latter group—the executive officers and high-ranking administrators—constitutes a special kind of party cadre whose every assignment, lateral move, or promotion (as well as demotion) is controlled by the party's personnel offices. The names of these people are on the *nomenklatura* rosters. The official biographies of prominent Soviet government functionaries usually contain such statements as "was dispatched by the party to work in the Soviet administration," "assigned by the party to work in the government," and so on. In other words, all of them are political appointees.

For many years unwritten Soviet protocol had demanded that in all public references in which the Communist Party and the Soviet government are mentioned together, the party must be first. And as every Soviet citizen knows, on any given level of administration—district, city, region, and all the way up—the focal point of political power is not the official government authority but the party committee. The same pattern is found on the very top of the Soviet pyramid, where the Central Committee of the CPSU and its ruling councils are more important than the Council of Ministers and the Supreme Soviet. The relative unimportance of the state apparatus was underscored when the office of the chief of state (Chairman, Presidium of the Supreme Soviet) remained vacant for several weeks at a time following the deaths of Brezhnev, Andropov, and Chernenko. In 1985, Gorbachev further downgraded the office by his decision to yield it to Andrei Gromyko.

In a typical Soviet city, routine problems and grievances are handled by officials of city hall, called "excom." But in the case of special problems (for example, the discovery of corruption in high places or an anticipated production shortfall in a local firm) the office that is immediately contacted and must resolve the situation is the city committee of the CPSU. Now, following Gorbachev's own example, the two offices are often combined: The first secretary of a city party committee serves concurrently as the chairman of the city soviet. This is the ultimate form of the party's control over the government.

Now let us return to our hypothetical Soviet city. The operation of every enterprise and institution in the city is controlled by the party in more than one way. For instance, let us say that the firm facing a production shortfall is a furniture factory employing 250 people. It can be taken for granted that the director of the factory and his top assistants are party members in good standing, who are thus subject to party discipline. The director, because he owes his position to a political appointment, would be expected to maintain close ties with the city party committee, most likely as a member of its bureau. The factory would have its own primary party organization, consisting of approximately thirty-five members, which include most of the factory's engineers and supervisors. (The percentage of card-carrying Communists among urban industrial personnel is about 15.) The organization is headed by a secretary accountable to the city party committee, thus bypassing the director. The factory, as a whole, would also be under the jurisdiction of the city party committee's industrial section presided over by a special subsecretary. All other local factories, schools, trade organizations, and various offices, including that of the mayor, are in the same multilevel relationship to the party. The same situation exists in every Soviet town or urban and rural district.

The Soviet system of government does not have an internal check-and-balance mechanism for regulating relations among its three branches: the legislative, executive, and judicial. Instead, an "outside force," the Communist Party, directs and coordinates the work of the entire government. But the Communist Party, and the Soviet government are apart from each other only in theory. In practice, they are inseparable. Remember that in the party program the state administration (government) is defined merely as a tool with which the CPSU is building Communism (see page 124).

How much is this traditional party-state relationship changing under *perestroika*? Signals coming from the big country are mixed. On the one hand, there is much evidence that the CPSU continues to act as the ruling party and card-carrying party members dominate the all-union legislative bodies (The Congress of People's Deputies and the Supreme Soviet) and the executive branch (only one cabinet level official—in charge of environmental protection—is a non-party member). On the other hand, Gorbachev seems to be shifting his main base of support and prestige from the party to the state, the CPSU's constitutional monopoly on power (Article 6) has been revised, and many non-Communists have won elections to republic-level and local legislative bodies.[9]

[9]Non-Communist candidates did especially well in local elections of February and March 1990 in the Baltic and Transcaucasian union republics.

## GLOSSARY

**Bourgeoisie:**  middle class.
**Cheka:**  original name of the Soviet secret police in Lenin's era.
**Deputy:**  member of the Soviet legislature.
**Gulag:**  (Russian) Chief Administration of Camps.
**KGB:**  Soviet (secret) security agency.
**Krai:**  province, territory.
**Oblast:**  region, land.
**Oprichnina:**  Ivan the Terrible's political police.
**People's Assessors:**  lay judges.
**Presidium:**  steering committees of supreme soviets and councils of ministers.
**Procurator:**  prosecutor, state attorney.
**Soviet:**  council, legislative assembly.

## RECOMMENDED READINGS

BARRY, DONALD D., and CAROL BARNER-BARRY, *Contemporary Soviet Politics*. Englewood Cliffs, NJ: Prentice-Hall, 1978.
BRZEZINSKI, ZBIGNIEW, and SAMUEL P. HUNTINGTON, *Political Power: USA/USSR*. New York: Viking Press, 1964.
HAZARD, JOHN N., *The Soviet System of Government*. Chicago: University of Chicago Press, 1968.

# CHAPTER
# 6
# THE ECONOMY

## NATIONAL ECONOMY

The central role of economics in Marxist ideology is reflected in the country's name, the Union of Soviet Socialist Republics, in which the word "Socialist" refers to the prevailing type of economic relations. Article 10 of the Soviet Constitution defines the national economy of the USSR as a public enterprise "based on the Socialist ownership of all means of production," including the land. According to the constitution, Socialist ownership assumes two forms during the transition to Communism: the all-national or state economy and the collective or cooperative economy. At present, state ownership embraces the bulk of the Soviet national economy, including all large industrial enterprises, banking, transportation and communication, the larger portion of trade and public services, and a large segment of agriculture. Persons working in this sector of the economy and the members of their families amount to about 85 percent of the population. Cooperative ownership extends to small artisan workshops, some retail trade and services, and much of the country's agriculture. This sector accounts for the remaining 15 percent of the population and it is growing under *perestroika*.

For several decades, it was believed that, during the transition from Socialism to Communism, all cooperative enterprises were to be gradually converted into state enterprises. From the standpoint of Marxist ideology, the latter represents a "higher stage" due to the fact (or rather claim) that it involves all members of society as co-owners, whereas the former stands for a "lower stage" because cooperatives belong to relatively small groups of individuals.

In his pragmatic approach to economics, Gorbachev has totally ignored this ideological distinction and has been treating cooperatives as a great source of hope for his version of "socialism with a human face." The scope of cooperative business has expanded to include both agricultural and urban enterprises producing goods and services. Individual business activities—such as moonlighting by various artisans, tutoring, private medical practice, family land-leasing, and street vending—have been completely legalized within certain limitations. It is expected that by the early 1990s the share of the GNP produced by the cooperative and private sector of the national economy would rise to 25 percent.

Until very recently, private ownership and use of the means of production—that is, private enterprise with hired help—was illegal in the Soviet Union on the grounds that it produces "unearned material gains" and creates economic inequality, the root of all social evil. Now, under Gorbachev, legal restrictions and limitations regulating such activities have been considerably relaxed. In 1990, a new law was passed legalizing small private business and property under the euphemism "citizens' ownership."

Soviet citizens may also legally own, buy, sell, will, and inherit personal property, such as an apartment, a house, or a car, but it is illegal for them to use such property to make a profit. Actually, various exceptions to this rule are quite common, and quasi-private business transactions have always been significant on the consumer level, which has traditionally been given a low priority in the overall economic development.

In the past, Soviet economic policy always favored the development of heavy industries at the expense of everything else. Justified in terms of Marxist economic theory, this one-sided approach produced a huge economy characterized by uneven levels of achievement in its various branches. Today, the Soviet Union is the second largest economic power in the world, with a GNP (gross national product) estimated at close to two thirds that of the United States. The USSR produces about 20 percent of the world's industrial output, but in such areas of economic endeavor as the quality of consumer goods and services and housing and highway construction, it is comparable to the underdeveloped countries of the Third World. The Soviet Union's awesome military might rests on the growing capacity of its science and technology to produce highly sophisticated weapons. But the same science and technology have so far been unable to prevent the periodic failures of Soviet agriculture. Despite a half century of experience in central planning, the Soviet Union is still chronically beset by shortages of the most

**BOX 6–1** *Definition of the USSR Economy*

> From the *Soviet Constitution, Article 16:* The economy of the USSR is an integral economic complex comprising all the elements of social production, distribution, and exchange on its territory.
>
> The economy is managed on the basis of state plans for economic and social development, with due account of the sectoral and territorial principles, and by combining centralized direction with the managerial independence and initiative of individual and amalgamated enterprises and other organizations, for which active use is made of management accounting, profit, cost, and other economic levers and incentives.

basic consumer commodities. During the last several decades, there was no mass unemployment in the Soviet Union, but low labor productivity and wages point to the existence of a "hidden unemployment"—the wasteful use of labor. The demonstrated ability of the USSR to control inflation contrasted with the high retail prices and frequent unavailability of many manufactured goods. The achievement of considerable equality in the distribution of property was in conflict with the unequal distribution of privileges.

Many other similar contradictions and paradoxes characterized the Soviet national economy—"The USSR, Inc."—in the mid 1980s, when it came under the leadership of the new chairman of its "board of directors," Mikhail S. Gorbachev, who lost no time declaring that what he had inherited was a "pre-crisis situation" calling for drastic reforms—*perestroika.*

So far, Gorbachev's reforms have produced mixed and inconclusive results. By emphasizing some of them and ignoring others, it is possible to portray the Soviet economy as improving and gaining strength or as weak and not responding to Gorbachev's remedies. Before judging *perestroika* and its chances to succeed, let us briefly review the history of Russia's economic development.

## HISTORICAL VIEW

At the turn of this century, Russia was a predominantly agricultural country only beginning to develop, with help from foreign investments, its extracting and manufacturing industries. But on the eve of World War I, it already rated fourth or fifth in the world in terms of overall economic production. Between 1918 and 1921, the new regime tried to carry out a complete socialization of the country's economy, seriously weakened by World War I, revolutions, and a civil war. Known as "War Communism," this short-lived experiment involved poorly coordinated measures dictated by a combination of the dire exigencies of the day and fundamentalist interpretations of Marxism. The three years of War Communism brought Russia's economy to the brink of ruin, forcing Lenin to call for a "temporary retreat" and to announce his New Economic Policy (NEP) in April 1921. Under the NEP, private enterprise was encouraged within set limitations in the areas of agriculture, domestic trade, light industries, and public services. The state, however, retained its monopoly over the so-called commanding heights: banking, heavy industries, transportation and communication, and foreign trade.

The proclaimed purpose of the NEP was to restore the country's economy to its pre-World War I level. Once this had been accomplished (by the late 1920s), the regime undertook its second attempt at socialization. In 1928, it was declared that the entire nationalized economy was to be rapidly developed in a highly centralized manner through five-year stages called five-year plans. The First Five-Year Plan (1928–1933) envisaged a rapid industrialization accompanied by the complete collectivization of the countryside. It was expected to release from agriculture the cheap labor needed for the construction and operation of new industrial projects and to increase the amount of marketable agricultural produce.

Carried out in the name of Stalin's promise to build "Socialism in one country," this change amounted to a "second revolution," which rivaled the first in terms of the human suffering it inflicted. The forced mass collectivization of agriculture was completed by the early 1930s, and industrialization continued at a rapid pace up to the time of the German invasion in 1941. During the four war years, much of the Soviet economy was destroyed or severely crippled by the advancing and retreating armies of both sides. The war also forced Soviet leaders to relocate many industrial enterprises and disperse them throughout the Asian part of the country. The postwar five-year plans not only rebuilt the economy in record time but also ensured its continued rapid growth until the end of the 1960s. Among the more spectacular achievements of the Soviet economy during that period was the development of its atomic and nuclear capacity and its pioneering efforts in space exploration. After the death of Stalin, and, once again, after the ouster of Khrushchev, far-reaching reforms were introduced to ensure the continuing growth of the economic base. During the 1970s, however, the upward momentum of the Soviet economy, in terms of quantitative growth, began to slacken. The Tenth Five-Year Plan (1976–1980) emphasized efficiency, productivity, and quality over quantity. Instead of a further expansion of the already vast industrial base, the plan called for relatively modest quantitative increases. The Eleventh Five-Year Plan (1981–1985) produced only 3 to 4 percent growth per annum. The Twelfth Five-Year Plan, which began in 1986, calls for renewed effort to increase the rate to about 5 percent, while improving the quality of goods and services. By all indications the Soviet Union has reached the point at which it must find a more effective use for its vast but not unlimited resources. Gorbachev and his aides have admitted as

**TABLE 6–1**    Declining GNP growth, 1965–1985

| | |
|---|---|
| Eighth Five-Year Plan, 1966–1970 | 41% |
| Ninth Five-Year Plan, 1971–1975 | 28% |
| Eleventh Five-Year Plan, 1981–1985 | 16.5% |

*Source:* Compiled by author from Soviet data.

much in their public speeches. But they also seem to be determined to solve this basic problem by changing from extensive to intensive economic development.

The overall economic ambition of the Soviet Union remains the same: to catch up with, and surpass, the United States. The overly optimistic Khrushchev thought that this could be done by 1981. His more realistic heirs, the current Soviet leaders, appear to have concluded that several additional five-year plans would be needed to achieve this "historic goal," which is supposed to tip the world scale in favor of Communism. They also know that the Soviet national economy is in a dire need of change.

## ECONOMIC REFORMS

Karl Marx's belief that economics determines everything else in the life of a nation throughout its history may or may not be correct. But there is no doubt that Gorbachev's *perestroika* will succeed or fail depending largely on his ability to cope with the existing economic problems. In the final analysis, all other reforms undertaken by Gorbachev, including *glasnost*, are merely tools, means, and even concessions for achieving this end. The economic problems of utmost concern, as they have been identified in the Soviet press, are as follows:

1. Reordering priorities and deciding on trade-offs among capital investments (economic growth and modernization), consumption (goods and services), and armaments (including related space projects).
2. Changing from extensive to intensive mode of development in both industry and agriculture.
3. Finding an optimal balance between central planning and free market forces, and improving information flows.
4. Reforming and rationalizing the system of prices, wages, and salaries.
5. Boosting incentives, encouraging individual initiative, and raising labor productivity.
6. Solving the food problem by encouraging quasi-private farming.
7. Raising the quality of manufactured goods and services.
8. Decentralizing the economic decision-making process and giving more power to territorial units of the system such as union republics, autonomous republics, and regions.

To resolve these problems is a formidable task, comparable perhaps to an attempt to overhaul the engines of a ship on the high seas without the benefit of a dry dock. Likely solutions appear to be interlocked in a chain which, to paraphrase Lenin, is only as strong as its weakest link. In other words, to be successful, they must be carried out concurrently, in a coordinated effort.

The two main legislative instruments needed for the proposed economic changes have been in place since early 1988: "The Law on the State Enterprise (Association)" and "The Law on the Cooperatives." The former law is aimed at giving a significant degree of independence from central authorities to factories, plants, and other state-owned enterprises. It gives them power and responsibility to deal directly with such matters as selection of managers, production decisions, distribution of profits, and budget allocations. The latter law encourages the liberalization of existing and establishment of new forms of cooperative business, including some quasi-private commercial activities. Most of the proposed remedies have already been tried with various degrees of success in Eastern Europe.

Gorbachev and his supporters are optimistic that the economic reforms are making progress, as appears to be borne out by statistical indicators. However, they complain that the progress is too slow due to lingering conservatism and even outright sabotage by remaining "imperious bureaucrats." Gorbachev's critics, on the other hand, profess to see no progress at all. According to some of them, the Soviet economy is a terminal "basket case" of misdirection and mismanagement. And their frame of reference, usually, is real economic life in the USSR: continuing shortages of basic goods, long shoppers' lines, poor services. The truth is probably somewhere in the middle. The jury's verdict on economic *perestroika*, however, is still pending.

The jury in this case consists of tens of millions of Soviet workers, peasants, craftsmen, and employees. Unlike other reforms, most of the proposed economic changes cannot be just ordered from above since they require active support from below. The Soviet people must consider these changes to be sufficiently attractive and feasible before contributing the extra efforts required for their solution, or accepting the inevitably painful adjustments.

It is hard to tell whether there actually is an organized opposition to the ongoing economic changes, as is sometimes darkly intimated in the Soviet press. More probably, it is just a propaganda straw man and an excuse for the disappointingly slow pace of *perestroika*. Because *perestroika* concerns all—in a way everyone who is not part of the solution is part of the problem. Violent ethnic disturbances, protracted work stoppages, and mass strikes have been damaging to the operation and development of the economy. At least for the time being, these and similar side effects of *glasnost* often come in direct conflict with the aims of *perestroika*. In a manner of speaking, Gorbachev has not been able to give his people both "circuses and bread"— the former have been at the expense of the latter.

Another challenge to Gorbachev's *perestroika* comes from several ethnic republics with higher-than-average living standards. Authorities there claim the right to overrule Moscow's directives which, in their opinion, infringe on local economic interests.

## CENTRAL PLANNING

Central planning, a vital part of the Soviet economic system, was first tried on an experimental basis in 1920, when a long-range plan for the electrification of Russia was put into operation. A personal pet project of Lenin, it called for the construction of thirty large electric power plants to serve the needs of the new, still-to-be-built industries. Eight years later, in 1928, the concept of central planning was applied on a much larger scale to the projected development of new economic capacities and increments of production in all major branches of the nationalized economy. The traditional free-market mechanism of supply-and-demand was replaced by a command economy operating and developing on the basis of five-year master plans. The five-year period was chosen as a unit for planning and development because it was believed to be the usual cycle of better and poorer harvests in Russia's agriculture, and also because at the time it took (on the average) five years to build and commission major new industrial enterprises. Central planning grew more complex with each successive five-year period, requiring an ever-larger bureaucracy to work out, coordinate, and control detailed plans involving not only the volume of material goods and services for the whole country, but also their cost, distribution, energy requirements, labor needs, labor productivity, and the like. Early in the period (1921), a cabinet-level office charged with this activity was established under the name of the State Planning Commission, usually referred to as *Gosplan* ("state plan"). The current chairman of *Gosplan*, Y. Maslyukov, is a full-member of the Politburo.

*Gosplan* puts together draft proposals for each new five-year plan, presumably on the basis of target figures and priorities set by the Politburo. In the past, the draft was then channeled through the Central Committee of the CPSU and placed before a party congress for its endorsement. It was on this occasion that the new economic goals were officially finalized. Actually, by that time, the new five-year plan was already in operation. For example, the current five-year plan was given the final seal of approval only in March 1986 at the Twenty-seventh Party Congress, two months after its implementation. After ex post facto approval by the party congress, the new five-year plan was submitted to a joint session of the Supreme Soviet, whose automatic approval made it, retroactively, a legal instrument: a law that every ministry and agency concerned, every union and autonomous republic, region, city, district, factory, and so on, has been obliged to carry out.

This procedure is being "democraticized" under Gorbachev's *perestroika*. In the future, free market forces would presumably be taken into consideration, making Soviet "command economy" less rigid. In this way, the "visible hand" of the planners would be helped by the "invisible hand" of supply-and- demand forces.

Various economic units have traditionally been encouraged to propose their own "counterplans" promising to outdo the original goals sent from above and challenging other units to "Socialist emulation"—that is, to outdo each other. Because the new leadership stresses quality over quantity, this practice is declining, but references to various promises and pledges to speed up or exceed production quotas still appear every day in the Soviet mass media.

During the last sixty years, central planning has undergone many reforms and changes, including Khrushchev's decision in 1959 to extend its cycle from five to seven years, evidently to cover up some serious miscalculations. Since 1962, consumption has replaced production as the chief yardstick for each successive five-year plan. More emphasis is placed on long-range (fifteen year) planning. Currently, efforts are under way to introduce on a large scale mathematical economics and computer programming into the planning process to deal more efficiently with a huge information overload. At the same time, there is an effort to build more flexibility into the *Gosplan's* mode of operation, allowing lower echelons of the economic system, including individual enterprises, to make their own decisions. Managers of various factories and plants are no longer treated as virtual hostages to the plan.

Every five-year plan is broken down into annual, quarterly, and monthly installments to ensure smoother operation and greater accountability. The Soviet mass media carry progress reports on the fulfillment of various parts and segments of a current plan. All this is supposed to create a feeling of expectation and achievement. It is this built-in tendency to appear successful at almost any cost that often casts doubt on official reports of Soviet economic accomplishments.

Since its introduction in 1928, the system of central planning has produced not only successes, but also failures. Moreover, some of the most serious failures resulted not so much from mistakes and miscalculations as from conscious trade-offs made by economic planners and their political bosses.

## TWELFTH FIVE-YEAR PLAN

The current Five-Year Plan, which runs from 1986 through 1990, is believed to be a crucially important test of Mikhail Gorbachev's ability to revitalize the Soviet economy. In the official media, the plan is described as a historic

**TABLE 6–2**  Selected Targets of the Twelfth Five-Year Plan, 1986–1990 (In Percentages; 1985 = 100%, Base Year)

| | |
|---|---|
| Gross national product | 119–122 |
| Individual income (cash) | 113–115 |
| Fringe benefits | 120–123 |
| Industrial production | 121–124 |
| Agricultural production | 114–116 |
| Labor productivity | 120–123 |

*Source:* Compiled by author from Soviet data.

"turning point" and the "launching pad" for a long-range economic strategy that is expected to accelerate progressively the annual rate of growth and double the Soviet Union's national income by the year 2000. The quantitative goals set for this five-year period, however, are not overly ambitious: They only slightly exceed those that were reached during the preceding five-year plan (see Table 6–1). Conspicuous by their absence are references to giant "hero projects" and sensational "miracle drugs," which used to be the centerpieces of all previous blueprints for economic development. Quantitatively, the Twelfth Five-Year Plan has no promise of a "great leap forward."

But Gorbachev's plan does put unusually high emphasis on the qualitative aspect of the operation and development of the Soviet national economy, which it seeks to modernize and make more efficient. The most difficult problem facing Gorbachev and his team is the legacy of a national addiction to bad work ethics and practices. Gorbachev is trying to solve the problem by instilling a renewed sense of energy and excitement. The scheme combines economic, political, and administrative measures—some of them quite innovative by Soviet standards. His effort has already produced a spurt of perceptible results: a more optimistic mood, a tighter work discipline, closer ties between wages and productivity, a more rational price policy, and a modest improvement of services. What remains to be seen is how long this momentum will last and how much of the desired snowball effect it is likely to produce. It appears certain that under Gorbachev's next (Thirteenth) five-year plan the Soviet Union will remain committed to the system of central planning and control, though not as rigidly as in the past.

The Soviet economy, functioning like a giant state-owned corporation, is organized on an industrial-territorial basis. This means that every branch of industry is put under one central ministry, which has local offices at various administrative-territorial levels. The party's control over the operation of such a branch flows vertically through the ministry's hierarchy and horizontally through its own chain of local offices. However, party officials are now under strict orders to avoid making day-to-day economic decisions especially on the local levels.

Current economic planning calls for continuing preferential development of the Asian regions of the USSR. The influx of population to this part of the country reached its peak during World War II, when many industrial facilities had to be evacuated from the western parts of the USSR and moved eastward. After World War II, many plants and factories were left permanently in their new locations in a concentrated effort to speed up the economic development of the Asian part of the country, to bring manufacturing industries closer to the sources of raw materials and fuel, and to achieve a higher degree of economic dispersion for strategic reasons. During the postwar five-year plans, the bulk of the new industrial projects was built in these economic regions. In the late 1950s and early 1960s, a major campaign launched to expand wheat farming in Kazakhstan and West Siberia brought in several million migrants. Now Gorbachev is determined to develop further the economic potential of Soviet Asia with its tremendous natural endowments.

It is rather obvious that the goals of the Twelfth Five-Year Plan (Table 6–2) will not be met, diminishing chances for Gorbachev's ambitious economic reforms to be completed by the year 2000.

## ENERGY

The Soviet economy satisfies its energy needs almost exclusively from domestic sources.[1] In fact, the Soviet Union is a net exporter of oil, natural gas, and, to a lesser extent, electric power. As mentioned, its known and suspected deposits of fossil fuels are enormously large, and their exploitation has been growing quite fast. During the preceding three five-year periods (1965–1980), production of oil, natural gas, and coal increased more than two and a half times. There are no signs that the country is heading for an energy shortage, as has often been predicted in the West.

Oil and natural gas, derived from mineral fuels, are the main sources of energy: They account for almost 70 percent of total output. At more than 600 million metric tons per year, the Soviet Union's oil production is the largest in the world, although it went down slightly between 1982 and 1985. While new oil-bearing areas are constantly being discovered in Siberia, more efficient techniques make possible further exploitation of partially depleted old fields in the Caucasus, Volga Valley, Ukraine, and Central Asia. About 75 percent of the extracted oil goes to Soviet refineries for domestic consumption, and the rest is used for export. Currently, the USSR produces approximately 12 million barrels of oil per day.

Natural gas production, which is currently growing faster than any other branch of the Soviet national economy, exceeds 450 billion cubic meters per year. A few years ago, the Soviet Union surpassed the United States and

[1]The Soviet Union imports some uranium for its atomic reactors from East Germany.

became the world's primary natural gas producer. Gas is carried mainly by an extensive system of pipelines crisscrossing the USSR. Some of them go beyond Soviet borders and serve as channels for foreign trade.

Coal is another important source of energy for the Soviet Union, although its share of total production is decreasing (less than 30 percent at present). The known deposits of coal are huge and dispersed all over the country, and its production is relatively inexpensive, especially when employing open-pit mining. This less expensive method accounts for about 35 percent of the more than 735 million tons of coal produced annually. Of lesser importance is the production of other solid fuels, like peat and shale.

Hydropower is used mainly as a source of energy in the production of electricity. Hydropower stations produce more than 20 percent of the electric power. The share of electricity obtained from atomic reactors is relatively small—about 10 percent of the total. The remaining three fourths of electricity is produced by thermopower stations. The total yearly production is approximately 1,750 billion kilowatt-hours—much less than in the United States.[2] Production of solar energy is limited to a few experimental projects located in the Caucasus, Crimea, and Central Asia.

The growth of electric power production is the most important single indicator in the entire Soviet national economy, because it is a prerequisite for further industrialization, urbanization, and modernization of agriculture and transportation. Its current annual rate of growth is about 1 percent (1989). At this rate, one of the most frequently displayed mottos in public places—Lenin's assertions that "Communism is Soviet power plus the electrification of the whole country"—will not be tested for some time to come.

An extensive network of high-voltage transmission lines interconnects regional systems, ensuring their coordinated operation in the entire country, as well as in parts of Eastern Europe.[3]

The impressive figures on the production side of energy in the Soviet Union tend to hide that, until now, their use of fuels and electricity has been notoriously wasteful, partially due to artificially low prices. The cost of energy, of course, is an important factor in the price formation for many industrial and agricultural commodities, as well as transport.

## INDUSTRIAL BASE

The Soviet industrial establishment is administered by a large number of union and union-republic ministries operating as state monopolies for the production of oil, coal, steel, automobiles, machine tools, and other major items. Smaller enterprises in food, housing, and light industries are under

[2]About 65 percent of the United States' production of electricity.
[3]This is called the Soviet Unified Power Grid. Several ministries and lesser agencies are in charge of the operation and development of Soviet energy resources.

**TABLE 6–3**   Industrial Growth Since 1913 (In Percentages)

|  | 1913 | 1940 | 1960 | 1970 | 1980 | 1986 |
|---|---|---|---|---|---|---|
| All production | 100 | 770 | 4,000 | 9,200 | 17,800 | 19,700 |
| Production, Group A | 100 | 1,300 | 8,900 | 21,400 | 42,900 | 45,000 |
| Production, Group B | 100 | 460 | 1,500 | 3,000 | 5,500 | 7,200 |

*Source:* Compiled by author from Soviet statistics.

the jurisdiction of republic-level ministries and local soviets. Individual plants and factories are run by managers or directors. More than 35 million blue- and white-collar workers are employed in the industrial sector, which consists of over 50,000 enterprises organized into "combines" (associations) and "trusts" (conglomerates). Over the years, periodic attempts have been made to decentralize and centralize industry by various administrative reforms.

The growth of the Soviet industrial base has been spectacular. Today the overall industrial output of the Soviet Union is estimated to be more than 80 percent of that of the United States, compared to about 12 percent in 1917. For the purpose of planning, Soviet industries are divided into Group A and Group B. Group A includes heavy industries, defined as "production of means of production" (making machines that make machines), mining and power industries, and armament and related industries. This group of industries has always received preferential treatment in the development of the Soviet economy. As a result, Group A has developed much faster than Group B, which includes food and light industries. For example, according to Soviet statistics, the total volume of industrial production increased 197 times between 1913 and 1986 (see Table 6–3). During the same period, Group A production increased 450 times, whereas Group B production went up only 72 times. Today, Group A industries contribute approximately 75 percent of the total industrial production. In 1913, this contribution was less than 35 percent. The vast difference between Group A and Group B extends not only to the quantity but also to the quality of their respective outputs. Soviet citizens may be proud patriots of a militarily powerful nation, but satisfied consumers of high-quality commodities they are not; almost without exception, products of the Soviet light and food industries are shabby and crude, as well as in short supply. For the average Soviet citizen, chronic scarcity of consumer goods is an acknowledged way of life. Some substantial discrepancies are also evident in the performance and quality of different industries within Group A. For example, compared to the United States, the Soviet Union is ahead in coal, oil, iron ore, pig iron, mineral fertilizer, natural gas, and steel output. But the Soviet Union is lagging far behind in electricity production, as well as in production in almost every branch of high technology. As a rule, the factor by which the Soviet economy is lagging behind is directly proportional to the level of complexity and sophistication of the machinery and equipment manufactured. Even by Soviet statistics, labor productivity in Soviet industry stands at about 55 percent of that in the United States. Here again, the difference between the two countries in labor productivity is much larger for more sophisticated industries manufacturing such finished products as electronic instruments, cars, and machine tools. Among the major problems facing the Soviet industrial establishment are: (1) obsolescence of plant equipment;[4] (2) insufficient production specialization; (3) bureaucratic resistance to innovation; and (4) low labor productivity. An estimated 10 percent of all industrial enterprises operate at a loss. The current reforms, started by Gorbachev and his team, are supposed to resolve or at least alleviate these and other formidable problems.

## AGRICULTURE

The feudal system of agriculture based on serf labor was formally abolished in Russia only in 1861, although many remnants of it lingered for almost fifty more years. Not until 1906 could the majority of peasants get legal titles to the land. By the end of the 1920s, more than 20 million small family farms existed in the USSR. They were poorly equipped, inefficient, and marginally productive of marketable goods. It was promised that the mass collectivization that followed would modernize agriculture almost overnight. This promise still remains unfulfilled.

For more than sixty years, agriculture has been a source of constant hardship and disappointment for millions of Soviet people and of embarrassment for their leaders. Stalin preferred simply to ignore the sad realities of the Soviet countryside. Khrushchev, on the other hand, not only talked about them, but tried all kinds of "miracle drugs."[5] His more practical successors have decided to invest huge sums of money in agriculture to make it independent of the unstable weather that affects about 60 percent of the arable land. Yet Soviet agriculture, which employs about 20 percent of the entire labor force, continues to be inefficient. For example, labor productivity in Soviet agriculture is estimated at one fifth to one third of that in United States agriculture (much of this discrepancy, however, is due to the difference in climatic conditions).

Following Gorbachev's ascent to power, overall responsibility for agriculture was first concentrated in a superagency called Agroprom, but was

[4]On the average, the equipment in Soviet plants and factories is almost twenty years old (compared to twelve years in the United States).

[5]Among the best-publicized measures of this kind were Khrushchev's campaign to cultivate vast "virgin lands" in Kazakhstan and his promotion of corn in various parts of the Soviet Union.

later relegated to the republic and local authorities. There are two basic types of agricultural enterprise in the Soviet Union today: the collective farm or *kolkhoz*[6] and the state farm or *sovkhoz*. The collective farm is a cooperative of producers, and as such represents the "lower" form of the Socialist economy. There are approximately 26,000 collective farms of different sizes. Collective farms are gradually decreasing in number because of their consolidation and conversion to state farms, the "higher" form of the Socialist economy. A typical collective farm has about 450 "households"—that is, members who, with their families, live in a village or several neighboring villages. The farm is run by an elected chairman. It usually has a motor pool, some cows, horses, sheep, pigs, and other livestock. The land that it cultivates (an average of about 16,000 acres) is assigned to it rent-free by the state. Every member of the collective farm is obliged to perform a specified minimum of units of work per year. His or her income is determined by the number of such units performed and their value, which depends on the harvest. But a large portion of the estimated income is payable in advance on a monthly basis. Each collective farmer's family can supplement its income by engaging in quasiprivate farming on small, individual plots of land cultivated by family members in their spare time. Historically, such small-scale family farming has helped millions of collective farmers to survive and has provided an important source of foodstuffs for the population at large. It still accounts for more than one fourth of the average collective farmer's total income.[7]

Compared to collective farms, state farms are much larger in size (an average of 50,000 acres) and are better equipped and mechanized. They are also more efficient. An average state farm employs about 750 wage-earning workers. Unlike multipurpose collective farms, most of the 23,000 state farms specialize in one particular branch of agriculture: grain, dairy products, vegetables, or whatever. State farms are run by appointed directors. At present, the state farms' share of marketable output almost equals that of the collective farms. State farm workers are also allowed to have small private plots.

As noted previously, until recently, collective farms were gradually consolidated, made into "agrofactories," lumped into regional consortiums, and changed into state farms. This process slowed shortly after Gorbachev's rise to power. Perhaps because he was born and raised on a farm, Gorbachev has a more realistic approach to agricultural problems. Without changing the framework of collective and state farms, he is promoting purely economic incentives: family subcontracting specific jobs, family leasing land

---

[6]The term *kolkhoz* also applies to various other producers' cooperatives: fishermen's, hunters', and so on. At various times in the past, other types of agricultural cooperatives, including "communes," were tried in the USSR. *Kolkhoz* or *artel* won out as a compromise between too much and too little socialization.

[7]Private plots of collective farmers average up to 0.5 hectare (1.25 acres). State farm employees are allowed to have smaller private plots.

and equipment, profit sharing, and, in general, tying earnings to actual labor productivity of individual farmers. Several thousand nonprofitable collective and state farms have been put on probation to shape up or face the possibility of going out of business. Gorbachev has also reduced the bureaucratic overhead on all levels of the agricultural establishment, while encouraging farmers to experiment with self-management. Yet it is too early to say whether this will provide an effective and lasting solution for the protracted crisis in which Russia's agriculture has been kept for the last half century by a combination of harsh and capricious climate, systematic neglect, and periodic experimentation with dubious stopgap measures. The current five-year plan promised but failed to increase agricultural output by 20 percent.

## FOOD PRODUCTION

As in most other countries, grain is the mainstay of food production in the Soviet Union. During the late 1970s and early 1980s, grain production in the Soviet Union averaged approximately 200 million metric tons per year. The current five-year plan was supposed to boost it to an annual average of 250 to 255 million metric tons. This goal has not been met, despite solemn promises of Soviet leaders coupled with various extraordinary measures that were supposed to increase the quantity and improve the quality of grain production. In 1986, production was 210 million metric tons; in 1987, 211 million; in 1988, 195 million; and in 1989, 211 million.

There are several interconnected reasons that compel Soviet leaders to urgently seek a permanent solution to the grain problem. First, the insufficient quantity, poor quality, limited assortment, and unreliable distribution system of food have been among more conspicuous failures of the Soviet economy. As Gorbachev must fully realize, it is by far the most visible aspect of the USSR's relative backwardness, casting a shadow of doubt on all his claims about the supposed superiority of Socialism.

Second, the current level of grain production is inadequate to sustain and develop animal husbandry. Acute shortages of fodder can cause shortages of bread—for which, in theory, there is more than enough grain (see Figure 6–1). This happens when peasants begin to buy large quantities of bread, sold at low subsidized retail prices, as a substitute for the animal fodder in short supply.

Third, current attempts to ease the problem by relying on large-scale grain imports have led to serious political repercussions. When viewed from a purely economic principle of relative advantages, a dependence on imports may not be such a bad idea. But it is much more dangerous politically, because at least in the past, the Soviet Union has had tense relations with the United States and other grain-exporting countries.

Finally, there is another kind of agricultural dependence which, at least in the past, was a source of worry for Soviet leaders. It deals with the

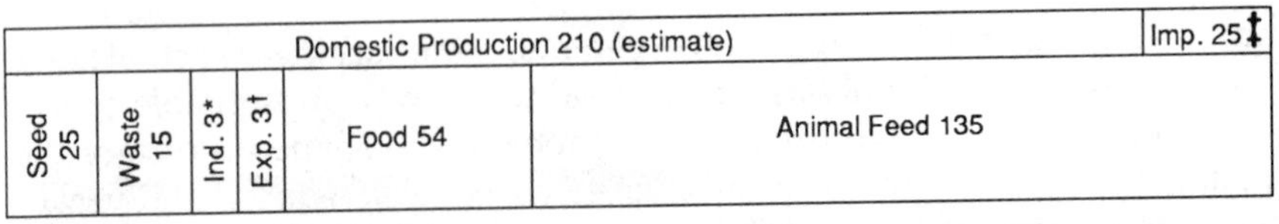

| Domestic Production 210 (estimate) | | | | | | Imp. 25‡ |
|---|---|---|---|---|---|---|
| Seed 25 | Waste 15 | Ind. 3* | Exp. 3† | Food 54 | Animal Feed 135 | |

*Industrial use—production of alcohol;
†Export—mainly wheat shipments to E. Europe;
‡Import—mainly coarse grain purchases from Argentina, Canada, and USA.

**FIGURE 6–1**    Estimated Grain Supply and Demand in the USSR (In Million Metric Tons). *Source:* Compiled by author from Soviet statistics.

individual plots of land assigned to collective farmers and state farm workers, which amount to quasi-private family businesses. The importance of their share of production has been disproportionate to their share of the land area, and, therefore, ideologically embarrassing.[8] Even according to Soviet statistics, the private sector accounts for very large portions of the total agricultural produce other than grain, potatoes, and sugar beet: eggs—33 percent; meat—29 percent; milk—29 percent; fruit—45 percent; vegetables—30 percent; and honey—50 percent.

Gorbachev's approach to this problem has been pragmatic: He simply redefined the term Socialism to include much of the quasi-private family farming on the grounds that the "means of production"—the land and heavy machinery—are only leased out to the farmers while legally remaining property of the state. How much fast relief this measure could bring to the protracted food crisis is uncertain at this time. Meanwhile, the Soviet Union continues to buy large quantities of food—mostly grain—abroad.

## TRANSPORTATION

The largest country in the world, the USSR has a relatively weak system of transportation, which is controlled by several ministries. Almost 75 percent of freight and passenger traffic is carried by a system of intensively used railroads, which includes the world's longest line, crossing most of Europe and all of Asia from Kaliningrad to Vladivostok (6,200 miles). The total railroad mileage, however, is less than 100,000 miles (compared to more than 200,000 miles in the United States). Several new railroads are currently under construction as part of an ambitious effort to develop further remote regions of Siberia, which are rich in natural

[8]Individual plots comprise less than 3 percent of the land currently under cultivation.

**TABLE 6–4**   Private Cars Per 100 People, 1986

| | |
|---|---|
| USSR–5 | USA–56 |
| (incl. Estonia–10 | France–36 |
| Lithuania–10 | England–33 |
| Tadjkistan–3) | Japan–22 |

*Source:* Compiled by author from Soviet statistics.

resources. The telephone system is poorly developed, serving only about 33 million instruments in the whole country.

Sea and river transportation is another important linkage between the great distances the Soviet Union spans across two continents, Europe and Asia. During the last sixty years, several canals have been built to connect the large river systems of the European USSR, and to thus enhance the use of inexpensive ways of hauling large amounts of cargo. The long rivers of Siberia are also being used increasingly as transportation channels for raw materials, fuel, lumber, and so on. The Soviet Union has a rapidly growing merchant fleet which serves the needs of both domestic and foreign economic activities. In Soviet foreign trade, more than 90 percent of shipping is done by ships flying the Soviet flag.

Gas and oil pipelines connect several major mineral fuel deposit sites to industrial centers in the USSR itself and in east Europe. New long-distance pipelines have been recently commissioned in the Asian part of the USSR. In all, pipelines extend for more than 200,000 kilometers.

Large cities, including Moscow, have extensive and efficient public transportation systems. Private cars, which only now are beginning to be produced in fairly large numbers,[9] are seldom used for commuting to work. As the USSR is just entering the automobile age, modern highways are few and far between, and most truck hauls involve relatively short distances. But a few years ago the Soviet Union commissioned *Kamaz*, the largest truck-manufacturing plant in the world, which was built with some Western help in the Tatar ASSR.

Air transportation is of special importance to a country as vast as the Soviet Union. It is provided by a single state-owned airline called Aeroflot, which operates some 2,500 jet airliners and flies more than 120 million passengers a year. The Soviet Union is one of very few countries in the world that manufactures large transport airplanes for both commercial and military uses. Aeroflot's fleet includes Soviet-built supersonic airliners.

---

[9]The USSR produces about 1.5 million passenger automobiles per year. Most of the auto vehicles manufactured in the USSR are trucks.

## BUILDING INDUSTRY

During almost the entire half-century of central planning, the building industry, which has been one of the busiest branches of the Soviet national economy, has concentrated chiefly on the construction of industrial projects. Only in the last two decades has more attention been given to the badly neglected housing needs of the fast-growing urban population. Although capital construction has been slowed, it is expected that by the end of the current five-year plan the overwhelming majority of urban families will live in small, private apartments consisting of two rooms, a kitchen, and a bath. At present, prefabricated, high-rise apartment buildings are rapidly replacing older buildings in which two or three generations of Soviet citizens had to be content with extremely crowded conditions and a communal way of life. Modest as it is by Western standards, this change marks an important milestone in the lives of a large number of ordinary Soviet citizens. For the more privileged members of society a larger, more comfortable, and attractive cooperative apartment is a realizable ambition today.[10] As part of the *perestroika*, residents of urban communities are being urged to build their own apartments in cooperative housing projects or individual homes. The best-known status symbol in the USSR today is to have a summer cottage or *dacha* in the country, in addition to having a city apartment.

The building industry, which currently employs approximately 11 million people, including many women, consists of large and small state-owned companies specializing in different types of construction: industrial plants, roads, bridges, and housing. Operating under annual and five-year plans, such companies undertake construction jobs required by various branches of the national economy. The allocation of building materials is also controlled and rationed. Exceptionally large construction projects may establish temporary companies to take care of their special needs. For example, a number of construction teams were put together to work on one of the most ambitious road building projects of the Soviet era, which was recently completed in east Siberia. It is called BAM (the Baikal-Amur Mainline) and its purpose is to provide a second railroad connecting the trans-Baikal region with the Far East. The road had to go through extremely mountainous terrain. Along with the construction of the road, new settlements were built with service and industrial facilities. This difficult and very costly project, 3,200 km. long, is of great economic and strategic importance. The former concerns the exploitation of Siberia's resources and the latter China's proximity to the Soviet Far East. The road is already open for traffic. Now the USSR and PRC (China) are jointly building a new railroad link between the two countries.

[10]In Moscow, a one-bedroom cooperative apartment costs about 10,000 rubles. Required down payment is one third.

Several other large construction projects are also under way in the USSR. Some of them are nearing completion, whereas others extend beyond the Twelfth Five-Year Plan. New gas and oil pipelines, including those connecting Siberia with west Europe gas pipelines, are under construction. But with the shift of emphasis from quantity to quality and from extensive to intensive use of the physical plant, demands on the building industry are decreasing.

The building industry is managed by several ministries and lesser bureaucracies. The overall control and coordination of these agencies are the responsibility of a senior vice chairman of the USSR Council of Ministers.

## FINANCIAL SYSTEM

The Marxist vision of the future promises the abolition of money. Today, money is still much in use in the Soviet Union, but Soviet currency differs in several respects from the traditional norm. First of all, the Soviet ruble is strictly an internal currency that may not be legally taken in or out of the country. Soviet foreign trade transactions outside the Socialist system of states are usually calculated in U.S. dollars, and foreigners, such as tourists and businesspersons, who need to have rubles for internal use in the Soviet Union must purchase them from Soviet banks at fixed rates of exchange. (Much higher prices for hard currency are usually offered by the black market.) Second, and more important from the point of view of ordinary Soviet citizens, the nominal value of money is drastically reduced by the chronic scarcity of available goods. Consequently, second-hand items, including cars, often cost more than new, comparable items because the latter, being in short supply, are either immediately sold out or must be ordered for future delivery long in advance. At present, the waiting time for a new car is about four years. Third, the purchasing power of Soviet money depends on the status of the purchaser. For example, one of the problems of knowing the real size of the Soviet military budget is that in the Soviet economic system wholesale prices for such industrial commodities as rolled steel and pig iron depend on which industry is buying them. By the same token, special retail stores in which better-quality consumer goods sell at discount prices cater only to selected groups of privileged Soviet citizens, while others are stuck with so-called "empty rubles"—excess money which cannot be spent meaningfully because of a lack of opportunity.[11]

Fourth, it is illegal in the Soviet Union to use money as profit-producing capital. There are very few investment opportunities such as funds. Citizens, however, are encouraged to maintain interest-bearing savings accounts (2 percent for regular, 4 percent for five-year certificates) in state banks and to

[11]Under Gorbachev, this condition has been improving.

buy state-loan bonds and lottery tickets. Finally, many commodities and services simply cannot be bought with money, either because they are not available for sale (such as private planes, fancy foreign cars, enrollment in better schools, or land), or because they are not distributed through regular commercial channels (such as trips abroad, accommodations in resort hotels, or chauffeur-driven limousines). On the other hand, such things as education, medical services, and dental care are free. Certain other services and goods are heavily subsidized and available at nominal cost: day-care centers, summer camps, housing, utilities, public transportation, publications, entertainment, and staple foods.

All this does not make money unimportant in the life of the average Soviet breadwinner, but the function of the ruble is perhaps more comparable to ration coupons or food stamps than to money in the West. The "empty rubles" represent a special kind of national debt: goods and services that the economy owes to consumers because of its protracted failures to deliver on time. It is estimated that such forced savings come to about 1,000 rubles for every person.

The Soviet monetary system is run by the union-republic Ministry of Finances and a network of state banks that take care of various transactions involving official organizations and enterprises. Private citizens, on the other hand, deal only in cash; individual checking accounts are virtually unknown, and buying on credit is limited to certain durables.

The ministry prepares the annual state budgets that operate as part of the five-year development plans. The main sources of revenue are the profits of state enterprises and indirect taxes on manufactured goods (called "turnover tax"). The personal income tax, which is quite low, brings in less than 10 percent of the revenue. As a rule, budgetary expenditures are listed under very general categories. Nevertheless, the published expenditure pattern holds the key to many seeming mysteries of the Soviet national economy: Successes and failures are directly traceable to generous and skimpy investments, respectively. In 1988, it was admitted for the first time that the state budget could not always be balanced. The budget for 1989 included a projected deficit of 36 billion rubles (7 percent of the total budget) blamed on mismanagement, lingering aftermaths of the Chernobyl nuclear disaster, and lower oil prices.

## WAGES AND PRICES

Because the Soviet state is concurrently the employer, supplier, and banker of its citizens, it can achieve the desired pattern of income distribution by manipulating any of the three leverages: salaries, prices, or taxes. The choice is usually between the first and the second of these options.

Historically, three different combinations of salary-price policies have been used. Until 1947, the policy was inflation of the ruble by a rapid rise of retail prices combined with a slower climb of salaries. This was accompanied by chronic shortages of goods leading to the accumulation of large amounts of almost useless rubles in the hands of Soviet citizens. A monetary reform wiped out much of these "forced savings."

From 1948 to 1954, there were annual reductions of retail prices while salaries remained unchanged with the exception of some upward adjustments for the low-paid categories of workers and employees. Beginning in 1955, the policy has been to keep the same retail prices but to grant periodic salary increases as a more effective way to demonstrate the improvement of living standards. During this period the work week has been gradually reduced to the present average of forty hours.

This purely material incentive is reinforced by all kinds of symbolic rewards such as medals, honors, titles, publicity, and constant appeals to patriotism and ideological commitment. The emphasis, however, is on cash payments on the basis of Socialist distribution, "to each according to his work."

Except for the early period immediately after the revolution (until 1931), different wages have been paid for different "quantities and qualities of work." This has resulted in a wage structure that generally favors persons with executive and professional skills. Since the introduction of the minimum wage in 1956, systematic efforts have been made to narrow the salary spread by raising the wages of the people on the bottom. At present, the minimum cash wage for state employees is about 100 rubles per month, and the average salary is about twice that amount. High salaries are 400 to 500 rubles per month. The maximum wage, assuming that there is such a fixed limit, has never been made public. It is believed that several thousand top-ranking party and government functionaries make about 1,000 rubles per month. Leading scientists probably command comparable salaries, and a few of the most successful intellectuals, such as writers and poets, may be outdoing everybody else. On the opposite end of the scale are millions of collective farmers; remember, however, that they are expected to earn additional income from their private plots. The minimum pension for a retired state employee and a collective farmer is 60 rubles and 40 rubles per month, respectively. On the average, old age pensions are approximately one third of the individual's former earning (wages or salaries).

Fringe benefits are estimated to be 30 percent over and above a worker's cash income, which brings the average compensation of a state employee to about 270 rubles per month. The fringe benefits, called Social Consumption Funds, include free education, medical and dental care, social security, paid vacations, and various other public services that are completely or partly subsidized by the state and made available to all on a supposedly equal basis. Actually, members of the privileged class enjoy many extra free benefits: access to chauffeured cars, country homes, exclusive clubs, and special clinics.

During the last two or three decades, a steady rise of wages, particularly those in lower brackets, has been slowly narrowing the income gap. During the same time period, the state has kept retail prices for essentials—staple foods, rent, utilities, transportation, and others—at a low level, often below cost. Official price increases have affected only so-called luxury items.[12]

The insistence on maintaining artificially low retail prices and relatively uniform salaries and wages is directly responsible for the existence of special stores and other privileges enjoyed by select groups of Soviet citizens, which cannot be effectively hidden behind the façade of egalitarianism. For ideological reasons, this arrangement is preferred to letting the price-wage structure more fully reflect the relative scarcity of goods. In theory, everybody can afford to buy everything. However, in practice, because of the scarcity of goods, only the privileged have the opportunity to do so in their special stores.

As mentioned, a reform of wages and prices is very high on Gorbachev's wish list. He is trying to make earnings and prices reflect more accurately the actual economic value and cost of services and goods produced. This measure is supposed to eventually affect the bulk of both wholesale and retail prices. Here the Gorbachev regime faces a potentially very serious political problem because the state subsidies for basic foods, housing, and utilities constitute an essential component of the unwritten social contract under Soviet socialism.

Gorbachev's promotion of cooperatives has created a second level of consumer economy with higher prices for goods and services these new ventures produce, and higher rates of income tax for quasi-private businessmen who operate them. This dichotomy is blamed for an increase of a peculiarly Soviet variety of creeping inflation (7 percent in 1989) caused by chronic shortages of less expensive (subsidized) goods and services.

## DOMESTIC TRADE

The main mechanism for the distribution of food and consumer goods in the Soviet Union is a network of state and cooperative retail stores and eating establishments. This sector of the national economy employs approximately 8 percent of the entire labor force and is supervised by the union-republic Ministry of Trade and a number of lesser agencies. By Western standards, Soviet stores and restaurants offer limited selections of poor quality goods.

[12]Included in this category are jewelry, hard liquor, tobacco, cars, furs, and many other consumer goods.

The availability of even the most basic staples is erratic, the service slow, and the prices for many consumer goods quite high. Despite oft-repeated promises to give a higher priority to retail trade, for ordinary Soviet citizens daily shopping continues to be a time-consuming and tiring chore. Standing in lines and being satisfied with a monotonous diet are especially common for consumers in provincial towns and cities.

According to official statistics, food accounts for about one half of all sales in state and cooperative stores. This ratio is slowly declining while the volume of sales is increasing. There is no indication, however, that the trend has so far seriously diminished the importance of another source of food and supply in small and large Soviet communities: the collective farmers' market in which peasants as individuals and as groups (collective farms) are allowed to sell their produce directly to consumers at prices determined largely by supply and demand. As a rule, prices at farmers' markets are higher than those posted in retail stores for produce that is similar, but is of lower quality and uncertain availability. Because of the shortcomings of the state trade system, these markets thrive. Published Soviet surveys admit that these outlets of semiprivate trade account for 25 to 30 percent of all foods sold. But well-informed foreign observers' estimates are considerably higher. In part, this discrepancy may exist because the markets are used by both individual farmers and collective farms, the latter of which are not included in Soviet statistics.

Collective farmers' markets have counterparts dealing in factory-made consumer goods. The visible portion of this enclave of private commerce includes consignment stores, swap shops, and "flea markets" ostensibly trading only in secondhand items, but actually also offering (at a premium) new things obtained through connections.

Traditionally, it is here that people who can afford exorbitant prices and who are willing to take certain risks can get in touch with black marketeers dealing in various luxuries, including new foreign imports, detoured or stolen goods of domestic origin in critically short supply, valuable antiques, and collector's items. The black market even buys and sells foreign currencies. The existence of the black market is not necessarily proof that the official system, which is supposed to provide for the material needs of the people, is not working well. But it is nevertheless embarrassing for the regime.

No less embarrassing and therefore just as thoroughly concealed is the existence of special stores catering exclusively to members of the Soviet power elite. In a sense, these comprise a kind of black market in reverse, because they provide the privileged individuals and their families with foods and consumer goods of better quality at discount prices. Such special stores, without display windows and signs, are operating in all Soviet administrative centers from Moscow down. In the spirit of *glasnost*, this

TABLE 6–5 Some Prices in State Stores, 1986 (In Rubles)

| | | | |
|---|---|---|---|
| Cafeteria meal | 0.75–1.25 | | |
| Cigarettes (20) | 0.30 | Ready-made man's suit | 100.00 |
| Beer (mug) | 0.22 | Tailor-made man's suit | 150.00 |
| Coffee (cup) | 0.08 | | |
| Bread (lb.) | 0.06–0.12 | Movie theater tickets: | |
| Potatoes (lb.) | 0.05 | day | 0.25 |
| Sugar (lb.) | 0.44 | evening | 0.40 |
| Haircut (man's) | 0.50 | children | 0.10 |
| Beef (lb.) | 1.00 | Transportation fares: | |
| Butter (lb.) | 1.50 | bus | 0.05 |
| Milk (ltr.) | 0.25 | metro | 0.05 |
| Vodka (ltr.) | 9.50–10.50 | monthly pass for metro | 3.00 |
| Newspaper | 0.03–0.05 | monthly pass for all | 6.00 |
| Pay telephone call | 0.02 | | |

Source: Compiled by author from Soviet data.

practice is being exposed and denounced in the mass media, and at least the more flagrant and demonstrative economic privileges of the party elite have been eliminated or reduced. And, as a stopgap measure, food packages are now being made available to the white- and blue-collar workers alike at selected enterprises.

Cities frequented by foreign visitors also have exclusive stores in which anyone who has hard currencies from Western countries can purchase better-quality Soviet goods at prices much closer to the rate of exchange offered in the black market than to that prevailing in Soviet state banks. They also offer much more selection. The same is true about the newly opened cooperative and quasi-private outlets for retail trade such as stores, street vendors, and coffee shops. But their prices in rubles are very high compared to those charged by state enterprises.

The current five-year plan is supposed to make the life of Soviet consumers easier by providing for the construction of larger and better stores, including self-service supermarkets. The actual improvement appears to be quite slow and modest. The chronic uncertainty of supply leads to overbuying and hoarding that further aggravate shortages.

## LIVING STANDARDS

The cash income of more than 100 million Soviet citizens working for the state consists of wages, usually paid twice a month in cash, and such related compensation as bonuses, various differentials, child-support subsidies, per diem allowances, and so on. Members of collective farms and other cooperatives receive compensation based on the profit realized by their enterprises. Farmers also make profits from their individual plots. A large majority of full-time college and vocational school students receives stipends, and a growing number of retired persons receives pensions.

To get a taste of Soviet life, let us imagine a hypothetical case of an urban family of five—parents, two children, and a grandmother—living in Moscow. To justify their better-than-average income, let us assume that the husband and wife are in their thirties; both hold semiprofessional jobs outside the home; their young children already attend school; and the children's grandmother is retired. Their monthly income, then, consists of two, better-than-average salaries and a pension, and totals 550 rubles. Out of this sum they pay a low income tax of 30 rubles (about 7 percent) and a small charge of 20 rubles (4 to 5 percent) for their modest apartment and utilities. They pay 4 rubles for labor union membership (we assume they are not party members), about 12 rubles on inexpensive public transportation (their children walk to school), and approximately 60 rubles on lunches and pocket money. Basic foods for a family of five cost about 260 rubles per month. Their daily diet is quite nutritious—about 3,300 calories—but monotonous and heavy on starch. It costs them almost 60 percent of their budget (including the "lunch money").

By now our hypothetical family has spent more than three fourths of its budget: 30 + 20 + 4 + 12 + 60 + 260 = 386. They are left with less than 170 rubles to cover all other expenses: the purchase and repair of clothing, shoes, household appliances, furniture, and other manufactured goods. All such things cost at least as many rubles in Russia as dollars in the United States. In other words, Soviet citizens not only receive less money than their American counterparts, but on a one-to-one basis the ruble has no more purchasing power than the dollar when it comes to manufactured goods. Only basic foods—bread, milk, potatoes, sugar—cost less in rubles than what they cost in dollars.

In addition, prices for slightly fancier foods are higher in the USSR than in the United States. On the other hand, books, magazines, and tickets to theaters and sports events are quite inexpensive. When balanced out, the purchasing power of the ruble and dollar is approximately the same. This means that even if we add the official cash value of the fringe benefits (30 percent) to the combined salaries of our Soviet family, their monthly income will be 665 rubles or about $1,000. Although an accurate comparison is very difficult, the best estimates put the overall living standards in the Soviet Union at between one half and one third of those in the United States.[13] This gap is slowly decreasing.

Average Soviet breadwinners, who are more likely to compare their living standards of today with those of yesterday, know that for the last four

[13]A comparison between the USSR and the United States is possible only in rough quantitative terms. The quality of U.S. goods and services is much higher than anything generated by the Soviet economy.

**BOX 6–2**   *Soviet Underground Humor*

> Question:     What are the labor-management relations in the USSR?
> Answer:       We pretend that we work, and they pretend that they pay.

decades their real income has been going up by a small percent every year, a modest but steady improvement. They also know that although prices have remained almost unchanged, there has been a change for the better in the quality of consumer goods and services. The official propaganda, which they do not entirely trust, promises them an even better tomorrow with bigger salaries and an increasingly larger number of free goods and services. But what they do know for sure is that their generation already enjoys the highest living standards in Soviet—and Russian—history and that conditions are slowly but steadily improving all the time. They and their families are also quite unconcerned about their economic security in years to come: They have no great need to save for the rainy day, and no fear of unemployment. In fact, before too long there may even be a shortage of labor in the USSR.

## LABOR FORCE

From the point of view of labor resources, the population of the Soviet Union in 1989 consisted of the following categories (in round figures):

|   |   |   |
|---|---|---|
| A. | Persons employed full time in the national economy | 139,000,000 |
| B. | Dependents of persons in Category A | 95,000,000 |
| C. | Nonworking persons subsidized by the state | 55,000,000 |

Category A represents approximately 46 percent of the total population, or 82 percent of the work-age portion of that total. The number of full-time employees has been growing during the last several years.

The labor force (Category A) consists of some 106 million blue-collar workers, including peasants, and about 33 million white-collar workers. Approximately one fifth of the entire labor force is still employed in agriculture. Slightly less than three fourths of the labor force is engaged in the production of material goods; only one fourth produces services. This ratio is, however, slowly changing in favor of the service sector.

Categories B and C consist of dependent children, housewives, retirees, invalids, full-time students, members of the armed forces (estimated at 4 million), and some prisoners. All of these groups of people contribute only marginally to the labor force: They do, for example, seasonal work, part-time jobs, and special construction projects.

Because of the relatively low rate of population growth, the annual supply of the new labor force is already insufficient to replace the retirees on a one-to-one basis. But the incoming workers will be better educated and trained to work with modern equipment. Moreover, there are considerable "hidden reserves" of labor within the Soviet national economy itself in the form of low labor productivity, overstaffing, and general inefficiency. The big question is whether or not this potential will be realized in time to avoid possible labor force shortages.

As a result of the ongoing effort to retool and modernize Soviet industries, approximately 20 million manual jobs are expected to disappear by the end of this decade. This would allow a major shift of the labor force to the service sector by 2000. The military personnel may be further reduced to increase the labor pool and help with vacancies (2 million in 1989).

It is unlikely, on the other hand, that the Soviet leaders would try to expand the labor force by simply raising the retirement ages, which are currently quite low: 60 for men and 55 for women. But a way probably could be found to encourage more retired people to do part-time, seasonal, or even regular full-time work. About 8 million—one out of every seven—retirees hold full-time jobs. It is estimated that for the rest of this century, approximately 15 million workers would have to be dislocated and moved. New cooperatives are supposed to absorb many of these people.

A major labor problem facing the Soviet leadership concerns the relocation of new industries in Siberia and other sparsely populated parts of the country. Better incentive programs, offering higher pay and extra fringe benefits, are being worked out to induce people to go to these areas and to stay there long enough to justify the considerable transportation and relocation expenses. As we know, the fastest growing components of the population are the ethnic minorities of Central Asia. These people, as a rule, do not like to relocate from their traditional habitats, creating pockets of rural overpopulation and "temporarily unemployed" workers (4 million in 1989).

Another major labor problem has to do with poor labor ethics, which cause absenteeism, tardiness, negligence, low labor productivity, and similar practices. The urgency of this problem is intimated by Gorbachev's effort to make it the number one priority of his administration. In one of his public speeches, Gorbachev made it very clear that low labor productivity is at the root of the poor economic performance and living conditions: "We live the way we work, no better and no worse."[14]

The principle of electing enterprise directors and other managerial personnel from slates of eligible candidates is now widely used in various branches of the national economy. Vacancies and job requirements are advertised in the mass media and the applicants are asked to appear before search committees and general personnel meetings. Secret ballots are used

[14]*US News and World Report,* September 22, 1989, p. 33.

to choose among the finalists subject to approval by the appropriate state and party authorities.

## "UNDERGROUND ECONOMICS"

The seamy side of the Soviet economy is not limited to the already-mentioned black and gray markets and special stores and other facilities for the privileged groups, which make economic inequality much more pronounced than is officially admitted and reflected in the salary scale. The chronic scarcity of goods and services has produced a high degree of public tolerance to numerous forms of petty (and sometimes not so petty) corruption and profiteering practiced by practically everyone in the country. Called by an untranslatable world, *blat*, this type of economic activity ranges from the exchange of favors among various officials to outright bribes, and from epidemic pilferage by blue-collar workers to the padding of expense accounts by their white-collar colleagues. Although incessant propaganda and written laws emphasize the sanctity of public property, the average Soviet citizen appears to be much less likely to commit a crime against private property belonging to his or her peers than to take illegal advantage of opportunities offered by his or her public job.

For several decades, free-lance artisans, called *shabashniki* (moonlighters), have been rendering various services in short supply: automobile repairs, housepainting, plumbing, and others. More often than not, they use for their private projects tools and materials diverted from the state-owned shops. The annual "take" (untaxed income) generated by such activities has been estimated at about one billion rubles.

A uniquely Soviet kind of economic wheeling and dealing provides badly needed lubrication for the central-planning mechanism. Every major enterprise has to watch its staff. Usually called "special assistants," these watchmen are professional troubleshooters whose jobs are to find ways to compensate for the inevitable inadequacies of the planners. The troubleshooters, known as "pushers," improvise on a grand scale swaps of supplies, spare parts, equipment, and other under-the-counter deals—all for the sake of fulfilling the plan. For a long time, one of the paradoxes of the Soviet

**BOX 6–3**  *The Strange Ways of Soviet Economics*

A second-hand Soviet car often costs more than a new one. Reason: The former car is available for immediate delivery, whereas the waiting time for the latter may be years.

A winning state lottery ticket can be sold on the black market for much more than the amount won. Reason: People with illegally amassed cash seek ways to "legitimize" the spending of their fortunes.

**BOX 6–4**   *Soviet Underground Humor*

| | |
|---|---|
| Question: | What would happen if central planning were to be used in the Sahara Desert? |
| Answer: | Nothing during the first few years, but then an acute shortage of sand would develop. |
| | |
| Question: | What is alive, 100 meters long, and feeds on potatoes? |
| Answer: | A line of shoppers in front of a meat shop in Moscow. |
| | |
| Question: | What is Soviet Socialism? |
| Answer: | It is the longest way from capitalism to capitalism. |
| | |
| Question: | Under capitalism man exploits man. How is it under Socialism? |
| Answer: | Under Socialism the situation is reversed. |

economy has been that its central planning seems to work only with the aid of various unplanned and even illegal measures.

Periodically the Soviet leadership has launched public campaigns against selected varieties of economic abuses and corruption. The mass media supports such campaigns with avalanches of factual data. Yet not much changes. Just as the collective agriculture continues to depend to a certain degree on the auxiliary engine of private farming, so the entire Soviet economy appears to be in constant need of stimuli that the official system cannot provide.

Gorbachev and his team are using a twofold approach to this unwelcome inheritance: On the one hand, they have decriminalized many such activities as moonlighting; on the other hand, they have cracked down on various types of official corruption. They must realize, however, that in the long run a lasting solution to this problem would not be possible without a substantial improvement in the Soviet economy's performance.

On the borderline of legality are various promotional inducements widely used throughout the Soviet economy to increase productivity and efficiency. In the past, they included almost obligatory end-of-year bonuses, the so-called thirteenth-month pay, and various prizes for alleged overfulfillments of production quotas that made everybody look good—including, of course, the management. The new administration is doing away with economic abuses of this kind.

## FOREIGN TRADE

For the first three decades of its existence, the Soviet Union did not often exercise its state monopoly on foreign trade. The Soviet Union was a pariah

BOX 6–5    *A Tale of Two Factories (An almost true story)*

There is a Soviet town with two factories; the Marx Hemp Fiber Factory and the Lenin Rope Factory. For many years, the two socialist enterprises have fulfilled and overfulfilled their production plans earning high honors and medals. Mysteriously, there has never been any rope to buy in the town's stores.

The mystery was finally solved when *glasnost* revealed that all rope produced by the Lenin Rope Factory is being shipped to the Marx Hemp Fiber Factory to be used there as a raw material for making hemp fibers. It is hoped that *perestroika* would reverse this peculiar production process, but first it must overcome the resistance of the conservatives at both factories who argue that it is easier to make hemp fibers by unweaving rope and make rope which can be used for this purpose regardless of its quality.

In the meantime, there still is no rope in the town's stores.

Compiled by author from Soviet underground humor.

of the international business community, which was angered by the new regime's flat refusal to honor Russia's World War I debts. During most of the Stalin era, "building Socialism in one country" meant trying to develop a national autarchy, with complete economic independence from the outside world, which at that time was called "capitalist encirclement." Major departures from this go-it-alone economic policy occurred at the very beginning of the big industrialization effort, when factory equipment had to be purchased abroad, and in the course of World War II, when large quantities of military and economic aid were sent to the embattled Soviet Union by its Western allies.

After the war, east Europe, Finland, North Korea, and, later, China were brought into the Soviet economic orbit, but the idea of isolation continued to prevail. In 1949, the USSR and its east European dependencies formed the Council for Mutual Economic Assistance (CMEA)[15] in a move designed to counteract the Marshall Plan, in which they refused to participate. Under this arrangement, the national economies of several Communist countries have been thoroughly integrated and tied to the Soviet economy. Together these countries constitute the USSR's largest trading partner.

Only after Stalin's death, when "peaceful coexistence" became Moscow's new policy, was there a marked change in the Soviet view of trade and business relations with non-Socialist countries. In the 1960s, the Soviet Union embarked on an economic offensive that included stepped-up trade with the West and Japan and a number of economic-aid projects in Third

---

[15]In the West, the Council for Mutual Economic Assistance is often called "Comecon." Its full members are the USSR, Bulgaria, Cuba, Czechoslovakia, East Germany, Hungary, Mongolia, Poland, Romania, and Vietnam.

World countries. The upward trend continued into the 1970s, and from 1970 to 1975 the volume of Soviet foreign trade doubled. In part, this was accomplished by huge deals involving Western countries, such as the well-publicized construction of an automobile factory in the USSR by the Italian Fiat Company. However, until 1979, more than one half of Soviet foreign trade was with the CMEA and other Socialist countries, and the total trade with the West and Japan accounted for only 35 percent. During the 1980s, there has been a modest increase in trade and business relations with the West and Japan. But even if the current volume of trade should be doubled, which appears unlikely in view of the continuing political tensions, the Soviet Union's imports from these countries would account for no more than 2 or 3 percent of its GNP—not enough to make the country vulnerable to economic sanctions.[16]

The Soviet Union's exports consist mainly of raw materials: oil, coal, metal ores, mineral fertilizers, lumber, and gold. Industrial products included in Soviet exports are limited primarily to weapons and some agricultural machines. In exchange, the USSR imports machine tools, computers, electronic equipment, and even whole industrial projects such as truck factories, gas pipelines, and steel mills. Often, this is done in cooperation with foreign firms and with credit secured abroad. Foreign equipment, capital, and technological know-how are considered desirable but not absolutely essential to the advancement of the Soviet economy. For the last several years, annual Soviet trade with the West has shown a small deficit due to the falling prices of the two major items of export, gold and oil. But Moscow's "strategic reserves" are estimated at $35 billion.

In the past, consumer goods had the same low priority in Soviet foreign trade as in the national economy in general and were not imported in large amounts, except in cases of dire necessity, such as serious agricultural failures. Limited reserves of foreign currencies and gold were spent primarily, if not exclusively, on the "production of means of production." As a rule, Soviet imports from the West were aimed at eliminating temporary deficiencies in the national economy, rather than at establishing a long-lasting dependency on foreign trade, which was unacceptable on ideological grounds.

The likelihood of extensive borrowing in the West to finance *perestroika* is rather slim because it would still be considered too much of a political gamble. But the Gorbachev administration is trying to expand business contacts with the West and Japan and make it more attractive for foreign capital to invest in joint enterprises operating in the USSR. Laws have been changed to facilitate such ventures. As a temporary stopgap measure, the USSR may start to import large amounts of consumer goods.

[16]In 1986 Soviet trade with the West (including the United States) and Japan was only about 1.5 percent of the USSR's GNP.

**TABLE 6–6**    Cooperative Business Under Gorbachev

|  | 1988 (January) | 1989 (January) |
| --- | --- | --- |
| Urban cooperatives | 23,000 | 48,500 |
| Coop labor force | 300,000 | 800,000 |
| Proportion of all retail trade and services | 0.1% | 0.83% |

*Source:* Soviet statistics

## ECONOMICS AND IDEOLOGY

Marx's contention that economics is the "base" that shapes and determines the ideological "superstructure" implied his criticism of free-market societies. It is, therefore, not surprising that in the Soviet Union this relationship has been reversed: Economics, like everything else, has been subordinated to the ideology of Marxism-Leninism.[17] The main ideological feature of the Soviet national economy is the official ban on large-scale private business, which is condemned as both illegal and immoral. On the Soviet scale of values, self-interest comes close to being equated with greed, whereas concern for the common welfare, as it is defined by Soviet leaders, is held to be the highest virtue. For purely ideological reasons, it is also taken for granted that, in establishing economic priorities, "scientific" central planning is far superior to the supply-and-demand process—though the latter is now taken into consideration.

As a mechanism for the production and distribution of material goods and services, the Soviet state-owned and centrally planned national economy has both relative advantages and disadvantages. Among the advantages is, first of all, the demonstrated ability of the Soviet Union to achieve and maintain steady economic growth. It is this characteristic that makes the Soviet economic model so attractive to many Third World leaders. Other advantages of the Soviet economy include its ability to avoid wasteful overproduction, costly advertising, and disruptive labor disputes; to ensure full employment and a more rational use of resources; to control inflation; and to achieve and promote a greater degree of economic equality. So far, the Soviet national economy has been depression-proof.[18]

Many serious shortcomings exist because the Soviet economic system rests on theoretical assumptions of what people, in their roles as producers and consumers, should be, rather than what they actually are. Other problems relate to the Marxist notion of social values. Most prominent among these shortcomings are such tendencies as a lack of personal initiative, low labor productivity, poor quality and a limited selection of goods, and bu-

---

[17]In Lenin's words: "Politics cannot but have primacy over economics."

[18]Although it became stagnated under Brezhnev.

reaucratic red tape. Furthermore, there can be little doubt that the economic system, which denies free choice, negatively affects the individual rights and freedoms of the Soviet people in general. In this sense, economics does influence ideology. Ultimately, the USSR's ideological legitimacy depends on the success of Soviet economics.

The ideology is behind the Soviet ordering of such economic priorities as forced reinvestment and development over consumption, industry over agriculture, and heavy industries over consumer goods production. All of this was and still is considered essential for building Communism. Any future reforms affecting the structure and operation of the economy that are or may be undertaken by Gorbachev or even his successors are likely to occur within certain ideological constraints. However, Gorbachev has already demonstrated that the ideology can be quite elastic.

For decades, one of the main functions of Soviet propaganda was to conceal, explain away, or minimize the liabilities of the national economy while taking maximum advantage of all its positive aspects. *Glasnost* has changed that by coming up with a more balanced score sheet. But even today, when celebrating Soviet economic achievements, the official media tend to give too much credit to Marxism-Leninism as a "guiding force" and to ignore the numerous natural assets of the huge nation that made these accomplishments possible. By the same token, some Western observers are quick to blame Communist ideology for even natural disasters that periodically befall the Soviet national economy. Over the last seventy years, there have been frequent, and so far unfulfilled, predictions of an imminent collapse of the Soviet economic system because of its dependence on ideological tenets.

To the degree that the Soviet Union is in a state of ideological war against the capitalist world, the Soviet national economy is a "war economy." From the point of view of Marxism, it is the economic sphere that will ultimately decide the historic contest between capitalism and Socialism (Communism). The contest is obviously far from being over. But it is just as obvious that the position of the Soviet economy vis-à-vis the West has not been improving. Today, the Soviet promise to "catch up with and surpass America" is still very far from its goal.

The new Soviet leader's apparent pragmatism on economic matters has very real ideological limitations. Gorbachev is quoted admonishing in 1986 a group of visiting East European officials:

> Some of you look at the [free] market as a lifesaver for your economies. But, comrades, you should not think about lifesavers but about the ship, and the ship is Socialism."[19]

---

[19]Quoted in *Newsweek*, March 3, 1986, p. 45.

Since then, most East Europeans have, indeed, abandoned their flimsy vessels. But the ship of soviet Socialism, with Gorbachev at the helm, is still afloat and, according to its skipper, is about to regain full speed through tighter labor discipline, better management, and accelerated development of modern science and technology—the topic of the next chapter.

## GLOSSARY

**Aeroflot:** the Soviet airline.
**Agroprom:** agro-industrial complex.
**Artel:** cooperative.
**Blat:** illegal dealings.
**Combine:** group of industrial enterprises.
**Comecon:** Council for Mutual Economic Assistance (CMEA). Established in 1949.
**Gosplan:** state planning authority.
**Kolkhoz:** collective farm.
**NEP:** New Economic Policy during the 1920s.
**Ruble:** Soviet currency (1 ruble = 100 kopecks); official exchange 1 ruble = $1.64.
**Shabashnik:** free-lance artisan, moonlighter.
**Socialist emulation:** "friendly competition."
**Sovkhoz:** Soviet state farm.

## RECOMMENDED READINGS

BERGSON, ABRAM, and HERBERT S. LEVINE (eds.), *The Soviet Economy: Toward the Year 2000.* Winchester, MA: Allen and Unwin, 1983.
WALKER, MARTIN, *Waking Giant: Gorbachev's Russia.* New York: Pantheon, 1987.
NOVE, ALEC, *The Soviet Economic System* (3rd ed.). Winchester, MA: Allen and Unwin, 1986.

# CHAPTER

# 7

# SCIENCE
# AND TECHNOLOGY

## SCIENTIFIC ESTABLISHMENT

Behind the impressive, although uneven, development of the Soviet economy stands the world's largest scientific complex, consisting of approximately 3,000 research institutes and several more thousand experimental laboratories and field stations. Staffed with 4 million scientists and technical personnel, this vast, highly centralized, regimented, state-owned enterprise is run in accordance with the five-year plans. Its objective is to provide a cutting edge for the development of the national economy. Currently, almost all areas of human knowledge and technology are being probed, investigated, and perfected in one or several Soviet research and development facilities that, on the whole, are well funded. One out of every four scientists in the world is a Soviet citizen.

The overall quality of the vast Soviet scientific effort does not, however, live up to the standards of that of advanced Western countries. This is especially true of those areas of scientific endeavor that have low political priority. But in selected fields deemed vital to the national security, Soviet science and technology have repeatedly demonstrated their ability to achieve spectacular results. For example, it was chiefly owing to their own efforts, rather than to the exploits of superspies or the forced labor of captured German scientists, that Soviet researchers and engineers managed to produce an atomic bomb as early as 1949, much earlier than was thought possible, and to launch the first artificial satellite, the famous Sputnik, in 1957, stunning the world at large.

Like everything else in the USSR, its scientific establishment operates under an elaborate system of political controls, a situation that occasionally has been responsible for serious failures. For example, during the Stalin era, research in traditional genetics and cybernetics was almost completely abandoned for purely ideological reasons.[1] As a result, the Soviet Union is still lagging behind in these two fields. Simultaneously, however, the same political controls were instrumental in encouraging Soviet researchers to make significant advances in other fields, thus giving the Soviet scientific landscape a highly uneven character. In the much more rational climate that distinguishes the contemporary USSR from that of the Stalin era, there is very little political interference with actual research in such fields as physics, engineering, chemistry, or mathematics. And just as before, the development of science and technology continues to receive full political support.

By all evidence, the quality of Soviet science in general is improving, and the number of areas of demonstrated excellence is growing. But there are also many problems that remain unsolved, and prominent among them is the contradiction between ideological constraints and the freedom of

**TABLE 7–1**  Famous Russian Scientists (Before 1917)

| Name | Dates | Scientific Field |
| --- | --- | --- |
| Mikhail Lomonosov | 1711–1765 | Mechanics, linguistics, chemistry, physics |
| Nicholai Lobachevsky | 1792–1856 | Mathematics |
| Nicholai Karamzin | 1766–1826 | Historiography |
| Nicholai Pirogov | 1810–1881 | Medicine |
| Alexander Mozhaisky | 1825–1890 | Aerodynamics |
| Ivan Sechenov | 1829–1905 | Physiology |
| Dmitri Mendeleev | 1834–1907 | Chemistry |
| Vasili Klyuchevsky | 1841–1911 | Historiography |
| Kliment Timiryazev | 1843–1920 | Botany, physiology |
| Ilya Mechnikov | 1845–1916 | Biology, biochemistry |
| Vasili Dokuchaev | 1846–1903 | Geosciences |
| Pyotr Yablochkov | 1847–1894 | Physics, electricity |
| Nikolai Zhukovsky | 1847–1921 | Aerodynamics |
| Ivan Pavlov | 1849–1936 | Physiology, psychology |
| Konstantin Tsiolkovsky | 1855–1935 | Aerospace dynamics |
| Alexander Popov | 1859–1906 | Physics, radio |

*Source:* Compiled by author from Soviet data.

[1]Traditional genetics was declared to be too slow to produce desired results in agriculture. It was replaced by a "new" genetics championed by Stalin's favorite, Trofim Lysenko, who posited that gross anatomical changes acquired in a parent generation would be passed on genetically. Lysenko's theory of genetics was disproven.

scientific inquiry, especially in the realm of the social sciences. A related problem is how to reconcile the requirement of continuing political isolation from the West with the need for international scientific cooperation. When applied to scientific research, centralized planning tends to discourage supervisors and the researchers themselves from accepting the risk of innovation, which creates a serious problem. Other problems concern priorities and funding, administration and organization, personnel training, and even ethnic quotas. We say more about these problems later.

Note that the Russian term *nauka*, which is usually translated as "science and technology," actually has an even broader meaning that includes "scholarship," "learning," and "knowledge." As we already know, Marxism-Leninism is officially called a science.

## HISTORICAL RECORD

As we have already seen and are about to discuss in more detail, Soviet historiography has always been subject to heavy ideological pressure. The interpretation of the history of science in Old Russia is no exception to the rule. It underscores and seeks to reconcile dialectically two seemingly contradictory claims: On the one hand, it blames the reactionary czarist regime for having ignored the need for science; but on the other hand it maintains that in spite of this, many talented Russian researchers and engineers actually made important discoveries and inventions that are being unfairly attributed to foreigners by Western historians. Under Stalin, this special kind of xenophobia often reached the outer limits of the ridiculous, giving the Russians credit for all the important breakthroughs. Such claims have been considerably toned down during the last quarter century, but some of the questionable Russian "firsts" remain. It is, for instance, claimed that radio was invented and first successfully tested by Russian physicist Alexander Popov, and that the world's first airplane was designed and built by another Russian, Alexander Mozhaisky. Of course, much of the outside world associates these turning points in the history of science and technology with different names.

It is generally agreed that the beginnings of Russian science and technology date from the era of Peter the Great. In 1724, Peter founded the Russian Academy of Sciences and charged it with the promotion of research and scholarly activities. The first generation of scientists and scholars was imported from western Europe. And it was also mainly western Europe that educated the subsequent generations of native Russian learned men. Among them was Mikhail Lomonosov (1711–1765), who earned international recognition for original contributions to such diverse fields of knowledge as astronomy, education, mechanics, and linguistics. By the early 1800s, Russia produced the first of many outstanding mathematicians, Nikolai Lobachevsky, the creator of a new geometry.

BOX 7–1    *Stalin on Russia's Technological Backwardness*

> In a speech delivered on February 4, 1931, Joseph Stalin gave a long enumera-
> tion of Old Russia's military defeats—from the Mongol invasion to World War
> I—caused by its technological backwardness. He then made the following
> remarkable prediction:
>
>> We are fifty or a hundred years behind the leading countries. We must
>> make up this distance in *ten years*. Either we do it, or we shall perish.
>> (emphasis added)
>
> I. V. Stalin, *Sochineniya* [*Works*] (Moscow: Politizdat, 1951), vol. 13, p. 39.

During its last 100 years, imperial Russia's most important single
contribution to world science was probably the periodic table of elements,
which was invented by Dmitri Mendeleev. Several prominent Russian researchers pioneered in the fields of soil science and geology. Another major
area of significant Russian achievement was physiology, thanks to Ivan
Sechenov and Ivan Pavlov. In aeromechanics and aerodynamics, important
breakthroughs were made by Nikolai Zhukovsky and Konstantin
Tsiolkovsky. In biology, Russia's contributors were Kliment Timiryazev and
Ilya Mechnikov.

Several other internationally recognized Russian researchers worked
in different fields. But on the eve of the 1917 Revolution, the overall reputation of Russia's relatively small scientific community was not great, either at
home or abroad. The total number of scientific research establishments was
only about 300, and in all they employed no more than 12,000 people.

A total commitment to scientific progress was one of the new regime's
promises meant to be carried out at any cost. From the very start, the top
priority given to scientific achievement ensured scientists and scholars of the
high prestige and special material privileges that they have been enjoying
ever since. During the first postrevolution decade, they even had a considerable degree of independence from politics, which they have never completely lost, even during the Stalin era. In the 1930s and later, however, the
already sizable scientific establishment was repeatedly ravaged by political
purges, mass arrests, and worse. Perhaps the best-known cases of political
persecution involved the famous airplane designer, Anatoli Tupolev,[2] and
the world-renowned physicist, Pyotr Kapitsa,[3] both of whom spent several
years under house arrest. Other prominent scientists and engineers were put
in special jails that included research facilities.

[2]Anatoli Nikolayevich Tupolev was the chief designer of numerous models of Soviet
planes, called in his honor ANT and TU.

[3]Pyotr Kapitsa was a famous Soviet nuclear physicist.

By comparison, Soviet scientists and scholars have been enjoying material privileges and popular esteem during the last thirty-five years. On the other hand, even in the more rational society that the Soviet Union is today, the huge scientific establishment is still treated politically pretty much like any other important segment of the national economy. Science and technology, now staffed almost exclusively with graduates of the Soviet higher education system, no longer enjoy the freedom from politics that the regime had to grant them in the past.

According to the official point of view, the last quarter of the twentieth century marks the beginning of a scientific-technological revolution (NTR, in Russian abbreviation) of unprecedented magnitude. It is considered to be a historical opportunity for Soviet science to achieve major breakthroughs in a number of important areas of research and development.

## GORBACHEV'S QUEST

According to Karl Marx's aphorism, in history every major event occurs twice: first as a serious drama or tragedy and then as a comedy or farce. Something like that—but in reverse order—has been happening in the post-Stalin era of Soviet history. First, there was Nikita Khrushchev, who tried to heal and reform his country through all kinds of sensational stunts and "voodoo cure-alls," enlisting the help of real scientists as well as pseudoscientists. The latter often made him look comical, although, of course, not everything about Khrushchev and what he did was funny. Mikhail Gorbachev, who is quite serious, is counting heavily on the help of the most respectable among Soviet scientists with his ambitious *perestroika* campaign. To him, this is logical since the scientists and engineers were responsible for the Soviet Union's surprising the world in space in the late 1950s, and for then managing to achieve parity with the United States in strategic weapons systems within the next ten years. Gorbachev appears confident that during the coming decade the same kind of modern miracle could occur in other important areas of the Soviet economy, making his country an all-around superpower. He believes that Soviet scientists could and would come up with badly needed major scientific breakthroughs and technological shortcuts to modernity.

Gorbachev's special relationship with the scientific community began immediately after his ascent to power. The honorable return to Moscow of academician Andrei Sakharov from internal exile in Gorky was highly symbolic, and it gave an impetus to the development of very close personal ties between the General Secretary and some leading scientists and scholars.[4]

[4]In October 1988, Sakharov won still another token of recognition when he was elected to the prestigious presidium of the USSR Academy of Sciences and later allowed to visit the United States. In 1989, the year of his death, he was elected to the new legislature.

BOX 7–2    *Gorbachev on Perestroika and Science*

*Perestroika* is a decisive turn toward science, a practical and businesslike partnership with it for the purpose of achieving the highest end results, an ability to put every undertaking on a solid scientific basis, and readiness and eager desire of scientists to actively support the party's course toward a renewal of society; at the same time, *perestroika* also means taking care of the development of science, the growth of its personnel, and their active participation in the process of the fundamental change.

Speech at the 1987 January plenary meeting of the CPSU Central Committee.

Several of these intellectuals even became informal advisers to Gorbachev, supplementing, if not outright replacing, more traditional ideological gurus. Scientists and intellectuals in general are among the more enthusiastic supporters of *perestroika* and Gorbachev's rational, common-sense approach to problems. This segment of the USSR's population has benefitted most directly from *glasnost*, which has made possible free discussion, unfettered debate, and criticism. At least the younger members of the scientific elite appear to support fully the ongoing reforms aimed at reducing the bureaucratic overhead of the huge research establishment, streamlining its operation, and rejuvenating its aging leadership.

There are some definite signs of improvement in such important areas as the R & D cycle, which used to be notoriously slow because of bureaucratic red tape and excessive secrecy. But, so far, there has been little evidence that Gorbachev's effort to quickly close the scientific and technological gap between the Soviet Union and the West (including Japan) is working. In 1957, after only four years in power, Khrushchev was able to reap the political and psychological benefits of a major Soviet scientific and engineering achievement—the launch of *Sputnik*, the first man-made orbital satellite. No such luck for Gorbachev, who is still waiting for his moment of glory in the realm of science while Soviet scientists and engineers are presumably working on new "*Sputniks*."

## ACADEMY OF SCIENCES

In the centralized world of state-owned research and scholarship, the USSR Academy of Sciences plays the role of national headquarters. It is responsible for the guidance and supervision of research conducted anywhere in the country. Founded in 1724 in St. Petersburg (Leningrad), it was moved to Moscow in 1934, where its administrative offices are housed in an impressive-looking building—like those usually occupied by national ministries. In fact, the Academy has ministerial rank, and it serves as an advisory body,

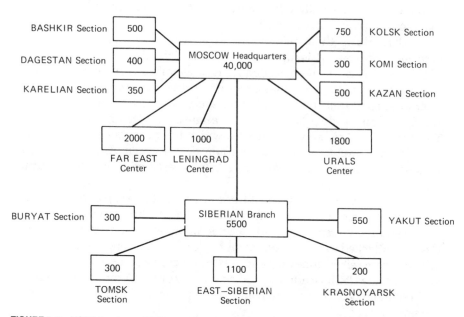

**FIGURE 7–1** USSR Academy of Sciences (Approximate Numbers of Scientists)

with the State Committee on Science and Technology, to the USSR Council of Ministers. The Academy is entrusted with much of basic research, whereas the committee directly controls all applied research. Historically, the Academy symbolizes that Russia's science has developed from the "top down."

The Academy consists of about 330 full members, called "academicians," and about 600 corresponding members who usually meet once a year as the "general assembly" to discuss major problems of national scientific development, to vote on organizational issues, and to elect new members.[5] The real seat of power is a permanent committee of the assembly, called the "presidium," which is chaired by a president. The members of the presidium and the president are elected by the assembly, which also elects by secret ballot new members from approved lists of candidates.

The Academy has four divisions: (1) physical sciences, engineering, and mathematics; (2) chemistry and biology; (3) geosciences; and (4) social sciences. Since 1957, the Academy has had a special Siberian Branch set on the banks of the Ob River in a new town called Akademgorodok (near Novosibirsk). There are also two major academy research centers, one in the Urals and the other in the Far East, as well as some thirty local sections in charge of specialized research activities scattered over the entire country. Leningrad has a major scientific center. About 300 of the most prestigious

[5]The USSR Academy of Sciences also has about 100 honorary foreign members.

research institutes are directly subordinate to the Academy. Altogether, the Academy employs more than 55,000 people.

All fourteen ethnic union republics have their own general academies of sciences whose work is supervised and coordinated by the USSR Academy of Sciences.[6] Each of these academies has several research institutes. As a rule, union-republic academies concentrate either on problems germane to their local conditions or on traditional areas of strength. For example, the Azerbaijanian Academy of Sciences specializes in petrochemical research. The Armenian Academy of Sciences, which has observatories high in the mountains, is well known for its astrophysical research. And the Georgian Academy of Sciences, by tradition, excels in research in low-temperature physics.

Of almost 3,200 research institutes, about one half are part of the system of academies just described. The other 1,400 institutes belong, and are administratively responsible, to various ministries and agencies. Some of them are attached to institutions of higher learning, although relatively little scientific research is done on campuses. But they, too, must coordinate their work with the USSR Academy of Sciences and/or the Committee on Science and Technology. Other research and development facilities are managed in the same way.

The language of Soviet science is Russian, although ethnic languages are also used in scientific periodicals and books published in union republics. A growing share of the world's scientific information, currently estimated at about 15 percent, appears originally in Russian (compared to more than 50 percent coming out first in English). The USSR Academy of Sciences publishes more than 150 journals.

The USSR Academy of Sciences has the responsibility for four specialized national academies located in Moscow: the USSR Academy of Agricultural Sciences, the USSR Academy of Arts, the USSR Academy of Medical Sciences, and the USSR Academy of Pedagogical Sciences. These major research organizations, in turn, have branches and institutes in many different places.

## RESEARCH AND DEVELOPMENT

The institute, officially called a "Scientific Research Institute" (SRI), is the basic unit of the Soviet research and development effort. The SRIs vary in prestige and size, but they have approximately the same organization. They are headed by appointed directors and staffed with researchers and technical personnel. The researchers, called "scientific fellows," hold ranks that de-

[6]The Russian Federation (RSFSR) is in the process of getting its own separate academy of sciences. It also has a specialized academy called the RSFSR Academy of Urban Economy.

pend on advanced degrees and experience and that correspond to the permanent academic ranks found in the institutions of higher learning. Vacancies are usually filled on a competitive basis from among applicants responding to announcements in professional journals.

Larger institutes may have branches in different towns or laboratories and field stations. An institute's internal structure usually includes permanent sections or departments and temporary project teams (groups). Some more reputable institutes have their own training programs and may award advanced degrees. As a rule, an institute is charged with a rather narrow and specific mission. Because of a Soviet obsession with secrecy, much scientific research and development is classified, making cooperation and cross-fertilization between institutes or even parts of the same SRI difficult. At least nominally, even the SRIs that operate under the cloak of secrecy are responsible to the USSR Academy of Sciences.

Basic research in pure science and theory is done primarily in the SRIs operating directly under the USSR Academy of Sciences and its various affiliates. These institutes are considered to be more prestigious and can be quite selective in hiring their staffs. The SRIs that are not directly affiliated with academies of sciences and that are more involved with applied research and development often have to be satisfied with second-best personnel.

Periodic attempts have been made to reduce this dichotomy and to bring theory and practice closer together. The current measure that is supposed to accomplish this goal provides for the creation of science and production associations. A typical association consists of a research institute, a design bureau combined with a workshop or pilot plant, and a mass-production factory. So far, not much has been written in the Soviet press about the success of this experiment, which is expected to improve and speed up the production cycle.

Budgetary expenditures on research and development are estimated at 3 to 3.5 percent of the GNP. This is a very high rate of investment in science and technology, rarely reached elsewhere in the world. It appears, however, that in a typical Soviet way of setting priorities, only about one third of the funds is earmarked for civilian research, whereas twice that amount is poured into defense-oriented fields of science and technology.

Until very recently, most Soviet research and development was done without the benefit of modern information retrieval systems, computers, instant copying machines, and other similar equipment that is standard in the West. The situation is slowly improving, thanks chiefly to imports of foreign equipment. The USSR Academy of Sciences has (since 1952) a special translation and information-distribution center, called the Institute of Scientific Information. Still, the flow of scientific information, both domestic and foreign, appears to be too slow. Soviet professional journals carry frequent complaints about this situation, as well as promises to do something about it. Perhaps part of the problem is that so many people are engaged in scientific research in the USSR. Because most of them are expected to write and publish, channels of communication often become glutted with contributions of marginal value. As part of Gorbachev's efforts to promote scientific progress, teaching faculties are encouraged to engage more in research and development, both on their own campuses and as outside consultants.

## SCIENTISTS

Approximately 1.5 million people officially identified as "scientific workers" are employed by SRIs, design bureaus, laboratories, experimental stations, and the like. As a group, these people and the members of their families command advantages and privileges that are denied to the overwhelming majority of their fellow citizens. They receive better-than-average salaries, housing, medical care, summer vacations, and opportunities for travel abroad. In a society that, though still backward in many respects, is so totally dedicated to scientific progress, scientists obviously enjoy high esteem and self-respect. In the eyes of at least some Soviet scientists, they have yet another relative advantage: Those who are in "hard sciences" are under less pressure to participate actively in various political campaigns.

It is for these and similar reasons that science as an expanding profession attracts large numbers of superior individuals in the USSR. It is considered by many gifted young people to be the best career opportunity that their system can offer. For most of them, to become a scientist means to surpass their parents in education and social status.

The elite of the profession consists of the members (full and correspondent) of the USSR Academy of Sciences and the other academies. They total perhaps 10,000 people, age 40 and over, who dominate the administrative offices of various research organizations, editorial boards of scientific periodicals, organizing committees of conferences, and headquarters of professional associations, which are called "learned societies." Many of them, as well as lesser scientific figures with advanced degrees, "candidate" and "doctor," combine their research work with teaching, an officially encouraged and profitable form of "moonlighting."

**BOX 7–3**   *CPSU Program on Soviet Science*

The party's policy in the field of science is designed to provide favorable conditions for dynamic progress of all areas of knowledge; concentrate personnel, material, and financial resources in the more promising areas of research called upon to expedite the achievement of planned economic and social tasks and society's cultural advancement; and ensure reliable defense capability for the country.

Many members of the scientific establishment are recipients of assorted official honors: medals, titles, prizes, elected offices, and similar trappings. A few leading Soviet scientists are Nobel Prize laureates. The USSR Academy of Sciences makes an annual award of its own, the Lomonosov Prize, for demonstrated scientific accomplishment.[7] Travel abroad is also considered, and indeed is, a token of recognition. It is afforded to relatively few scientists and scholars, usually as part of official exchanges. Most Soviet researchers have a reading knowledge of English, the chief language of modern science.[8]

The ethnic composition of various scientific bodies is treated by the Soviet authorities as a delicate issue. Lately, it almost exclusively concerns Jewish scientists and scholars, held to be disproportionately numerous for their share in the total population and potentially unreliable because of the continuing Jewish emigration. From an official point of view, the problem is compounded because many of the most valuable Soviet scientists are Jewish. A mass exodus of Jews, therefore, holds the threat of a potential brain drain.

Generally speaking, all European ethnic groups have higher ratios among scientists than their proportions in the total population. This is understandable, given that many of the Soviet Asian minorities were largely illiterate only two or three generations ago. More than one third of the scientific community is composed of women, and their share is rising. However, relatively few women have reached the upper levels of the scientific establishment.

## QUALITY AND INNOVATION

The quality of Soviet science and technology is very uneven. Just as in the national economy, the emphasis in the research and development effort has been on quantitative growth; the result has been to produce a scientific establishment approximately twice as large as that of the United States. The big question is how to transform quantity into quality, which until now has been seriously sought only in a few selected areas vital to national security. There appears to be no reason to think that Soviet scientists and engineers, who have managed to manufacture first-rate military hardware, should not be able to do the same in the civilian field, provided that they are given sufficient funds.

The funds allocated at this time to civil science and technology are far from adequate, making it unlikely that the Soviet Union could expect to overcome its considerable qualitative lag behind the advanced Western

[7] Actually, two Lomonosov Prizes are awarded every year: One goes to a Soviet scientist and the other to a foreign scientist.

[8] An estimated 80 percent of Soviet scientists can read English, but relatively few of them have sufficient fluency to use it at conferences.

**FIGURE 7–2**    *Lenin*, the first atomic icebreaker in the world.

countries and Japan. The technology transfer from these countries to the Soviet Union may be of considerable help in providing models for "reverse engineering," charged with copying and imitating finished products. But the cost of mass producing such products would still have to be borne by the Soviet national economy, which currently simply could not afford it without first thoroughly reordering priorities.

A modest improvement in the quality of Soviet civilian science and technology is occurring nevertheless. The rate of progress is, most probably, directly proportional to the money invested. Less convincing are the views offered by some foreign observers who blame the continuing inferiority of Soviet scientific endeavor on such peculiarities of the whole system as its insufficiently competitive character, an innovation-resistant bureaucracy, a relative lack of material incentive, and the imposition of political controls. The only real prerequisite for enthusiasm, creativity, and the urge to excel is challenge. And there is no evidence that the Soviet system can no longer offer its scientists and engineers continuing challenges in various areas, including the huge and badly neglected realm of civilian needs. Quite the opposite: The goal-oriented Soviet society's main strength is its ability to create challenges; for this purpose it uses, among other sources, a deep-seated historical feeling of technological inferiority and a desire to overcome it.

The uneven quality of Soviet science and technology—peaks of excellence and depths of mediocrity—reflects a familiar pattern of traditional Soviet priorities. Every scientific activity proceeds, or at least is supposed to proceed, in accordance with the five-year plans. The current plan calls for special efforts to speed up the research and development cycle: pure research—applied research—development and production. Other urgent problems to be solved deal with industrial efficiency and public health.

## PRIORITIES

Areas of science and technology given the highest priority include pure research into the structure of the atom, low-temperature physics, aerodynamics, variable mass dynamics, and the molecular state of solids. Also high on the list of priorities are areas of applied science and engineering such as space exploration, nuclear energy, and, of course, strategic weaponry. Institutes and industries directly responsible for these areas of research and development have the best possible equipment and materials that money, both rubles and hard currencies, can buy. Their budgets are fat, and they have the first choice in selecting and recruiting scientific and engineering talents.

Because for many years the concept of top priority was almost synonymous with the definition of national security, much of the work in these areas is still classified. From the limited available information, it appears that the basic research is conducted in highly specialized institutes operating along the lines of the usual compartmentalization. However, complex problems requiring input from several scientific disciplines are sometimes handled by task forces consisting of leading specialists with different institutional affiliations. Innovative approaches and creative initiative are encouraged and rewarded.

Soviet strategic weapons, nuclear warheads, and various systems for their delivery are generally believed to possess awesome destructive power and sufficient accuracy to perform their intended mission in case of a global conflict. The impressive record of Soviet space exploits supports this contention. Depending on who counts and what is counted, the USSR has scored more, or at least as many, important "firsts" in space exploration as the United States. Space exploration of the magnitude and sophistication already achieved must be based on a high level of metallurgy, mechanical engineering, applied mathematics, radio electronics, and other branches of science and technology.

Soviet accomplishments in the realm of nuclear energy are also quite impressive. They include numerous atomic power stations, atomic-powered ships, and at least two functioning breeder reactors that produce both electricity and enriched plutonium for commercial use. The world's first

TABLE 7–2    Soviet (Russian) Nobel Prize Winners in Science

| Name | Field | Date |
|------|-------|------|
| Ivan Pavlov | Physiology | 1904 |
| Ilya Mechnikov | Biological immunity | 1908 |
| Nikolai Semyonov | Kinetics | 1956 |
| Pavel Cherenkov | Cosmic rays | 1958 |
| Igor Tamm | Cosmic rays | 1958 |
| Ilya Frank | Cosmic rays | 1958 |
| Lev Landau | Low-temperature physics | 1962 |
| Nikolai Basov | Laser electronics | 1964 |
| Alexander Prokhorov | Laser electronics | 1964 |
| Leonid Kantorovich | Economic analysis | 1975 |
| Pyotr Kapitsa | Low-temperature physics | 1978 |

Source: Compiled by author from Soviet data.

plant for the assembly-line production of atomic generators is now under construction in the Soviet Union.[9]

Soviet scientists and engineers are doing pioneer work in thermonuclear fusion by laser beam. They are also developing new methods for casting and rolling steel and other metals.

## PHYSICS AND MATHEMATICS

The Soviet Union has been doing exceptionally well in practically all subareas of theoretical physics and mathematics. Soviet scientists have made especially significant advances in mathematical logic, topology, the theory of differential equations, and functional analysis. They excel in aerodynamics and hydrodynamics, for which there is a long tradition dating from the beginning of the century.

This impressive theoretical research has so far produced spotty results in its application to production technology. For example, the Soviet Union is estimated to be at least ten years behind the West in the production and use of computers in civilian fields. The bulk of commercial calculations and office work is still done by hand with the help of the old-fashioned abacus. In applied mechanics, the quality of equipment and machines ranges from good to poor, depending on the military utility of a given item. Thus, the USSR produces high-quality trucks and tractors (and presumably also tanks), but poor-quality cars. Soviet jet planes are among the world's best, but elevators in some new buildings are notoriously bad. Many mechanical gadgets used widely in the West—such as office machines, home appliances,

[9]The first operational atomic power station in the world was commissioned in the USSR in 1954. Currently, the USSR is selling its atomic generators on the international market. In spite of the Chernobyl accident, construction of new atomic power stations is proceeding.

**TABLE 7–3**    Growth of Scientific Establishment

|                                              | 1940 | 1965 | 1970 | 1977 | 1982 | 1986 |
|----------------------------------------------|------|------|------|------|------|------|
| Scientific researchers (in millions)         | 0.1  | 0.7  | 0.9  | 1.3  | 1.4  | 1.5  |
| Expenditures on science (in billions of rubles) | 0.3 | 6.9  | 11.7 | 18.3 | 25.1 | 29.3 |

Source: Compiled by author from Soviet statistics.

and power tools—are simply nonexistent in the Soviet Union. This situation is improving quite slowly.

Just like the successes, Soviet failures and shortcomings in science and technology usually have rational explanations. Both successes and failures result from conscious decisions concerning the choice of priorities. There is little that is erratic or mysterious about either of them.

It appears that on this level of research and development the main emphasis is currently on further automation of various production processes. The Soviet Union is shopping abroad for the technical know-how and equipment that could expedite the matter. It is also developing its own sophisticated computer systems, having overcome problems inherited from the Stalin era when cybernetics was banned on ideological grounds. (Cybernetics was rejected for allegedly challenging Marxist dialectics of the thinking process.)

## CHEMISTRY AND BIOLOGY

The main concentration in chemical research in the USSR is currently on petrochemistry and the chemistry of petroorganic compounds vital to the production of various kinds of plastics, synthetic rubbers, and polymers. But in the daily use and variety of synthetic materials the Soviet Union is far behind the West. The development of large-scale chemical industries did not begin until the late 1950s, as a concomitant to major reforms designed to upgrade agriculture.

Other major areas of Soviet chemical research are alloys and nonorganic compounds. In chemical physics, Soviet scientists have pioneered in research on combustion and explosion, and research on the chemistry of natural and artificial radioactive elements is also a priority.

Soviet biology, which was badly crippled during the Stalin era, has made a respectable comeback during the last thirty years. Here too, the turning point was the inauguration of a new agrarian policy by Stalin's heirs. In addition to the traditional fields—genetics, physiology, botany, zoology, and medicine—Soviet researchers are doing quite well in such new areas as molecular biology, radiation genetics, and space biology. The practical application of biological research has yielded some significant benefits for the country's medical services and agriculture. Agricultural sciences have their own national headquarters: The Academy of Agricultural Sciences (founded in 1929). The main direction of research deals with practical problems of agriculture in developing drought-resistant crops, fighting plant diseases, and experimenting with new fertilizers.

As mentioned, perhaps because the country is so huge and its national wealth seemingly unlimited, the Soviet Union has been rather slow in developing a concern for the protection of the environment. Ecology and other environmental sciences still seem to merit a low priority.

## MEDICAL RESEARCH

The record of Soviet medical research and its practical application is spotty. Soviet medics excel in such important areas as coronary surgery and rehabilitation, organ transplants, and the implementation of artificial prostheses. They are also doing quite well in cancer research and in a number of other important areas involving major health concerns and communicative diseases. Soviet scientists are credited with developing and perfecting new microsurgical techniques. Moscow and other large cities have first-rate research facilities, including experimental laboratories and clinics, working in several selected areas of health care and disease control. Perhaps not surprisingly in view of the advanced ages of Soviet leaders, during the 1970s and early 1980s lavish support was given to extensive studies of gerontology and geriatrics.

But several lines of medical research receive little attention in the Soviet Union. For example, Soviet scientists appear to be years behind their Western colleagues in work on prenatal treatment, genetic engineering, artificial organs, and test-tube implantation. Pharmaceutical research in the Soviet Union is another weak area and a source of serious problems for public health, which we shall discuss later.

Since World War II, the Soviet Union has cooperated in various international ventures concerned with medical research: conferences, symposia, and exchange programs. The overall planning and coordination of research and development are provided by the USSR Academy of Medical Sciences (established in 1944).

## GEOSCIENCES

Sciences dealing with the earth, such as geology, geography, seismology, oceanography, and meteorology, are quite important in a country that is so large and rich in natural resources not yet properly mapped and developed. The main goal of research in this area is to discover the governing principles of the distribution of various natural deposits: oil, gas, coal, and metal ores.

This is being done in numerous institutes and laboratories on the basis of data produced by geological, geophysical, and geochemical investigations.

A whole army of geoscientists and technicians—more than a half-million people—is engaged in fieldwork mostly in little-explored parts of the country: Siberia, the Far East and Far North, and Central Asia. Specially equipped artificial satellites are used to scan large areas in the continuing, intensive search for new natural deposits. Geoscientific expeditions are well armed with modern tools, sensitive instruments, cross-country vehicles, airplanes, and helicopters. Many Soviet marine expeditions venture far from the shores of the USSR. For several years, a Soviet scientific station has been operating near the South Pole in Antarctica.

Soviet geoscientists are pioneering in the technique of predicting earthquakes—a field that has an important practical application in many parts of the USSR, such as Central Asia, the Caucasus, the Crimea, and the Far East. The branches of geoscience dealing with the study of soils constitute another field of traditional excellence, dating back to old Russia. In fact, the modern international terminology for soil classification contains many Russian words.

Research in geosciences has found an important practical application in civil engineering and road construction in areas of permafrost, mostly in Siberia. An extremely ambitious project, which is still on the drawing board, is supposed to reverse the flow of several Siberian rivers from north to south to irrigate the deserts of Central Asia.

The Siberian Branch of the USSR Academy of Sciences (shown in Figure 7–3) serves as the headquarters for complete geological survey and research conducted east of the Ural Mountains.

FIGURE 7–3  Akademgorodok, the Siberian Branch of the USSR Academy of Sciences.

## SOCIAL SCIENCES

In Soviet usage this broad term includes such disciplines as economics, politics, jurisprudence, sociology, history, anthropology, philosophy, international relations, and even literary criticism. Another peculiarity of the Soviet social sciences is the fact that the entire field is very close to official ideology and propaganda. As we have seen, all societal phenomena are viewed by Marxism-Leninism as interrelated and interacting parts of the whole, called the "superstructure." Social sciences are supposed not only to analyze the superstructure but also to enable the Soviet leaders to "scientifically administer" their society. The ideology of Marxism-Leninism tells the leaders what is to be done; the social sciences are expected to tell them how it can be done best with regard to particular aspects of society. It follows that the social sciences must function within ideological boundaries.

Given this framework for operation, Soviet social scientists must proceed cautiously with their scholarly inquiry. In selecting their research topics, expressing opinions, and offering value judgments and conclusions, they must be mindful of purely ideological considerations. They know that their findings must be consistent with ideology and fall within its limits. To be sure, after the death of Stalin, the interpretation of the ideology has become less rigid, and its limits have been considerably widened. As a result, published research in the social sciences is more factual and diverse, even though it does retain its ideological bias.

The cream of the social science crop is composed of the Soviet philosophers, the high priests of Marxism-Leninism. It is their job to analyze current events and interpret them in an ideologically appropriate manner. Products of their efforts are either published in authoritative sources or incorporated into important policy statements by the Kremlin leaders. In official language, all this is called "a creative development of the Marxist-Leninist theory." The most important philosophers work in a special "think tank" of the Central Committee of the CPSU called the CC Academy of Social Sciences.

There is now a division of labor between Marxism-Leninism and specialized disciplines of the social sciences: The former retain the strategic heights and the last word on all important sociopolitical issues, and the latter take over problems of everyday tactics. Thanks to this arrangement, sciences, which were completely submersed in the past (even criminology), are now back in good graces. The case of criminology as an academic discipline is a good example of the changed climate of the Soviet social sciences. For many years, no research in this field was allowed because, according to the ideological point of view, under Socialism all objective reasons for criminal behavior were absent. The same theoretical principle is maintained today, but the emphasis has shifted to the well-known Marxist qualification that the people's conscience lags behind sociopolitical changes. This time lag justifies investigations of motives and causes for criminal activities as long as the results are not added up to give an overall statistical picture of crime in the country. In a similar way, it is now possible for Soviet sociologists to conduct objective opinion polls on specific issues without being concerned that their findings may be at variance with general ideological assumptions.

Study of international relations on the basis of empirical data has become a full-time occupation of many scholars gathered in several "think tanks." The two most prestigious research centers are the Institute for Study of the U.S.A. and Canada and the Institute of the World Economy. Classified analyses conducted by these institutions are believed to be used by Soviet leaders for making foreign policy decisions.

Next in importance after the Marxist philosophers among Soviet social scientists, although much more numerous, are the economists. Actually, the overwhelming majority of Soviet economists (sometimes called "engineer-economists") consists of college graduates who took a prescribed mix of courses in Marxist economics, business management, and public administration. A large subgroup of Soviet economists specializes in economic planning. Theoretical research in economics is considered an ideologically sensitive area to be handled with great care by experts thoroughly versed in both Marxist philosophy and economics.

Many other Soviet social scientists, such as anthropologists, historians, jurists, literary critics, and sociologists, take a back seat because of the relative unimportance of their fields of expertise to the superstructure.

## HISTORIOGRAPHY

The story of Soviet historiography epitomizes the difficult past and uncertain present of the Soviet social sciences in general. Already under Lenin, who defined history as "politics turned backwards," the study and interpretation of past events had become a topical political concern. All history was rewritten with emphasis on the economic interpretation. In the new textbooks the past was presented as humankind's long and painful illness arising from purely economic causes, but manifest in political and national symptoms. As the illness progresses, surgical interference—revolution—becomes inevitable. In other words, history was written backwards, as reflected in the rearview mirror of the 1917 Revolution.

Under Stalin, all history texts, and first of all those dealing with Russia, were repeatedly modified, revised, expanded, or contracted to keep up with the changing political demands of the day. Russia's past became almost as unpredictable as its future, and Soviet historical research began to rank among the most hazardous occupations in the country. Many historians paid dearly for veering, usually inadvertently, from the zigzagging party line. Outright falsifications of the historical record, both by commission and omission, were commonplace. Stalin must have had strong suspicions that, as a collective memory, history was not helping, but hurting, his cause. According to underground Soviet humor of the day, it became increasingly difficult "to predict Russia's past."

As part of the de-Stalinization campaign beginning in the mid-1950s, Soviet historiography was put on a much more rational basis. During the next three decades, the quality of historical research in the Soviet Union was steadily improving, the historical perspective presented in published sources was broadening, and more humanistic attitudes toward the past were gaining momentum.

This relative improvement, impressive as it was, did not signal a break between Soviet historiography and politics. The revised historical texts continued to serve current political needs and, therefore, were still subject to frequent recalls for further modifications. The past as depicted in these texts was not appreciated on its own terms but was evaluated for its relevance to, and utility for, the present. As a result, many themes remained off-limits to Soviet historians—for example, Trotsky's role in the 1917 Revolution, the peasant resistance to collectivization, the mass purges of the 1930s, and the secret provisions of the Nazi-Soviet pact (1939). Together with Trotsky, many other losers in the struggle for power continued to be treated as "nonpersons" in Soviet textbooks, and still others' historical roles were minimized. The latter category of "has-beens" included Nikita Khrushchev, who was the most important person in the Soviet Union for more than ten years (1953 to 1964). On the other hand, Lenin continued to be treated as a superman.

After the emergence of *glasnost*, a change for the better occured in the treatment of the country's past by the native historians. Since then, efforts have been undertaken to fill in "blank pages" of history books and give more balanced accounts of controversial events and figures, including the victims of Stalin's purges.

## HUMANITIES

As it is used in the Soviet Union, the term "humanities" covers entirely most disciplines dealing with language, literature, and fine arts, but only some parts of philosophy and history. The last two disciplines are divided between the humanities and social sciences, roughly along the classical-modern line.

During the Stalin era, practically all branches of the humanities were subjected to frequent ideological interferences. Many specific areas of scholarly research were periodically declared irrelevant to the cause of building Socialism, and were thus suspended. Crude attempts were made to inject the humanities with large doses of Marxism in efforts to make them more "progressive." Thus, for example, for a number of years, Soviet linguists were obliged to adhere to a class theory of the nature of language, according to which language is a part of "superstructure," and members of the same nationality but different classes speak different languages. There were several competing variations of this theory, and it took no lesser authority than Stalin himself to put an end to the ensuing controversy. He even wrote a lengthy article, entitled "Marxism and Problems of Linguistics" (1950), which brought all further research in linguistics to a virtual halt.

Currently, only slight political demands are made upon the humanities: paying lip service to the "classics of Marxism-Leninism," using Marxist terminology, and observing such official taboos as staying away from discussions of religious issues. There is a certain ambivalence about the status and quality of the ongoing research in this whole area of Soviet scholarly endeavor. On one hand, because the humanities have little social utility in the eyes of the regime, they are not receiving much support. On the other hand, however, some of the more esoteric humanistic fields, such as rare languages, histories of ancient cultures, and studies of obscure literary heritages, seem to attract exceptionally gifted scholars, at least in part because they offer an escape from politics. It would probably be fair to say that, as a rule, achievements in the Soviet humanities have occurred despite, rather than because of, the Communist system.

## POLITICAL CONTROLS

The 1917 Revolution and the ensuing civil strife all but destroyed Old Russia's modest scientific community, and it forced many leading scientists to emigrate. Most of their colleagues who stayed in Russia showed little liking for the new regime in spite of its proclaimed commitment to scientific progress. Faced with this situation, Soviet leaders had to bend over backwards to secure the cooperation of these people and to create the scientific base essential to their ambitious economic goals. Scientists not only were given better creature comforts but were also extended a limited immunity to various political harassments that were rapidly becoming the norm of Soviet life: forced attendance at meetings, rallies, propaganda lectures, and so on. Very important scientists could even openly indulge in such "antisocial" behavior as going to church and observing religious holidays.[10] But all their professional activities were closely supervised by political administrators in charge of institutes and laboratories.

The special status of scientists began to erode in the 1930s when neither an international reputation nor the title of academician was a guarantee

[10]Academician Ivan Pavlov, Nobel Prize-winning physiologist of international fame, was a devout Christian. His parish in Leningrad was carefully preserved by the authorities.

against police terror. From the point of view of the regime, there was a rational reason for the change: The first generation of new Soviet-educated scientists was waiting in the wings ready to take over. In fact, some of these new scientists were also quite ready to denounce their older colleagues and mentors and bring ideological charges against them. In 1936, in an important symbolic move, the USSR Socialist Academy[11] merged with the USSR Academy of Sciences, becoming its division of social sciences and drastically changing the political composition of the membership.

The death of Stalin improved the lot of Soviet scientists as individuals, but it did not reverse or even slow down the disintegration of their special apolitical status as a group. On the contrary, under all five heirs of Stalin, the huge scientific establishment, including the USSR Academy of Sciences, has been treated more and more like just another branch of the national economy, important but not different in regard to political controls. Today, with approximately one third of its members belonging to the Communist Party, the scientific establishment has the political controls and trappings typical of the Soviet Union as a whole. Thus, every research institute or similar operation is headed by an administrator who is a party member. It also has a primary party organization headed by a secretary. All scientific personnel are expected to attend periodic meetings and political lectures. Since 1961, presidents of the USSR Academy of Sciences have been members of the Communist Party.[12] Apparently, as a group, Soviet scientists of recent generations have taken for granted this integration into the mainstream of Soviet life. They appear to be neither inclined nor specially fitted to make political decisions. Of course, there are exceptions to this rule.[13]

There are still a few lingering exceptions to the total politicization of Soviet science. A handful of the older senior scientists, mostly well-known academicians, are allowed to live with a minimum of political pressure. Those of their younger colleagues who are engaged exclusively in theoretical research are permitted a certain degree of eccentric behavior and are treated as a Soviet version of absent-minded "eggheads." For example, relatively little pressure is put on the young theoretical scientists to join the party. And, although they are expected to conduct themselves within the prescribed ideological constraints, there is practically no political interference in their professional research.

---

[11]It was founded in 1919 as the Communist Academy and later, in 1924, was renamed the Socialist Academy.

[12]The first party member to be president of the USSR Academy of Sciences was Mstislav Keldysh (1961–1975). His successors—Anatoli Aleksandrov (1975–1986) and Guri Marchuk (present)—are also party members. About 65 percent of "candidates of science" and 70 percent of "doctors of science" are CPSU members.

[13]The best-known Soviet scientist to become deeply involved in the politics of dissent was Academician Andrei Sakharov.

**BOX 7–4**   *Soviet Leaders Talk About Science*

BREZHNEV (at the celebration of the 250th anniversary of the USSR Academy of Sciences):

We have no intention of dictating to you the details of your research subjects, or how to go about it—that is a matter for the scientists themselves.

GORBACHEV (at the Twenty-seventh Party Congress):

The Party attaches foremost importance to the task of greatly accelerating scientific and technological progress.

## SCIENTIFIC EXCHANGE

Until World War II, Soviet science was almost completely cut off from the rest of the scientific world. Then, as part of cooperative efforts, Soviet scientists and technicians began to develop limited contacts with their colleagues in the allied nations. With the advent of the Cold War in the late 1940s, this first international connection faded away. It was, however, replaced by the role of scientific supervisors that Soviet scientists were assigned to play in postwar east Europe. Formalized within the framework of the Council for Mutual Economic Assistance (CMEA), this unequal relationship has remained intact and is currently expressed in various multilateral cooperative arrangements: joint scientific projects, exchanges of scientific and technical information, and exchanges of personnel. Perhaps the best-known joint projects, supervised by Soviet scientists, are the Dubna Atomic Research Institute and the manned space flights that include East Europeans in their crews.

Under the CMEA arrangement, Moscow has been able to maintain a complete monopoly on research and development related to nuclear weapons within the Soviet bloc of nations.

**BOX 7–5**   *Soviet Underground Humor*

Official:   Your request for an exit visa to go to the West is denied because you know a state secret.

Scientist:   But in my field of science the USSR is ten years behind the West.

Official:   That is the state secret you know.

A much more important international connection was established by Soviet science in the mid-1950s when "peaceful coexistence" became the basis of Soviet foreign policy. Since that time, the USSR has concluded scientific exchange agreements with many different countries, including the United States. Soviet scientists and engineers attend many international congresses, visit research centers and laboratories of the most advanced Western nations, collect scientific data, observe experiments, and participate in joint projects. All of this is supposed to be reciprocal, to give Western visitors to the USSR the same opportunities. The consensus among Western scientists is that the Soviet side gets more than it gives. There is, however, less unanimity on the question of how much of this shortchanging is due to the relative inferiority of Soviet science and how much is caused by deliberate actions of Soviet authorities preoccupied with secrecy and considerations of national security.

Even more controversial is the question of technology transfer. Many observers believe that the Soviet Union accrues unilateral benefits by purchasing in the West advanced "soft" (licenses, blueprints, patents) and "hard" (equipment) technology. Although this too is supposed to be a two-way street, the lopsided results appear to favor the Soviet side. As long as the West holds a technological edge, this situation probably could not be expected to be otherwise. Given the competitive nature of free-market economies, it is far from clear whether an effective limited selective embargo to curb the transfer of technology to the USSR could be devised.

It has been suggested that in the broader context of East-West relations, the transfer of technology makes the Soviet Union dependent on the West and also encourages the dissemination of Western ideas among the Soviet people. There is, however, not much concrete evidence supporting either of these wistful notions.

## SCIENCE AND IDEOLOGY

In an effort to make an abstract concept comprehensible to the masses, Lenin once defined Communism as "the Soviet power plus electrification." This well-known cliché, in which the word "electrification" stands for the gamut of modern scientific and technological miracles, attests to the centrality of science in Marxist-Leninist ideology. As a matter of fact, the ideology itself is constantly identified as the most important and advanced science of them all. In the past, the Soviet mass media portrayed ideology and science as two natural, inextricably integrated partners working hand in hand and giving Marxism-Leninism much of the credit for all spectacular breakthroughs, such as space exploits. This kind of bragging has been curbed now.

There is no question that the ideology has been the main moving force in the development of Soviet science. The actual division of labor between

**BOX 7–6** *CPSU Program on Scientific Research*

> Dialectical materialistic methods have been and remain the fundamental, tried-and-tested basis for progress in natural sciences and social studies. They should be creatively further developed and skillfully applied in research.

ideology and science is also clear: The former sets goals and measures the progress made toward them, whereas the latter is expected to find ways and means to expedite their achievement. The ideology is the master and science is its important, perhaps currently the most important, servant. But they are not equal partners.

There is also an interaction between ideology and science justifying such frequent Soviet semantic compounds as "scientific Communism (Socialism)" and "Communist (Socialist) science." Of the two expressions, the first appears to be chiefly a public relations device and a tribute to our scientific age. The second expression, on the other hand, has much real meaning: Both the whole and the major components of the Soviet science machine are thoroughly permeated by ideology, although the same may not be true about all individual scientists. The term "Soviet science" refers to more than just geography. The Soviet system definitely has no use for an independent "temple of knowledge" or an apolitical "ivory tower." And Soviet science is neither of these; rather, it is a service establishment.

Divergence of priorities and interests between ideology and science must occur quite often. But on the theoretical level, Marxism-Leninism prescribes only one limitation on the unquenchable thirst for knowledge in the realm of natural sciences: The continuing search for new facts must be confined to the material universe.[14] In Soviet educational literature, scientific data and atheistic proof are usually equated.

In recent years, Soviet leaders have been successful in enlisting the support of the scientific community for their public stand against nuclear war. Soviet scientists seldom remain neutral or differ with each other and their government on such issues as the so-called nuclear winter or Star Wars. Many of them play leading roles in various international peace organizations sponsored by Moscow. There seems to be little doubt that in Mikhail Gorbachev many Soviet scientists see a very reasonable and pragmatic leader who puts concrete results above ideological rhetoric.

As we shall see in the next chapter, a concurrent emphasis on ideology and science characterizes the entire system of Soviet education.

---

[14]Actually, Soviet scientists are researching at least some areas of parapsychology. The ideologically proper name for this research is the study of "biophysical effects."

## GLOSSARY

**Akademician:** member of the USSR Academy of Sciences.
**Candidate of science:** lower of two graduate degrees.
**Doctor of science:** higher of two graduate degrees.
**Nauka:** science and technology, learning, scholarship.
**Reverse engineering:** copying and imitating mechanical devices.
**Sputnik:** satellite (literally, "fellow traveler").
**Technology transfer:** flow of sophisticated Western technology to the USSR.

## RECOMMENDED READINGS

GRAHAM, LOREN R., *Science and Philosophy in the Soviet Union*. New York: Vintage Books, 1974.
KNAUS, WILLIAM A., *Inside Russian Medicine*. New York: Everest House, 1981.
MEDVEDEV, ZHORES A., *Soviet Science*. New York: W. W. Norton, 1978.

CHAPTER

# 8

# THE EDUCATIONAL SYSTEM

## SOVIET EDUCATION

Like almost everything else in the USSR, its educational system is very large: more than 100 million people—every third person in the country—are enrolled in various kinds of schools, colleges, universities, or training programs. More than one half of them go to school full time. The Soviet Constitution (Article 45) not only guarantees free, multilingual education, but also makes completion of secondary school, the equivalent of high school, compulsory for all young people. Illiteracy has been almost completely eliminated, and the number of people with high school diplomas employed in the national economy has passed the 50 million mark. In numbers of college students, the USSR is second only to the United States.

To be fully appreciated, this impressive record must be seen against the background of Old Russia, a country in which three fourths of the people were illiterate, and enrollment in a high school or college was an almost exclusive privilege of the rich. The Soviet educational system differs from that of Old Russia in many other important ways: All Soviet schools are run by the state,[1] offer free tuition, teach the same curricula, exclude religious

[1]Actually, churches are now allowed to offer Sunday schools. Seminaries, belonging to various licensed churches, have a total enrollment of several hundred full-time students.

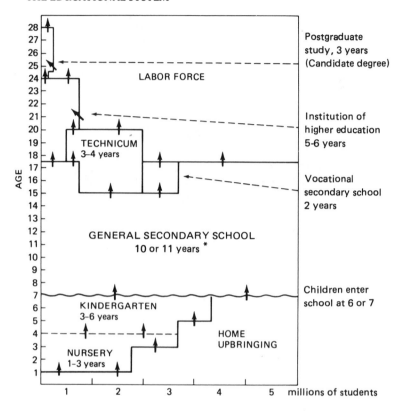

Note: The middle school curriculum is now being gradually changed from 10 to 11 years.
*Source:* Compiled by author from Soviet data.

**FIGURE 8–1**   Structure of the Soviet Educational System

instruction, and use standardized methods and textbooks. Depending on the level, education is available in as many as sixty languages, in accordance with the formula "National in form, Socialist in content." The "Socialist content" is a hallmark of Soviet education on every level, from kindergarten and elementary school to university and postgraduate studies. In addition to mandatory courses in Marxist ideology, the history of the USSR, and the history of the Communist Party, elements of political indoctrination are incorporated into practically all other courses of instruction, even those dealing with highly technical matters. The stated mission of Soviet schools is not only to educate, but also to "mold and rear the new Communist man." To accomplish this twofold goal, every bit of knowledge is presented from the point of view of Marxism-Leninism.

A related feature of Soviet education is the rigidity of its curricula. Beyond the prescribed general schooling, instruction offered by vocational schools and institutions of higher learning is compartmentalized and packaged in the form of narrow professional specializations allowing for only a few electives. Soviet students are taught on a kind of need-to-know basis, and the availability of various educational opportunities is determined not by student demand, but by the same central planning mechanism that determines the production of material goods. It is education by the state, of the state, and for the state.

With the exception of military schools, all Soviet learning facilities are coeducational. As could be expected of a society preoccupied with economic development, technical disciplines, engineering, and sciences are given a high priority in the Soviet educational effort. The quality of education is quite uneven, and, as a rule, large cities have much better secondary schools than do smaller towns and the countryside. Because admission to most institutions of higher learning and professional schools is highly competitive, certain groups of the population have considerable advantages over others. About 8 percent of the Soviet GNP is spent annually on education.

Education is high on Gorbachev's list of priorities for both economic and social reasons. The ongoing reforms of general education and of higher and specialized secondary education appear to have his touch of pragmatism about them. Two huge ministries and several lesser bureaucracies have been consolidated and merged into a single agency, the USSR State Committee on Public Education. Universities and other institutions of higher learning have been granted more autonomy.

## HISTORICAL REVIEW

Until the beginning of the eighteenth century, virtually no secular education was available in Russia, and literacy was limited to the clergy and the upper-level state bureaucracy. As part of Peter the Great's (1689–1725) concentrated efforts to modernize Russia, many young men of aristocratic birth were sent to Europe to learn various professions; equally large numbers of foreign scholars were recruited to come to Russia to teach at newly established schools. In 1755, the first Russian university, staffed mostly with foreign professors, was founded in Moscow. More colleges opened their doors in other large cities during the following fifty years. But the main mode of education for the sons and daughters of the rich elite was instruction by private, live-in tutors, usually imported from France and Germany.

Learning opportunities increased considerably during the nineteenth century, which saw the development of a comprehensive educational system consisting of state, parochial, and private schools. The number of students among the urban population rose sharply. The emancipation of the peasants in 1861 was followed by a number of reforms intended to further liberalize and broaden education on all levels. Some benefits of learning began to come down to the countryside level. It was, however, a slow process: On the eve of the 1917 Revolution, an estimated 75 percent of Russia's population was still illiterate. The incidence of illiteracy was especially high among peasant women and members of many ethnic minorities, some of which did not even have writing systems for their native tongues. By and large, high school and university education continued to be accessible only to members of the privileged classes. Before the revolution, Russia had only about 100 colleges with a total enrollment of no more than 130,000.

Soon after the revolution, the new regime launched a massive campaign to wipe out illiteracy in the adult population and to provide free schooling for all children. In many ethnic territories this ambitious effort required the creation of alphabets. New, politically colored textbooks had to be written, translated, and printed in huge quantities, and a whole array of teachers had to be retrained or educated from scratch on a crash basis. Very impressive results were achieved during the first postrevolutionary decade, but there were also many problems brought about by too much experimentation and improvisation in the search for quick solutions. An entire generation of Soviet professionals graduated from various schools that taught almost no general education courses.

The present Soviet educational system began to take shape during the early 1930s, when the regime decided on a back-to-basics approach to education. The main changes that have occurred since that time have been in the following areas: (1) strengthening political indoctrination; (2) increasing the number of years of compulsory schooling from seven to eight, ten, and now eleven (1984); (3) placing progressively more emphasis on natural sciences, mathematics, and engineering; and (4) improving the overall quality of education.

During the same period numerous other reforms did not prove practical and had to be abandoned. They included the separation of sexes in secondary schools, the addition of an extra year to the high school curriculum, and the insistence on a two-year work experience between high school

**BOX 8-1**  *CPSU Program on the Educational Reform*

The CPSU will continue improving the public education system, taking into account the need to accelerate social and economic development and the requirements of scientific and technological progress. The reform of the general education and the vocational school systems now being effected in the country is based on creative development of Lenin's principles of a uniform poly-technical labor school. It is geared toward raising still higher the standards of instruction and education of the young, to make them better prepared for their future labor activity and to gradually introduce universal vocational training.

and college. After two decades in operation, the so-called campaign of bringing education closer to real life, which was once one of Khrushchev's pet projects, appears to have lost much of its momentum, but it is still officially in use.

Now Gorbachev wants to add computer science to the secondary school curriculum in spite of severe constraints on the availability of hard and soft wares. Only about 15 percent of all schools have computer laboratories. As part of his educational reforms, most of responsibility for day-to-day decisions has been taken away from various bureaucratic agencies and given to schools, technicums, institutes and universities.

## EDUCATION AND UPBRINGING

Soviet education differs from its contemporary counterparts in the West in two aspects: (1) the Soviet school accepts a greater share of responsibility for the general upbringing of children besides teaching them various subjects; and (2) the centralized educational effort closely fits into Soviet society as an integral part, interconnected with politics, economics, mass media, and culture. To find comparable situations in America's educational experience one would have to look at the more conservative parochial schools or military academies.

As an upbringer of the young, the Soviet school seeks to supplement rather than to supplant the family. The need for the loving care of the family is fully realized by Soviet educators, who stress the importance of cooperation between school and home. It is, however, usually the school that leads the family in developing personal qualities deemed desirable in the "new" Soviet citizen: "Communist morality," Soviet patriotism, devotion to socially useful labor, and a feeling of being part of a social group. The main challenge in "character building" is to teach young people how to be competitive and ambitious as well as altruistic and comradely at the same time. School routine is filled with a special kind of friendly competition in which the winners are supposed to help the losers, and everybody is expected to be a good sport.

Education is by far the most important tool for providing the sociopolitical cohesion for a culturally diverse, huge country, and for molding the supernational Soviet character demanded by the ideology. As a part of society, the Soviet school is the supplier of future "builders of Communism." Both classroom instruction and extracurricular activities are designed to prepare the young to become disciplined and well-adjusted citizens. The extracurricular activities are channeled through the two previously mentioned youth organizations with strong links to the Communist Party: the Octobrists (Oktyabriata) and Pioneers. Practically all school children belong first to the former (ages 5 to 9) and then to the latter (ages 10 to 15). The Octobrists and Pioneers are organized into "detachments" based on school classes. Their activities are guided and supervised by upper classmates and members of the Komsomol.

A large body of published Soviet research sets forth the ways and means of bringing up the young. Prominent among many authors are the names of Anatoli Lunacharsky, the first Soviet minister of public education, and Anton Makarenko, a pedagogue who developed a methodology for rehabilitating and reshaping young minds and hearts by applying group pressure and gentle persuasion. A convinced Communist, Makarenko (1888–1939) devoted much of his life to making useful members of society out of hardened juvenile delinquents. His theories and methods are widely used throughout the Soviet educational system.

## METHODOLOGY

Currently, the responsibility for research and development in education rests with the USSR Academy of Pedagogical Sciences, which was mentioned previously. The Academy oversees and coordinates the work of thirteen research institutes and several experimental facilities in Moscow and other parts of the country. The main thrust of ongoing efforts is twofold: (1) development of the new "Communist mentality"; and (2) integration of classroom learning with various practical skills that, together, constitute the so-called polytechnical education.

The former task concerns itself with the development of various teaching methods designed to increase moral motivation, reinforce conformity and positive behavior, strengthen Marxist values, and instill patriotism. As in commercial advertising, these goals are sought by use of clever semantic formulas that relate—consciously or subliminally—all life experience to the blueprint for "building Communism." These formulas are then carefully implanted in various curricula from kindergarten through university, and in the extracurricular activities supervised by the Komsomol, which helps with the proper ideological upbringing of the young.

The latter area of concentration deals with problems related to the growing needs of the national economy in trained blue-collar labor. Ways have to be found to provide young people with practical work experience and vocational training during their entire schooling, without creating the impression in their minds that blue-collar work is inferior to more scholarly pursuits. The trouble with this contention is that it runs contrary to the prevailing scale of values in Soviet society today.

Other areas of research and development include teaching Russian as a second language, educational psychology, special education for the handicapped, testing methodology, teacher training, teaching machines, and preparation of textbooks and audio-visual aids. There is a modest amount of exchange and cooperation in the field of pedagogical research with other countries, mostly those of the Communist bloc.

On the whole, the Soviet approach to teaching and learning methodology is quite conservative. New ideas are usually slow in percolating through several layers of bureaucratic inertia. In January 1984, a reform was introduced which would gradually add a year to secondary schooling by lowering the enrollment age; this would allow expansion of the school curriculum.

## PRESCHOOL EDUCATION

The fact that the Soviet educational system is geared to serve the state, rather than the individual, is hardly noticed by those who enter this system early in life—the earlier, the better. This is one reason for the existence of a vast network of preschool training facilities that are generously subsidized by the state. Another reason is economics: As we know, in the overwhelming majority of Soviet families, both husband and wife hold full-time jobs.

More than 122,000 nurseries and kindergartens in the country take care of more than 15 million young children. These numbers are constantly growing. A typical institution enrolls from 100 to 120 children from a neighboring residential area. Its staff consists of twelve to fifteen persons, usually women: teachers, coaches, and a paramedic. Children are divided into several age groups, each of which follows its own schedule of activities, including outdoor sports, various games, arts, and music. The schedule provides for a warm midday meal, several snacks, and a nap period. Children's parents are expected to be actively involved with the program, show interest in the daily routine, talk to their sons and daughters about it, and have frequent meetings with the teachers. Complete medical and dental care is part of the overall program for which only the more affluent parents pay a nominal monthly fee.

The main objective of Soviet preschool education is to instill in young children a sense of group belonging and collective living. The children are

**TABLE 8–1**   Students in All Types of Education at the Start of 1986/87 Academic Year (million)

| | |
|---|---|
| Total number of students | 108.1 |
| including: | |
| In general education schools | 43.8 |
| In vocational training schools | 4.1 |
| In specialized secondary schools | 4.5 |
| In higher educational establishments | 5.1 |
| Those being trained for new professions; upgrading their skills at work; and covered by other types of training | 50.6 |

*Source:* Compiled by author from Soviet statistics.

taught to be orderly, cooperative, helpful, obedient, and conforming. This is achieved by a combination of friendly persuasion, individual attention, and carefully programmed conditioning involving speech training, group games, and media effects. By almost all accounts, Soviet methods of organized child rearing are quite successful. The children enrolled in preschool institutions appear to be healthy, cheerful, and content. Soviet educators are convinced that the nursery and kindergarten experience makes further socialization in the regular school easier.

## GENERAL SECONDARY EDUCATION

Preschool education in nurseries and kindergarten combined with day care is available to only 50 to 55 percent of children aged 1 to 6. The rest of them get their preschool training at home from parents and grandparents. Then comes school. For Soviet children, compulsory universal education begins at age 6 or 7 when they enter the first grade.[2] More than 50 million students receive secondary education. Most of them are enrolled in general secondary education expecting to finish a ten- or eleven-year course of study, and receive the equivalent of a high school diploma at age 17. But many students take alternative routes that are available to them at the turn of their eighth year—that is, at age 14 or 15. The first of these alternatives consists of about 5,000 professional-technical schools with an ever-increasing enrollment which currently stands at close to 4 million students. In these three-year schools a watered-down version of general education is combined with the teaching of various practical skills (trades) geared to the needs of industry and agriculture.[3] As a rule, students in these vocational schools do not plan to continue their formal education. We discuss the other alternative, called "specialized secondary education," later.

Currently, about three fourths of the children go through the complete curriculum of regular secondary education. In cities and towns most secondary schools include all grades, but in rural areas the schools are smaller, and have only eight or four grades. Some urban schools offer evening classes for students in the upper grades who combine their study with work. The entire country has a standardized curriculum that calls for a six-day-per-week class schedule, five to six class periods per day, a heavy emphasis on mathematics and natural sciences, and much homework. Some secondary schools offer an "extended day" for children of working parents, which enables about 11 million students to remain in school after hours to do homework under

[2]The age is gradually being lowered to 6.

[3]By the end of the Twelfth Five-Year Plan, approximately two thirds of all young people aged 14 to 17 are supposed to be enrolled in the professional technical schools. The slow growth of enrollment in these schools was, in the past, due to their reputation as a dumping ground for poor learners and a dead-end street, meaning that graduates from these schools had no chance to be admitted to colleges or universities.

supervision and to receive warm meals. Some secondary schools located in sparsely populated rural areas also provide room and board at a nominal cost.

Students wear prescribed clothing at school, discipline is strict, and parents are held responsible for their children's behavior. A standard grading system consisting of numbers from five down to one is used in all schools. In cities, schools are usually located within easy walking distance from the students' homes, although enrollment is not based on any residence requirement and parents may send their children to any school they choose. All schools follow the same calendar: The academic year begins on the same day early in September, is interrupted by the same official holidays and vacations, and ends late in May. For graduating seniors, this is followed by several weeks of standardized examinations.

Besides Russian, secondary education is available in about fifty languages of the USSR. However, in all schools using minority languages for instruction, Russian is taught as a mandatory second language. Such schools are chiefly in ethnic territories: union republics and autonomous republics, regions, and areas. On the other hand, secondary schools that use Russian as the language of instruction can be found practically everywhere in the country.[4] Since the mid-1980s, the teaching of Russian as a second language has been intensified and, presumably, improved. At the same time, the learning of local languages by nonnative residents (mostly Great Russians and Ukrainians) has been receiving much more attention than before.

There are no elected boards of education in the Soviet system. Individual schools—about 130,000 of them—are run by appointed directors (principals). Now, more public involvement in education on the grass-root level is being encouraged.

## SPECIAL SCHOOLS

There are three types of special schools in the Soviet system of secondary education: schools for especially gifted children, schools for pathologically retarded children, and military academies. The existence of schools for gifted children presents a problem from the point of view of Marxist pedagogical theory, which maintains that hereditary traits are secondary in importance to environmental factors. Intelligence quotient (IQ) tests are not used in the Soviet Union, and differences in aptitudes and learning abilities are attributed to such controllable conditions as motivation, learning opportunities, and interest—in other words, "nurture" over "nature." In spite of this theoretical position, children who show unusually high learning abilities and talents are encouraged to enroll in special schools emphasizing mathe-

---

[4]In a few rural areas within ethnic territories, schooling is available only in local languages.

**TABLE 8–2**   Soviet Secondary Education

Classes Per Week

| Subjects          Grades: | 1 | 2 | 3 | 4 | 5 | 6 | 7 | 8 | 9 | 10 |
|---|---|---|---|---|---|---|---|---|---|---|
| Russian language | 12 | 10 | 10 | 6 | 6 | 3 | 3 | 2 | 1 | — |
| Literature | — | — | — | 2 | 2 | 2 | 2 | 3 | 4 | 3 |
| Mathematics | 6 | 6 | 6 | 6 | 6 | 6 | 6 | 6 | 5 | 5 |
| History | — | — | — | 2 | 2 | 2 | 2 | 3 | 4 | 3 |
| Social studies | — | — | — | — | — | — | — | — | — | 2 |
| Nature study | — | 2 | 2 | 2 | — | — | — | — | — | — |
| Geography | — | — | — | — | 2 | 3 | 2 | 2 | 2 | — |
| Biology | — | — | — | — | 2 | 2 | 2 | 2 | 1 | 2 |
| Physics | — | — | — | — | — | 2 | 2 | 3 | 4 | 5 |
| Astronomy | — | — | — | — | — | — | — | — | — | 1 |
| Technical drawing | — | — | — | — | — | 1 | 1 | 1 | — | — |
| Chemistry | — | — | — | — | — | — | 2 | 2 | 2 | 3 |
| Foreign languages | — | — | — | — | 4 | 3 | 3 | 2 | 3 | 2 |
| Art | 1 | 1 | 1 | 1 | 1 | 1 | — | — | — | — |
| Music | 1 | 1 | 1 | 1 | 1 | 1 | 1 | — | — | — |
| Physical education | 2 | 2 | 2 | 2 | 2 | 2 | 2 | 2 | 2 | 2 |
| Home economics | 2 | 2 | 2 | 2 | 2 | 2 | 2 | 2 | 2 | 2 |
| TOTALS | 24 | 24 | 24 | 24 | 30 | 30 | 30 | 30 | 30 | 30 |
| Additional electives | — | — | — | — | — | — | 2 | 4 | 6 | 6 |
| Days of summer practice (fieldwork) | | | | | 6 | 6 | 12 | 12 | 24 | — |

Note: Soviet schools meet for classes six days a week. The curriculum is now being gradually changed from 10 to 11 years. Classes in computer science are being added.
*Sources:* Compiled by author from Soviet data.

matics, natural sciences, or foreign languages. In special schools emphasizing mathematics or sciences, these subjects receive intensive treatment, while other standard subjects are given normal coverage. In special foreign-language schools, English or another foreign tongue is used as the language of instruction for about half of the subjects. Such schools, found only in Moscow and other big cities, are most prestigious, and successful graduation from one of them greatly enhances a student's chances of being accepted by the better institutions of higher learning.

In compliance with the official educational theory that deemphasizes innate abilities and limitations, there are no separate schools or tracks for slow learners. Instead, underachieving students are usually encouraged to enroll in vocational schools with less demanding academic requirements. In larger school systems, children with learning problems are given professional counseling and guidance, as well as free extra tutoring. In addition, various techniques of group pressure are used to shame laggards into studying harder.

**TABLE 8–3**   Educational Level of the Population as of 1987 (million)

| | |
|---|---|
| Higher education | 20.8 |
| Incomplete higher education | 3.5 |
| Specialized secondary education | 30.9 |
| General secondary education | 65.5 |
| Incomplete secondary education | 43.6 |

Pathologically retarded children attend separate schools staffed with professional personnel trained in special methods. Special school facilities also exist for physically handicapped children. Officially known as the "second section's schools," these two types of institutions are seldom mentioned in the voluminous Soviet statistics on education. It is known that there are about 2,500 special schools of both types in the USSR, but the number of students enrolled in them is not made public.

The third type of special schools are the military, army and navy, academies for boys aged 15 to 17. These are boarding schools that combine the general secondary education of grades nine and ten with basic military training, to prepare young boys for officers' schools. Sons of career military officers are admitted to these schools on a priority basis.

## SCHOOL CURRICULA

The standardized secondary school curricula allow little flexibility to either the teachers or the students. Basic requirements governing subject matter, methodology, tests, and the like are the same across the entire country. All schools use almost identical textbooks, although they are written by different authors and printed in different languages. In ethnic territories, secondary schools teach local languages, literature, and history. However, students in such schools are also required to learn Russian as a second language and to take courses in Russian culture. Local ethnic studies and Russian studies receive approximately the same number of class periods. In schools in which Russian is the language of instruction, this entire portion of the curriculum is devoted to Russian studies.

The study of both history and literature, taught in the seven upper grades, is highly politicized through selection and interpretation.[5] In literature, the main emphasis is on the Russian nineteenth-century classics and Soviet writers. Foreign literature is limited to translated works of selected

[5]At the end of the 1987–1988 academic year, final examinations in Russian (Soviet) history were suspended in almost all schools in a tacit recognition of serious deficiencies in how this subject had been taught in the past. New textbooks of history and other social disciplines are being introduced at different levels of the educational establishment.

classics and modern "progressive" authors. The teaching of history, which is dominated by the history of the Communist Party and the Soviet Union, includes a survey of the world's past as reflected in the rearview mirror of "historic materialism." Another vehicle for the introduction of political, social, and economic issues is provided by five years of geography and one year of social studies. This bloc of courses emphasizes the Soviet Union, but it also includes a more general treatment of the world at-large.

The most commonly taught foreign language is English. (It was German before World War II.) Studying a foreign language is required in the six upper grades. But the graduates of the regular Soviet secondary schools usually possess only a reading knowledge of their foreign languages. To be sure, their chances of ever speaking with foreigners are slim anyway.

The main emphasis in the curriculum is on mathematics and natural sciences: biology, chemistry and physics. These and related disciplines take up approximately one third of the weekly course load in grades seven through ten, justifying the official description of secondary education as "polytechnical." Efforts are under way to introduce a large dose of computer science into the school curriculum. But there are not enough personal computers to do this consistently.

As a rule, boys and girls receive separate instruction in home economics and most physical education, including some basic military training. Boys, for example, take drill practice while girls take first-aid instruction. They usually also attend separate classes in sex education and personal hygiene. Class periods are forty-five minutes long with ten-to-fifteen-minute breaks between them. Student enrollment in classes is not supposed to exceed thirty, and now this limit is being lowered to twenty-five.

## SPECIALIZED SECONDARY EDUCATION

Specialized secondary education is a uniquely Soviet institution. It encompasses a network of more than 4,000 schools that combine in their curricula the last two years of general secondary education, equivalent to the junior and senior years of high school, with specialized training in engineering, economic planning, medicine, agriculture, or education. Usually called "technicums," these schools currently enroll about 4.6 million full-time and part-time students who, upon graduation, work as paraprofessional specialists such as preschool and elementary school teachers, medical technicians, and factory supervisors. More than 17 million such paraprofessionals work in various sectors of the Soviet national economy. Their level of education is roughly comparable to two years of college.

Prerequisites for admission to technicums include completing eight years of general secondary education and passing entrance examinations. The course of study in technicums takes three to four years, depending on the field of specialization. Those who have completed ten years of regular secondary school may be admitted to technicums with advanced standing. Approximately 75 percent of the full-time technicum students receive stipends of 40 to 60 rubles a month and dormitory accommodations at a nominal fee. The amount of the stipend depends on the specialization, grades, year of study, and, to a lesser extent, the financial status of the family.

Specialized secondary education is available in more than 450 majors, mostly in technical and engineering fields, which also command larger stipends. In many national territories, instruction in technicums is given in local languages. Most technicums and similar paraprofessional schools are coeducational, and more than 50 percent of the students are women. The sole exception to the rule is military officers' schools on this level, which admit only men.

Graduates of technicums must accept positions assigned by the placement offices of their schools, and they must remain there for at least two years before they can move to other jobs.[6] Holders of diplomas signifying completion of specialized secondary education are eligible for admission to institutions of higher learning and are accorded a certain preferential treatment in this respect over graduates from general secondary schools. They are usually also entitled to admission with advanced standing.

Some paraprofessionals combine their work with part-time or correspondence studies at institutions of higher learning. However, they are exceptions. Most of these people do not continue their education beyond the level they have already achieved. On the Soviet scale of social values, graduation from specialized secondary education stands for membership in the lower middle class. In Stalin's days, when analogies with the military establishment were fashionable, the recipients of specialized secondary education used to be called the "noncommissioned officers of the Soviet economy."

## HIGHER EDUCATION

The Soviet system of higher education consists of two basic types of institutions: universities and institutes. Universities which number more than seventy, are located in large cities. A Soviet university consists of several "faculties" (schools) that are further subdivided into "chairs" (departments). Major programs offered by universities include natural and mathematical sciences, social and political sciences, humanities, and jurisprudence (law schools). Institutes, of which there are about 800, are professional schools with narrow specializations in such fields as medicine, education, electrical

[6]Exceptions to this rule are made in cases of family hardships, poor health, and similar situations. Personal connections and even bribes are sometimes used to secure more desirable positions.

engineering, civil engineering, agriculture, or foreign studies. Institutes usually offer a very limited choice of closely related majors. They enroll more than 75 percent of all students. Other institutions of higher learning include art academies, musical conservatories, and some military schools.

Admission to all these schools is by standardized competitive examinations, which have become more objective and are now staggered over the June–August period, allowing applicants to apply to more than one school. To be allowed to take the examinations, applicants must have completed secondary education, general or specialized. Depending on the popularity of a given institution, competition can be quite fierce—only a fixed number of candidates are admitted, about 650,000 full-time students per year out of a much larger number of eligible applicants.

There are more than 5.3 million students altogether, but only about 60 percent of them study full time. All first-year students are admitted to a preselected major, and beginning with the first semester, they must take prescribed blocks of courses related to their major. Soviet higher education—universities and institutes—offers about 400 different majors organized into twenty-two groupings, most of which are in engineering and the natural sciences. General requirements are largely limited to courses on Marxism-Leninism and foreign languages. Very few electives are available, and they may be taken only as overloads.

The course of study usually lasts five years, and practically all majors require four summer internships and a research project during the senior year, at the end of which students must also take a standardized state examination. Changes of majors or transfers from one school to another are difficult.

Tuition is free and approximately 75 percent of the full-time students receive stipends of 40 to 70 rubles per month, depending on major, grades, year of study, and financial status of the family. This money is barely enough to pay for simple food, other necessities, and dormitories. Exceptionally good students who make the equivalent of the dean's list receive larger "individual stipends."

There are still some "closed" college level institutes where admission is by invitation only. One of these schools is the Institute of International Relations in Moscow, specializing in preparing future Soviet diplomats.

Successful completion of all requirements is rewarded by a diploma; there is no bachelor's degree. Graduates are obliged to accept for a period of two years jobs in any place to which their institution's placement service may assign them. The national economy of the USSR employs almost 13 million university and institute graduates. About three quarters of a million people get their diplomas every year. The largest group of graduates (more than 35 percent) consists of engineers and technicians, followed by economists.

## LEARNING INSTITUTIONS

The most prestigious institution of higher learning is the Lomonosov University in Moscow (named after Mikhail Lomonosov, its official name is The Moscow State University). It is the oldest university in Russia proper and the largest in the USSR. Of its seventeen constituent schools, sixteen are called "faculties" and one other is the "Institute of African and Asian Studies." These large teaching units are divided into 274 departments (chairs), some offering several related majors. The university library contains more than 6.5 million volumes. The faculty numbers more than 7,000 and the student body exceeds 30,000, which is unusually large for Soviet universities.

As is true of practically all Soviet institutions of higher learning, the Lomonosov University does not have an American-style campus. Instead, its various teaching units, administrative offices, and dormitories are scattered over a large area of the city. Its main and best-known building is a wedding-cake-shaped high-rise structure located in southwest Moscow (see Figure 8–2). This fairly modern facility is not typical of the overwhelming majority of Soviet learning institutions, which are housed in rather simply

**FIGURE 8–2**
The Moscow State Lomonosov University

constructed buildings, and which lack any claim to esthetic appearances. It appears that Soviet "supply side" higher education feels no need for attractive packaging and wrapping.

All institutions of higher learning—universities and institutes—are located in larger cities, including the capitals of union and autonomous republics. Their greatest concentrations are in Moscow (about 80), Leningrad (about 50), and Kiev (about 30). All together there are only about 100 Soviet metropolises that offer higher education. Conspicuous by their absence are small-town colleges typical of America. The idea seems to be that higher learning must be as much as possible a part of everyday life in large industrial communities.

The seventy-odd universities and about 400 pedagogical, medical, and social science institutes, together with the art and music academies, are known collectively as VUZs. In Russian, this abbreviation stands for "Higher Educational Institutions." The other 400 college-level establishments are polytechnical institutes (about 60) and specialized engineering and natural science institutes. They are called VTUZs—"Higher Technical Educational Institutions." The difference between a degree from a VUZ and VTUZ is roughly the same as between a B.A. and a B.S. degree in America, and just as imprecise.

Universities and polytechnical institutes are entirely under the jurisdiction of appropriate agencies of higher and specialized secondary education. Institutes in both VUZ and VTUZ categories usually operate under a dual jurisdiction of the same educational authorities and various branch ministries—public health, oil industry, machine-building industry and others—depending on their specialization. This reveals that the institutes are considered to be training facilities for young persons already committed to professional careers in specific areas of the national economy. Recently, accreditation reviews have closed several institutes found deficient in their academic performance.

Universities and polytechnical institutes have considerably larger student bodies than do specialized institutes. On the average, they enroll 6,000 to 7,000 full-time (day) students each. For specialized institutes, in contrast, this figure stands at about 3,500. Many, but not all, institutions of higher learning have evening (part-time) and correspondence (in absentia) divisions.

Technicums and other learning institutions on the level of specialized secondary education are also concentrated in larger cities, although their distribution encompasses more than 200 locations. Each of these "junior colleges," numbering about 4,000, enrolls about 500 full-time students. A typical technical institute, or technicum, occupies a building or a part of a building in the middle of an urban community. A few of them are on the premises of large industrial plants appropriate to their specializations so that classroom study can be easily combined with practical work.

## SOVIET STUDENTS

The young[7] men and women studying full time at Soviet universities and institutes total about 3 million, only slightly more than 1 percent of the USSR's population. Officially, they are selected on the basis of their scholastic performance in secondary school and competitive entrance examinations, and on the strength of an official recommendation that each applicant must secure from his or her last place of study or employment (school, factory, military unit, office, or whatever). Unofficially, the final selection of those to be admitted is also determined by a complex quota system designed to ensure a politically desirable ethnic, sex, age, and social origin distribution. Even more unofficially, the status and personal connections of the applicant's family can be quite helpful in borderline cases.

Small categories of applicants—those with excellent grades, disabled veterans, distinguished workers—may be admitted without being required to take entrance examinations or on a priority basis upon satisfactory completion of all or some of the examinations. Every year, a few technical majors are put on the list of critically needed specializations. Qualified students may be admitted to such majors directly, without taking entrance examinations.

The quota system of admissions is, in theory, supposed to lessen a disproportionately large ratio of students with white-collar family backgrounds and to ensure a more representative ethnic composition of the student body. In practice, it appears to contribute to the power of school administrators to discriminate against undesired applicants.

To stay enrolled, the student must earn grades of satisfactory or better in all subjects. The normal load is five courses per semester, and class attendance is compulsory. Except for mathematical subjects, examinations in Soviet schools take the form of either oral interviews or written essays. Failing grades must be removed within prescribed short grace periods and, as a rule, cannot be successfully appealed. Readmission or even transfer to another school is difficult. As important as it is, academic performance alone does not guarantee the successful continuation and completion of one's studies. Soviet students, who receive free tuition and in most cases are even paid to study, are fully expected to realize that their special status is contingent on the continuous evidence of political loyalty. Unlike compulsory secondary education, Soviet higher education is clearly not a right, but a privilege extended to relatively few individuals. The best insurance against losing this privilege is provided by membership in the Young Communist League (Komsomol), even if it adds to the already considerable burden of higher learning. Some upper-class students join the party.

---

[7]The age limit for full-time admission to undergraduate and graduate study is 35. There is no age limit for enrollment in part-time or correspondence programs.

**TABLE 8–4**    College Graduates by Type of Study (In Thousands)

|  | 1940 | 1965 | 1970 | 1975 | 1977 | 1985 |
|---|---|---|---|---|---|---|
| Graduating class including: | 126.1 | 403.9 | 630.8 | 713.4 | 751.9 | 902.0 |
| full-time | 97.8 | 224.8 | 334.8 | 433.3 | 462.2 | 541.6 |
| part-time | 4.4 | 43.5 | 82.1 | 79.7 | 84.7 | 107.3 |
| correspondence | 23.9 | 135.6 | 213.9 | 200.4 | 205.0 | 253.1 |

*Source:* Compiled by author from Soviet statistics.

Although physical education is compulsory for all first-year and second-year students, competitive collegiate sports receive relatively little attention. There are no fraternities and sororities, but students are encouraged to join various clubs (called "circles") promoting hobbies, crafts, and amateur arts. Entertainment comes mostly in the form of movies and concerts. Women comprise about 50 percent of the student body.

Students' social life is limited, not so much by any formal rules as by the heavy academic demands. Personal relations are subject to relatively few restrictions, such as curfew hours in dormitories. Marriages between students, especially upperclassmen, are not infrequent. There are approximately 100,000 invited foreign students, mostly from the developing countries in the USSR. About 30 percent of them attend Moscow's special institution, the Patrice Lumumba University. Smaller groups of foreigners are enrolled at many regular schools as well.

Only a few Soviet students are sent to study abroad. At home, Soviet students are strongly discouraged from establishing close relations with foreign students attending Soviet universities and institutes.

## ADVANCED DEGREES

Soviet universities do not have separate graduate schools or departments. A relatively small number of graduate students, called "aspirants," are admitted every year to universities and selected institutes.[8] Their programs of study are highly individualized. As a rule, full-time graduate students combine their studies with duties as teaching or research assistants. There are currently only about 100,000 full- and part-time graduate students in the USSR. Most of them have returned to academia after fulfilling their two-year work assignments. But a select few with exceptionally good academic records are invited to continue their studies without interruption upon graduation from a university or institute.

[8]Admission to graduate study is on the basis of competitive examinations in three areas: (1) foreign language; (2) philosophy (mostly Marxism-Leninism); and (3) field of specialization.

For full-time students, the first phase of graduate study usually takes three years to complete. It is rewarded by the lower of two academic degrees, called "Candidate of Science." Full-time graduate students receive larger stipends than those paid to undergraduate students. The requirements of graduate study include preparing for three comprehensive examinations and writing a thesis that has to be defended publicly before a special faculty committee. There are approximately 500,000 recipients of the candidate's degree in the USSR, most of whom are faculty members at universities and institutes or members of scientific research organizations.

The higher academic degree, called "Doctor of Science," is currently held by no more than 45,000 scientists and scholars. It is awarded on the basis of significant original research, often in the form of a major published work, evaluated and accepted by a committee of recognized experts. Research required for the doctorate is usually done on the job as a byproduct of the candidate's teaching or other professional activity. To write and defend the doctoral thesis, an approved candidate is entitled to a one-year, paid leave of absence from his or her place of work. Recipients of the doctorate, usually persons in their thirties or older, are the elite of the Soviet scientific establishment and academe.

In addition to about 360 designated select institutions of higher learning, some of the more prestigious research institutes are given the authority to award degrees of candidate and doctor in the fields of science appropriate to their expertise. In terms of the average time and effort required for their completion, probably the lower of the two Soviet academic degrees, that of candidate, comes closer to the American Ph.D.

## CONTINUING EDUCATION

The concept of continuing education that allows people to combine work and school has always been an essential part of the Soviet educational system. More than one half of all students pursuing diploma and degree programs in technicums, institutes, and universities, about 5 million people, study on a part-time (evening) basis or in absentia (by correspondence). By law, all employers must encourage and assist working students in this endeavor by giving time off with pay for study and examinations, adjusting work schedules, and even paying for transportation to and from school. Studying part time or in absentia is so demanding that it could not be pursued successfully by most working students without such special arrangements. For example, both part-time and correspondence students must complete all degree (diploma) requirements in no more than six years, which is only 20 and 50 percent longer than full-time study at universities and technicums, respectively. The average course load of working evening students is fourteen hours of lectures per week.

**TABLE 8–5**  Study of Foreign Languages in Soviet Schools (1986)

|  | | INCLUDING | |
|---|---|---|---|
|  | Total (million) | English | French | German |
| The number of students and pupils studying foreign languages | 30.7 | 16.4 | 3.3 | 10.8 |
| including: in higher educational establishments | 2.8 | 1.6 | 0.2 | 1.0 |
| in specialized secondary schools | 1.2 | 0.6 | 0.1 | 0.4 |
| in general education schools | 25.7 | 13.7 | 2.9 | 9.0 |
| in vocational schools | 1.0 | 0.5 | 0.1 | 0.4 |

The Soviet system of education in absentia is also quite demanding. It requires an intensive effort, adherence to an exact timetable, and attendance in person at periodic examination sessions. There are correspondence divisions in many regular universities and institutes. In addition, about twenty special schools offer this type of education exclusively.

Graduates from divisions of continuing education receive diplomas that entitle them to the same employment opportunities as those students who have completed their studies by going to school full time. The three types of education—full time (day), part time (evening), and in absentia (correspondence)—are supposed to be completely coordinated, to enable students to switch from one track to another. Evening classes are available not only on academic sites but also at other locations more convenient to students enrolled in them. About 80 and 150 major specializations in somewhat broader fields than those pursued by day students are available to evening and correspondence students, respectively. As in all Soviet education, the main stress in continuing education is on science and technology.

**TABLE 8–6**  College Graduation by Majors (In Thousands)

|  | 1940 | 1965 | 1970 | 1975 | 1976 | 1985 |
|---|---|---|---|---|---|---|
| Graduating Class including majors in: | 176.9 | 403.9 | 630.8 | 713.4 | 734.6 | 902.0 |
| engineering and mechanics | 32.3 | 157.4 | 237.7 | 432.8 | 289.9 | 340.3 |
| agriculture | 12.9 | 33.9 | 58.3 | 53.9 | 56.7 | 88.0 |
| economics and planning | 10.1 | 40.8 | 75.6 | 95.6 | 93.7 | 127.2 |
| medicine and public health | 20.7 | 31.0 | 43.8 | 53.6 | 55.3 | 69.7 |
| education | 78.5 | 99.3 | 152.2 | 154.7 | 161.9 | 179.8 |
| arts and humanities | 16.7 | 34.6 | 55.1 | 61.9 | 63.9 | 78.0 |
| law | 5.7 | 6.9 | 8.1 | 13.1 | 14.1 | 19.0 |

*Source:* Compiled by author from Soviet statistics.

Certain professions—for example, medicine—are completely excluded from this type of education.

Besides programs leading to diplomas and degrees, the system of continuing education offers many short-range refresher and retraining programs for different professions, as well as various courses, workshops, lecture series, and seminars. Much of this system operates today within a loose framework called "People's Universities." In addition to educational institutions, special organizations disseminate popular scientific knowledge through lectures at factories, plants, collective farms, community centers, and in military units. An extensive educational program is a permanent feature of daily television and radio broadcasting, conducted both in Russian and many ethnic languages. Opportunities for self-study and guidance are provided by numerous clubs, community centers, and public libraries.

## TEACHERS AND TEACHING

The State Committee on Public Education employs in its 200,000 schools, administrative offices, and research organizations more than 2.5 million teachers, about three fourths of whom are women. In grades one through three, a teacher teaches all subjects, but above that level the teaching assignment usually consists of one or two related subjects. The normal teaching load is sixteen to eighteen classroom hours per week plus preparatory work and other duties. Overloads for extra pay are common, especially among younger teachers whose starting salary may be as low as 140 to 150 rubles per month. In general, secondary school teaching is not one of the better-paid professions in the Soviet Union. Perhaps as a kind of compensation, teachers are among the most decorated and bemedaled Soviet white-collar workers.

Teachers' training is provided by about 500 technicum-level teachers' schools and more than 200 college-level pedagogical institutes. In addition, graduates from universities often become teachers in the upper grades.[9] Besides the State Committee on Public Education, the Academy of Pedagogical Sciences also supervises teachers' training. The standardized teachers' education curriculum consists of three parts: (1) sociopolitical subjects, including Marxism-Leninism, which take up one sixth of the time; and (2) education and applied psychology courses, which occupy another sixth of the time; and (3) subjects pertaining to specialization, which are allocated the remaining two thirds of the time. Continuing education for teachers includes methodology workshops, upgrading and refresher courses, retraining programs, and various professional seminars and conferences.

In comparison to school teachers, members of faculties of institutions of higher and specialized secondary learning receive much higher salaries. Numbering about three quarters of a million, this group is divided into three

[9] Most universities require students to take courses in teaching methodology.

ranks: those of professors, associate professors, and assistant professors. In skill-developing disciplines, such as foreign languages, there is an additional permanent rank called "instructor." Faculty members are paid on the basis of their rank and seniority; they also receive a fixed bonus for advanced degrees of "candidate" or "doctor." Only about one third of faculty members (approximately 220,000) are women.

The Soviet system of education has no provisions for academic freedom and tenure to protect faculty from political pressures. On the contrary, it is assumed that to have a successful academic career, a faculty member must set an example of unswerving loyalty to the regime. A very high percentage of academic administrators, as well as many rank-and-file educators, are members of the Communist Party.

As a rule, standardized textbooks for various subjects and for various schools are written by members of the teaching profession and are published by the State Committee on Public Education or its various branches. Faculty members are strongly encouraged to publish in professional periodicals printed in different languages of the USSR. Practically every branch of academe has its own monthly or quarterly journal. Many faculty members combine their teaching with sponsored research and consulting. Small numbers of selected faculty members participate in foreign exchanges.

## QUALITY OF EDUCATION

Marked differences in the theory, goals, and structure of Soviet education make it difficult to compare its quality with that of education in Western countries. It is quite obvious that Soviet educational effort is unimpressive in such areas as the liberal arts, humanities, and jurisprudence. These disciplines suffer the most from ideological bias and command relatively low priorities in the overall master plan for "building Communism." In many other areas, considered to be more important to achieving the goals set by the Kremlin leaders, the six decades of Soviet education have produced several generations of various professionally trained specialists: engineers, agronomists, medics, scientists, and economists. Given the large number of these specialists, it is not surprising that their average quality is not high, as has been shown by many recent Soviet émigrés who settled in Israel, the United States, and western European countries. But even with this emphasis on quantity necessitated by the rapid growth of the national economy, the Soviet educational establishment has been able to produce a considerable number of top quality experts in many important branches of knowledge.

The important "firsts" scored by Soviet science and technology during the last thirty years have been accomplished primarily by graduates of Soviet learning institutions. From the point of view of the Soviet leaders, the Soviet educational system has done quite well by producing, in record time, a large

**BOX 8–2**   *Reasons for Educational Reform*

---

The following are some of the most frequent complaints about the state of the
Soviet education:

1. Boring and uninspiring instruction on all levels;
2. Too much emphasis on learning by rote;
3. Too much centralization in curricula;
4. Not enough individual attention given to students;
5. The existence of elite schools;
6. Depreciation of high school and college diplomas;
7. Shortage of male teachers (as "role models") in secondary schools;
8. Shortage of modern equipment and teaching aids;
9. Poor state of the physical plant (school houses, dormitories, etc.);
10. Low teachers' salaries.

Compiled by author from Soviet data.

---

number of "builders of Communism" with both a sufficient professional
know-how and a sense of political loyalty. The Soviet educational system,
however, has not done well—nor has it been expected to—for individuals;
it has not liberated their minds, broadened their intellectual horizons, introduced them to different sets of values, or expanded their knowledge of the
world at large. From the beginning, it has been education by the state and
for the state, not for individuals.

Internally, the quality of Soviet education is uneven: Urban communities have much better secondary schools than villages; large cities have better
institutions of specialized and higher learning than provincial towns; universities carry more prestige and employ better faculties than most institutes;
and some institutes are officially "equated to universities" but others are not.
As a rule, full-time day students receive a better education than those who
attend evening classes or study by correspondence. Opportunities for quality education are also unequal, despite official pronouncements to the contrary. Children of the elite have several advantages denied children of the
average citizens: the urban locations of their schools; the connections of their
important parents, which can help even if competitive entrance examinations are supposed to be objective; and private tutoring obtainable for
substantial fees, which can enhance their chances for admission to better
schools. Nationality—ethnic belonging and linguistic preference—can also
affect educational opportunities for students.

Many problems face Soviet schools. But the overall quality of Soviet
education appears to be rising. Expanding contacts with the West are definitely contributing to this trend. There is, however, little evidence in the

USSR to support the theory that better education automatically leads to more democracy by fostering liberal thinking.

## POLITICAL ASPECTS

The giant Soviet educational effort is fully and quite openly used for ideological propaganda, which is blended into every academic curriculum, course of study, and even individual lesson. In Lenin's words, "the Soviet school has a political function," and, therefore, there cannot be any "petty bourgeois talk about the autonomy of education from politics." As we have seen, from a Marxist point of view, human knowledge can never be objective, neutral, or apolitical. It follows that before reaching the minds of the people to be educated, knowledge must be carefully selected and properly interpreted to produce politically desired results. This practical application of Lenin's words about education's political function ensures the safety of knowledge. And the more knowledge that is imparted to a person, the larger must be the dose of ideological medicine calculated to minimize the risk involved. For example, one of the three fields of comprehensive examinations required of all Soviet graduate students, regardless of their professional interests, is always Marxism-Leninism.

Less sophisticated political indoctrination begins much earlier in the lives of all Soviet students and remains with them as a permanent and indispensable part of education. Under Stalin, a well-known young Soviet writer publicly pledged that the first word of his expected baby would be "Stalin."[10] It is a measure of both continuity and change in the Soviet educational effort that Soviet children today begin to learn politics not as babies but at the age when they first enroll in kindergarten, and that they learn about Lenin long before they learn about Stalin. As they grow up and move through the prescribed phases of the educational system, stories of Lenin's boyhood give way to his full biographies, to the history of the USSR, and to the history of the Communist Party. By the time they complete their secondary education, they have been exposed to a lot of patriotism presented in the form of countless heroic stories about the Revolution, civil war, and especially World War II. If they continue with their studies, they also learn the all-important tenets of Marxism-Leninism, presented as the ultimate and absolute truth: the class struggle, the inevitability of Communism, the evils of individualism, the virtues of collectivism, and so forth. Gradually, students are conditioned to accept the subjective Marxist version of the world, and it does not take long for them to understand that the behavior that is rewarded both in and out of school calls for noncritical conformity and manifest loyalty to this theory. In school, from the first grade through

[10]Alexander Avdeyenko made this promise in his speech at the First Congress of the Soviet Writers' Union in 1934.

**BOX 8–3**   *Rules For Octobrists*

---

1. Octobrists are future Pioneers.
2. Octobrists are diligent; they study well, love their school, and respect their seniors.
3. Only those who love work are called Octobrists.
4. Octobrists are honest and truthful children.
5. Octobrists are congenial; they read, draw, and have fun.

---

graduate studies, this behavior is constantly reinforced by a multitude of extracurricular activities sponsored by the Octobrist and Pioneer organizations and the Komsomol under the watchful supervision of the Communist Party, which has its primary organizations in virtually all educational institutions. On the university-institute level, primary party organizations include not only administrators and faculty members but also more active and politically ambitious students.

By guaranteeing free tuition, the Soviet Constitution protects education from becoming a commercial commodity. There is, however, nothing in the Soviet system to protect education from extreme politicization. On the contrary, the mission of all Soviet schools is to provide the national economy with specialists well indoctrinated in Marxist tenets. Together with the mass media, literature, the arts, and other means of influence, Soviet education is expected to create a "new Soviet man," for whom the Marxist perception of the world would be both a common-sense necessity and a high moral virtue.

**BOX 8–4**   *Rules For Pioneers\**

---

1. A Pioneer cherishes the memory of those who have given their lives in the struggle for freedom and the thriving of the Soviet Motherland.
2. A Pioneer is friends with children of all the nations of the world.
3. A Pioneer studies diligently, is disciplined and polite.
4. A Pioneer loves to work and takes good care of people's property.
5. A Pioneer is a good friend who cares for those who are younger and helps those who are older.
6. A Pioneer grows to be a courageous person and is not afraid of hardships.
7. A Pioneer tells the truth and treasures the honor of his group.
8. A Pioneer conditions his body and does physical exercises.
9. A Pioneer loves nature and protects every day the planted trees, useful birds, and animals.
10. A Pioneer is a model for all children.

\*These rules are printed on the back cover of standard notebooks for Soviet school students.

---

In the meantime, an improved system of education is supposed to produce a more competent and better-qualified labor force urgently needed for the realization of Gorbachev's ambitious economic reforms.

### GLOSSARY

**Aspirant:** graduate student, graduate assistant.
**Attestat:** high school diploma.
**Faculty:** school, major division of a university.
**Institute:** college, professional school.
**Technicum:** junior college, paraprofessional school.
**VTUZ:** institution of higher technical learning.
**VUZ:** institution of higher learning.

### RECOMMENDED READINGS

BRONFENNER, URIE, *Two Worlds of Childhood*. New York: Russell Sage Foundation, 1970.
JACOBY, SUSAN, *Inside Soviet Schools*. New York: Hill and Wang, 1974.
ROSEN, SEYMOUR M., *Education and Modernization in the USSR*. Reading, MA: Addison-Wesley, 1971.

# 9

# THE MASS MEDIA

## INFORMATION OR PROPAGANDA

Closely related to the educational effort and, until very recently, just as much politicized were the Soviet mass media: the press, radio, and television. [According to an official definition, media's main mission was not to inform, but rather to "organize and mobilize the masses for the fulfillment of the tasks set by the Communist Party and the Soviet government."] Dissemination of information was subordinated to this mission, which determined what news was reported and how it was interpreted and presented. The regime claimed a complete monopoly on the mass media.[2] For many years, freedom of the press as promised by the Soviet Constitution (Article 50) was an empty promise, indeed, because the existence of an official ideology set severe limitations on all forms of public expression. Under Gorbachev this is being done in a less obvious and assertive way, and private individuals and groups are allowed to collect, report, and broadcast information. However, their means for carrying out such activities are severely limited.

---

[1] V. A. Golikov (ed.), *Sovetskii Soyuz* [The Soviet Union] (Moscow: Politizdat, 1975), p. 340.

[2] Officially recognized churches were allowed to publish limited editions of religious periodicals of restricted distribution among parishes.

The official mass media are managed by several cabinet-level agencies, including a special office in charge of censorship, known by its abbreviated Russian name—*Glavlit*.[3] Even under *glasnost*, nothing can be printed, said over the radio, or shown on the TV screen without having first been checked by *Glavlit* to make sure that no state secrets are being disclosed. In fact, much of the responsibility for what is published today in the Soviet Union has shifted from shadowy "central authorities" and "competent organs" to the editors of various media outlets and ultimately to the individual journalists themselves.

The mass media's establishment is huge and its message is intended for a large audience. Almost 8,400 newspapers, written in about sixty different languages, have a combined circulation of more than 190 million copies. Approximately 650 of these papers are issued daily or six days a week. Their total circulation exceeds 80 million copies on any one day. The Soviet Union also publishes about 5,500 weekly, monthly, and quarterly journals, with a total circulation almost as large as that of the newspapers. In a similarly big way, multilingual radio broadcasting logs in more than 1,400 hours per day and reaches practically every locality within the Soviet borders. And an even more powerful and effective modern medium at the complete and exclusive disposal of the regime is television. A vast network of television stations brings programs originating in Moscow to about 90 percent of the area occupied by the huge country: mountain villages in the Caucasus, remote collective farms in Central Asia, frontier settlements in the Far East, and even weather stations above the Arctic Circle. At this time, there are already more television sets in the Soviet Union than there are family households—about 100 million.

Other outlets for disseminating information and propaganda include various public lectures and seminars, numerous billboards and posters, as well as large publishing houses that turn out inexpensive books, brochures, and visual aids. Closed meetings of party members are sometimes used to disclose information considered too sensitive for the general public.

There are two official news gathering and reporting agencies in the USSR—*TASS* (Telegraph Agency of the Soviet Union) and *Novosti* (News)—with correspondents stationed throughout the world. Soviet news agencies, periodical publications, and radio and television stations are served by approximately 85,000 professional journalists, members of an exclusive and privileged organization called the Soviet Journalists' Union. Because of the importance and sensitivity attached to their work, Soviet journalists are expected to belong to the Communist Party or its youth organization (Komsomol).

---

[3]*Glavlit* stands for "Chief Administration on Matters of the Press and Literature." In the USSR, its existence is seldom even mentioned and never discussed in official sources.

## HISTORICAL PERSPECTIVE

The first Russian newspaper was founded personally by Peter the Great at the beginning of the eighteenth century. Called *Vedomosti* (Official Reports), this newspaper had set a precedent for the dependence of the Russian press on the government that lasted for more than two centuries. Only the last decade of the czarist era witnessed the emergence of a freer and more competitive press, reflecting, within the limits prescribed by censorship, different political opinions and even exposing corruption in high official circles. In 1917, during the short reign of the Provisional Government, freedom of the press finally became a reality in Russia. But this freedom abruptly ended as soon as Lenin and his followers took power.

In fact, the new regime was just two days old when it issued its first "Decree on the Press" (November 9, 1917), which closed down all non-Socialist newspapers on the grounds that "the bourgeois press is one of the strongest weapons in the hands of the bourgeoisie."[4] It is significant that the attack against the press took place six weeks prior to the establishment of the secret police and several months prior to the forming of the permanent Red Army.[5] During 1918, further restrictions on the press were proclaimed, and some 350 Socialist (but non-Bolshevik) newspapers were closed down "to end once and for all the dependence of the press on capitalism."[6] By May 1919, the regime had nationalized all printing presses, duplicating machines, and similar equipment. During the early 1920s, the last non-Bolshevik newspapers were banned, and new, stricter rules of censorship were introduced, narrowing the range of themes and topics allowed to be covered by the official press.

At the same time, as more and more people became literate, the number of publications and their circulation continued to increase. By the mid-1920s, there were newspapers in many different ethnic languages, but all of them carried the same official message. Even earlier, in July 1918, the new government took over and monopolized embryonic radio facilities with the hope of using them for the promotion of Communist ideas not only at home but also abroad. In 1922, the most powerful radio station in the world, Comintern (Communist Internationale), was built in Moscow and began to beam multilingual revolutionary messages to all four corners of the earth. On the eve of World War II, the USSR already operated an extensive network of radio stations.

During the early 1930s, experimental television was in use in the Soviet Union. In 1939, a TV center was opened in Moscow to broadcast regular programs to a limited number of receivers located in clubs and other public buildings. Interrupted by the war, efforts to make television a mass commu-

[4]Reported in *Pravda* (November 10, 1917), p. 1.

[5]The secret police, then called the "Cheka," was founded on December 20, 1917. The Red Army (Soviet Army) was established on February 23, 1918.

[6]V. I. Lenin, *Sobranie Sochinenii* [*Collected Works*] (Moscow: Politizdat, 1960), vol. 36, p. 143.

nication medium were resumed in 1945, but not until the early 1960s did the Soviet economy begin to mass produce relatively inexpensive TV receivers. Today, there are more television sets in the USSR than in any other country except the United States.

After Stalin's death, the de-Stalinization campaign produced some marked improvements in the quality of the Soviet mass media. The scope of news coverage was broadened, reporting became less monotonous and boring, and more space and time were allocated to such lighter aspects of life as sports, entertainment, romance, family problems, and leisure. The reason for this welcome change was quite obvious: The new Soviet leaders had decided to shift the main burden of their control over the masses from terror to propaganda that, therefore, had to be made more effective. An even more radical change in the same direction occurred with the introduction of Gorbachev's *glasnost* in the mid-1980s.

## CENTRAL NEWSPAPERS

The 8,400 Soviet newspapers—including about 650 dailies[7]—are divided into two major groups: central or all-national newspapers and local newspapers. Central newspapers are published in Moscow by various components of the official establishment for distribution throughout the country. The most important among them is *Pravda* (Truth), the organ of the Central Committee of the Communist Party. It is the oldest (established in 1912) and the most important daily, with a circulation of several million. The next in importance is the Soviet government's paper, called *Izvestia* (News). Other

**TABLE 9–1**   First Steps toward Press Monopoly

| Date | Step |
| --- | --- |
| November 9, 1917 | "Decree for the Press": closing down "…organs of the press which (1) call for open resistance of nonsubordination to the workers' and peasants' government, (2) spread confusion by means of obvious distortions of facts, and/or (3) call for obviously criminal acts subject to legal prosecution." |
| January 28, 1918 | Establishment of the "Revolutionary Tribunals" for the press. These "tribunals" were charged with the responsibility of preventing the press from committing "crimes and misdemeanors against the people." |
| April 5, 1918 | Obliging all newspapers to publish "decrees and ordinances of the organs of the Soviet Power." |

*Source:* Compiled by author from Soviet data.

[7]Actually, most Soviet "dailies" are published six days a week. Of the big papers, only *Pravda* and *Izvestia* are issued every day.

Пролетарии всех стран, соединяйтесь!

# ПРАВДА

*Газета основана*
*5 мая 1912 года*
*В.И.ЛЕНИНЫМ*

**Орган Центрального Комитета КПСС**

№ 41 (26124)  •  Суббота, 10 февраля 1990 года  •  Цена 4 коп.

*Proletarians of all countries, unite!*

# PRAVDA

*The paper was founded*
*on 5 May 1912 by*
*V. I. LENIN*

**The Organ of the Central Committee of the CPSU**

No. 41 (26124)  •  Saturday, 10 February 1990  •  Price: 4 kop.

**FIGURE 9–1** *Pravda's* new name plate (since January 1, 1990).

central newspapers with large circulations include such publications as *Trud* (Labor), put out by the trade unions; *The Red Star*, the organ of the Defense Ministry; *The Literary Gazette*, published by the Soviet Writers' Union; and *Komsomolskaya Pravda*, a youth daily, published by the Central Committee of the Komsomol. Altogether, there are about thirty central papers.

Compared with American dailies, Soviet newspapers are much smaller in format. They carry almost no commercial advertisements or classified ads, and do not publish comics. A typical issue of *Pravda*, for example, has only six pages. On any average day, its front page carries several official reports and two or three photographs pertaining to the latest economic achievements in the USSR: commissioning of a new factory, overfulfillment of coal-mining production quotas, a record harvest of sugar beets, or completion of a major construction project. Next to them, in the left-hand column, is a usually unsigned editorial commenting on either economic progress or some specific political issue of the day. The front page also contains a number of brief foreign-news items and official announcements concerning visiting dignitaries, comings and goings of various delegations, and exchanges of diplomatic messages. As part of *glasnost*, a portion of the front page is sometimes reserved for readers' letters. On the very top of the front page, *Pravda*, as well as most other Soviet periodical publications, displays Marx's famous appeal: "Proletarians of all countries, unite!" which first appeared in the Communist Manifesto. (In English, the word "workers" is usually used instead of "proletarians.")

The second page of *Pravda* normally contains several signed articles of "criticism and self-criticism" pertaining mostly to party and economic matters. Similar critical articles appear on the third page. They are interspersed with articles and illustrations praising various new accomplishments and achievements to ensure that the overall impression from any given issue of the paper is positive and optimistic, although currently the balance between good and bad news is often very close. Now the main message of each issue of *Pravda* is twofold: to convey to readers the sense of a dire need for change, and to assure him or her that decisive steps to meet this need are underway.

The fourth and fifth pages are normally devoted to foreign news: good things about the Socialist countries and their friends, and bad things about the capitalist countries and their dependencies. The sixth page is devoted to sports news, TV schedules, weather forecasts, and similar information. It may also contain a few human-interest stories.

A daily issue of *Pravda* contains seventy-five to ninety separate headings of news reports, commentaries, and articles. Approximately one half of this material is devoted to economic themes. Slightly more than one third of all items deals with foreign news. A regular issue carries eight to ten photographs and, usually, at least one political cartoon. Sometimes *Pravda* even prints artistic prose and short poems. *Pravda* is a morning paper.

*Izvestia* is officially the newspaper of the Supreme Soviet and the Council of Ministers. In its format and appearance, *Izvestia* closely resembles *Pravda*. The contents of the two big papers are not very different either. An underground Soviet joke used to put it this way. "In the News (*Izvestia*) there is no truth, and in the Truth (*Pravda*) there is no news." Actually, both papers have about the same proportions of the Soviet versions of these two ingredients, but *Izvestia* puts more emphasis on stories and information pertaining to purely governmental matters. It also provides slightly more detailed coverage of sports and cultural events. The Sunday issue of *Izvestia* includes a magazine supplement called *Nedelya* (Week). *Izvestia* is an afternoon paper.

As a rule, the two leading Soviet papers share exactly the same editorial opinion on all important issues. To find even minor deviations from this norm, one has to go back to the periods of intense power struggle in the Kremlin following the deaths of Lenin and Stalin. The editors-in-chief of these two papers are high-ranking party functionaries.

Other central papers follow the same general pattern, except that they emphasize special areas of interest and themes assigned to them. Most of them are published two to three times a week. Central papers are available throughout the country, both at newsstands and by subscription for home or office delivery through the regular mail. Their single copies sell for the

BOX 9–1   *Ten Important Central Papers*

*Pravda* (Truth) The most important paper; organ of the Central Committee of the CPSU; circulation of several million; published every day (printed in twenty cities); emphasis on party affairs and general news.

*Izvestia* (News) The second most influential daily; organ of the Soviet government; circulation of several million; carries official information and general news. Its Sunday edition has a supplement with news analysis, feature stories, and artistic prose.

*Trud* (Labor) The organ of the trade unions; published six days a week; very large circulation; concentrates on labor and economic information; some general news.

*Komsomolskaya Pravda* (Komsomol's Truth) The daily (six days a week) of the Komsomol Central Committee; large and growing circulation. This paper is especially designed for young readers.

*Krasnaya Zvezda* (Red Star) The organ of the Ministry of Defense; of particular interest to military personnel. Its lead stories reflect the official thinking on strategic matters.

*Literaturnaya Gazeta* (Literary Gazette) The voice of the Writers' Union; carries the most authoritative opinions pertaining to literary life, stage, screen, and other cultural outlets.

*Sovetskaya Rossiya* (Soviet Russia) The largest newspaper in the RSFSR (Russian Federation), which it is supposed to serve; printed simultaneously in several cities; has the same attribution as *Pravda:* the Central Committee of the CPSU.

*Za Rubezhom* (Abroad) Weekly paper; reports exclusively about international events and foreign news.

*Sovetski Sport* (Soviet Sport) Carries comprehensive summaries of all important sports events; well illustrated.

*Selskaya Zhizn* (Rural Life) Designed primarily for farmers; carries agricultural news, articles, and stories.

Compiled by author from Soviet data.

equivalent of 3 to 5 cents depending on the number of pages in a given issue. A subscription to *Pravda* or *Izvestia* costs about $12.00 a year.

Several times a year, *Pravda* changes its format to dramatize a special topic: a CPSU Central Committee meeting, an important speech by the top leader, or a report on the state of the national economy. Special topics of this kind sometimes occupy almost the entire daily edition, leaving little room for anything else. On rare occasions, *Pravda* carries commentaries on vital issues, signed by pseudonyms, which are assumed to belong to one or more members of the ruling elite. Under Andropov, *Pravda* began to carry brief reports about regular meetings of the Politburo. Other papers followed suit.

**TABLE 9–2**  Publication of Newspapers by Union Republics (1982)

| Union Republic | In Russian | In Ethnic Languages |
|---|---|---|
| RSFSR (Russian Federation) | 4,100 | 303 |
| Ukranian SSR | 446 | 1,353 |
| Byelorussian SSR | 58 | 128 |
| Uzbek SSR | 87 | 173 |
| Kazakh SSR | 226 | 157 |
| Georgian SSR | 19 | 123 |
| Azerbaijan SSR | 25 | 95 |
| Lithuanian SSR | 24 | 94 |
| Moldavian SSR | 87 | 66 |
| Latvian SSR | 36 | 56 |
| Kirghiz SSR | 46 | 55 |
| Tajik SSR | 11 | 47 |
| Armenian SSR | 10 | 72 |
| Turkmen SSR | 12 | 24 |
| Estonian SSR | 11 | 31 |

*Source:* Compiled by author from Soviet statistics.

During Gorbachev's tenure, these reports became more detailed but still limited to the end results of such meetings—saying nothing about any debates, arguments, or disagreements among the top Kremlin leaders.

## LOCAL PRESS

Local papers are published on the republic, region, city, district, and other administrative levels by appropriate government and party offices, sometimes jointly and sometimes separately. Many local papers appear only in ethnic languages, whereas others have both a Russian and a non-Russian edition. The use of ethnic languages by the local press has sharply increased due to the growing local nationalism.

Because it is expected that people everywhere in the country read central dailies to keep abreast of national and international events, local papers do not carry much news about events outside their localities. As a rule, their circulation and availability are also limited to their immediate areas. Their main fare used to consist of local economic news selected to create an overall positive impression: completion of an industrial project, construction of a modern apartment house, renovation of a school, opening of a new sports center, and similar stories. All kinds of local heroes of the day—a worker who exceeded his production quota, an engineer who came up with a technical innovation, or a teacher whose students achieved high scores—were featured in print and photography. Shortcomings and failures of local significance were usually reported in the form of expanded letters to the editor. Now many local papers, especially those published in ethnic republics, are openly critical of even the most basic aspects of the Soviet system. Some specialize in negative news. On the lighter side of the news are only sports events, cultural happenings, and literary and artistic achievements of local talents. Compared with the central papers, the local press is more likely to at least briefly mention serious crimes, accidents, and disasters occurring in a given locality.

Many local papers carry limited numbers of concise personal advertisements and notices. On occasion, such papers may also display a few illustrated commercial advertisements of a new movie or of a subscription campaign for state bonds.

Like all other large cities, Moscow has its own local press. The most popular local papers are a daily, called *Evening Moscow*, and a weekly tabloid, *Moscow News*, which is published in Russian and several foreign languages, including English. *Moscow News* is considered to speak for the extreme liberal wing of the Gorbachev reform administration.

## SOVIET MAGAZINES

Soviet journals and magazines come in the same two large categories as the newspapers: central and local. The most important political journal, published by the Central Committee of the Communist Party, is called *Kommunist* (Communist). A plain-looking, monthly periodical, it contains articles by leading Soviet ideologists who have the final word on the application of Marxism-Leninism to current events. *Kommunist's* editorials are closely watched by all party members. Other specialized monthly and quarterly publications are devoted to problems of economics, engineering, medicine, education, and so on. They are put out either by appropriate ministries or various branches of the academic establishment.

Very important in the Soviet scheme of periodical publications are the so-called thick monthly literary reviews. Traditionally, they provide the best possible exposure for new poets and writers, and they thus serve approximately the same function as the bestseller lists in the United States. The most prestigious "thick journals" are *Novyi Mir* (New World) and *Oktyabr* (October). For example, Alexander Solzhenitsyn made his famous literary debut in the pages of *Novyi Mir* in 1962.[8] More recently, the magazine has been publishing prose and poetry that were formerly banned.

The best-known pictorial weekly publication is called *Ogonyok* (Little Light). It contains a mixture of political, cultural, and economic news items, commemorative articles, human-interest stories, personalities' profiles, poetry, humor, and sometimes installments of new fiction. Even in this most popular and diversified pictorial the main emphasis of both the stories and

[8]The title of Solzhenitsyn's first published story was *One Day in the Life of Ivan Denisovich*. It describes life in one of Stalin's concentration camps.

the color illustrations is still on economic issues. *Ogonyok* has a growing circulation of several million copies. This periodical has earned a reputation as one of the most outspoken and consistent adherents to *glasnost*. During the last several years, *Ogonyok* has scored many "firsts" in opening up formerly forbidden themes and lifting taboos from sensitive subjects, such as prostitution, youth gangs, AIDS, drugs, and official corruption. It thrives on sensational and controversial topics.

Several all-national satirical magazines, the best-known of which is called *Krokodil* (Crocodile), give special twists to the "criticism and self-criticism" theme. They also carry satirical exposés of the international scene, or rather of that portion of it that is populated by bad capitalists and their puppets. Top Soviet leaders now in power and major failures of their domestic or foreign policy are still not permitted to be satirized in print or drawing. Unlike so many other things, humor continues to be subject to strict ideological constraints under Gorbachev's policy of *glasnost*, although the severity of ideological restrictions has been considerably relaxed.

There are also special periodicals for different age groups of youth, as well as for women. Numerous other Soviet periodicals are devoted to various kinds of sports, recreation, and hobbies. Conspicuous by their absence are periodical publications devoted to violence, horror, sex and pornography, the occult and mysticism, and religion. But there are now periodicals featuring criminal stories and detective work.

The Soviet Union publishes several magazines in foreign languages for distribution abroad. As already mentioned, many local journals and magazines are published in ethnic languages. Like the newspapers, all Soviet periodicals are quite inexpensive. They are available at newsstands and by subscription.

There are now discernible differences among various periodicals on questions pertaining to various aspects and issues of *perestroika*, such as: desirability of certain changes, need for further revelations of the Stalin era's crimes, and ethnic politics. Sometimes it seems to be even possible—or so it is claimed by eager observers—to detect in the Soviet press a weak echo of the power struggle in the Kremlin. The latest new shortage, creating long lines and leaving many buyers-to-be disappointed, involves the sale of the more controversial publications: *Ogonyok, The Moscow News, and Novyi Mir.* Just as before, Soviet publishing undertakings are not expected to be profit-making businesses, and their circulations are determined by political considerations rather than readers' demand.

## RADIO

At the beginning of the Soviet era, Lenin initiated a special campaign to promote radio as a promising new medium, which he compared to a magic newspaper that could overcome the illiteracy and great distances of Russia. Radio has indeed served the regime well as a modern instrument of mass political propaganda and education. This was especially true during the 1920s and early 1930s when radio existed in the Soviet Union chiefly in the form of cable networks with individual receivers in every community that were wired to relay stations operated by trusted technicians who had complete control over the selection of broadcasts. Later, the growing number of wireless radio receivers in the hands of private citizens began to present the regime with the formidable problem of preventing people from listening to undesirable broadcasts from abroad. The problem, which became acute during World War II and the Cold War, remained unsolved, because there was no way to make the Soviet borders soundproof or to enforce a complete ban on the reception of foreign broadcasts short of confiscating millions of radio receivers.

As a result of this situation, Soviet radio is the only mass medium that must deal with healthy competition to attract and hold the attention of the listeners. And, of course, it must also stay within the limits of the official ideology. Soviet radio broadcasters try to meet this challenge by constantly increasing the volume and diversity of their programs. Broadcast in more than seventy languages, and totaling more than 1,500 hours per day, the radio programs include summaries of Soviet newspapers, live interviews, news, panel discussions, and comments on important events—none of which is very exciting fare by Western standards. In recent years, sportcasts and popular music have become daily features on Soviet radio. The most important portion of the programming, about 180 hours of it, originates in Moscow, which operates eight radio channels for domestic consumption by special categories of listeners: young children, teenagers, young adults, women, peasants, and others.

It is doubtful, however, that the Soviet leaders really believe that they are winning the radio-wave battle. Lately, there·have even been reports of an illegal variety of citizen's band (CB) radio in the USSR. Branded "radio pirates" and "radio hooligans," these daring Soviet amateurs use homemade transmitters to rebroadcast recorded Western jazz and rock-and-roll music. This is happening in spite of strict controls imposed on all ham radio operators.

## TELEVISION

Television, on the other hand, has so far been an ideal vehicle for the official message. Unlike radio, television can be fully controlled. It is not surprising, therefore, that for the last two decades the emphasis in the USSR has been rapidly shifting in favor of television. By and large, the approximately 100 million TV sets scattered over the entire country can receive only domestic signals originating in Moscow or in local studios.[9] The Soviet Union has more than 350 television stations and approximately 1,400 relay facilities served by cable and a telecommunications satellite system called *Orbit*.

Much prime television time is given to the direct broadcasting or replaying of central programs transmitted on four channels from Moscow and providing more than fifty hours of news, commentaries, education, and entertainment per day. About one fifth of this time is allocated to news and commentaries on current events, including a daily program called *Vremia* (Time). Purported to be the most watched regular TV program in the world, *Vremia* outwardly resembles a traditional Western news broadcast with two announcers, prerecorded film clips, interviews, and various visual aids. But because everything shown and said on this broadcast represents the official position of the Soviet leadership, the program is watched with great attention by millions of viewers throughout the Soviet Union. Ethnic republics and lesser territories have their own television stations.

The general character of the material shown on Soviet television resembles that of American educational programs: serious in tone, serving utilitarian purposes, free from sex and violence, and uninterrupted by commercials. The resemblance, however, does not go much further than that, because Soviet television programs, including entertainment, always have strong ideological overtones. The same is true for travelogues, sports shows, and practically everything else. On a typical day, Soviet viewers may be able to choose, in addition to news, from the following list of programs: (1) daily or weekly economic series, such as "Construction Sites of the Twelfth Five-Year Plan," "Winners in Socialist Emulation," "Reports from Leading Collective Farms," or "How to Put Your Heart into Your Work"; (2) travelogues and weekly installments from "Animal Kingdom"; (3) musical and family variety shows; (4) World War II combat and spy stories with a strong patriotic flavor; (5) special shows commemorating various important events on the Soviet calendar; (6) old Soviet movies; (7) coverage of sports events; (8) various lectures, including regular high school and college instruction; (9) children's programs, including nonviolent cartoons; and (10) relatively few game shows and contests, emphasizing desirable social values and behavior; (11) panel discussions and interviews involving leading personalities; and (12) investigative reports dealing with various problems. Special programs range from heated discussions of controversial issues (crime, prostitution, drugs) to beauty contests, and from fashion shows to "tele-bridges" between the USSR and the USA. As a "populist leader," Gorbachev often uses television for direct personal appeals to the people at large. A very special treat for Soviet TV viewers would be a rare satirical show or an old foreign movie. There is as yet very little cable television in the USSR.

[9]In parts of the Baltic union-republics and near Leningrad, it is possible to receive television programs from Scandinavian countries.

**BOX 9–2**  *Five Important Central Journals*

*Kommunist* (Communist) With a circulation of close to 1 million, this plain-look-ing monthly contains the latest interpretations of various developments from the Marxist-Leninist point of view. It is "must" reading for all party executives.

*Krokodil* (Crocodile) The most popular (circulation 6 million) periodical. Published every ten days, it is devoted to humor and satire. It carries numerous political cartoons and has many talented artists on its staff.

*Ogonyok* (Little Light) A widely distributed, illustrated weekly magazine with a very large circulation. It carries political news stories, human-interest items, serialized fiction, and pictorial reports.

*Novyi Mir* (New World) The leading "thick" literary review, which has much prestige and influence among better-educated people. It is believed to be liberal. Its monthly circulation of approximately 2 million copies features new prose, poetry, criticism, and commentary.

*Oktyabr* (October) Another important monthly review with about the same circulation and similar content as *Novyi Mir*. This journal is identified with conservative tastes and opinions, as opposed to *Novyi Mir*, which is supposed to be more liberal.

In terms of circulation, the leading magazines are *Argumety i Fakty* (Argu-ments and Facts), *Krestyanka* (Peasant Woman), *Zdorovye* (Health), and *Nedelya* (Week). Each one of them comes out in tens of millions of copies.

Compiled by author from Soviet data.

Compared with other Soviet-produced appliances, television sets are not expensive—the least expensive black-and-white set sells for about 170 rubles—and are readily available. Almost every household has a "blue screen"[10] as its treasured possession. Recently, the first generation of Soviet-made videotape recorders made a belated appearance.

Just as it is elsewhere in the world, in Gorbachev's USSR television is rapidly becoming the most effective and influential mass medium, which reaches millions of people, including those who seldom, if ever, read news-papers. Because of this, it also is the most tightly and completely controlled propaganda tool in the country. Mikhail Gorbachev is the first Kremlin leader to make full use of this medium in his efforts to revitalize Soviet society. In turn, *glasnost* has greatly benefited television, making its pro-grams more lively, diverse, and interesting. Many formerly banned topics are now part of the daily fare. Television equipment has been upgraded and the amount of daily broadcasting has been increased. News programs now often include direct man-on-the-street reporting and live interviews.

[10]"Blue screen" and "silver screen" are the Soviet press's nicknames for television and movies, respectively.

## JOURNALISTS

In the Soviet Union, the word *journalist* denotes a profession that only remotely resembles its counterpart in the West. The functions and responsibilities of Soviet journalists are comparable to those of public relations officers in a private corporation or of copywriters working for an advertising firm.

During the first six months of the Soviet era, there was even a special ministry of the press in charge of all existing periodical publications and the people employed by them. The eventual decentralization of the mass media left all news outlets in the hands of various party and state authorities, a situation that has prevailed ever since. And from the very beginning, Soviet journalists have been the official mouthpieces of the regime, trusted with its intimate secrets. Of more than symbolic importance to the profession has been the fact that Lenin, the founder of the Soviet state, considered himself a journalist, although he was educated as a lawyer.

Because information in the USSR is treated as a sensitive political commodity, its handling is entrusted only to party members in good standing and with solid backgrounds in various aspects of Marxism-Leninism. Soviet journalists are constantly involved in areas of Soviet life in which contradictions between theory and reality are the most flagrant and obvious. At times, it is their duty to rationalize, minimize, or even completely gloss over these contradictions. At other times, for example, they have been called upon to completely reverse themselves and criticize, denounce and condemn their own views of yesterday. This is how they earn their living, which, on the average, is quite good by Soviet standards.

Approximately 50 percent of professional Soviet journalists are graduates of Moscow University's department of journalism or of a special Moscow institute that offers a program of studies dominated by political subjects. Many other journalists originally started their careers as political propagandists or party functionaries who later switched to full-time work in the mass media. They all belong to a special organization called the Union of Soviet Journalists, which has about 85,000 members: print journalists, broadcasters, editors, and the like.

Within the Soviet journalistic profession, the status of foreign correspondent carries much prestige, and only some 500 of the most politically reliable individuals are stationed abroad. In addition to the *TASS* and *Novosti* agencies, which maintain permanent offices in many foreign countries, correspondents from *Pravda, Izvestia,* and the central Soviet radio and television networks are found in about fifty major capitals and cities of the world. Although most of the foreign news coverage appearing in the Soviet mass media is based on abstracts and excerpts from Western sources, byline contributions of Soviet correspondents stationed abroad can be found in every issue of *Pravda* or *Izvestia.* And the names of some of these correspon-

BOX 9–3    *Soviet Underground Humor*

---

At a newspaper kiosk in Moscow:

| | |
|---|---|
| Customer: | *The Truth [Pravda]*, please. |
| Vendor: | We don't have *The Truth*. |
| Customer: | *The News [Izvestia]*, then. |
| Vendor: | *The News* is late today. |
| Customer: | *Rural Life?* |
| Vendor: | It's finished. |
| Customer: | *Soviet Russia?* |
| Vendor: | It has been sold out. |
| Customer: | What's left? |
| Vendor: | *Labor [Trud]* for 2 kopeks. |

---

dents are well known in their country. *Pravda* alone has about fifty correspondents stationed abroad.

Much of the information that Soviet foreign correspondents manage to collect is for official use only. This does not mean that they are necessarily engaged in gathering secret intelligence information, but rather points to the fact that information in general is still handled with the utmost care in the USSR.

Every major Soviet paper has numerous volunteer correspondents who report on local issues and happenings. Close to 50 percent of the published information comes from these correspondents and, after thorough editing, it appears in papers over the names of amateur correspondents. This is supposed to testify to the democratic nature of the Soviet press. But every news outlet is managed by professionals.

## NEWS MANAGEMENT

In deciding what to report, Soviet journalists and editors are guided neither by a need to sell their product nor by a belief that the public has the right to know. Instead, their chief concern now is "what is good for *perestroika*."[11] When news is selected, interpreted, and reported on this basis, the public is informed mainly about events and stories that are considered to be good for the ongoing reforms. Happenings that do not fall into this category are either ignored or, if they are too obvious, reported in such a way that their significance is minimized. A somewhat similar attitude toward the news existed perhaps in the United States and other Western countries during

[11]To be sure, there is no consensus on this point among them.

BOX 9-4    *Gorbachev on the Western Media's Coverage of the Chernobyl Accident*

---

They launched an unrestrained anti-Soviet campaign. It is hard to imagine what was said and written during those days: "thousands of casualties," "mass graves of the dead," "desolate Kiev," that "all of the Ukraine's soil has been poisoned," and so on and so forth.

To sum it up, we faced a veritable mountain of lies—most vile and malicious lies. It is not pleasant to recall all this, but it must be done. The international public must know what we had to face. This must be done to answer the question: What, in actual fact, was behind that highly immoral campaign?

Gorbachev's television address on May 14, 1986, as reported in *Pravda*, May 15, 1986, p. 2.

---

World War II, when journalists reporting from battlefields slanted their stories because of both military censorship and their own sense of patriotism.

Given this approach to news reporting, it is no wonder that the world depicted by the Soviet mass media is significantly different from the image familiar to the Western reader and viewer. In Soviet news coverage, the emphasis is on optimism from the Communist ideology's point of view. In covering the domestic scene, the daily news typically includes reports and stories on many negative aspects of Soviet life, problems and failures. But all of this is counterbalanced by messages about new economic achievements and advances in the Soviet national economy, exemplary "labor heroism" of individual workers, innovative efforts of progressive administrators, and promising initiatives and experimentation under *perestroika*. The purpose of the messages is to reassure, instill optimism, and invite imitation of worthy precedents that help to move the nation faster toward Gorbachev's version of "Socialism with a human face." As a rule, all these reports and stories are based on actual happenings and use names of real people. Crimes, disasters, major and minor setbacks, and failures are reported in a special "constructive" way called "criticism and self-criticism." In spite of Gorbachev's personal pledge to support public candor, Soviet life continues to be shown as more harmonious than it actually is, and *perestroika's* chances for success almost always get the benefit of the doubt. The Soviet theory of mass media holds that good news affects positively not only people's beliefs, but also their behavior. It is maintained that, as a result of receiving good news, people are more cooperative, optimistic, and hopeful—characteristics desired by their leaders.

News coverage of the nuclear catastrophe at Chernobyl in April–May 1986 dramatically demonstrated the basic difference between the Soviet and Western approaches to journalism. To Soviet journalists, their own reporting of the tragic events was professionally responsible and sufficiently frank. But in the opinion of their Western counterparts, the Soviet media were guilty of withholding information to cover up a dangerous failure. Soviet journalists condemned the West for what they called sensationalism and gloating over a human tragedy. Western journalists claimed that any false reporting or exaggeration on their part was a direct result of excessive Soviet secrecy.

In covering the world at large, the same selective method is still used to create the impression that "progressive forces" are steadily gaining the upper hand over "reactionary elements" on all continents of the globe. Usually, this means stressing the positive news from Socialist countries and the negative news from major capitalist countries, including the United States. Although Soviet correspondents are posted in all major capitalist countries, the negative information about these countries is usually quoted from foreign mass media, as if to dispel any doubts concerning its credibility. Appropriate comments are supplied to connect news-making events with the Marxist theory of history, leaving no room for speculation or controversy. On the other hand, Soviet coverage of major disasters and near-disasters—space mishaps, train derailments, fires, or hijackings—has been steadily improving in terms of time and detail, earning more trust for Soviet journalists.

The Soviet media's approach to news is strictly formal and official. Personal lives of news makers, including Soviet leaders, are almost never reported. As a result, relatively few Soviet citizens know such things as, for example, the name of the General Secretary's daughter or how many children the head of the Soviet government has.[12] Soviet journalists take their profession very seriously as if their reports and articles were to be used as rough drafts of history.

## SEMANTICS OF COMMUNISM

To convey their message, the Soviet mass media employ many verbal signals, euphemisms, clichés, and terms that, even when they look quite familiar to people in the West, often have different meanings. As we have already seen, even such words as "party," "democracy," and "election" mean different things in the Soviet Union than in the West. Of course, Soviet citizens are quite used to the semantics of Communism.

Until the advent of *glasnost*, the most widely used euphemism in the Soviet mass media was probably the expression "the cult of personality," meaning the last two decades of Stalin's rule, characterized by police terror, mass deportations, and blood purges. Serious economic problems were customarily minimized in the media as passing "growing pains" or "temporary difficulties." Any admission of failure was usually prefaced by lengthy, stereotyped enumerations of achievements, illustrated by appropriate statistics calculated to absorb the shock. One-sided value judgments were often

---

[12]Gorbachev's wife, Raisa, is sometimes shown in the Soviet mass media, but she is seldom identified by her name or her relationship to the General Secretary.

introduced with such phrases as "Everybody knows that..." or "In accordance with the world's public opinion...." In the realm of international relations, mass media coverage was based on the use of generalizations, black-and-white contrasts, and standard labels that left no doubt in the minds of readers and listeners of the official Soviet position vis-à-vis any given event. Prominent among these labels were the following: "peace-loving nations of Socialism," "progressive forces of peace and Socialism," "peaceful coexistence," "lessening of tensions" (détente), "the just cause of national liberation," "reactionary circles," "imperialist warmongers," "neo-colonialism," "supporters of the Cold War," and "Zionist elements." Special terms were used to define the character of Moscow's relations with foreign Marxist parties. The term "Communist and workers' parties" signaled official Soviet approval, whereas the word "revisionists" was reserved for heretics, such as the Chinese and Albanian Communist leaders. Among the most frequent clichés were expressions like "cares of the party and government," "Communist internationalism," "high Communist morality," "fraternal friendship of Soviet nations," "Leninist principles of administration," "collective leadership," and "the unity of the party and the people."

Some of these terms and clichés are continued to be used along with quite a few new ones. Next to *glasnost* and *perestroika*—which are the catchwords for everything good and progressive—the most frequently mentioned word in the current political vocabulary is "stagnation" denoting the "basket case" economy inherited from the Brezhnev era. The term "cooperative" often refers to small family businesses. The large Soviet army in Afghanistan was called a "limited contingent," and the soldiers who have served there are said to have carried out their "internationalistic duty." Gorbachev's foreign policy is called "New Thinking."

The monotony of a single "correct" interpretation of events, imposed by ideology, used to be compounded by the sameness of the language found in all Soviet periodical publications, on the radio, and in television broadcasts. Mass media's vocabulary was a strange mixture of bureaucratic terms, "big words," and colloquialisms. The style of the Soviet mass media continues to be formal and at times even pompous. Rhetorical extravaganzas, a specialty of *Pravda*'s editorials, are still imitated and paraphrased by lesser broadcast and print news outlets not only in Russian, but in all other languages employed by the Soviet mass media. A number of especially high-sounding and emotional epithets are still reserved for references to such official sacred cows as Karl Marx, Vladimir Lenin, and the October Revolution.

But, in general, there has been a marked improvement in the use of language, making reporting more candid and straightforward. A much more subtle approach to information is used and the reporting is no longer done in black and white. There are indications that the Soviet press is changing to a more businesslike tone, presumably in accord with the desired public image of the Gorbachev leadership.

## CRITICISM AND SELF-CRITICISM

As we have seen, according to historic materialism, under capitalism the moving force of history manifests itself through destructive explosions of the class struggle. Under Socialism, the class struggle ceases, and the forces of history are harnessed and put to constructive use through a special thesis-antithesis mechanism called "criticism and self-criticism." On the theoretical level, this is supposed to explain how progress continues under Socialism. On the practical level, this mechanism has provided badly needed excuses for the shortcomings of the Soviet system.

As a standard feature of every Soviet information outlet, criticism and self-criticism is a carefully couched and controlled counterpart of the investigative exposé found in Western journalism. For a long time, the chief rule of the game was that Soviet journalists may engage in criticism only on a specific cue coming from above. The Soviet mass media could go for years completely ignoring some of the most patent failures and abuses. Then, upon receiving their orders, Soviet journalists suddenly subjected some obvious outrage to a broadside attack, which, however, was seldom aimed higher than the middle-echelon executives of the bureaucratic hierarchy believed to be responsible. The attack was usually led by appropriate central newspapers—*Pravda, Izvestia, Trud,* or whatever—and then supported by the local press and all other media. This was the first phase, called "criticism." To be constructive, charges had to always be defined as deviations from or misinterpretations of the correct "party line." This way the responsibility could be put squarely on the shoulders of a few individuals, who were normally identified by name. Then came the second phase, with its own rules. All those who had been accused and named were expected to immediately confirm the validity of the charges, confess their guilt, and promise to return to the correct course, from which they had strayed. This second round was called "self-criticism." The final round came when the mass media proudly reported that the criticism and self-criticism campaign had resulted in a decisive improvement of the original bad conditions. In other words, virtue had to always triumph over any evil.

During the Stalin era, the most morbid variety of criticism and self-criticism was periodically supplied by the infamous show trials of so-called enemies of the people involving fabricated charges, forced confessions, and calls for blood. The most celebrated and unusual case of this routine was Khruschev's denunciation, behind the closed doors of the Twentieth Party Congress, of the misdeeds of the Stalin era. The unusual thing about this attack was that it was aimed at the very top. But the blame was placed, as usual, on a few individuals—Stalin, Beria, and their helpers—rather than on the system. The story of this dramatic event, purposely leaked to foreign observers, made its first sensational appearance in the West. Only several weeks later were the Soviet mass media allowed to release a short summary of Khrushchev's famous "secret" speech. At the same time, privileged members of Soviet society were given oral briefings and allowed to listen to passages from the speech. Because this occurred in 1956, Stalin, who had died three years earlier, could not confess his guilt. But the mass media played their customary role by solemnly announcing in due time that the appropriate measures had been taken to correct all wrongdoings of the past.

Under Gorbachev, a new round of de-Stalinization has been coupled with denunciations of various forms of power abuse, corruption, and decline during the Brezhnev era. The code word for this is *glasnost*. As was suggested earlier in this book, Gorbachev's *glasnost* is nothing like the First Amendment to the U.S. Constitution: It does not promise freedom of information for information's sake. Instead, the official media continue to deliver information for the sake of Socialism. But *glasnost*, nevertheless, has resulted in a tremendous change of all Soviet mass media, greatly broadening their scope of coverage and their ability to criticize. Many taboos have been lifted and life in the USSR is now presented more as it actually is with all its warts, wrinkles, and contradictions, than as it pretended to be under the rules of the old make-believe game. At least for now, the prescribed boundaries allow criticism of practically all party and government officials.

On lower levels, criticism and self-criticism reports are usually generated by readers' letters to the editors, which contain various personal complaints about poor consumer services, bureaucratic snafus, and the like, and which give the editorial staffs ample choice for their daily exposés. Many grievances that do not get published are, nevertheless, investigated by correspondents who act as quasiofficial inspectors and are feared by small-time bureaucrats. *Glasnost* has opened up the gates for a real avalanche of such grass root criticism which was pent-up for a long time.

## KEEPING INFORMED

The Soviet people are now considered to be more mature and ready to handle a larger amount of unpleasant information. Still, those of them who depend primarily on the official mass media for information get a subjective and one-sided picture of the world in which they live. As for the domestic aspect of this picture, most of them can usually figure out the "distortion factor" and, therefore, are not much misled by what they read in Soviet papers, hear on Soviet radio, and see on Soviet television. To a degree, this is comparable to the reaction of an experienced consumer to the exaggerations and overstatements of commercial advertising. It is the world at large, and especially

**BOX 9–5** *Death in the Kremlin and Soviet Mass Media*

Leonid Brezhnev was almost 76 when he died on November 10, 1982, at about 8:30 A.M. Because of his advanced age and poor health, his death did not come as a surprise, but it took Soviet radio and television more than twenty-six hours to report the sad news.

Yuri Andropov died on February 9, 1984, at 4:50 P.M. after a long and grave illness. His death was reported on Soviet television and radio three hours later.

Konstantin Chernenko, who was both old and in poor health, died on March 10, 1985, at 7:20 P.M. His death was reported by Soviet media almost immediately.

Compiled by author.

life in the West, about which average Soviet citizens continue to be misinformed, because even if they suspect that the official mass media do not tell them the whole truth, there is no easy way to get more objective information, fill omissions, and correct distortions.

In the past, a combination of pervasive official secrecy and the skimpy and incomplete information available to average people turned the wheels of many rumor mills that more often than not produced grossly inaccurate accounts of actual happenings. It seems entirely plausible that on occasion the Soviet security authorities (KGB) had a hand in manufacturing and disseminating misinformation designed to confuse both their own citizens and public opinion outside the USSR. Now, under *glasnost*, there is even a special television program designed to combat, explain, and dispel rumors.

Still another, not too reliable, source of information in and about the Soviet Union resulting from excessive secrecy has been the art of reading between the lines of official Soviet texts, watching for minute changes in the rhetoric of Soviet leaders, and scrutinizing their group photographs for hints and clues. In the past, silent signals—real or imagined—discovered in this manner have caused great excitement not only in the USSR but also outside its borders. Known as *Kremlinology*, this method for analyzing Soviet politics has been aptly defined as "the strange science that sought to understand Soviet policy by piecing together a jigsaw of facts and hints about the Soviet leadership." The author of this definition is a noted British journalist[13] with Soviet experience who uses the past tense ("sought") because he optimistically believes that Gorbachev's *glasnost* has "killed Kremlinology." It appears to be a somewhat premature conclusion: actually, the guessing game about Soviet leaders' secret motives and intentions goes on.

[13]Patrick Cockburn in "R.I.P. Kremlinology," *The Washington Post*, February 14, 1988, p. C-1.

Members of the privileged groups are better supplied with information, just as they are better provided with material goods. But even the high-ranking officials receive their information on a "need-to-know" basis in the form of special foreign news summaries prepared daily by *TASS* and printed on paper of different colors indicating the degree of detail and distribution. Sensitive domestic news is usually conveyed orally at closed briefings of those considered entitled to know it. All information received through these restricted channels is treated as state secrets that are not supposed to be copied, repeated, or discussed with unauthorized persons.

Soviet propagandists down to the district level have access to a special foreign news summary called *Atlas*, which prints abridged translations of stories from international wire services. They are, however, explicitly forbidden to quote or even paraphrase the information contained in the summary. Why should they know more than they can tell? Because Soviet people at large are not completely dependent on the official sources of information alone. It follows that, to be effective, propagandists need to know at least as much as their audience does.

## PUBLIC OPINION

Soviet leaders have always claimed that their decisions and actions enjoy wide support among the masses. Important policy statements usually contained references to people's wishes, popular mandates, and public opinion. Because there were no independent opinion polls in the Soviet Union, such assertions could not be measured with any degree of accuracy. Indeed, just like the results of Soviet elections in the past, the officially reported Soviet public opinion was not usually a true expression of popular preferences but merely an echo of the views voiced by the Soviet leadership. The mass media served to amplify and carry this echo near and far.

What it means is that, for many years, the cause-and-effect relationship between high-level decisions and public opinion was the reverse of what it was claimed to be. The process of forming a desired public response followed an established scenario, every phase of which was closely supervised by full- and part-time propagandists assisted by local political activists. It proceeded approximately as follows: Let us say an important decision was announced in the name of the Central Committee of the CPSU and the Council of Ministers of the USSR. The decision may have concerned a domestic issue or a foreign policy action. Almost immediately after the announcement, general meetings of employees were organized at every factory, collective farm, office, and so on, to discuss the important event and adopt appropriate resolutions. Similar meetings were called together at universities, institutes, and sometimes even secondary schools. If the occasion was considered to be exceptionally important, work or study was interrupted, making it obliga-

**BOX 9–6**  *Gorbachev on Public Opinion*

---

Direct contacts with citizens and their letters have become an important "feed-back" link between the Soviet leadership and the masses. Letters are being sent to newspapers and magazines (many of them are published), to the government, and to the Supreme Soviet. Especially many—to the party's Central Committee.

Gorbachev, M.S., *Perestroika i Novoye Myshlenie* (*Perestroika and the New Thinking*) (Moscow: Political Literature Publishing, 1987), p. 65.

---

tory for everyone to attend the meetings. Otherwise the meetings were held after quitting time, making attendance voluntary but implying that all patriotic citizens were still expected to be present, and any unexcused absence would not go unnoticed.[14] The meetings usually began with a presentation by a professional propagandist who outlined the issue, repeating almost verbatim an appropriate editorial from *Pravda*. Then a few local activists in a prearranged order stepped forward to voice their support for the announced policy. Other participants were invited to take the floor, and some of them usually felt obligated for various personal and career reasons to go on the record speaking briefly in favor of the measure. The "silent majority" simply remained uninterested and passive, wishing for the whole farce to come to its predictable end. Finally, one of the local activists moved to adopt a stereotypical resolution of full support, which had been prepared in advance, the meeting then adopted it by a show of hands. At that point everybody could go home.

A variation of this routine could be used to produce, instead of a resolution, a letter or petition signed by all those present. Of course, the final product could be not only *for* something but also *against* almost anything. Soviet mass media used to carry reports and statistics of such staged grass-roots level actions, calling them "spontaneous" expressions of public opinion. Publication of carefully "seeded" and selected letters to editors was also used for the same purpose: to "educate and mobilize" the public.

This does not mean, however, that in the past Soviet leaders were uninformed about the people's feelings and thoughts. Such information was readily available to them from such sources as the KGB. But it was used to measure the effectiveness of their propaganda efforts, rather than as a basis for policy decisions.

The situation is very different now: Gorbachev and his top aides actually urge the masses to meet and openly express their opinions on all important issues. Free debates and disputes are encouraged and disagree-

---

[14]Underground Soviet humor refers to this as "voluntary but on a compulsory basis."

ments with official points of view are tolerated. There is much evidence that the regimes is no longer immune to public opinion.

## UNOFFICIAL SOURCES

The chief unofficial information channels are still foreign radio broadcasts, especially those narrated in Russian and in the ethnic languages of the USSR. As has been noted, the fact that Soviet borders could not be made soundproof has been a serious concern for the Soviet authorities. In the past, they have used various drastic methods to cope with this challenge to the official monopoly on information; harassing and even legally prosecuting listeners, confiscating radio receivers, jamming undesirable radio signals, manufacturing only short-range receivers, and exerting diplomatic pressure on the foreign countries responsible for the broadcasts. None of these, or similar measures, was completely satisfactory.

With the advent of *glasnost*, futile attempts "to beat them" were replaced by a much more successful effort "to join them" in order to neutralize their effectiveness and remove the mystique of the "forbidden fruit." Such stations as "Radio Liberty,"[15] "Voice of America," and the "British Broadcasting Corporation" have been allowed to open permanent bureaus in Moscow.

With the exception of some Communist periodicals, newspapers and magazines published in the West cannot be purchased easily in the Soviet Union. Such publications are not available even in public libraries, unless one has special permission to do authorized research.

Such Russian-language periodicals as *America*, put out by the U.S. Information Agency and delivered to Russia in quantities controlled by written agreements, end up in the hands of the privileged Soviet citizens entitled to know more than others. More successful as sources of eagerly sought information about the United States are mobile exhibits that have been periodically organized by the same agency as part of the USA–USSR cultural exchange.

Clandestinely produced underground publications, called *samizdat*,[16] made their appearance in the Soviet Union soon after Stalin's death in 1953. In the past, production, distribution, and even possession of such material were severely punishable as "aiding and abetting hostile propaganda." Now, such activities, though no longer illegal, are controlled by less drastic, but apparently effective measures limiting their impact. For example, it is very difficult for unofficial publishers to secure supplies of paper and printing or broadcasting equipment. Besides, *glasnost* took the sting out of

[15]Located in West Germany, this radio station is financed and controlled by the United States.

[16]*Samizdat* is a Russian abbreviation that means "self-publishing."

BOX 9–7   *Soviet Underground Humor*

| | |
|---|---|
| Question: | What is a Soviet optimist? |
| Answer: | A poorly informed Soviet pessimist. |
| | |
| Doctor: | Are you complaining about your eyes or ears? |
| Patient: | I do not know which it is, doctor. But I hear and see different things. |

many formerly controversial issues, which used to be the main subject for the underground press. Here too, the mystique of the "forbidden fruit" has largely disappeared.

The expansion of two-way tourism between the USSR and the West has the potential for making Soviet citizens better informed about the world at large and, by comparison, about their own country. Also very helpful in this respect have been various exchanges between Western and Soviet media outlets: televised debates ("space bridges"), parallel articles, documentaries, and candid interviews.

## FOREIGN CORRESPONDENTS

In a strange way some 500 foreign correspondents stationed in Moscow are part of the mechanism that supplies the Soviet public with unofficial information about its own country. News items and stories reported by these correspondents and made public in the media outside Soviet borders are sometimes used in shortwave radio broadcasts beamed back to the Soviet Union. It is in this complicated manner that Soviet citizens used to learn about such news as the apparent health problems of their top leader, a fire in a Moscow hotel, a crash of a Soviet airliner, or an act of defiance by a group of dissidents in Moscow. In the past, the echo effect underscored the importance of the presence of foreign journalists in Moscow. But as one of its byproducts, foreign journalists were often made targets of Soviet harassment. In recent years several Western journalists have had to face Soviet courts on charges of libel. Others were accused of becoming involved with dissident groups and unlawfully interfering in Soviet domestic affairs.[17]

There is no denying that on occasion Western correspondents have traded their roles of neutral witnesses for those of direct participants in cases involving Soviet dissidents. Although this proves that their hearts are in the right places, there is also a danger of runaway emotions resulting in exaggerations and distortions of the importance of the dissident movement to the

---

[17]In 1986, an American journalist, Nicholas Daniloff, was arrested and expelled from Moscow in retaliation for espionage charges against a Soviet U.N. employee in New York.

total picture of Soviet life. In some instances, foreign correspondents may have been used by desperate individuals, not necessarily representing anybody but themselves, or even manipulated by the secret services, including the KGB.

In the past, the difficult situation of foreign correspondents in Moscow dramatized the different perspective on information and news values prevailing in the Soviet Union. Included in this perspective is the Marxist-Leninist attitude toward freedom of the press, which is at the root of many problems pertaining to international communications. For example, many topics that in the West would be considered legitimate for news stories are treated as national security matters in the Soviet Union. And what is headline news in Moscow often would not be newsworthy in New York or London. Foreign journalists are expected to find ways to satisfy their sensation-hungry public at home while keeping peace with their supersensitive official hosts in the Soviet Union. At times this must seem almost impossible. During recent years, many Western journalists have written books based on their frustrating experiences in the Soviet Union.

But reporting from Moscow has been made much easier for Western journalists by increased access to factual information under Gorbachev's *glasnost*, although many restrictions are still in place. This relative openness has made Moscow a less exotic and exciting date line: most of what is reported from there nowadays is simply derived, translated, and summarized from the official Soviet press which carries richer and more reliable information. As a rule, it is also much less sensational.

## FREEDOM OF THE PRESS AND IDEOLOGY

Although many writings of Marx, Engels, and Lenin contain lip-service praises of freedom of the press, both the theory and (particularly) the practice of Marxism-Leninism clearly demonstrate that this freedom is deemed desirable only when it helps to promote the Socialist (Communist) cause. Freedom of the press is considered to be a means rather than an end, a natural human right and an absolute value. As has already been noted, the Soviet Constitution (Article 50) flatly states that "freedom of the press" must serve a specific purpose: It must "strengthen and develop the Socialist system." Of course, real freedom is not compatible with any prescribed conditions for its use. Under *glasnost*, the official view of what is "good for Socialism" has been broadened to include much criticism of the Stalin and Brezhnev eras and, the lingering negative remnants of those times.

In terms of Marxist-Leninist ideology, the correct attitude toward freedom of the press depends on "concrete historical conditions." For example, before the 1917 Revolution, Lenin was always in favor of such freedom for Russia. But, as we know, only two days after the revolution Lenin decided that the conditions were no longer favorable, and he banned all opposition newspapers. For political reasons, Lenin called his decision a "temporary measure" and promised that with the final victory of the new order the press would be given full freedom within the boundaries of legal responsibility "in accordance with a law broadest and most progressive in this respect." Needless to say, no such law has ever been enacted in the Soviet Union, and the victory of the new order there has resulted in not more, but less freedom of the press. In fact, even this promise of Lenin's is seldom reprinted in the USSR today, except as part of his complete works, which occupy some forty-seven hardcover volumes in the most recent (fifth) edition.

As for broken promises, Lenin's record is, perhaps, not worse than that of many other twentieth-century politicians. The point here is that the restoration of unlimited freedom of the press in the Soviet Union is the promise most unlikely to be fulfilled by any Soviet leader under almost any conditions. To see why is easy. Marxist-Leninist ideology demands from its followers a total commitment to a goal alleged to be the ultimate truth. Any freedom to deviate from the truth would be wasteful, confusing, and harmful to the cause. What is needed instead is a concentrated effort to get the one and the only correct message across to as many people as possible. The Soviet mass media are doing just that.

Because Marxist-Leninist ideology is in essence a self-serving prophecy, all significant occurrences and events are treated by the Soviet media, not as surprises, but as events long anticipated and consistent with earlier developments. Soviet journalists and editors do not pretend to foresee the future in terms of "whats," "whos," "whens," and "wheres," but they do claim to know in advance the "whys." It may be said that, thanks to Marxism-Leninism, they have interpretations for things before they happen. Or, to put it differently, all news-making events are interpreted by the Soviet mass media either as anticipated symptoms of a completely diagnosed disease or as expected effects of the prescribed cure for this disease. Because it is a serious but curable disease, the patient—humanity—should be encouraged by optimistic progress reports.

Given this openly biased (in the name of the ideological goal) attitude toward the news, it is no wonder that information and propaganda are completely blended in the Soviet mass media. As we see in the next chapter, ideological propaganda is also an inseparable ingredient of Soviet artistic expression. As seen from the West, this is a flagrant suppression of freedom. But in the eyes of a Communist, it signifies a commitment to a lofty goal.

Under *glasnost*, the Soviet press and other mass media have not become free and independent from the "Powers That Be." But their collective mission, which was formerly to protect and embellish the status quo, has now become more complex and diverse. Now the media serve as different instruments of change: investigative reporting, critics at large, loyal opposition, and even "devil's advocates." Their current task is to prime the pump of a public debate about *perestroika* and to keep it going, which is not an easy thing to do after seventy years of one-party rule. This involves some careful stage managing and role playing. Unlike before, various media outlets sing now with different voices, but they are all part of the same choir.

## GLOSSARY

**Glavlit:**  Soviet censorship authority.
**Izvestia (News):**  major paper; organ of the Soviet government.
**Novosti:**  Soviet news agency.
**Pravda (Truth):**  most important Soviet newspaper; organ of the CC of the CPSU.
**Radio Liberty:**  U.S. funded radio broadcasting to the Soviet Union.
**Samizdat (self-publishing):**  unofficial, "underground" press.
**TASS:**  Soviet news agency.

## RECOMMENDED READINGS

HARASYMIW, BOHDAN (ed.), *Education and Mass Media in the Soviet Union and Eastern Europe*. New York: Praeger, 1976.
HOPKINS, MARK W., *Mass Media in the Soviet Union*. New York: Pegasus, 1970.
MICKLEWICZ, ELLEN P., *Media and the Russian Public*. New York: Praeger, 1981.

CHAPTER
# 10
# SOVIET CULTURE

## PEOPLE'S CULTURE

The overall performance of the Soviet cultural establishment can perhaps best be compared with that of a brass orchestra playing mostly merry tunes and inspiring marches, or an artist whose palette contains bright colors, or a writer whose specialty is stories with happy endings. For a long time, the main task of Soviet art has been to celebrate and glorify the past, present, and future triumphs of the Communist cause, to instill optimism, and to invite imitation of model heroes. State-owned and party-controlled, Soviet culture may very well be the greatest (in size) show on earth. Readily available official statistics on the numbers of books published, movies made and shown, theatrical plays performed, and other cultural achievements proudly make this point.

Soviet culture shares many characteristics with the educational system and mass media. As a tool of the official ideology, it seeks to indoctrinate and educate as many readers, viewers, and listeners as possible. It is a mass culture in both its relatively low level of appeal and its equally low cost of availability. For these reasons, it is officially called the "people's culture." But for almost fifty years—first under Stalin and then under Brezhnev—it was actually a "court culture" rather than "people's culture."

Actually, even today people at large do not have much to say about decisions affecting Soviet culture, because its successes are not measured by box office receipts or by the number of books sold. Instead, all important decisions concerning cultural activities are made by high-ranking officials, sometimes including even the members of the ruling elite. Such decisions are never based on considerations of profit or public demand, although on the levels of production and distribution of cultural goods and services these two factors usually play a significant role. In the marketplace of Soviet culture, the traditional supply-and-demand relationship is reversed: Politically motivated supply determines, or at least tries to determine, popular demand.

The central bureaucracy entrusted with the management of Soviet culture consists of a special section of the Central Committee of the CPSU, a union-republic ministry (called the USSR Ministry of Culture), and several lesser agencies in charge of particular activities. On lower levels, cultural organizations function under the dual supervision of appropriate party committees and government offices. In ethnic territories, various cultural outlets adhere to the already familiar formula: "National in form, Socialist in content." Because the "form," as we know, includes local languages, Soviet culture is a multilingual phenomenon. Its chief means of expression, however, is the Russian language. Only the Russian variety of Soviet culture is readily available everywhere in the USSR: In all ethnic territories, Russian

**BOX 10–1**   *Major Writers of the First Half of the Nineteenth Century*

---

Alexander PUSHKIN (1799–1837): the greatest Russian poet and writer of all times; the founder of modern Russian literature. Pushkin's works and ideas played a major role in the development of Russia's culture and literary language. His works include: *Eugene Onegin* (a novel in verse); *A Captain's Daughter* (a short historical novel); *Boris Godunov* (a historical drama); also many long epic poems, lyrical poetry, songs, short stories, and dramatic works. Many works of Pushkin have served as themes for musical compositions, paintings, and stage adaptations.

Mikhail LERMONTOV (1814–1841): a moody ("Byronic") poet and writer, second only to Pushkin. His works include several epic poems, lyrics, and a novel entitled *A Hero of Our Time*. Mostly because of Pushkin and Lermontov, the first half of the nineteenth century became known as "the Golden Age of Poetry."

Nikolai GOGOL (1809–1852): a humorist and author of many short stories, several dramatic works, and novels. His best-known works are: *Inspector General* (play), *Overcoat* (short story), *Taras Bulba* (short historic novel), and *Dead Souls* (satirical novel).

Compiled by author.

theaters, movie houses, libraries, and other cultural facilities operate side by side with those using local languages.

Next to the mass media, the cultural establishment has been most profoundly affected by *glasnost*. The best way to appreciate the changes of the last few years is to compare the present situation with how things were before Gorbachev's ascent to power.

## CULTURAL HERITAGE

The Russian component is also the cornerstone of the historic foundation on which Soviet culture has been built. This component consists chiefly of the nineteenth century's rich heritage in literature, theater, music, and other artistic forms that developed within the framework of "critical realism." Formulated by a brilliant literary critic, Vissarion Belinsky,[1] critical realism demanded that artists and writers use their creative talents and power to influence the public to struggle against the sociopolitical status quo. This made Russian culture, especially literature, into a kind of surrogate politics— a tradition that is a hallmark of Soviet culture even today, although now its mission is to support rather than to oppose the existing system. On the other hand, the legacy of Russia's modernistic culture, which developed as a powerful challenge to critical realism just before the revolution and then

BOX 10–2    *Major Writers of the Second Half of the Nineteenth Century*

Ivan TURGENEV (1818–1883): a major writer and author of some of the most famous Russian social novels: *Rudin, The Nest of Gentry, On the Eve, Fathers and Sons, Smoke,* and *The Virgin Soil.* He also wrote many short stories, including *Sportsman's Sketches.* A liberal Westerner, he spent much of his life in western Europe as Russia's unofficial "cultural ambassador."

Fyodor DOSTOYEVSKY (1821–1881): one of the two internationally best-known Russian writers (the other one is Leo Tolstoy). He is famous for the deep psychological studies of his characters. He wrote many novels with extremely acute and explosive plots. His most important works are: *Notes from the Underground, Crime and Punishment, The Gambler, The Idiot, The Possessed,* and *The Brothers Karamazov.*

Leo (Lev) TOLSTOY (1828–1910): possibly the most important writer in any language during the last two centuries. A very prolific writer of novels, short stories, plays, essays, and articles on a great variety of subjects. His three most famous novels are: *War and Peace, Anna Karenina,* and *The Resurrection.*

Compiled by author.

[1]Vissarion Belinsky (1811–1848) inspired and led a large group of young writers who shared his view that Russian literature had a sociopolitical mission to perform. Other arts followed suit.

continued during the early 1920s, is being deemphasized in the contemporary Soviet Union.

The cultural heritages of the ethnic minorities are treated on an even more selective basis. The criteria for acceptance of ethnic heritages include a provision that automatically bars artistic works with anti-Russian overtones. This test applies to ethnic folklores that, together with Russian folklore, constitute another important source of the Soviet people's culture.

The concept of Soviet culture did not come into existence overnight. At the beginning of the Soviet era, a halfhearted attempt was made to foster an instant cultural revolution. To this end, there was a first to be a complete break from all traditional cultural values produced by "rotten bourgeois cultures," followed by the emergence of a new literature and arts created from scratch by the true proletarians. Individual creativity was to be replaced by a "higher form of teamwork" and "creative collectives." The new superior culture was to be known as "Proletarian Culture" (or "Proletcult," for short).

To be sure, the idea of Proletcult never had the support of Lenin and other top Soviet leaders, who tended to be conservative in their cultural tastes. Toward the end of the power struggle among Lenin's heirs, it was even officially condemned as a "leftist deviation." Already, much earlier, with the introduction of the NEP in 1921, the organizers and leaders of this movement were forced to compete in a relatively free artistic marketplace that was resurrected along with private enterprise. Before long, Proletcult was reduced to a rather insignificant fringe group, completely overshadowed by the many larger and much more influential artistic movements vying with each other and thriving in the climate of relative liberalism. During much of the NEP era, only works of art that openly challenged the ruling regime were barred, a condition that had also characterized the history of Russian arts before the revolution.

## SOCIALIST REALISM

The creative climate began to change for the worse during the late 1920s, immediately after the inauguration of the planned economy. This was not by coincidence. Having first consolidated its political monopoly and then nationalized the entire economy, the regime was ready to extend its total control over the remaining major sphere of human activity—culture. Cultural pluralism had to be eliminated, just as political freedom and private business had been eliminated a few years earlier.

As the most important field of artistic creativity, literature was chosen to lead the way. In 1932, a party-government decree abolished all writers' groups and associations, and replaced them with a single official organization called the "Union of Soviet Writers." From that time on, every professional writer in the USSR had to be a member of the union. Membership in the union requires adherence to its policy, which has been known since 1934 as "Socialist realism." The same conditions must be met by artists, composers, architects, and sculptors, who have their own "unions."

In the Union of Soviet Writers' constitution, Socialist realism is defined as "the historically truthful depicting of reality in its revolutionary development." The key words are the last four, "in its revolutionary development." They have been generally interpreted to mean that Soviet reality must be shown in the process of becoming better than it is, being perfected, and reaching its ideal in accordance with Communist ideology. In presenting Soviet reality, writers and artists, and even composers, are supposed to be guided by four rules:

1. Their work must be realistic in content and form.
2. It must have mass appeal.
3. The message must be an optimistic one.
4. And it must follow the party line ("partiynost").

In the West, similar rules may perhaps guide the work of a scriptwriter or a commercial artist employed by an advertising agency, a public relations firm, or a political candidate. The analogy is valid precisely because Soviet writers

**BOX 10–3**   *Other Major Writers of Prerevolutionary Russia*

Anton CHEKHOV (1860–1904): Russia's best short-story writer. He successfully challenged the notion that only lengthy novels can show the complexity of the human condition. Chekhov is also considered to be one of the founders of modern realistic drama. His best-known plays include *Ivanov*, *Uncle Vanya*, *The Sea Gull*, *Three Sisters*, and *The Cherry Orchard*.

Maxim GORKY* (1868–1936): the first important Marxist writer of short stories, plays, and novels. He is credited with founding Socialist realism.

Leonid ANDREYEV (1871–1919): writer of short stories and plays.

Ivan BUNIN (1870–1953): writer of short stories, novels, and poetry; the first Russian Nobel Prize winner.

Alexander KUPRIN (1870–1938): writer of short stories and novellas.

Ivan GONCHAROV (1812–1891): writer of social novels.

Nikolai NEKRASOV (1821–1878): writer of "civic" poetry.

Alexander OSTROVSKY (1823–1886): playwright.

Alexei TOLSTOY (1817–1875): writer of poetry, historic novels.

Nikolai LESKOV (1831–1875): writer of short stories, novels.

Mikhail SALTYKOV-SHCHEDRIN (1826–1889): satirist.

*The pen name of Alexei Peshkov. The name can also be spelled Gorki.

Compiled by author.

**TABLE 10–1**  Ten Best-Known Soviet Poets

| Name | Dates | Name | Dates |
|------|-------|------|-------|
| Alexander Blok | 1880–1921 | Osip Mandelshtam | 1891–1938 |
| Vladimir Mayakovsky | 1893–1925 | Alexander Tvardovsky | 1910–1973 |
| Sergei Yesenin | 1895–1925 | Andrei Voznesensky | b. 1933 |
| Anna Akhmatova (Gorenko) | 1889–1960 | Robert Rozhdestvensky | b. 1932 |
| Boris Pasternak | 1890–1960 | Yevgeni Yevtushenko | b. 1933 |

*Source:* Compiled by author from Soviet data.

**BOX 10–4**  *Gorbachev on "Socialist Realism"*

"Problemless" depicting of reality has done us a disservice: it created a gap between the word and the deed which has bred public passivity and a lack of faith in the proclaimed slogans.

Gorbachev, M.S., *Perestroika i Novoye Myshlenie* ("*Perestroika and the New Thinking*") (Moscow: Political Literature Publishing, 1987), p. 16.

and artists are, for all practical purposes, employed through their unions by the Soviet state, which happens to be the only employer in the country.

Under Socialist realism, state censorship—a familiar feature of the Russian cultural scene—changed from proscriptive to prescriptive. Instead of being told what not to write, paint, or compose, Soviet artists began to be given orders to create specific plots, themes, and heroes.

## SOVIET LITERATURE

By tradition, the central place in Soviet culture belongs to literature. Since the introduction of Socialist realism in 1934, Soviet literature has been a "command literature"—that is, a state-owned activity with a special mission to perform. To a degree, it is comparable to any other manufacturing branch of the Soviet national economy, except that in place of machines or tools the Soviet literary establishment produces books. In a sense, these books too are machines and tools; they are used in social engineering to make their authors, in Stalin's words, "engineers of human souls."

Who tells the engineers what kinds of literary machines and tools they are to produce? A Nobel Prize-winning writer and the long-time dean of Soviet writers, Mikhail Sholokhov, answered this question as follows: "Our adversaries in the West claim that we, Soviet writers, write what the Party dictates to us. It is not quite so. Actually we write what our hearts dictate us

**BOX 10–5**  *Soviet Underground Humor*

> Socialist realism is when you tell your superiors pleasant things they like to hear, using simple words which they can understand.

to write. But our hearts belong to the Party."[2] A growing majority of some 10,000 professional Soviet writers indeed belongs, at least formally, to the party. For their books to be accepted, every one of these writers must first get his or her inspiration from the current party line and then write in accordance with the other principles of Socialist realism.

Under Stalin, this minimum requirement was often all that was needed for moderate literary success. If beyond being ideologically correct, a book proved to be good reading, its author was entitled to special privileges and bonuses and was treated like a genius. Such writers were indeed rare among the big crowd of professional hacks busily churning out countless "industrial novels," "boy-meets-tractor" short stories, and versified glorifications of Stalin. The huge volume of these works was supposed to compensate for their marginal readability. As in so many other areas of early Soviet civilization, the emphasis was on quantity rather than on quality of literary production.

The big change in Soviet literature after Stalin's death stems from the insistence that books must contain enough human interest to be, if not exciting, at least readable. From afar, it may not look like an earthshaking demand, but for both writers and readers in the Soviet Union the difference was real and significant. In retrospect, it is easy to see that the de-Stalinization campaign marked a turning point in the history of Soviet literature and

**TABLE 10–2**  Ten Best-Known Soviet Writers

| Name | Dates | Works |
|------|-------|-------|
| Maxim Gorky | 1868–1936 | Novels, short stories, plays |
| Aleksei Tolstoy | 1882–1945 | Novels, short stories |
| Mikhail Sholokhov | 1905–1984 | Novels, short stories |
| Nikolai Ostrovsky | 1904–1936 | Novels |
| Leonid Leonov | b. 1899 | Novels, plays |
| Alexander Fadeyev | 1901–1956 | Novels, short stories |
| Konstantin Fedin | 1892–1978 | Novels, short stories |
| Valentin Katyev | 1915–1986 | Novels, plays, short stories |
| Mikhail Bulgakov | 1891–1940 | Novels, plays, short stories |

*Source:* Compiled by author from Soviet data.

[2]Mikhail Sholokhov is best known for his two long novels, *Quiet Flows the Don* and *Virgin Soil Upturned*. The passage is from the *Sobranie sochinenii* [Collected Works] (Moscow: Gosizdat, 1969), vol. 8, p. 292.

caused palace revolts, protracted strife, and even casualties inside the literary establishment.[3] The resulting availability of better-quality reading matter had definitely benefited the readers.

On the whole, the Khrushchev regime that initiated and managed this change during the first post-Stalin decade retained at all times its control over Soviet literature. In the process, however, it had to accept the risk of coping with certain lingering side effects: so-called underground literature, writers' protests and defections, and periodic challenges to censorship. These relatively new phenomena, even the more sensational of them, did not greatly affect the mainstream of Soviet literature, which continued to feature prose and poetry written in accordance with the canons of Socialist realism, though of a less restrictive variety. Under the Brezhnev regime (1964–1982), oppressive political controls were gradually tightened up and, as a result, the Soviet literacy landscape became once again lifeless and sterile. Many talented writers chose to emigrate or were forced to leave the country. Among them were two winners of the Nobel Prize in Literature: Alexander Solzhenitsyn and Iosif (Joseph) Brodsky. In the mid-1980s, *glasnost* brought a significant change for the better: Ideological restrictions were softened and many taboos were lifted. The quality of Soviet literary production has been steadily improving since then.

The mainstream of contemporary Soviet literature carries an impressive variety of readable, even if not great, novels, novellas, short stories, and plays, and a rich assortment of poetry. Artistically better works tend to be just inside the new outer limits of official tolerance. As before, such questions as the number of copies to be published, distribution, reprinting, and new editions are not decided by popular demand or cash-register success. Instead, these decisions are based first of all on political considerations, and second, on the limitations imposed by economic planning on printing shops' production and paper supply. The publishers in the USSR are not expected to make profits, although they are encouraged to break even. They are primarily concerned with the publication of certain numbers of books in specific categories: new books, classics, translations, and others. But both writers and readers are now exercising considerable influence on the question of what books should be published and in how many copies. The former have even been allowed to form writer's publishing cooperatives.

Just as before, Soviet literature's chief function is ideological propaganda. But the propaganda message has become more subtle, more entertaining, and, hence, probably also more effective.

## THEMES AND HEROES

In the late 1950s and early 1960s the groping for vaguely defined, new limits of tolerance often caused many literary controversies. Some writers, such as

---

[3]For example, the head of the Writers' Union, Alexander Fadeyev, committed suicide (1956), presumably because he was unable to cope with new demands.

**TABLE 10–3** Russian Nobel Laureates in Literature

| Name | Date | Works |
|------|------|-------|
| Ivan Bunin | 1933 | Prose and poetry |
| Boris Pasternak | 1958 | Prose and poetry |
| Mikhail Sholokhov | 1965 | Prose |
| Alexander Solzshenitsyn | 1970 | Prose |
| Iosif (Joseph) Brodsky | 1987 | Poetry |

*Source:* Compiled by author.

Ilya Ehrenburg,[4] managed to probe without ever crossing the invisible line. Others, such as Vladimir Dudentsev,[5] who went, probably inadvertently, just a bit too far, were publicly scolded and then allowed to recant their transgressions. Still others, like Alexander Solzhenitsyn, resolutely pushed beyond the point of no return and were ultimately expelled from the USSR. Boris Pasternak's case fell between these last two categories.[6] By trial, error, and design, the new boundaries were gradually drawn, firmly enclosing a much larger territory for the same old game of Socialist realism, played by the same rules. The source of inspiration and guidance was also the same: the party line. As mentioned, during the next twenty years this newly gained realm of creative freedom shrank back to almost what it had been under Stalin.

There was a time when practically all Soviet writers concentrated on a few selected themes concerning such momentous current events as industrialization, collectivization, or World War II. The party line then meant an actual listing of desired topics in order of their priority.

Thanks to *glasnost*, the situation is different now, and the party line offers a broader interpretation of the overall purpose of Soviet literature. Individual writers are fully expected to use their own imaginations and to come up with suitable themes that would best serve this purpose. They do not, of course, have unlimited choice because of the ideological constraints and because, as is the case with writers throughout the world, the majority of them follow the lead of a few true innovators who introduce fashions and fads.

Among the fashionable themes in Soviet literature of the late 1980s is the challenge presented by ambitious economic projects: the development of newly discovered natural deposits, the construction of giant plants, or the mass introduction of modern technology. The plot usually revolves around the complexity and sophistication of the problems involved, including purely human problems dealing with conflicting emotions, feelings, and

[4]Ilya Ehrenburg's short novel, *The Thaw* (1954), gave its name to this entire period of more tolerance toward literature.

[5]Vladimir Dudentsev wrote a novel, entitled *Not by Bread Alone* (1954), for which he was publicly scolded by Khrushchev.

[6]Boris Pasternak's novel *Doctor Zhivago* (1956) was at first accepted for publication but was later banned in the USSR.

**TABLE 10–4**  Ten Glasnost "Bestsellers"

---

*Children of Arbat*—An anti-Stalin novel by Anatoli Rybakov (1987).
*We*—An anti-Utopian novel by Yevgeni Zamyatin (1921).
*Lolita*—Vladimir Nabokov's seductive novel about sexuality (1955).
*Doctor Zhivago*—Boris Pasternak's famous novel about Russia's civil war (1957).
*Construction Pit*—A political satire on Socialism by Andrei Platonov (1932).
*White Robes*—Vladimir Dudintsev's expose of Stalin's pseudoscientists (1987).
*The Bison*—A novel about an abused Soviet scientist by Dannil Granin (1987).
*1984*—Russian translation of George Orwell's anti-Utopian classic (1948).
*Requiem*—An anti-Stalin poem by Anna Akhmatova (1956).
*Dog's Heart*—Mikhail Bulgakov's satirical treatment of efforts to create a new "Soviet man"
    (1928).

---

*Source:* Compiled by author.

strivings. Difficult things are not made to look easy, and the heroes who face them are not superhuman. They are, as a rule, not necessarily what the average readers are either, but rather what the readers believe themselves to be: tough, sometimes moody, not always satisfied with themselves, but with their hearts in the right place. The most popular works in this genre of Soviet "high tragedy" tend to be melodramatic. A variation of this theme, called *derevenshchina* (ruralism), has the heroes nostalgically long for the more wholesome and simpler country life of the past while groping for the future. Under Gorbachev, Soviet writers have been encouraged to be more critical about various aspects of contemporary society, and to deal with real life hardships.

Soviet readers have benefited from *glasnost* in three important ways: (1) so-called desk drawer manuscripts—works of current Soviet writers written some years ago when they could not have been published—have appeared in magazines and as books; (2) prose and poetry of many (but not all) Russian émigré writers have begun to be published in the Soviet Union; and (3) politically controversial—and for a long time banned—works of early Soviet poets and writers have now been "rehabilitated" and republished (or published for the first time). As a result, after years of starvation diets, Soviet readers find themselves deluged and forced to choose from many conflicting attractions.

Popular on the lighter side are sentimental stories of marital problems, broken families, and the search for personal happiness. The variations of these themes deal consciously with alcoholism, juvenile delinquency, and women's place in Soviet society. The stories no longer must end happily, as long as they manage to convey the generally optimistic view that Soviet society as a whole is going along smoothly. The bulk of contemporary Soviet poetry is written in this split-level style, which allows personal pessimism in the perception of intimate life. But there are definite limits of how much "apolitical reading" may be included in any given magazine issue, anthology, or book-publishing plan. Editors are held responsible for holding the line.

A relatively new phenomenon is the appearance of novels and plays dealing with the more sensational pages of Russia's prerevolutionary history. Taking liberties with historical facts and often lacking in artistic quality, these Soviet thrillers seem to owe their existence and considerable popularity chiefly to the large doses of Great Russian nationalism worked into their melodramatic plots.

Many themes remain completely taboo: violent crimes, explicit sex, homosexuality, the supernatural, or anything having to do with the possible existence of God. Other themes appear to be strictly rationed: detective stories, high adventure, spy thrillers, and humor and satire. There is a growing interest in science fiction, which has to be politically correct and optimistic.

## WRITERS, EDITORS, CENSORS, AND CRITICS

All 10,000 professional "engineers of human souls" are doing rather well for themselves by Soviet standards, and a few score of them have made it to the very top of Soviet society. Their royalties are large, medals and titles numerous, and names famous. Among them are a dozen or so surviving old timers, including Sergei Mikhalkov and Leonid Leonov. Born around the turn of the century, they are beyond their most productive years. The so-called soldier generation, people who were of draft age during World War II, is represented by more than a score of eminent writers and poets, including several women. Best known among them are Yuri Bondarev, Bulat Okudzhava, and Vasil Bykov. A larger group of talented writers consists of people in their late forties and early fifties: Andrei Voznesensky, Robert Rozhdestvensky, Yevgeni Yevtushenko, and many others. It was primarily this group of "angry young men" that attracted much attention to the literary renaissance following Stalin's death, when poets led the way by reacting quickly to sociopolitical changes.

There was no such "poetry explosion" for the debut of Gorbachev's *glasnost*. Instead—perhaps, because the window of opportunity was opened so widely and the amount of accumulated frustration so great—writers and poets first immersed themselves in heated political debates and criticism of the surviving old leaders of the literary establishment.

Since then, the leadership has passed to a younger generation of writers who have little or no personal memories of the Stalin era. Some of them show great promise. Many others are in the process of making their literary debuts, which by long-standing tradition take place in the pages of thick monthly reviews: *Novyi Mir* (New World), *Oktyabr* (October), *Moladaya Gvardia* (Young Guards), *Yunost* (Youth), and others. Before being considered for

**TABLE 10–5** Ten Currently Popular Soviet Writers

| Name | Dates | Name | Dates |
|------|-------|------|-------|
| Fyodor Abramov | 1920–1982 | Yuri Kazakov | 1927– |
| Chingiz Aikmatov | 1928– | Yuri Nagibin | 1920–1985 |
| Victor Astafyev | 1924– | Valentin Pikul | 1928– |
| Yuri Bondarev | 1924– | Valentin Rasputin | 1934– |
| Vasil Bykov | 1924– | Vladimir Soloukhin | 1924– |

*Source:* Compiled by author.

membership in the union, a beginning amateur writer is usually expected to have published in the pages of a literary review.

Editors of such literary reviews, as well as editors of various fiction publishing houses, are normally professional writers distinguished not so much by their creative talents as by their political reliability. Armed with "blue pencils," they have the right and duty to reject manuscripts and to delete or change texts. Evidently believing that there is safety in numbers, they make their more difficult decisions in committees designated as "editorial boards." In the past, high-ranking party ideologues sometimes were brought in as consultants or final judges.

Although editors are responsible for both the artistic value and the ideological correctness of all manuscripts, they in turn are double-checked by nameless representatives[7] of *Glavlit*—the censorship organ. The second editing, which is ostensibly designed only to make sure that no state secrets are being divulged, is known as the "red pencil" procedure.

The blue-red pencil censorship formula dates back to the birth of Soviet literature. Its substance, however, has undergone considerable changes. Today, there is much greater reliance on writers' self-censorship, more emphasis on artistic quality, and considerably less fear of accepting risk. The postpublication verdict is made chiefly by literary critics who are more often than not another variety of the not-too-successful writers with impressive political credentials. Their reviews determine what should or should not be republished. Readers, on the other hand, have only a limited say on this question by buying or not buying a given book. The word *byestseller* (bestseller) has made its way into the Russian language, but it has lost its original meaning: It stands for an officially praised book that is published in huge quantities primarily because of its political message, rather than because its sells well.

---

[7]Soviet censors use code numbers rather than names. These numbers usually appear on the last page of Soviet publications.

## READERS AND READING

Of course, the really important test of any literary work is whether or not it is being read, and by how many people. Neither successful sales nor critical acclaim are the equivalent of this test, but in the West, the former comes close to it. In the Soviet Union, where most publishing is subsidized and books are quite inexpensive, a successful sale of a book is less directly related to its reader appeal. The authorities, no doubt, have ways to find out which books are in demand and make their decisions with this information in mind. Other factors being equal, the more a book is in demand, the more copies of it are printed. More often than not, official praise, reader demand (in bookstores and in libraries), and large editions go hand in hand. But there are also exceptions: many editions of politically desirable books not in demand, or few editions of books deemed less desirable regardless of actual demand.

Reading is encouraged not only by making books readily available in stores and libraries but also by emphasizing its importance in the secondary school curriculum. As a result, reading is a mass phenomenon. The regime is proud of this fact and also feels obliged to make sure that the choice of available reading materials is controlled and meets ideological requirements as much as possible. This is primarily done by its owning all printing facilities, manipulating circulation and distribution, and closing borders to literature printed in other countries. Auxiliary and, currently, not often used measures include removing books from public libraries. Large libraries have restricted holdings that can be used only by people with special permits. Only a few years ago, private possession of officially banned books often led to criminal charges, even though lists of such books were never made public. A loyal Soviet reader apparently was expected to exercise self-censorship on the basis of his or her intuition.

Now legal restrictions apply only to foreign books with strongly anti-Communist content and pornographic literature. Works written by "underground" Soviet authors and printed in the USSR or abroad and works of several prerevolutionary Russian and ethnic (non-Russian) authors as well as such controversial figures as Trotsky are all but officially forbidden. This means that they are not available in libraries and stores, but their old editions may be kept in private collections and sold in second-hand bookstores.

The overwhelming majority of Soviet readers is unlikely to even realize that the choice of books available to them is restricted. Given the large selection of books readily available, this attitude is not surprising. The vast selection includes works of contemporary Soviet authors, Soviet and Russian classics, world classics, and a growing number of translated modern foreign writers, including many Americans. Many of these works are available not only in Russian but also in the different ethnic languages of the USSR. In its entirety, Soviet literature consists of more than seventy national (ethnic) literatures, some quite old and others new: this makes literary translation a big and thriving industry.

Those Soviet readers who object to the restrictions on the availability of books probably find some consolation in the fact that, as far as classics are concerned, the regime has never had a complete choice of what not to publish. For example, under Stalin it definitely would have preferred not to publish several major works of Fyodor Dostoyevsky because of their strongly anti-Socialist overtones.[8] But all earlier efforts to ban or ignore Dostoyevsky's legacy were counterproductive and had to be abandoned. At present, all works of Dostoyevsky are being published, but the most objectionable ones among them are either made available only in complete sets of collected works or are printed in smaller numbers. From an official point of view, neither solution must seem quite satisfactory.

## HUMOR AND SATIRE

Another problem, for which there also appears to be no easy solution, concerns literature that appeals chiefly to the readers' sense of humor. The history of Soviet humor and satire is a rather humorless story. The best authors writing in this vein were severely persecuted during the Stalin era. For some of them—for example, Mikhail Koltsov, Mikhail Bulgakov, and Mikhail Zoshchenko—the ultimate fate was an untimely death, forced silence, or public disgrace. Their younger colleagues, though no longer physically abused, continue to have a difficult time publishing works that ridicule and satirize anything above the ground floor of Soviet society. At least in the past, the regime, aware of the infectious nature of laughter, felt ill at ease with the satirical works of even such classical Russian and foreign satirists as Gogol, Saltykov-Shchedrin,[9] Swift, and Molière. Although their books were published and their plays were produced, special care was taken to try to convince readers or viewers that the exposed gaps between pretense and reality were not applicable to Soviet society.

Actually, the opposite is true: Because Soviet society has such great ambitions and strives so hard to show constant progress toward their fulfillment, it has always been beset by false appearances and bogus claims. But in the past most of them were taboo topics for the probably well-founded fear that the ensuing disillusionment and skepticism could seriously undermine the fragile official enthusiasm. Unlike the proverbial emperor, Soviet Communism may not be stark naked, but it certainly does not wear all the regal clothes that are claimed by official propaganda. It took a long time for this to be admitted. Even today *glasnost* stops short of licensing humor and

---

[8]This is especially true of Dostoyevsky's novels *Notes from Underground* and *The Possessed*.
[9]Mikhail Saltykov-Shchedrin was a major Russian satirist of the nineteenth century.

**TABLE 10–6** Five Best-Known Soviet Satirists

| Name | Works |
|------|-------|
| Yevgeni Zamyatin | Short stories, novels |
| Mikhail Zoshchenko | Short stories |
| Vladimir Mayakovsky | Plays, poetry |
| Mikhail Bulgakov | Novels, plays, short stories |
| Ilya Ilf (Feinsilberg) and Yevgeni Petrov (Katayev) | Novels, short stories |

*Source:* Compiled by author.

satire at the expense of many ideological "holy cows," including the current Kremlin leadership.

In the foreword to one of the last truly satirical novels to be published in the Soviet Union (1931), its authors related the following conversation that they purported to have had with an unnamed high official:[10]

> "Tell me, why do you write funny? How can you make fun of things during the reconstruction period? Have you gone crazy or what?"
>
> After this, he gave us a long and angry argument that right now laughter is harmful.
>
> "To laugh is sinful," he said, "Yes, you should not laugh! And you should not smile! When I see this new life and these changes, I do not feel like laughing. I feel like praying!"

The only punching bag that has always been available to Soviet satirists is the bad capitalist world. In the past, glaring contradictions of that world had to be treated carefully, however, so as not to invite comparisons and to suggest analogies close to home. Today, too, the new regime definitely does not view the human condition as a comedy.

As compensation for the dearth of officially available humor and satire, there has always been in the Soviet Union a steady trickle of anonymous political jokes aimed at the Soviet system and its leaders. Even in the darkest days of the Stalin era, the authorities could not completely stop such jokes from being invented and circulated among close friends. Today, such grin-and-bear-it jokes still cannot be published in print, presented on stage, or said on television, but they can be safely told in larger groups of friends. Big Brother pretends not to hear them.

## "UNDERGROUND LITERATURE"

The pre-Gorbachev regime was more effective in controlling so-called *samizdat* (self-publishing) and *tamizdat* (over-there publishing). Those two Russian

---

[10]Ilya Ilf and Yevgeni Petrov, *Sobranie sochinenii* [Collected Works] (Moscow: Gosizdat, 1961), vol. 2, pp. 7–8.

words of recent coinage stand, respectively, for works unofficially reproduced inside the USSR and works by Soviet or ex-Soviet writers published abroad and then smuggled into the USSR. The former sometimes became the latter, and vice versa, neither kind reached many readers.

*Samizdat* (which was mentioned in previous chapters) was a ripple effect of Khrushchev's de-Stalinization campaign. Aside from police persecution, its chief limitation stemmed from a lack of privately owned printing or duplicating equipment in the USSR. Even most optimistic estimates have seldom claimed the existence of more than a handful of typewritten copies of any work produced in this manner. Typically, these manuscripts consist of a few political poems or a short satirical story of modest artistic value. After having been circulated among some close friends, a copy of such a work sometimes found its way into the hands of a foreigner and became known abroad.

*Tamizdat*, in a broader sense, means anything written by émigré or Soviet authors and printed abroad. Among this type of literature, which has existed since shortly after the 1917 Revolution, is some first-rate poetry and prose. In fact, the first Russian Nobel Prize laureate (1933) was an émigré writer, Ivan Bunin,[11] who lived in exile in France. Among several Russian émigré writers who came to the United States was Vladimir Nabokov, author of the best-selling novel, *Lolita*.[12] The most famous émigré writer recently to come out of the Soviet Union is Alexander Solzhenitsyn. Expelled from the USSR in 1974, he has made his home in the United States. He, too, has won a Nobel Prize.

In a narrower sense, *tamizdat* stands for a contemporary variety of this literature published abroad and then brought into the USSR for distribution there. Special pocket editions of suitable books, including Solzhenitsyn's works, have been published for this purpose, and presumably some copies of them are currently circulating in the USSR. "Thick" émigré literary reviews, were supposed to have clandestine channels for distribution inside the Soviet Union. Now several émigré periodicals intended for this purpose have gone out of business as casualties of *glasnost*.

Some, so far not very successful, attempts have been made to start publication of unofficial magazines in the USSR. In the late-1970s, a number of prominent Soviet writers tried openly to publish an apolitical magazine called *Metropol*, featuring poetry and prose with explicitly sexual and vaguely mystical references. There have been many similar publishing ventures during the last decade that have not produced much interest among Soviet readers at large nor much alarm in official quarters.

---

[11]Ivan Bunin is best known for his short novel, *A Gentleman from San Francisco*.

[12]*Lolita* was first published in the United States in 1955. A few years later it was made into a movie. Nabokov's real name was Sirin (1899–1977).

Paradoxically, in the past, both types of dissident literature, internal and external, attracted more attention abroad than in the Soviet Union. It is easy to see why: These acts of literary defiance demonstrate that the natural, nonconforming artistic spirit survives and keeps cropping up under almost any conditions. A work of Soviet *samizdat*, regardless of its artistic quality, often seemed comparable to a cluster of vegetation stubbornly struggling for its place in the sun amidst the asphalt and concrete wasteland of a modern city. But neither *samizdat* nor *tamizdat* presented a real threat to the monopoly of official Soviet literature. Their existence, however, offered something at least resembling competition and also provided Soviet writers with a means for applying pressure on their ideological overseers.

In a more liberal climate of the Gorbachev era, the so-called underground literature has lost much of its special attraction as a forbidden fruit. As was noted earlier, many formerly banned works are now available to Soviet readers through normal channels.

## STAGE AND SCREEN

Socialist realism's requirements apply to all other artistic forms of expression, and theater and cinema are no exceptions. But the application of Socialist realism to these two chief forms of the performing arts has not been uniform. Stage and screen, in fact, may be seen as representing the extremes: the broad liberal and the narrow conservative viewpoints, respectively. More liberal stage plays, are usually produced only by selected avant-garde theaters in Moscow and Leningrad known for their innovation and experimentation.

The theatrical tradition has deep roots in Russia's prerevolutionary past. Some ninety years ago, the partnership between a playwright, Anton Chekhov, and a young actor-director, Konstantin Stanislavsky (Alekseyev), laid the foundation of modern realistic drama. Ever since that time, their successful experimentation, called the Moscow Art Academic Theater (founded in 1898), has been one of the world's leading stages.

Today, Moscow has several other excellent theaters; the total number of professional theatrical companies in the entire country is about 600. All theaters are subsidized by the state and are, therefore, independent of the box office revenues. Admission tickets are inexpensive, and performances attract large audiences, which, according to Soviet statistics, include many blue-collar workers. Major cities have special theaters for young people and children. In ethnic territories, many theaters give performances in local languages.

The repertoire of Soviet theaters consists of plays written by contemporary Soviet authors, Russian and foreign classical plays, and numerous works by "progressive" foreign playwrights. The last category includes selected plays of several contemporary American authors who show the darker side of life in the United States. Similar plays by Soviet authors writing about the tragic past of their own country are in great demand today. In many historical plays Stalin is cast as a villain. A relatively new vogue are experimental studio theaters that operate as artistic cooperatives and are self-financed.

Feature movies are produced in some twenty studios in Moscow, republic capitals, and other large cities. (There is no "Soviet Hollywood.") All studios belong to the state, which nationalized the industry in 1919. Together, they produce approximately 300 full-length films annually.[13] In films, designed to be shown to great numbers of people, the ideological propaganda is more relentless than in any other outlet of Socialist realism. Soviet moviegoers—and average Soviet citizens are said to attend their very inexpensive movie theaters more often than their Western counterparts do—are exposed to propaganda blended into dramatic plots. Some of the movies are very good. Beginning with such early classics as Sergei Eisenstein's *Battleship Potemkin* (1925), many Soviet movies have gained international acclaim for directing and acting. A limited number of carefully chosen foreign movies can be seen on the Soviet screen. Explicitly forbidden are pornographic and erotic films.

Movie directors, scriptwriters, and actors have their own union, with about 6,500 members, which is now under a new leadership of younger and more "progressive" persons. More daring films are being produced and shown. Both movie and stage actors are relatively well paid, and many are recipients of all kinds of honorific titles and medals that entail official esteem and privileges. And, of course, many of them have numerous fans and admirers, although the private lives of movie and stage personalities are almost never made public. There are no fan clubs, posters, or any other promotional publicity gimmicks.

A special high-level government agency, called the USSR State Committee on Cinematography, is in overall charge of the movie industry.

## MUSIC

Next to literature, music has always been Russia's chief artistic export and contribution to the world's culture. The traditional interest in music is evident in Soviet culture. There are about 2,000 professional composers organized in their own union. Moscow and other large cities have symphony orchestras, opera and ballet houses, and musical comedy (operetta) theaters. Altogether, there are more than forty opera houses and about 300 concert

---

[13]This number includes films in Russian and major ethnic languages.

**TABLE 10–7** Five Best-Known Soviet Composers

| Name | Dates | Works |
| --- | --- | --- |
| Dmitri Shostakovich | 1906–1975 | Operas, symphonies, songs |
| Sergei Prokofiev | 1891–1953 | Operas, concerts |
| Aram Khachaturian | 1903–1978 | Operas, concerts |
| Isaak Dunayevsky | 1900–1955 | Songs |
| Dmitri Kabalevsky | 1904– | Operas, songs |

*Source:* Compiled by author from Soviet data.

companies. Musical records and tapes are produced by several recording studios and retailed at low prices.

The official mission of Soviet musicians is "glorification of the heroic labor of the Soviet people."[14] This mission is carried out mainly on four distinctly separate levels:

1. Operas and symphony orchestra concerts. Their repertoire consists of Russian and foreign classical music and a large number of operas and other musical works by contemporary Soviet composers. Socialist realism applies even to this level, and in the past, during Stalin's era, Dimitri Shostakovich and other leading composers were often severely criticized for deviating from its principles.
2. Musical comedies (operettas) and chamber music concerts. Here, too, one finds a mixture of compositions by prerevolutionary Russian, Soviet, and foreign authors.
3. Popular and folk songs. Usually performed at mass concerts, this type of music attracts by far the largest number of listeners. Countless songs by contemporary Soviet composers are filled with patriotism and optimism. With folk songs— Russian and those of ethnic minorities—these songs constitute the chief daily musical diet.
4. "Purified" domestic imitations of rock-and-roll and pop music are also in demand. There are now several Soviet rock groups that give regular—and officially sanctioned—performances before large audiences of mostly young people. On rare occasions, rock concerts are even shown on Soviet television.

Access to all these levels of musical performances is quite inexpensive. Each of them has its own stars enjoying not just the popularity and admiration of the audiences but also official titles and privileges.

All opera houses have their own ballet companies, the best known of which belong to the Moscow Bolshoi Theater and the Leningrad Kirov Theater. Various kinds of dancing are performed on the other two levels. Several professional song-and-dance groups constantly tour the country and make frequent trips abroad.

[14]Quoted from the official charter of the Composers' Union.

There is still another kind of highly popular entertainer in the USSR: the crooner who writes his or her own music and lyrics. Perhaps the best-known such poet-musician is Bulat Okudzhava, who sings and plays guitar. Another such entertainer was Vladimir Vysotsky (1938–1981).

## VISUAL ARTS

The impact of Socialist realism on visual arts has been exceptionally strong, giving contemporary Soviet painting and sculpture a distinctly non-Western character. To a lesser degree, this is also true of Soviet architecture. The main reason for this pronounced divergence is that Socialist realism completely rejects modern abstract art. In the history of Russian art, which was dominated by modernism during the first quarter of this century,[15] this presents a definite regression—a return to the nineteenth century.

Under *glasnost,* there has been a marked increase of official tolerance for more diversion in artistic expression. So-called unsupervised art exhibits and open-air art markets have become regular cultural events in Moscow and other large cities. Paintings, sculptures, and "pop art" on display range from the traditional to modern and from the depiction of Stalin's *Gulag* to religious symbolism.

The Soviet artistic establishment has its own headquarters in Moscow, called the USSR Academy of Arts. About 18,000 professional artists, members of a special union, are busily working on paintings, drawings, graphics, and sculptures in which their creative imagination is combined with the necessary minimum or more of Socialist realism.[16] Their mission, for which they are well paid, is to make canvas and granite into long-lasting testimonials to Soviet accomplishments. A hundred years ago, their predecessors used art in the same utilitarian way, except that they were criticizing and condemning Old Russia's socioeconomic failures.

**TABLE 10–8** Five Best-Known Soviet Artists

| Name | Date | Works |
|------|------|-------|
| Alexander Gerassimov | 1881–1963 | Portraits, heroic scenes |
| Vera Mukhina | 1889–1953 | Sculptures, monuments |
| Isaak Brodsky | 1883–1939 | Portraits, heroic scenes, historic themes |
| Alexander Deinika | 1899–1969 | Heroic scenes, historic themes |
| Nikolai Rerikh | 1874–1947 | Historic themes, exotic landscapes |

*Source:* Compiled by author from Soviet data.

[15]Vasili Kandinsky was a pioneer of modernistic art at the beginning of this century. Among other Russian artists of that generation were Shagal (Chagall) and Malevich.

[16]Some very well-known Soviet painters, for example, Ilya Glazunov, do not belong to the Artists' Union.

As a rule, paintings and sculpture produced by Soviet artists end up in public places rather than in the homes of private collectors. Among numerous museums and art galleries, the most impressive collections are found in the Tretyakov Gallery in Moscow and the Hermitage Museum in Leningrad, where contemporary Soviet art is displayed along with classical masterpieces of Russian and Western artists. Realistic sculptures, sometimes with a touch of symbolism, adorn the squares and parks of Moscow and other large cities. Many of them are memorials to the heroes and heroic events of the 1917 Revolution, the civil war, and World War II. The likeness of Lenin is by far the most frequent theme for publicly displayed Soviet monumental art.

Unlike painting and sculpture, Soviet urban architecture is not that much different from its modern counterpart in the West. During the Stalin era, there was an effort to develop a new style that called for the erection of huge wedding cake-shaped buildings, such as the main building of Moscow University. But this type of architecture, nicknamed "Stalin baroque," is no longer in fashion, having been replaced by less pretentious variations of high-rise structures emphasizing efficiency. Lately, there have also been a few modest efforts to resurrect some of the traditional Russian and ethnic architectural forms and to blend them with the modern simplicity of prefabricated apartment houses and office buildings. An informal public organization, called "Fund of Soviet Culture," and financed by private donations, was founded a few years ago for the purpose of preserving and restoring art and architecture. One of the executive officers is the Soviet "First Lady," Raisa Gorbachev.

## OTHER ENTERTAINMENT

Officially, Soviet culture has no room for either art for art's sake or entertainment for entertainment's sake. All cultural activities are supposed to contain redeeming social values, and the availability of various kinds of entertainment is determined on the same basis. This approach discourages such "bourgeois" types of entertainment as nightclubs, strip and porno shows, gambling, pinball-machine parlors, and pop music. But amusement parks and dancing halls, deemed to be socially useful institutions, operate in practically every Soviet community. In cities one also finds coffee shops, with musical entertainment designed specifically for young people, and discothèques. The postwar period has witnessed a revival of many folk customs and rituals thoroughly purged of any religious meaning.

A very popular form of entertainment with deep roots in the country's history is the one-ring circus. Moscow and other large cities have permanent circus companies that give year-round performances in specially constructed arenas. Several traveling circuses also tour smaller communities and

**FIGURE 10–1**    The Bolshoi Theater in Moscow, home of a famous opera and ballet company.

perform under the tent during the warm months of the year. A typical circus show features tamed animals, acrobats, magicians, clowns, and similar attractions quite familiar to spectators in the West. However, there are also some slight differences: scantily clad dancing girls are usually absent; clown routines contain mostly jokes satirizing minor economic failures; and safety nets are used with all attractions high above the ground. Violence of any kind and the thrill of mortal danger are banned from public shows.

Strict safety requirements render many kinds of car and motorcycle racing unacceptable. Horse races, however, are allowed and even include state-run betting offices. No betting or playing for money is permitted in pool rooms, which are usually located in clubhouses. Card games, dominoes, and a European variety of bingo, called "lotto," may be played in public places for fun. Some small-time illegal gambling and betting exist, but there is no organized numbers game.

Moscow has one of the largest zoos in the world, which contains many rare animals. Smaller zoos, found in other cities, provide opportunities for family outings and group visits by children. Children's entertainment includes numerous puppet theaters with vast repertoires of folk fairy tales.

## AMATEUR ARTS

Millions of Soviet citizens, young and old, participate in various amateur art activities, which are generously sponsored by their government. Every large industrial enterprise, profession, or neighborhood has its own clubhouse that features arts and crafts classes, singing and musical groups, dance and drama circles, and all kinds of hobby workshops. A typical Soviet town has several such clubhouses belonging to the local railroad workers, scientists, military personnel, Young Pioneers (boy and girl scouts), public health employees, and so forth. In addition, large sections of the town usually have community centers especially built and equipped to take care of amateur needs. Similar, although smaller, facilities exist in rural areas.

Participation in practically all amateur activities is free. The needed supervision and instruction are provided by professionals who either volunteer their services or work part time for small honoraria. But each club normally also has a small staff of full-time employees in charge of administration and housekeeping. Many amateur activities are involved in annual, multilevel contests culminating in all-national finals. The winning groups and individuals receive trophies and prizes, and sometimes are even invited to become professional entertainers or artists. A few Soviet amateur-turned-professional folk music groups have successfully performed in foreign countries. According to official statistics, more than 25 million people, about 10 percent of the entire population, are taking part in amateur activities.

Like continuing education, amateur activities fit well into the official concept of the new Soviet way of life, which emphasizes cooperative spirit, communal interests, and togetherness. Group sports are vigorously promoted for the same reasons. Neither activity is supposed to be rewarded with payments. In practice, some money does change hands surreptitiously to encourage the winners.

## HOBBIES

As a matter of ideological principle, the regime prefers its citizens to spend their leisure hours participating in collective activities with proper social content. Private hobbies, therefore, are permitted as a kind of concession to human weakness and a holdover from the past. Given the economic realities of Soviet life, the hobbies that are pursued by ordinary citizens seldom reach extravagant dimensions. Very few people in the Soviet Union, for example, can afford to collect expensive art items or antiques. Some people collect postage stamps and coins. In the past, for political reasons, stamps from certain countries (China, Israel, and Albania) were extremely difficult to obtain, and the trade and possession of gold coins are illegal. Others collect rare books, which can be bought and sold through numerous second-hand bookstores.

To promote a hobby more appropriate to the Soviet way of life, young people are encouraged to collect patriotic buttons and badges honoring various official campaigns and achievements. Music fans collect records and tapes, including those with tunes broadcast by foreign radio stations. There is even a black market for such recordings. Officially available videotapes are limited to old Soviet movies, but more racy foreign video fare can be obtained also through black-market channels.

Photography is a popular hobby with many Soviet people, but it, too, is subject to severe economic limitations. Movie cameras are owned by only a few privileged individuals, and home movies hardly exist. The same is true about home video cassette recorders.

Where living conditions permit, people keep house pets: dogs, cats, and birds. Some veterinary services are available, but things like special pet foods are not. Among the favorite seasonal pastimes of men are fishing and hunting; women and children enjoy wild berry and mushroom picking. Any one of these hobbies can add some welcome variety to the rather monotonous diet of the average Soviet family.

## SPORTS

Technically, everyone engaging in sports activities in the USSR is supposed to be an amateur. With the exception of coaches and instructors, no Soviet athletes are officially treated as professionals—a contention that has been periodically challenged at various international meets and competitions. Because in the West the distinction between amateur and professional athletes is expressed primarily in terms of sources of income, it is hardly applicable to Soviet citizens, who receive their income from the same source regardless of occupation. But from a functional point of view, Soviet athletes are easily divisible into a majority of part-time amateurs and a minority of full-time professionals.

As with just about everything else, sports in the USSR are centralized and placed under a special government agency, called the All-Union Council on Physical Culture and Sport, which supervises physical education in secondary schools and coordinates all sports activities. The agency is directly responsible to the USSR Council of Ministers, and it has offices on all administrative levels.

Sports activities are organized in nine national associations (societies), each catering to a large segment of Soviet society:

> *Burevestnik* (Stormy Petrel): more than 1.5 million students and faculty members;
>
> *Dinamo* (Dynamo): more than 2 million employees of the KGB and the Ministry of Internal Affairs; other government agencies;
>
> *Lokimotiv* (Locomotive): about 1.5 million railroad workers;
>
> *Spartak* (Spartacus): close to 7 million workers in trade, communications, and other services;
>
> *Trudovye Rezervy* (Labor Reserves): about 2 million instructors and trainers of professional schools;
>
> *Zenit* (Zenith): about 3 million workers of various industries;
>
> *Vodnik* (Mariner): several million merchant sailors and shipbuilders.
>
> The remaining two national associations belong to the Soviet Armed Forces and the DOSAAF (Voluntary Society for Promotion of Army, Aviation, and Navy).

These associations have thousands of teams and individual competitors representing more than seventy recognized competitive sports. Competition takes place within and among each society. A comprehensive system of levels for individual and team achievement is used to match and promote the competitors. Competitors reaching the top levels often become full-time, quasi-professional athletes for the duration of their sports careers, although officially they are considered to be on administrative leave from their normal jobs.

These winners are put on national and Olympic teams. Bemedaled and celebrated, these athletes are the counterparts of the professional sports stars of the West. But, although their material rewards are relatively high, they cannot turn their sports skills into monetary fortunes. And when they retire from sports, they either become coaches or return to their original professions and jobs.

It is small wonder that Soviet state-supported athletes have done exceptionally well in various international competitions, including the Olympics. So far, the biggest Soviet triumph was scored at the 1980 Moscow Olympic Games, which were well attended in spite of an American-led boycott by several nations. The USSR, in turn, boycotted the 1984 Los Angeles Olympic Games. In 1988, powerful Soviet teams won impressive victories in both the Winter and Summer Olympics. Under Gorbachev, Soviet athletes have been permitted to sign contracts with foreign teams.

The most popular spectator sport is soccer, followed by volleyball, basketball, and ice hockey. Conspicuous by its absence is American football.

But there is a sharp increase of interest in tennis, while baseball and golf are being tried on an experimental basis. Ethnic sports include a popular Russian game called *gorodki*.[17] Chess and checkers are classified as sports and are played by large numbers of people. Admission to all sports events, which are treated as nonprofit activities, is inexpensive.

As a means of promoting physical training, young people are strongly encouraged to complete physical fitness tests and are awarded badges signifying their readiness for "labor and defense." Several levels of achievement are included in this program. Higher levels of accomplishment are acknowledged by the special titles of "master of sport" and "meritorious master of sport." Most sports, including chess and checkers, are separated by sexes and divided into age groups.

## ARTIST BOHEMIA

Talent, recognition, and fame also give some top Soviet artists a certain license to follow a style of life that is markedly different from that of ordinary people. Thus, Moscow and a few other large cities have their modest counterparts of the artistic districts found in major cultural centers of the West. For example, one of Moscow's suburbs, Peredelkino, is known as a "writers' village." In the capital itself, some apartment houses and clubs are officially reserved for artists, and some restaurants and bars specialize in catering to their tastes, although they probably do not live up to all of their desires.

Many artistic celebrities, especially those who have been abroad, sport foreign clothing. Some even drive expensive foreign cars. As long as the regime is interested in the artists' services at home and abroad, it appears to be willing to tolerate a certain degree of nonconformity in the way the artists dress, spend free time, entertain each other, and behave in private. In their private lives, many members of the artistic elite are believed to be quite uninhibited and permissive. Rumors have it that sexual deviations and drugs are not uncommon in some circles.

But this Soviet version of Bohemia is far from being completely free-for-all and unlimited. Rather, it may be best characterized as a cynical deal involving the selling and buying of artistic talents. The price paid by the buyer does not include political freedom—just creature comforts and a limited license for indulgence. This arrangement is an obvious effort by the regime to lessen the temptation for top artists to defect to the West.

Probably only a small minority of the Soviet artistic elite has both the bargaining power and the inclination to use it for the purpose of obtaining this special status.

[17]*Gorodki* can be played by two teams or by individual players. The game involves knocking down small wooden sticks, arranged in various patterns, by throwing longer wooden clubs.

**FIGURE 10-2**
Vera Mukhina, "A Worker and a Collective
Farmer."

## CULTURAL EXCHANGES

Since the death of Stalin, the Soviet Union has been actively promoting
cultural exchanges with other countries. Included in these exchanges are
people and materials: artists, athletes, writers, and musicians; as well as
films, books, and art exhibits. During this time, the Soviet Union has also
been participating in various international cultural events such as conferences, competitions, matches, contests, and the like. Its most spectacular
achievements have probably been in sports. Soviet state-supported athletes
have completely dominated the last six summer Olympic Games and have
done exceptionally well in all kinds of other bilateral and multilateral contests, both abroad and at home. The staging of the Twentieth Summer
Olympic Games in Moscow, although surrounded by political controversy
and protests, nevertheless marked by far the biggest international sports
event ever held on Soviet soil.

On several occasions, cultural exchange has involved such joint undertakings as filmmaking, book publishing, and other projects. Of course, much
cultural intercourse has been occurring between the USSR and other Communist countries. But the Soviet Union also has cultural exchanges with

BOX 10–6   *Soviet Underground Humor*

---

Question:   What is a string trio?
Answer:      It is a Soviet string quartet returning from an overseas tour.

---

many non-Communist nations, including the United States. During the
1970s, the Soviet-American cultural exchange agreement specified sports
meets, exchanges of theatrical groups, art exhibits, and similar planned
activities. A new agreement was signed in 1985 and cultural exchanges
between the two superpowers appear to be gaining momentum with every
passing year.

Almost without exception, Soviet theatrical performances abroad have
been a great success, duly noted, of course, by official propaganda. However,
there is a price tag attached to this success: A number of outstanding Soviet
artists have used the opportunity of being abroad to defect to the West.
Others had to be allowed to emigrate, and a few were forcibly expelled from
the USSR for their political dissent. Given the volume of artistic gifts and
accomplishments available in such a huge country as the USSR, the artistic
egress does not represent a serious depletion of talent. The annals of history
are replete with both happy and sad stories of artists moving from one
country to another, changing citizenship, or becoming voluntary exiles. It is,
however, a source of considerable embarrassment for the Soviet leadership,
chiefly because they insist on treating culture and arts as official state
business. This makes the Soviet exodus different and gives a political connotation to all Soviet expatriates, even though the reasons for their individual
decisions to leave the country are diverse. It appears that when Soviet
citizens, and especially official bearers of the wonderful news about a para-
dise on earth, decide to leave or not to return, the credibility of the happy
message carried by Soviet arts in general suffers greatly with both the Soviet
public at home and foreign audiences abroad. With the improvement of
conditions for cultural and artistic expression in the USSR, the incidence of
defections has decreased. Some prominent émigré artists have even returned
to the Soviet Union as guest performers or for good.

## ART AND SOCIETY

It is rather obvious that Soviet literature and the arts have never been meant
to serve as a true mirror of Soviet society. On the contrary, all forms of art
practiced in the Soviet Union have a prescribed coefficient of favorable
distortion in their treatment of reality. To be sure, special care is taken
nowadays not to allow the distortion to exceed the point beyond which the
arts would rapidly lose their validity. But the relationship between the Soviet

**BOX 10-7**  *Solzhenitsyn on Literature and Politics*

> ...Then why do we need literature? Is not a writer supposed to teach other people? Is not this how it has been always understood to be? But a major writer in a country...is like a second government. This is why no regime ever likes major writers, just minor ones.
>
> Alexander Solzhenitsyn, *First Circle* (Bern, Switzerland: S. Fischer Verlag, 1968), p. 320.

arts and social reality remains approximately the same as the one that exists between the show-window display of a typical Soviet store and the goods actually available inside. What is written, painted, and performed on stage by Soviet artists is more attractive, bigger, and better than the real Soviet way of life. Their label of Socialist realism notwithstanding, the chief characteristics of Soviet arts are those of romanticism—that is, an artistic rendering of life not as it is, but as it ought to be in accordance with a certain ideal. The ideal is clearly defined, and Soviet artists are expected to follow it as best they know how. They are expected to produce works and performances that instill confidence and enthusiasm in all the Soviet people, who are supposed to strive toward the same ideal. From the point of view of faithful believers and those who are inclined to believe, this is a superior kind of artistic expression because it serves a lofty purpose. But, as viewed by skeptics and those who do not believe, this is sheer propaganda wearing the mask of art or entertainment. It seems probable that the overwhelming majority of Soviet people simply never try to make the distinction, and take for granted that art and propaganda always come blended together, and that the latter pays for the former.

Soviet arts are not a commercial commodity, and, thanks to that, they are easily accessible to the public. The ensuing wide distribution of cultural enrichment is, of course, a real social asset. There is, however, another side to this coin: Being kept on a kind of cultural welfare, the Soviet public has little opportunity to select the cultural benefits that it gets. Beggars—or welfare recipients—cannot be choosers. The selection is made by self-appointed experts and overseers of the arts who have impressive titles and

**BOX 10-8**  *CPSU Program on Artistic Freedom*

> The CPSU takes a careful and respectful attitude to talent and artistic quests. At the same time it has always fought and will continue to fight, relying on the unions of creative workers' public opinion and Marxist-Leninist literary and art criticism, against the lack of ideological principles, indiscriminating attitudes in world outlook, aesthetic dullness, and hack-work.

academic degrees. This makes Soviet literature and art into a didactic tool to be used to influence and mold society.

It would be tempting to say that, because Soviet literature and art are not produced by a free, creative process, they must be of inferior artistic quality. The truth, however, appears to be more complex than that. The entire history of literature and arts in both old Russia and the Soviet Union points to the fact that freedom is but one of many sources of artistic inspiration. On the whole, the quality of the Soviet cultural production is comparable to that of the rest of the contemporary world. So far, the Soviet civilization has not produced any artistic spectaculars of the *Sputnik* magnitude.

If Alexander Solzhenitsyn is right about the perception of major writers as rivals of governments (Box 10–7), it is doubtful that the Soviet leaders would even welcome truly great works of art, because such works could have an unpredictable impact on Soviet society. After all, the intimate tie between Russia's literature and art—"critical realism" or "Socialist realism"—and politics has long been a fact of life. This love-hate relationship is not about to disappear, though Gorbachev's pragmatic approach to arts and artists has cooled it down.

## CULTURAL REVOLUTION

The impressive results of Gorbachev's "cultural revolution" are a kind of deposit or down payment on his promise that, when completed, *perestroika* will have drastically changed Soviet society for the better. At the same time, Gorbachev uses liberalization of literature and arts as a tool to energize Soviet people and infect them with the enthusiasm necessary for his vital economic reforms to succeed. Or, if we were to compare the post-Brezhnev Soviet Union with a seriously ill person in urgent need of major surgery, the "cultural revolution" is a shock treatment designed not to cure but to convince the patient about the seriousness of his condition. New or formerly banned books, plays, movies, and other works of art recently made public in the Soviet Union certainly bring home this point.

On this point, Gorbachev is being applauded by some of his countrymen, especially members of the creative intelligentsia. But he is also criticized by others who see it as a dangerous overdose of "cultural medicine." Some rejoice or fear that a point of no return has been reached and passed, others have equally strong and divided feelings, believing that the process may still be stopped or even reversed. After all, this is what happened to the "thaw" in literature of the Khrushchev era, which was followed by a very real "freeze," though not a complete reversal.

Since Gorbachev's *perestroika* is a "revolution from above" and its application to culture amounts to a "command liberalization," any outcome of the ongoing changes is possible, though a return to Stalin's or Brezhnev's past appears unlikely. Remember that Gorbachev and his team have greatly expanded but not given up ideological limitations governing literary and artistic expression in the Soviet Union. Just as under his predecessors, under Gorbachev Soviet culture enjoys no autonomy. Not yet, anyway. If other major components of Soviet society cannot be changed as fast as has been planned by the reformers in the Kremlin, ways may have to be found to slow down the liberalization process in the realm of culture. As the artistic aspect of *glasnost*, Gorbachev's "cultural revolution" is hostage to the rest of his ambitious reforms, but for the time being it is a window of opportunity for both producers and consumers of literature and art in the USSR.

## GLOSSARY

**Byesteller:** bestseller.
**Derevenschchina:** rural themes and moods.
**Gorodki:** sport game.
**Partiynost:** adherence to the party line.
**Proletcult:** proletarian ("new") culture.
**Socialist realism:** prescribed rules for art.
**Surrogate:** substitute.
**Tamizdat:** external (outside the USSR) publication.

## RECOMMENDED READINGS

BILLINGTON, JAMES, *The Icon and the Axe*. New York: Alfred A. Knopf, 1966.
BROWN, DEMING, *Soviet Russian Literature Since Stalin*. New York: Cambridge University Press, 1977.
SIMMONS, ERNEST J. (ed.), *Continuity and Change in Russian and Soviet Thought*. Cambridge, MA: Harvard University Press, 1955.

CHAPTER

# 11
# SOVIET SOCIETY

## NEW SOCIETY

The official self-image holds that Soviet society is a new and distinctly different human community, free from traditional class antagonisms and contradictions. It is supposed to consist of only two classes, the workers and the collective farmers, and a special social "stratum" rooted in both of them, the "intelligentsia." The distinction between the classes is based entirely on the two forms of Socialist ownership of the means of production: all-state and cooperative. The difference between belonging to either class or to the intelligentsia derives from the type of work or occupation: blue-collar or white-collar, respectively. According to this simple classification, hired hands on state farms and members of collective farms who perform the same work and make approximately equal wages belong to two different classes. But a lowly collective farm bookkeeper or a government clerk and a mighty head of a state ministry or a four-star general are considered members of the same social stratum—the intelligentsia. The two classes and the stratum are supposed to be nonantagonistic and equal components of Soviet society, structured on a horizontal plane.

As we have seen already, Soviet society is actually much more diversified and complex, being stratified on a vertical scale to a degree comparable

**BOX 11–1**  *Preamble to the Soviet Constitution*

> It is a society of high organizational capacity, ideological commitment, and consciousness of the working people, who are patriots and internationalists.

to that found in contemporary societies in the West. Moreover, unquestionably the Soviet Union has a ruling elite—that is, a relatively small group of people exercising power and control over the masses—although it may not be a class in the traditional sense of the term.

Unable to deny completely the existence of vertical stratification in the contemporary Soviet Union, the official propaganda asserts that this stratification is based strictly on merit and that the privileged status of individuals derives from their high positions in society, rather than the other way around. The allegedly functional character of inequality is supposed to ensure an unusually high degree of upward mobility, which is hailed as a unique advantage of the new Soviet society.

Even more important than the official point of view is the claim that Soviet society is undergoing a transition from Socialism to Communism and that all its remaining contradictions, inequalities, and discrepancies are therefore temporary. As we have seen, the mass media and artistic outlets are geared to emphasize, sometimes at the expense of the objective truth, both the scope and speed of the social change that has occurred and is currently occurring in the Soviet Union. Yet there are many areas of Soviet society in which the forces of continuity appear to be just as strong as those of change. And in some of these areas an impartial observer can even detect evidence of occasional regression and backsliding.

In sum, contemporary Soviet society is based on a mixture of old and new, Russian and Marxist trends, attitudes, and relations. These various ingredients interact, compete, or merely coexist. Although Marxist-Leninist ideology provides a general blueprint for the classless and harmonious future society, the concrete shape of that promised future is far from clear. Soviet society continues to be goal-oriented and committed to controlled change, but there seems to be no way to tell with certainty how fast it is moving toward the goal and how far it still has to go. Signals coming from the Soviet Union are rather confusing. For example, there is some evidence that Soviet society is becoming more egalitarian and socialized as a result of Gorbachev's reforms against corruption and elitist privilege. But there is also an unmistakable striving on the part of the Soviet masses for personal gratification, because the same reforms seem to have encouraged more consumerism and individual self-interest.[1]

[1]"The Right Opposition" has challenged Gorbchev' preoccupation with the improvement of living conditions as a revision of "true Marxism-Leninism."

Gorbachev's version of Socialism, which his *perestroika* promises to usher in by the turn of the century, calls for a less authoritarian and paternalistic society characterized by more humane and democratic relations, fairness, mutual respect, self-discipline, and cooperation. This optimistic vision of the not-too-distant future assumes a significant improvement of the material well-being of the Soviet people.

In the past, an important special feature of Soviet society was its very close identification with the official political-economic establishment. All facets of social life were either directly controlled or closely monitored and guided by the appropriate offices. For better or worse, Soviet citizens were never left alone to take care of themselves. If under Stalin Soviet society was based on fear, later its main characteristic was a constant interference by big brother in everybody's affairs. The Soviet Constitution (Preamble) defines it as follows: "It is a society in which the law of life is concern of all for the good of each and concern of each for the good of all."

Today it is a society in flux and, to some degree, in disarray. And it has pretty much given up its ideological pretension of being superior to all other societies.

## HISTORICAL ROOTS

A major ingredient of contemporary Soviet society is the legacy of social norms and customs inherited from the former Russian Empire. This legacy, however, does not include the social structure. Old Russia's society was based on a rigid hereditary caste system, in which the two main castes (or estates) were the landed gentry (nobility) and the peasantry. Other estates, less important as historic factors, were: the clergy, the merchants, the townspeople, and the militarized frontier settlers called "Cossacks."[2] From the moment of birth and, almost without exception, throughout his or her entire life, every Russian subject belonged to one of these estates with its attendant obligations and privileges. For centuries, the distribution of social privileges was flagrantly unequal. To belong to the gentry meant to be rich, to receive a fairly good education, to possess various legal privileges, and to have access to the official positions of power and prestige. On the other end of the social scale were the peasants, entitled only to hard work, poverty, and a lack of the most elementary human rights.

During the nineteenth century, the traditional caste system slowly started to disintegrate under the pressure of industrialization, urbanization, and other modern trends. Two relatively small groups of people began to play increasingly important roles in Russia's changing society. One of them

---

[2]The Cossacks ("free men" in Turkic) emerged as a distinct group of frontier settlers during the fifteenth and sixteenth centuries. They were given a degree of autonomy and self-rule by the czars in exchange for this military service.

**TABLE 11–1** Class Structure (in percentages)

| 1917 Russia | | 1988 USSR | |
|---|---|---|---|
| Workers | 17 | Workers | 61.7 |
| Peasants | 66 | Collective peasants | 12.1 |
| Bourgeoisie | 17 | "Intelligentsia" | 26.2 |
| | 100.0 | | 100.0 |

*Source:* Compiled by author from Soviet statistics.

was the emerging class of capitalists coming from the ranks of the more enterprising nobles and merchants. The other extremely influential group was a new breed of intellectuals, both of gentle and nongentle (*raznochintsy*) origins. Proudly calling themselves by the borrowed French word *intelligentsia*, these well-educated and often very gifted people with strongly anti-government political beliefs became the undisputed leaders of Russia's cultural development and gave it a distinctly ideological character. All noted Russian revolutionaries, including Lenin, were supplied by the intelligentsia.

The 1917 Revolution not only did away with the caste system, but it also introduced a kind of "affirmative action" that granted various preferential considerations to those belonging to the "working classes," and severely limited the civil rights of the members of the formerly privileged estates: the gentry, the clergy, the merchants, and the Cossacks. For almost two decades, these people, and even their children, were officially labeled "deprivees" (*lishentsy*) and were barred from educational and career opportunities.

In 1936, the new Soviet Constitution put an end to this open discrimination against the "old classes." On that occasion, Stalin publicly declared that "the son is not responsible for his father,"[3] and since then it has been maintained officially that Soviet society consists of only two friendly classes, the workers and the collective farmers, plus a stratum of the Soviet intelligentsia. The 1977 Soviet Constitution had nothing new to say on this subject; it did, however, give the intelligentsia a new title, "people's intelligentsia," which emphasized that Soviet society was undergoing rapid changes on its way to becoming completely homogeneous.

## "NEW CLASS"

It was also in the mid-1930s that the process of vertical stratification of Soviet society gained momentum, and quickly produced a distinct upper echelon of senior bureaucrats and managers and a smaller elite group at the very top.

---

[3]This statement did not prevent retaliations against family members of the so-called enemies of the people during the mass purges of the late 1930s. During World War II, millions were subjected to discrimination because of their ethnicity. After World War II, residents of German-occupied territories and former POWs were officially blacklisted.

**BOX 11–2**   *Gorbachev on Inequity*

The Socialist way of life can have only one hierarchy—the hierarchy of personal merits based on abilities, knowledge and experience, strength of character and striving toward high public ideals. This is what the criteria for it should be.

Speech at the Twentieth Komsomal Congress, *Pravda*, April 17, 1987; p. 2.

Some thirty years later, a disillusioned Communist theoretician named these groups, which he expanded to include the entire Communist Party, the "New Class."[4] According to his theory, the political power possessed by the CPSU's members is equivalent to property ownership, making the party the new ruling class of the Soviet Union. Recall that in earlier chapters we used the analogy of the owner-manager relationship to explain the party-government duality in the USSR. We suggested that party membership may be compared to first-class Soviet citizenship. It is, however, doubtful that even the party's top bureaucracy, much less the entire CPSU's membership, can be called a ruling class in the traditional sense of the term, as long as the political power cannot be automatically passed from parents to children like monetary fortunes or hereditary titles in other societies.

Little evidence suggests that anything resembling power dynasties has developed in the Soviet Union. Communist bigwigs do possess all kinds of privileges that extend to the members of their families, and they are able to give their children (and even their grandchildren) special educational and career advantages. But most of this preferential treatment ends with the demise, physical or political, of the clan's founder. The record shows that, almost without exception, members of the second and third generations of Soviet leaders' families have had less than spectacular careers. If we compared the passing of power from one generation to another in the USSR to the inheritance of money in the West, we would have to conclude that the heirs of Lenin, Stalin, Khrushchev, and other top Soviet leaders seem to have inherited only small fractions of the power fortunes amassed by their predecessors.[5] Even such material perquisites as country *dachas* (cottages), automobiles, and luxurious apartments usually revert to the state rather than stay in the family of important Soviet has-beens, thus giving credence to the official claim about the functional nature of Soviet privileged groups.

---

[4]The expression "New Class" was made famous as the title of a book written by the disillusioned Yugoslav Communist leader Milovan Djilas.

[5]Here are some examples: Lenin's niece, Olga Ulyanov (Maltsev), is a professor of chemistry at Moscow University; her older brother, Victor Ulyanov, Lenin's nephew, works as a technician at an airplane factory in Moscow. Stalin's daughter, Svetlana, defected to the West in 1967, returned to the USSR in 1984, and then redefected in 1986. Stalin's oldest son by his first marriage, Yakov, an artillery officer, perished in a German POW camp during World War II.

The size of the expanding ruling group is estimated at several million, and that of the elite, merely at between 10,000 and 20,000 top functionaries plus their families. All members of this component of Soviet society are, of course, card-carrying Communists of long standing, and practically all of them have had higher education. As already mentioned, it is relatively easy for their children to continue meeting these two prerequisites. In fact, the coincidence of party members and college graduates among the offspring of the ruling group is almost 100 percent. Furthermore, the magic generated by the names of powerful persons definitely helps their children to move up the career ladders, but only to the level of middle-ranking bureaucrats and professionals. So far, exceptions to this rule have been of a temporary nature, lasting only until the death or political demise of the powerful person himself or herself. For example, such was the fate of Stalin's younger son, Vasili, and Khrushchev's son-in-law, Aleksei Adzhubei, and Brezhnev's son, Yuri.[6] Yuri Andropov's only son, Igor, is a middle-ranking diplomat. Chernenko's daughter, Yelena, is married to a diplomat, and his son, Vladimir, is a movie executive. Gorbachev's daughter, Irina, is a medical doctor in an ordinary Moscow clinic.

On the other hand, under Brezhnev there was a growing incidence of "high society" marriages between daughters and sons of the elite, suggesting the emergence of a hereditary "palace guard." This trend has been discontinued, though it is difficult to know what is happening because even under *glasnost* little light is shed upon the private lives of Soviet leaders and their families.

## CLASSES

In addition to being the uppermost part of the Communist Party, the ruling elite belongs to a much larger social group officially called the "people's intelligentsia," meaning the white-collar workers. The Soviet intelligentsia, which roughly corresponds to the middle class in the United States, currently contains between one fourth and one third of the entire population. This ratio is growing. Gainfully employed members of the intelligentsia number about 25 million and include all working-age people with a higher education and a majority of people with a specialized middle (paraprofessional) education. Their main occupations are the following:

Party and government bureaucrats;
Teachers, scientists, scholars;

[6]Stalin's younger son, Vasili, an air force general during World War II, was demoted after his father's death; he died of alcoholism. Khrushchev made his son-in-law, Adzhubei, editor of *Izvestia*. He was transferred to a lower position after Khrushchev's downfall. In the late 1970s, Brezhnev's son Yuri was appointed First Deputy Minister of Foreign Trade. In 1986, he was demoted and sent as commercial attaché to Bulgaria. In 1988, Brezhnev's son-in-law, Yuri Churbanov, was sentenced to hard labor for corruption.

Medical doctors and some paramedics;
Military and police officers;
Artists, writers, actors;
Business managers.

Approximately 30 percent of the eligible intelligentsia members belong to the Communist Party. Among the top layers of the group, party membership reaches almost 100 percent. It is also here that one finds people and families with the highest incomes and the most lavish privileges. These are the leading professionals, top military, and bureaucrats. On the other hand, members of a sizable lower portion of the intelligentsia receive smaller salaries and fringe benefits than those commanded by skilled blue-collar workers. As already mentioned, beginning medical doctors and schoolteachers often make less than the national average for state employees. The same is true of low-ranking clerks and bureaucrats, who are included in the intelligentsia.

Each of these occupational subgroups has its own hierarchical structure. The last one—managers of business activities—enjoys much higher living standards than its official status implies. Members of this subgroup, called *khozyaistvenniki* (business managers) and numbering several million, owe their good fortunes to their control of scarce goods and services. A new subgroup are businessmen who command unusually large income from cooperative ventures. The boundaries of this group are vague and its lower strata include many blue-collar employees.

In theory, the blue-collar workers are the most glamorous class. With their families, they constitute more than two thirds of the USSR's population. Being of worker origin used to be an important advantage in getting better educational and career opportunities. Today this is no longer so, but personal working experience in the production process does entitle people to receive preferential treatment for admission to colleges and universities. By and large, the claim that workers are the favorites of Soviet society is true only in terms of the incessant propaganda praise with which they are showered. As a group, the workers earn an average compensation—wages and fringe benefits—that is considerably below that of the intelligentsia. And the bulk of them are far removed from the real political power: On the whole, only one out of every fourteen or fifteen blue-collar workers belongs to the

**BOX 11–3**   *Soviet Underground Humor*

There were three classes of Soviet citizens under Stalin:

1. Those who were serving their time in prisons and camps
2. Those who already had served their time in prisons and camps
3. Those who were still expecting to serve their time in prisons and camps

Communist Party. This ratio, however, is higher among industrial workers. The educational level of the workers averages seven to eight years of secondary school, usually with a vocational slant, although an ever-growing number of younger workers are graduates from high schools or technicums. The number of blue-collar workers is increasing.

A majority of Soviet industrial workers are the children or grandchildren of peasants, who constitute the least privileged of the three officially recognized social groups. Smallest in size, this class has been declining faster than the rate of ongoing urbanization. This seeming paradox arises as a result of the official use of terminology: Every time a collective farm is converted into a state farm, which occurs quite often, all of its members are reclassified as agricultural workers. Both subgroups of peasants—collective farmers and agricultural workers—are on the bottom of the Soviet social pyramid. They receive the lowest incomes, the fewest fringe benefits, and the worst education. Relatively few members of the rural population belong to the Communist Party (approximately 5 percent of the adults). Gorbachev's efforts to improve peasants' lot have not been effective so far.

In the Soviet Union, there are no large numbers of such social outcasts as homeless drifters and so-called street people. For the regime, this is a source of considerable pride, high on the list of Soviet socioeconomic achievements that offer favorable comparisons with the West.

## UPWARD MOBILITY

One important reason that the Soviet system is not likely to breed revolt has been the upward social mobility, whose tempo continues to rise. Thanks to the steadily expanding national economy and the personnel gaps caused by periodic purges in the past, there has always been room on the top for ambitious young people who meet two basic requirements: ideological conformity certified by membership in the party and professional training, usually obtained through higher education. To be successful, social climbers must also possess a good deal of perseverance and character. Superior intelligence is desirable but not absolutely essential. Family and personal connections, as mentioned, can be extremely helpful, especially because the assignment of positions and promotions in the Soviet Union is almost never based on objective tests or evaluations. Nepotism and cronyism are widespread and cause much resentment and envy among the losers. Gorbachev has promised to remedy this situation.

Upward social mobility is always accompanied by a certain amount of disruption and tension. Contemporary Soviet society, though it is not an exception to the rule, seems to generate fewer adverse effects than might be expected. This is probably because the avenues for social mobility do not often change, and the patterns of success or failure are quite predictable. In other words, the rules of the game are well known in advance, and the game itself moves rather slowly. The Soviet Union is not an ideal setting for the rags-to-riches adventure or any other variety of instant success story. As we already know, the contemporary Soviet political system, which has its share of rivalries and power struggles, is nevertheless relatively devoid of high political drama. For a long time, for instance, not many people—either candidates or voters—spent sleepless nights waiting for early returns of elections to the Supreme Soviet. This has changed now, but political victories in the modern USSR usually still come in small installments and follow established routes. By the same token, even complete political failures, which under Stalin frequently had sinister consequences, have now become much less spectacular and less tragic. For example, several political has-beens live quietly in forced retirement and oblivion in or near Moscow.

The ongoing vertical mobility blurs the boundaries between classes and social groups in the Soviet Union. This is especially true with regard to housing. Only the top strata of the privileged groups live in fairly exclusive and better-appointed apartment houses. The rest of the people, regardless of their income or social station, are clustered closely together. Farmers live in villages rather than on individual farms, and in urban areas, home usually means a small apartment in a socially integrated high-rise building. Perhaps because of this togetherness, there is a distinct lack of feeling for rank and status among the majority of the people, giving Soviet society a desired egalitarian appearance. But below the surface of social uniformity many tensions are generated by such personal human weaknesses as envy and jealousy, as well as by national differences.

## COLLECTIVISM

The semicommunal type of living so widespread in the Soviet Union is not just an economic necessity caused by a shortage of housing. Ideologically, it is considered to be an environment most conducive to the desired social climate of collectivism. As practiced in the USSR, collectivism implies close social relations, emphasizes people's dependence on each other, puts social interests above the individual, and forces everybody to mind everybody else's business. Its motto is "One for all, all for one," which, as we should recall, is written in the "Moral Code of the Communist." Although collectivism is vigorously promoted as a basic principle of Marxism-Leninism, it also has deep roots in the many centuries of rural Russia's communal life. The basic unit of the serfdom system was a village community called the *mir*, which managed all internal affairs, periodically redistributed leased land, and bore collective responsibility toward its gentle landowners.

By emphasizing the common good over self-interest, collectivism is supposed to produce a friendly, cooperative, and, at the same time, efficient society. Because, under collectivism, giving is more virtuous than receiving, it is a producers' society rather than a consumers' society. Collectivism means that considerations of national security, state interests, community concerns, and the like must be put before any personal needs and aspirations. Public manifestations of individualism and self-interest are equated with egotism and are summarily condemned as antisocial behavior. Examples of unselfishness, readiness to help others, and self-sacrifice are exalted in the Soviet mass media and artistic outlets.

The net results of the heavy stress on collectivism are mixed and even contradictory. On the one hand, Soviet society as a whole displays a strong sense of cohesion and unity, especially in the face of such adversities as wars, economic hardships, and national disasters. As individuals, Soviet citizens tend to be more cooperative and to share a feeling of belonging to the same work team. Instead of striving toward self-sufficiency and worrying about individual security, they rely on others; they get, in other words, the "elbow feeling."[7] Keen competition is limited mostly to top-level white-collar professionals and especially to those with political ambitions.

On the other hand, the emphasis on collectivism appears to be the main source of such negative attributes of Soviet society as an appalling lack of initiative, widespread contempt for official rules and regulations, and a large degree of alienation. Somewhat contrary to its popular image in the West as a huge hard-labor colony, the USSR has a social environment often conducive to idleness, goldbricking, and cynical indifference. Although its system of relatively moderate punishments and rewards keeps most of the people in line, it seems unable to deter a sizable minority of alienated citizens from going astray and neglecting their duties. This annoys others who believe that their lazy fellow citizens are getting a free ride from a society committed to collectivism and communal spirit.

As realized by Lenin (and even by Marx before him), the Russians, as a nation, are not the best material for an efficient collectivist economic system. Somewhat ironically, the system appears to work much better today in such "Germanized" parts of the Soviet Union as Estonia, Latvia, and Lithuania. Gorbachev's reform campaign has been going faster and achieving more tangible results there than anywhere else in the country. In fact, underlying much of the local nationalism is the suspicion that the Baltic republics contribute more to the Soviet economy than they get.

## SOCIAL RELATIONS

Individualism is seen as the antithesis of collectivism, and its manifestations are, at best, tolerated, while being blamed on social atavism. As products of society, Soviet people are expected to feel, think, and act alike on all major

---

[7]The "elbow feeling" means having close friends beside you on whose help you can readily depend. It is a striking contrast to the notion of "elbow room," which is deemed desirable in the United States.

issues. But the insistence on conformity usually stops short of interfering with interpersonal relations, and people are free to select their friends, mates, and acquaintances. Social relations in general tend to be quite informal, a trend consonant with both the Russian peasant tradition and Marxist-Leninist ideology. Introductions and self-introductions are simple and brief. In addressing each other, complete strangers most frequently use the words "citizen" or "comrade," though the latter word has a more official connotation. Either word can be used with or without the last name of the person to whom it refers. Children call grownups whom they do not know "uncle" or "aunt." Older people may be addressed as "grandfather" or "grandmother."

The Russian language has two forms of "you," formal and informal. The latter is used by children and to children, by young adults to each other, and by closer relatives and friends. In theory, all party members are supposed to use this informal "you" (ty, in Russian) with each other. In practice, however, superiors address their subordinates by ty, but subordinates reply with the more formal vy (formal "you").

Next to the family, the smallest units of Soviet society are groups that consist of fellow workers and neighbors. The former, called a "working collective," is more formally structured and is supervised by the "triangle": the official boss, a party secretary, and a trade union representative. The latter is a looser group that includes the tenants of each apartment building and is usually presided over by voluntary activists. Both primary groups make it their business to be involved in the private lives of their members and exercise various kinds of pressure to correct any aberrations in their behavior. Their other important function is to serve as bridges between individuals and families, on the one hand, and society at large, on the other. In this sense, the working collectives and neighbor's associations are similar to the primary organizations of the party and the Komsomol.

In addition, most Soviet people participate in other group activities such as professional associations, amateur clubs, and study projects. This appears to be officially encouraged as an expression of the new Soviet democracy. During the last few years, the number of informal organizations dedicated to various causes has mushroomed to tens of thousands. Some of them claim nation-wide membership and have branches in different cities, while others limit their activities to local interests and issues. Proclaimed goals and objectives of these groups range from environmental concerns to efforts to preserve and promote ethnic cultures. Most active in the latter category are mass movements, called "popular fronts," in the Baltic republics. The informal groups have no primary party or Komsomol organizations and some are openly anti-Communist.

For many years, the official position maintained that there were no lonely or lonesome people in the Soviet "society of optimism," as it was often called by the mass media. Because of this supposition, there were few social services and activities specially designed to cope with such human conditions. Religious groups, all of which are constantly watched by authorities, used to limit their activities strictly to religious services and rituals, for fear of being accused of engaging in propaganda. Nonregistered religious and spiritual cults, sects, and groups were forbidden to operate in the open and their members risked legal prosecution. This has been changed and the public-at-large is now urged to actively participate in donations and services to charities and fund-raising campaigns. Churches are welcome partners in efforts to help those in need.

On the grass-roots level, there is a microstructure of small circles of friends: mostly men, and usually neighbors or co-workers, who get together in their spare time to chat and drink. For many, such meetings are a form of escapism from and passive protest against the regimentation and drudgery of everyday life.

Theoretically, intimate relations between people are their own private business. There is, however, not much privacy for anybody or anything in the Soviet Union. As a result, courtships, love affairs, and quarrels seldom remain secret. Heterosexual relations outside marriage are tolerated, provided that the parties observe rather old-fashioned (by Western standards) conventions and appearances. Homosexuality, which is seen as a perversion, is subject to legal prosecution and public condemnation. Consequently there are no openly gay groups or societies though this may be changing.

## ALCOHOLISM

For a long time, excessive drinking, with all the attendant complications (disorderly conduct, absenteeism, domestic fights, accidents, and so forth), was one of the most serious problems facing Soviet society. Because of the lack of privacy in the Soviet way of life, much drinking was done in public places, and its ugly side effects were routine sights: drunken street brawls, alcoholics sleeping it off on park benches, and various other forms and degrees of alcohol-induced misbehavior. Although reliable statistics on the production and consumption of alcoholic beverages were hard to find, even some Soviet authorities admitted that during the 1970s the alcohol problem increased. This made it difficult to label alcoholism a "remnant of the capitalist past," which was too far behind to have affected most of the alcoholics even in their infancy.

The embarrassing aspect of the problem was that, except for some illegally homemade vodka, all alcoholic beverages are manufactured and retailed by the Soviet state, which derives a substantial profit from this monopoly. The revenue, however, could not have been large enough to offset the damage to the national economy caused by alcoholism. Why then did the Soviet state, which is not known for catering to consumers' wishes, tolerate alcohol abuse for so long? It seems that, bad and embarrassing as it

**BOX 11–4**    *Soviet Underground Humor and Alcoholism*

> *Before the antidrinking campaign*
> Between CAPITALISM and COMMUNISM lies a long period of SOCIAL-ISM. And between SOCIALISM and COMMUNISM lies even a longer period of ALCOHOLISM.
> *After the antidrinking campaign*
> An important official is trying to get romantic with his new secretary; the young lady is willing, but wants to close the office door, which is wide open. "Don't do that, or people may think we're having a drink!" protests her boss.

was, mass alcoholism was considered by earlier Soviet leaders to be a lesser evil than—and even a solution to—the potentially greater problems of accumulated dissatisfaction and alienation.

It may be a measure of Mikhail Gorbachev's stature as a leader that he dared to declare war on alcoholism right after coming to power. Instead of imposing halfhearted and timid measures, like those that had been tried unsuccessfully in the past by his predecessors, he attacked the "green serpent"[8] from several sides: curbing production and sales of hard liquor, raising the legal drinking age, introducing stiff penalties for alcohol-related misconduct, prescribing compulsory medical treatment, and launching a vigorous educational campaign to promote temperance and even abstinence. Excessive drinking, especially in public places, is no longer accepted as normal social behavior. On a cue from high above, the Soviet mass media began to blame excessive drinking for poor workmanship, truancy, family breakups, and even crime. It seems the new leader has invested a lot in this "moral equivalent of war"—his personal prestige and the success of his ambitious economic reforms, which depend so much on what he calls the "human factor." His economic reforms emphasize the need for much greater labor productivity contingent on the overall improvement of work ethics.

There are conflicting reports concerning the effectiveness of the antidrinking campaign. Although outward symptoms of mass alcoholism are definitely on the wane, how much heavy drinking survives underground is unknown. Even official Soviet media have admitted to a sharp increase in bootlegging. The Gorbachev regime probably does not expect the campaign to be successful immediately; it assumes Soviet citizens drink heavily because of tradition and psychological need. Use of alcohol at every festive occasion is an old Russian custom; a more modern rationale is to use alcohol to escape the depressing reality of insufficient material goods and comforts. But a start has been made and the USSR is slowly moving away from its dubious distinction of being among the countries with high per capita

[8]One of many nicknames for alcohol addiction in Russian is "green serpent."

consumption of alcohol. In 1987, Americans brought AA meetings to the Soviet Union for the first time.

In contrast, drug abuse has never been a serious problem in Russia. Soviet authorities appear to be determined to keep it that way, by enforcing very strict controls. According to official statistics, there are fewer than 150,000 drug addicts in the country.

## CRIME AND PUNISHMENT

Although comprehensive crime statistics have never been published, most observers agree that the majority of crimes committed in the USSR are nonviolent. Very strict firearms control is vigorously enforced. Compared with major nations in the West, murders, rapes, and muggings, which are seldom even mentioned by the Soviet media, occur relatively infrequently.

Soviet sensitivity to crime statistics is the result of embarrassingly naïve and unfulfilled prophecies made by Lenin and other early Marxists, who claimed that because crime is caused by social inequalities, it would completely disappear with the advent of Socialism. An estimated 1 million convicted criminals in the USSR today belie that claim. The number of prisoners used to be much higher before Gorbachev's ascent to power in 1985 and his subsequent amnesties, but now it is rising again.[9]

Peculiar conditions of Soviet life have made certain kinds of crime almost completely nonexistent. For example, there is little organized violent crime and very few cases of kidnapping for ransom in the USSR. Crimes involving the use of private cars are rare, and the use of private planes for wholesale smuggling and similar illegal activities is even less frequent. But there are also categories of crime peculiar to Soviet society: illegal dealings in foreign currencies, black-market activities, violations of production plans, and other economic crimes. Avoidance of socially useful work or study, labeled "parasitism," is punishable as a crime. So are, even today, certain kinds of political dissent and religious practices.

Corrupt bureaucratic practices—influence peddling, bribery, extortion, favoritism—used to be (and to lesser extent still are) spread widely throughout the huge official establishment.

The incidence of serious crime is rising as an unwelcome byproduct of liberalization. It is considerably higher in cities, which evidently lack both strong police departments and the traditional communal ties of the countryside. The most frequent crimes are "hooliganism," which is defined as malicious actions against the public order, and vandalism, which usually involves public property. Close to one half of these crimes are committed by juvenile delinquents. In urban areas, juvenile delinquency is also blamed for

[9]At least in part, it is due to massive ethnic clashes in the Caucasus and in Central Asia.

**TABLE 11–2** Crime in the USSR, 1987 and 1988

| Major categories | 1987 | 1988 | %change |
| --- | --- | --- | --- |
| Premeditated murder | 14,651 | 16,710 | +14.1% |
| Aggravated assault | 28,250 | 37,190 | +31.6% |
| Rape (including attempted) | 16,765 | 17,658 | +5.3% |
| Armed robbery | 9,047 | 12,916 | +42.8% |
| Burglary | 46,485 | 67,114 | +44.4% |
| Theft (from state and private individuals) | 132,377 | 165,283 | +24.9% |
| Fraud (including bribery) | 23,897 | 21,543 | −9.8% |
| Embezzlement | 96,986 | 87,450 | −9.8% |
| Profiteering (black marketeering) | 43,372 | 45,235 | +4.3% |

Note: The total number of crimes committed in 1988 was 1,867,223—a 3.8 percent increase over the previous year. Included in this total were 362,096 crimes committed by persons acting under the influence of alcohol, and 183,953 crimes—committed by juveniles.

*Source: Izvestia,* Feb. 14, 1989, p. 6.

a large share of more serious crimes, such as muggings and robberies. In the past, excessive drinking was considered to be the main cause of this problem.

As for criminal, nonpolitical justice, the treatment of suspects, defendants, and convicts is, on the whole, comparable to Western fairness, understanding, and compassion. Sentences for violent crimes tend to be harsher in the USSR, which enforces the death penalty for a number of serious offenses. Conditions in prisons and labor camps can be extremely severe. But, on the other hand, the maximum length of imprisonment is only fifteen years. A wide variety of suspended sentences, combined with constructive rehabilitation efforts and community services, is widely used by Soviet courts to deal with relatively minor crimes, such as thefts of state or personal property, cheating, petty embezzlement, disorderly conduct, and similar offenses. In recent years, there has been a growing popular clamor for the abolition of capital punishment.

During the last few years, there has been a marked improvement in the dispensation of justice. Heavy emphasis is placed on the educational function of justice by encouraging open trials, public condemnations, confessions of guilt, and statements of remorse. Cases that offer redeeming social lessons are often tried at the place of work or residence of the accused. Co-workers and neighbors attending such hearings are expected to feel a moral responsibility for the misdeeds of their peer.

All minor offenders under age 14 come before special Commissions on Juvenile Affairs consisting of representatives from various official agencies and communal organizations. These commissions can punish both the juvenile delinquents and their parents. Punishments range from public reprimands and fines to confinement in juvenile labor colonies. The jurisdiction over cases involving minors aged 15 to 17 is divided between the commissions and regular courts depending on the seriousness of the alleged crimes. The Soviet press now admits the existence of youth gangs whose activities often involve unruly behavior, vandalism, and forms of violent crime.

In spite of the undeniable progress made by the Soviet judicial system during the entire post-Stalin era, until very recently, cases with political overtones continued to be treated with prejudice and bias. Pressure was applied to the accused, procedural norms were disregarded, and very heavy sentences were meted out based on the most tenuous interpretation of the written law.

## WOMEN'S ROLE

That women in the USSR have long been equal with men is one of the Soviets' proudest claims. The claim is supported not only by references to the Soviet Constitution (Article 35) but also by some very impressive statistical data on women's education, employment, and other social accomplishments. Women, who comprise more than half of the Soviet student body and labor force, occupy more than 73 percent of the jobs in education, about 84 percent of the jobs in public health, and 71 percent of the positions in various outlets of culture and entertainment. For many years, Soviet women have been successfully holding their own in such traditionally male occupations as mine engineering, space exploration, bricklaying, and commercial fishing. Approximately 90 percent of all work-age women, except those in school, have jobs outside their homes.

The number of women in high political, executive, and professional positions is, however, relatively small. Currently, there are very few women among the members of the Central Committee of the CPSU; one woman serves as a candidate-member on the Politburo 1990. There are relatively few women in the new USSR Supreme Soviet, and the USSR Council of Ministers. There are only about twenty women among the 330 members of the USSR Academy of Sciences. As we have already seen, women constitute less than a third of the party's membership, which is a recognized prerequisite for a successful political career. But all of this does not take away from the tremendous progress made by Soviet women, who some sixty years ago started from practically zero: About 80 percent of the women in Old Russia were illiterate.

Equal pay for equal work regardless of sex has long been a Soviet reality. Soviet women also receive sixteen weeks of maternity leave with full pay, and an optional leave up to one year at half pay to take care of infants. Women can retire with full pensions at age 55, five years earlier than men. An extensive network of nurseries, day-care centers, and kindergartens helps working mothers to bring up their children. Most of the more demeaning women's occupations, such as prostitution, stripteasing, and similar sex-oriented jobs, have been eliminated.

On the negative side are some formidable problems produced by the full integration of the sexes. As a not very funny Soviet joke puts it, women in the USSR are equal, not only with men, but also with bulldozers and tractors, although in recent years many physically difficult jobs have been closed to them. Because of a dire need to have two family incomes and also because of a strong social disapproval of not being employed by the national economy, Soviet women seldom stay home as full-time housewives. This means that they end up working all day on a job and still taking care of the housework, made especially difficult by chronic shortages of such consumer goods as baby foods, modern kitchen appliances, and clothing. More often than not, the grind of daily shopping falls on their shoulders too. No wonder that fewer and fewer Soviet women are willing to raise many children, which may be a byproduct of women's emancipation unexpected by the Soviet leaders. According to Soviet statistics, more than half of the fast-growing number of divorces are initiated by wives who do not feel economically dependent on their marriages. This may come as an unpleasant surprise to Soviet men, most of whom appear to have problems with the changing roles of the sexes.

## FAMILY LIFE

After a brief experiment with "free love" and extremely informal cohabitation arrangements, Stalin's Soviet Union settled down to rigid norms of traditional family life. Divorces were made difficult, abortions were outlawed, and illegitimate children were listed "fatherless" in official documents. All of this began to change again following the death of Stalin in 1953. Today the divorce rate is high: It affects at least one third of all new marriages. Divorces are simple and courts are involved only to settle questions of child custody and support. Unsuccessful marriages that end in divorce during the first two years are especially common among the young urban population. Abortions are once again legal and free of charge, and there is no longer any official stigma attached to children of unmarried mothers. Early marriages are encouraged. But living together without benefit of matrimonial procedure is not generally accepted by Soviet society, which remains basically conservative in its attitudes toward sex and family life. Such attitudes are strongly supported by educational and propaganda efforts, which depict the family as the building block of Soviet society. Today, there are relatively few single-parent families and children born out of wedlock. But the incidence of divorces is growing.

As a means of strengthening family life, marriages and baptisms, which used to be treated as bureaucratic formalities, have been made into solemn

**TABLE 11–3** Suicides in the USSR

| Year: | 1965 | 1984 | 1985 | 1986 | 1987 |
|---|---|---|---|---|---|
| Number: | 39,550 | 81,417 | 68,073 | 52,830 | 54,105 |

Note: The ratio between men and women committing suicide is approximately 3 to 1.
*Source:* Compiled by author from Soviet data.

occasions celebrated in special "palaces." The ceremonies, supervised by robed officials, closely resemble religious rites because they include various symbolic words, gestures, and actions. There is some free marriage and family-planning counseling. Professional advice and help on sex matters are usually available, on request, in public health centers and clinics. Since oral contraception is not available in the USSR, many women are forced to resort to abortion.

A typical urban family in the USSR seldom has more than two children. Today, only an estimated 20 percent of urban families have a live-in grandmother (*babushka*, in Russian) who helps to take care of the children and household chores. As a rule, both the husband and wife in urban families hold full-time, outside jobs. Peasant families tend to be larger; they have more children and almost always include members of three generations living under one roof. As noted, families with the largest numbers of offspring are found in rural areas of traditionally Muslim union republics: Azerbaijan, Kazakhstan, Kirgizia, Tajikistan, Turkestan, and Uzbekistan. It is in rural families with several children that the wives are least likely to have full-time, outside jobs, though the cause-effect relationship here may be the reverse of what it seems.

The number of families in the USSR is estimated at approximately 73 million. Despite the formal equality of the sexes, men continue to play, or at least are trying to play, the traditional role of head of the household. As part of Russia's agrarian heritage, members of the extended family are known by many different titles that denote the exact relationship of one relative to another. For instance, two different titles are used to denote the mothers-in-law of the husband and the wife.

## PUBLIC HEALTH

As a comprehensive system of public service, medicine vies only with mass education for the top spot on the list of officially claimed Soviet achievements. Both in absolute figures and on a per capita basis, there are more physicians in the USSR than in any other country in the world. An extensive network of hospitals and clinics covers the entire land. All medical and dental services, which come under the union-republic Ministry of Public Health, are free of charge and available on demand. Medical services include

**TABLE 11–4** Abortions and Live Births in the USSR

| Year | Abortions (mill.) | Live births (mill.) |
|------|-------------------|---------------------|
| 1989 | 6.5 | 5.6 |

Note: During the same year, an estimated 90% of first-time preg-
nancies ended in abortion.

*Source:* Compiled by author from Soviet data.

prenatal and baby care, unlimited hospitalization, and visits to doctors. Abortions are also included in the medical services and are available on demand. Soviet women resort to abortions very frequently, primarily because of the chronic shortage of other birth control options.

Heavy emphasis is placed on preventive medicine and health education. Periodical medical checks and various tests are obligatory for many professions, and there are numerous sanataria and rest homes with prescribed medical treatments and diets where millions of people spend all or part of their annual vacations. Thanks to a comprehensive system of vaccination, outbreaks of communicable diseases are rare. Reliable data on this aspect of Soviet public health are, however, difficult to obtain even under *glasnost.* The same is true about statistics on suicides, mental illness, and infant mortality. According to official statistics, there have been fewer than 200 cases of AIDS in the Soviet Union, involving mostly foreign residents.

The quality of Soviet medicine, however, is uneven. As a rule, members of the privileged groups and their families have access to better medical facilities and doctors, whereas their common fellow citizens must be satisfied with more crowded clinics, shoddier hospitals, and less experienced and talented doctors. Moscow and other large cities are better serviced than provincial towns, and the vast countryside is on the bottom of the scale. Large cities have, in addition to free medical facilities, pay clinics that provide faster and more personalized service. Drugs are either free (in hospitals and clinics) or very inexpensive (in pharmacies). But, as with so much else in the Soviet Union, often even the most essential medical products, including drugs, are in short supply. Large urban areas have modern emergency services, including trauma centers. Regular doctors and specialists make house calls as part of the free service. Nurses and paramedics also provide home services.

Doctors' salaries do not compare favorably with those of other professions. A young graduate from a medical school may receive considerably less than the overall national pay average. His or her starting salary is about 200 rubles per month. Private practice on the doctors' own time is officially tolerated, and this allows some general practitioners, and especially dentists, to supplement their modest incomes. As a rule, their fees are low. As part of the economic reform, cooperative pay clinics have opened in Moscow and other large cities.

The one area of medicine in which Soviet theory and practice sharply differ from those in the West is psychology. Analytic psychology, based on the theories of Freud and his disciples, is not in favor. Instead, Soviet psychologists stress physiological causes of mental disorders. At times, political nonconformity has been diagnosed and treated as a mental "illness." Modern theories of behaviorism are rejected, although some of the methods of Soviet propaganda appear to be based on them.

To have the highest ratio of medical personnel and services in the world is a source of much pride for the Soviet regime. There is, however, an ironic twist to this situation: Just as the absence of unemployment encourages low labor productivity, the availability of free public health services seems to contribute to a sort of mass hypochondria, which keeps Soviet doctors, clinics, and hospitals rather busy. Because medical care is free, there is no incentive to use the system prudently.

## ATTITUDES

In the early 1930s, Stalin is supposed to have observed that Socialism must be built first of all in the minds of people. Have Stalin and his successors succeeded in instilling a Socialist (that is, Communist) mentality in the minds of their people? The answer is both yes and no, because an inventory of typical Soviet attitudes contains at least as many of Old Russia's customs as new Marxist-Leninist tenets. In the minds of most Soviet people, these two originally different sets of values are probably no longer separable. This is especially true of the ethnic Russians.

Many current Soviet attitudes that have their roots in the millennium of Old Russia's history persist because the excessively rapid rate of change that was imposed on Soviet society from above affected form more than content. These attitudes often cause serious problems. For example, the masses of Soviet industrial workers who operate modern machines and produce sophisticated goods still appear to have the cultural metabolism and habits of the traditional Russian peasant used to the seasonal ups and downs of the agricultural cycle, rather than to the year-round factory routine. As a result, the fulfillment of yearly, quarterly, monthly, and even weekly production plans is subject to a peculiar kind of hazard, called *shturmovshchina* (crush tactics). In a nutshell, there is a strong tendency to mark time and postpone things as long as possible, and then desperately try to compensate for lost time by working extra hard, usually at the expense of quality.

A more serious problem stems from the lingering remnants of the serf's attitude toward labor in general, which must have been something like this: "Work only as much as is needed to survive." As we know, serfdom, formally abolished only in 1861, had been the lot of a majority of Russians for several centuries. Much of the educational and propaganda effort is spent on promoting new Communist attitudes toward labor and work ethics. It is one of Gorbachev's top priorities.

Not surprisingly for a nation with living memories of a most devastating war fought on its territory, the popular attitude is strongly antiwar; yet, at same time, it is also antipacifist. This distinction is emphasized by the official propaganda, which encourages pacificism only for those outside the borders of the Socialist bloc.

An ambivalent Soviet attitude of simultaneous contempt and admiration for the West is also a legacy of Old Russia. The same can be said about Russians' suspicion of foreigners, who, after all, have come to Russia more often as unwelcome invaders than as invited guests. Soviet patriotism derives much of its strength from this traditional feeling of being surrounded by potential enemies. This is encouraged by official propaganda.

The peasant background of much of Soviet society is probably no less responsible for the informal character of Soviet manners than is Marxism-Leninism, with its emphasis on "proletarian simplicity." The same is even more true concerning a traditional respect for old age. As we already know from previous chapters, much of the Soviet method of child care and upbringing stresses respect for grownups. But as was noted, the old custom and the new ideology clash on the question of women's equality.

Prominent among the new attitudes is a strong appreciation of education and culture. The latter term often has a curiously broad meaning, including personal behavior, public order, habits, and taste. Acts that do not comply with Soviet etiquette are labeled *nyekulturnyi* (noncultured), meaning vulgar or antisocial. The already-mentioned sense of dependency on society, the state, and the government has both historical and ideological roots. It is quite strong. In fact, because the overwhelming majority of Soviet people were born after the 1917 Revolution, their new attitudes, grounded in lifelong exposure to Soviet education and the Soviet way of life, all appear to have strong roots. These "internalized" attitudes include a sense of purpose, self-discipline, confidence, and accomplishment. On the negative side, the already-noted lack of personal initiative is coupled with inertness and unwillingness to accept risk.

The Soviet people's attitude toward authority is tied to their long experience of living under authoritarian regimes without questioning their mandates for power and legitimacy. The people generally accept the Communist leaders' inherent right to the last word, as prescribed by the so-called democratic centralism. Until recently, willingness to obey official orders from top to bottom was accompanied by ritualistic adulation of those in authority, and especially of the current General Secretary. But now Gorbachev has vowed to live by what he calls "Leninist modesty." Unlike some of his predecessors, Gorbachev seems to enjoy considerable popularity in the Soviet Union.

Ironically, this traditional attitude toward authority both helps and hinders the reform campaign. On one hand, a solid majority of Soviet citizens continues to display stoic patience and willingness to wait, though sometimes grumpily, for tangible benefits of *perestroika*. But on the other hand, when specific reforms—especially the economic ones—require active participation and initiative, old habits contribute to hesitation and inertia.

Perhaps the most important byproduct of this Soviet attitude toward authority is a traditional indifference to, and even mistrust of, formal democracy. In the past, this feeling was reinforced by ideological propaganda that ridiculed Western political processes and institutions.

## NEW SOVIET MAN

How many of the old and new attitudes exist, and in what proportions they are held by individual Soviet citizens, depends on a number of variables: age, education, ethnic origin, and others. The optimal combination of these properties, which is embodied in the "New Soviet Man" and probably exists only in the pages of Soviet fiction, envisages a person of undetermined but active age, young at heart, in excellent health, intelligent, sensitive, and rational. This ideal Soviet man is, of course, totally devoted to the principles of Marxism-Leninism, which have become his second nature. He is well educated in general and probably also in a practical (technical) professional field. He has a sense of purpose and direction. He is hard working, honest, sincere, and deeply motivated. He dialectically combines a feeling of true Soviet patriotism with a commitment to "proletarian internationalism." On top of that, he is a model citizen, a perfect organization man, a helpful comrade, a loyal friend, and an ideal family man. It goes without saying that a person with such sterling qualities would be a dedicated member of the Communist Party and a subject and tool of its discipline.

This kind of person will presumably inhabit the future Soviet society of plenty and complete equality, governed by the Communist principle, "From each according to his ability, to each according to his need." But what about the men who are living in the Soviet Union today? How does the label of the New Soviet Man apply to them? The answer hinges largely on the perspective. Compared with his grandfather or even his father, the average Soviet citizen has changed quite dramatically in the general direction of the envisaged ideal. But in comparison to the ideal self, he and his posterity have a long way to go. There can, however, be little doubt that in the eyes of many of his compatriots, Mikhail Gorbachev is a living prototype of the New Soviet Man. His stellar success makes him a role model for those aspiring to become

**TABLE 11–5** Soviet Orders and Medals

Few countries, if any, can compete with the Soviet Union in regard to the number and variety of official awards: orders, medals, and titles. These awards are given not only to individuals but also to factories, ships, newspapers (*Pravda* has three orders), and whole cities. The top awards come in two varieties, military and civilian.

| Military | Civilian |
|---|---|
| 1. Gold Star (Hero of the Soviet Union) | 1. Gold Star (Hero of the Socialist Labor) |
| 2. Order of Lenin | 2. Order of Lenin |
| 3. Order of the Combat Red Banner | 3. Order of the Labor Red Banner |
| 4. Order of the October Revolution | 4. Order of the October Revolution |
| 5. Order of the Red Star | 5. Badge of Merit |

Gold Stars are supposed to be worn at all times. Some individuals have several of them. Except for parades and similar formal occasions, colored ribbons are worn instead of all other orders and medals.

There are many other military and civilian medals. The latter variety includes a number of medals awarded to mothers for delivering and rearing several children.

In 1988, the Gorbachev regime publicly pledged to curb what it calls a glut of "inflated and devalued state honors." As far as is known, in sharp contrast to his bemedaled predecessors, Gorbachev has only two medals which he rarely wears in public: Order of Labor Red Banner (1949) and Order of Lenin (1981).

*Source:* Compiled by author from Soviet data.

leaders. For more adventurous individuals there is the example of Boris Yeltsin—a repentant party *aparatchik*—who made a dramatic political comeback as a populist candidate for the USSR Congress of People's Deputies. In ethnic republics, the new heroes are local nationalist leaders.

Not surprisingly, as individuals Soviet citizens appear much more alike than do their contemporaries in the West. This sameness is not merely in appearance; it also pertains to the fundamentals of their life philosophy—proof that various norms that affect Soviet society are powerful and effective. The uniform character of their education, upbringing, and life experience tends to cause individual Soviet citizens to have similar reactions to events and to share the same opinions on the major ideological, political, economic, and social issues. Besides, because of the mode of their upbringing and training, they are conditioned to follow appropriate cues from above, rather than to make their own choices and decisions. In the USSR, one thinks and does "as everybody else does," remembering that safety is in numbers. In the past big numbers offered Soviet individuals not only a sense of safety but also a feeling of righteousness.

But there is a "law of compensation" at work here too. As if to make up for their lack of disagreement on big issues in the recent past, Soviet people, especially the ethnic Russians, have been engaging in endless argu-

ments on everything since the beginning of *glasnost:* politics, music, literature, movies, the weather, sports, and a great many other things that are
excluded from the ideological compass. On the level of everyday life Soviet
citizens now feel free to take a stand and fight for it with all their might, no
longer willing to leave politics to the expertise of their former self-appointed
leaders. The Soviet Constitution (Article 50) gives them political rights—
freedom of speech, the press, and public assembly and demonstration—but
still limits their use to one specific purpose: "to strengthen and develop the
Socialist system."

## RIGHTS AND DUTIES

From a Western point of view, Soviet citizens may not be free. But this view
is not necessarily shared by Soviet citizens themselves. Indeed, most of them
probably have no real conception of what has been, in the eyes of outsiders,
so conspicuously missing in their lives for a long time—individual rights and
freedoms. Historically, the notion of individual freedoms never became part
of Russia's traditional scale of values, which has long been dominated by the
quest for national security. For its part, Marxism-Leninism, which is supposed to have all the correct answers to all the political issues, has little use
for any free contest of political opinions.

The "bill of rights" contained in the Soviet Constitution (Chapter 7,
Articles 39 to 69) is not a legal document that Soviet citizens can use in court
against undue pressure from their government, though *glasnost* has introduced a degree of legal protection. It is actually a detailed description of the
expected give-and-take relationship between the state and the individual.
As such, it deserves our examination. At the outset it states that, "Enjoyment
by citizens of their rights and freedoms must not be to the detriment of the
interests of the society or the state, or infringe on the rights of other citizens"
(Article 39). What follows is a long list of rights and freedoms (Articles 40 to
58) defined in such a way as to emphasize the common good that is expected
to be served. As a result, some of the most important rights—the right to
work and the right to education, for instance—actually become obligations.
And it also turns out that, because the promised freedoms can be used only
within narrow channels, by implication they forbid more than they purport
to allow. There then is a statement that further limits the use of rights and
freedoms: "Citizens' exercise of their rights and freedoms is inseparable from
the performance of their duties and obligations" (Article 59). The next ten
articles (60 to 69) enumerate the ways that individuals must serve their
society, including the obligation to work and serve in the ranks of the
military establishment.

Everything that is promised, demanded, allowed, and by implication
forbidden in the relations between Soviet citizens and their society underscores one fact: All matters of ideology are outside the scope of this relation-

ship and are, therefore, nonnegotiable. The bill of rights resembles a contractual agreement that may exist in a company town between the employer and his employees. The contract has no references to the employer's ownership rights or his freedom to make managerial decisions. But from the point of view of an employee who has no other choice but to live and work in the town, it is not a bad deal, because most of his basic needs are taken care of: a job, housing, medical care, school, annual leave, cultural outlets, and retirement. This is much more security than his forebears or he ever had before and it is for a price that looks reasonable in comparison. It may very well be the best deal anybody can remember and, therefore, a reason to feel fortunate and even happy.

Given Russia's historical record and the Soviet scale of social values, it is doubtful that Western ideas about human rights find many supporters among the ordinary Soviet citizens, whose daily concerns, worries, problems, priorities, and joys transpire on a different plane of existence. But Soviet people at large are becoming more demanding, sensitive to unfairness, and impatient. Protest meetings, mass demonstrations, strikes, and open acts of defiance have become very common. In the long run, this is incompatible with the normal operation of a society based on planning, organization, goal orientation, and social engineering—principles that are, of course, antonyms of individual freedom, but that do provide a high degree of security against unemployment, medical emergencies, and similar risks. One of Gorbachev's most controversial promises is to find a way to reconcile the seeming opposites.

## SOVIET WAY OF LIFE

How does the everyday operation of this society—the Soviet way of life—differ from that of the West? What does it mean to be a member of Soviet society? What kind of "mindset" do Soviet people have?

As we know, some answers to these questions are obvious. For example, there is no doubt that Soviet society is structured, organized, and centralized. Depending on one's value judgment, it is a planned Socialist or totalitarian society that does not recognize the autonomy of individuals or groups of individuals within its boundaries. The closest parallel in the American experience would be a career in the military service and life on a military post. (Currently, the post is headed by a liberal-minded general.)

We also know that Soviet life is inferior to that of the West in terms of creature comforts: clothes, food, gadgets and appliances, living quarters, personal means of transportation, and other material values. This scarcity of consumer goods and services was briefly experienced by the west European nations during World War II, but it has never been known in the United

**BOX 11–5** *Soviet Underground Humor*

> *Six paradoxes of Soviet life:* (1) there's no unemployment, but no one works; (2) no one works, but productivity goes up; (3) productivity goes up, but there's nothing in the stores; (4) there's nothing in the stores, but at home there's everything; (5) at home there's everything, but no one is satisfied; (6) no one is satisfied, but everyone votes yes.

States.[10] Economically the Soviet society is one of relatively low expectations. On the other hand, the economic risks that Soviet citizens must take are also low. Their society provides for them from the cradle to the grave. In effect, Soviet citizens are on a sort of welfare roll all their lives, but with no social stigma attached.

Psychologically, the welfare aspect of Soviet society compensates to some degree for the social regimentation and economic austerity that it imposes. For example, Soviet citizens—official visitors, tourists, and emigrants, alike—appear to be genuinely shocked to find out the cost of higher education, housing, or medical care in some of the Western countries. The relative equality in the distribution of visible wealth—that is, property and income—makes economic hardships more bearable. Also on the positive side, although difficult to measure, are such intangible feelings they have as national pride, accomplishment, and purposefulness. At least for some Soviet citizens, Marxism-Leninism fulfills the psychological function of a religious mystique.

On the negative side are nationalist tensions caused by ethnic antagonisms, which at times run high. Probably less menacing to the regime is a feeling of dissatisfaction with the way things are among the people at large. Although this feeling is widespread, in the people's minds the blame is usually put on individual aspects of the Soviet way of life rather than on the Soviet system as a whole. But if in the past open opposition was limited to relatively small groups of dissident intellectuals now organized forms of political protest often involve very large numbers of people from various walks of life. Tight controls and harsh laws against "vagrancy and parasitism" make it virtually impossible for Soviet citizens not to be part of the establishment. The Soviet way of life leaves little room for nonconformity, even in the era of *glasnost*.

Soviet status symbols are a mixture of traditional signs of material well-being and various new marks of distinction. Depending on the social level, the former may range from an imported dress or pair of blue jeans to a summer cottage (*dacha*) or a car, and the latter come with a variety of

[10]The gasoline shortage of the summer of 1974 gave Americans a taste of this kind of situation.

medals, titles, and similar trappings. Among the privileged, success is measured by such yardsticks as making trips abroad, spending summer vacations at exclusive resorts, and having live-in domestic help.

When everything is added up, the Kremlin leaders must feel confident
that their "technology of behavior"[11] keeps Soviet society on an even keel.
And from their point of view, it is a reasonably well-working society.

## TRANSITION

Gorbachev's ambitious reform campaign has shattered the notion that Soviet
society is "unchanging and unchangeable." Change is evident in all aspects
of Soviet life, although there are also strong elements of continuity which
provide a framework and set limits for the ongoing changes. What is not
clear at all, however, are many questions related to these changes: Where
would they eventually lead? How would they interact? How much are they
adhering to a laid out plan? How much improvisation and hit-or-miss effort
is involved? The types of problems facing Gorbachev are not solvable in a
smooth or neat way. Therefore, it is not surprising that the initial phase of
*perestroika* has produced confusion, contradictions, and paradoxes. Here are
some examples:

For decades, the Soviet Union was one of the most information-consti-
pated countries in the world. Now Soviet citizens are struggling under a
constant stream of news and revelations which they have not yet learned
how to digest or take in stride. Traditional adulation of leaders and self-con-
gratulation for alleged achievements have yielded to condemnation of the
recent past and unprecedented self-flagellation.

Gorbachev's efforts to energize his people appear to be often all but
futile in the face of formidable forces of inertia. And much of verbal support
for *perestroika* is not always backed up by action. This is especially true in the
economic sphere where promised changes and improvements have been
very slow and disappointing.

Some members of the older generations worry about what they see as
the darker side of *perestroika:* new tensions, disputes, complaints, mutual
accusations, and general uncertainty. In their opinion, Soviet society is losing
its ideological capital and becoming more fragmented and excessively permissive. Their usually younger opponents argue that *perestroika* is not going
fast and far enough.

The same people, who for several decades calmly accepted the so-
called functional inequality which bestowed privileges on a largely self-appointed political elite, are now showing resentment against their more

---

[11]The term "technology of behavior" is used by B. F. Skinner in his book *Beyond Freedom
and Dignity* (New York: Alfred A. Knopf, 1971).

enterprising peers who try to improve their own lot by engaging in cooper-ative and quasi-private business activities allowed under *perestroika*.

Pluralism now tolerated in the Soviet Union under *glasnost* allows people to hold and even express different opinions, but does not grant these opinions an equal status. Just as before, there is only one truth. But now the holders of this absolute Marxist value are more willing to let others err and stray from it. The Communist Party is willing to yield on the question of constitutional guarantee of its special status, but it firmly holds to power.

Activists in some ethnic areas see *perestroika* as an opportunity to push for more "home rule" or even independence, while in other non-Russian regions local nationalists seem to be nostalgically longing for the pre-Gorbachev times. Russians themselves are also divided into imperial-minded "internationalists" and nationalistic isolationists.

In short, it is a society at a crossroads undergoing a complex multi-directional process, a transition from a condemned past to an uncertain future.

## FUTURE CHANGES

For two decades between Khrushchev and Gorbachev, time seemed to stand still in Russia, making predictions about her immediate future relatively easy. Now that Gorbachev's ship of state is on the move through uncharted waters, the factor of predictability has been drastically reduced.

The current passing of power in the system to much younger people, often skipping an entire generation, has greatly accelerated the process of change that was set in motion by Stalin's death and Khrushchev's de-Stalinization efforts. However, if we are to assume, as we must, that the basic principles of the Soviet political and economic systems will remain intact, we should not expect that, by changing, Soviet society will necessarily become more like Western societies. Ours is not a two-dimensional world in which every move away from Stalin is a move toward Jefferson. There are many other alternatives.

This is not to say that it's unlikely during the next decade of *perestroika* that the Soviet Union would borrow and imitate some Western ways, methods, and trends in areas where it lags behind, such as high technology, retail trade, service industry and others. The need "to learn from other societies"[12] is openly recognized by the top Soviet leaders.

It would be enough to look at the history of Soviet society to find proof of both its ability to change and its ability to do so strictly within its own expanding context and on its own terms. In a relatively short historic period, Soviet society has undergone tremendous changes in such spheres as eco-

---

[12]This was emphasized in the first speech of the new CC secretary in charge of ideology, Vadim Medvedev (October 5, 1988).

**BOX 11–6**   *On Predicting Russia's Future*

We have been wrong on just about every major development in the U.S.S.R. since the Bolshevik revolution. We didn't anticipate the revolution; when it occurred, we didn't think it would succeed; when it was successful, we thought socialism was going to be abandoned; when it wasn't, we thought we wouldn't have to recognize the new Soviet state; when we did, we acted first as if it was like the Western democracies and then as if it was like the Nazis; when the Germans invaded, we thought the Russians could last only six weeks; when they survived the war, we thought they couldn't recover quickly from it; when they recovered quickly, we thought they didn't have the know-how to build missiles, and so on. This record would seem to suggest, at least just a little bit, that perhaps we should not be too positive in other assumptions we have made.

Fred W. Neal, *US Foreign Policy and the Soviet Union* (Santa Barbara, CA: Center for Study of Democratic Institutions, 1961) p. 7.

nomics, education, science and technology, and culture. Yet its political institutions and politics have changed much less, and its basic ideological tenets have remained almost completely intact. Future changes will probably follow the same pattern of selectivity.

Politically, the most significant change likely to affect Soviet society in the near future will be a gradual broadening of its power base, involving larger numbers of people, mostly party members, in the decision-making process. A possible chain reaction to this could be a concurrent decentralization of power, giving more authority to local governments and also increasing their responsibility for coping with various problems. But all of this will be done within the framework of "democratic centralism" and its emphasis on corporationlike subordination and discipline.

The most important visible changes that have been made by Gorbachev's reform so far are: openness of the press (*glasnost*), strengthening of legality, and loosening of ideological restrictions governing economic activities. Together, they represent a significant break with the past, and probably forecast the main directions of any future changes.

A continuing effort to improve the consumers' lot appears certain. It will probably be accompanied by measures designed to achieve a higher degree of class equality, not just in terms of nominal wages, but also in fringe benefits and privileges. A rather modest goal for a minimum cash income of 100 rubles per capita a month is currently being pursued.[13] Yet to achieve it, the economy will have to become considerably more efficient than it is today. Gorbachev promises to do this by raising labor productivity, modernizing

[13]In 1987, an estimated 70 percent of all Soviet people had a per capita income of 100 or more rubles per month. This is the unofficial "poverty line."

BOX 11-7    *Preamble to the Soviet Constitution*

---

The supreme goal of the Soviet state is the building of a classless Communist society in which there will be public, Communist self-government. The main aims of the people's Socialist state are: to lay the material and technical foundation of Communism, to perfect Socialist social relations and transform them into Communist relations, to mold the citizen of Communist society, to raise the people's living and cultural standards, to safeguard the country's security, and to further the consolidation of peace and development of international cooperation.

---

production, and introducing better management. As we know, his idea of a more efficient economy calls for more private incentives, opportunities, and rewards.

A residue of Stalinism, embodied by many thousands of high party and government officials, is about to be dissipated by natural deaths and retirements. It does not necessarily follow that this mass exodus of the most conservative bureaucrats will usher in an overall relaxation in Soviet life. What seems to be more likely is a mixture: relaxation in some areas, no significant changes in others, and even more restrictions in the remaining ones. For example, although in years to come immigration rules are likely to be relaxed and tolerance for internal dissent may gradually increase, more ethnic separation seems to be a certainty. At the same time, Russian nationalism may become more militant. More Russification, in the name of a homogeneous Soviet nation, appears to be a certainty, too. It is also quite conceivable that as a backlash to Gorbachev's liberalization, Soviet society will experience a partial return to ideological orthodoxy in matters of family life, marriage, and sex. As to the split-level quality of Soviet life, it is certain to endure until the ideological goals are either abandoned or fulfilled, though neither prospect appears to be imminent. But, with the passage of time, the divergence between official and private values could diminish. This is one of Gorbachev's solemn promises.

How does Gorbachev himself see the future of his society? He probably envisages a Soviet Union still ruled by the Communist Party, but with other interest groups exercising influence on the running of the government. He, most likely, accepts the idea of a much looser type of federation of the ethnic components making up the nation. His goal is to make Soviet society work better and to take better care of its members while retaining its basic socialist character.

In spite of their inability to predict the Soviet Union's future (See Box 11-6), there is no dearth of doomsday prophets who see Gorbachev leading his country to a terminal systemic crisis, a complete breakup of its multinational structure, a military takeover, or other calamities. A collection of such self-destructive scenarios, imaginative but not very convincing, is presented in a book by a recognized American expert.[14]

Future changes of Soviet society will both affect and be affected by many internal and external factors. As we have already seen, the Soviet Union has far-reaching global ambitions to change all other societies in its own image. Next, we look at the USSR's position in the world.

## GLOSSARY

**Babushka:** grandmother; old woman.
**Collectivism:** togetherness, spirit of togetherness.
**Cossack:** frontier settler (in Old Russia).
**Dacha:** country home, summer cottage.
**Hooliganism:** disturbance of peace, antisocial behavior.
**Intelligentsia:** intellectuals, white-collar workers, middle class.
**Khozyaistvenniki:** business managers.
**Lishentsy:** individuals deprived of civil rights.
**Mir:** close peasant community (in Old Russia).
**Nyekulturnyi:** uncultured, crude, unbecoming.
**Parasitism:** avoidance of socially useful work.
**Raznochintsy:** intellectuals of nongentry origin (in Old Russia).
**Shturmovshchina:** uneven, convulsive mode of work.
**Totalitarianism:** centralized, one-party political system.

## RECOMMENDED READINGS

FRIEDBERG, MANRICE, and HEYWARD ISHAM (eds.), *Soviet Society Under Gorbachev*. New York: M. E. Sharpe, 1987.
MILLER, WRIGHT, *Russians as People*. New York: E. P. Dutton, 1961.
RYVKIN, MICHAEL, *Soviet Society Today*. New York: M. E. Sharpe, 1989.

[14]Zbigniew Brzezniski, *The Grand Failure* (New York: Scribner's, 1989).

# CHAPTER

# 12

# FOREIGN RELATIONS

## GORBACHEV'S "NEW THINKING"

The Soviet Union, which Mikhail Gorbachev inherited in 1985, is one of the world's two superpowers as well as the metropolis of the "Commonwealth of Socialist nations"—a vast empire that consists of countries scattered over the entire globe. Moscow is also the recognized headquarters of the international Communist movement, which, although no longer wholly monolithic, claims to be the strongest common political cause in the history of humankind. It was a combination of these roles that Gorbachev's predecessors had played in their high-stakes game in the world's arena, culminating in the recognition of a strategic parity between the two superpowers, the United States and the USSR. Translated into various diplomatic and political moves, the changed "configuration of forces" and the newly acquired status of acknowledged strategic equality with the United States promised to increase Soviet influence in all corners of the world. It seemed that never before had the Soviet Union, or for that matter Russia, been riding so high in world politics. But the new Soviet leader was also keenly aware of the insecure power balance based on nuclear arsenals, and of the tremendous cost to the Soviet economy of the continuing arms race underlying this concept. He

**BOX 12–1**    *Gorbachev on International Security*

Security, if we speak about the USSR and U.S.A. can be only mutual, or, if we take international relations as a whole, only universal.

M.S. Gorbachev in the Introduction (p. 1) to his book in English, *Toward a Better World* (New York: Richardson and Stienmen, 1987).

knew that a dangerous impasse had been reached, and he was determined to break out of it. Besides, he also had some pressing domestic reasons.

Gorbachev likes to quote Lenin's truism that domestic and foreign policies of a nation must be—and ultimately are—closely interconnected. The counterpart of his *perestroika* at home is Gorbachev's "New Thinking" in the realm of international relations. The connection between the two is clear: To carry out far-reaching domestic reforms, he needs to secure peaceful coexistence with the rest of the world at the lowest possible cost to the Soviet economy. Conversely, his commitment to *perestroika* provides Gorbachev with collateral for securing better relations with the West.

Gorbachev's "New Thinking," which is actually a mix of both new and old Soviet positions, makes the following main points: (1) It assumes complete military equality between the two superpowers. Neither side should try to achieve superiority over the other. (2) It emphasizes the concepts of "collective security" and "shared destiny" as the only realistic option for the world's future (see Box 12–1). (3) It calls for "demilitarizing" international relations, especially relations between the East and West. Both nuclear and conventional weapon systems should be reduced to the level of "reasonable sufficiency"—enough for defense, but not for offense. (4) It encourages the use of the U.N. as an instrument for setting regional conflicts in the Third World. The U.N.'s role in world affairs should be strengthened. (5) It seeks to "exorcise" the public image of the USSR abroad. *Glasnost* should dispel any lingering fears of the "Red Threat."

Implicitly, Gorbachev's "New Thinking" appears to promise more restraint of the Soviet Union in fulfilling ideological commitment to help national liberation movements in Third World nations. It also hints that Moscow's more pragmatic leadership is ready to accept compromise and be willing to resolve difficult issues, such as the INF and Afghanistan.

Inasmuch as Gorbachev's domestic and foreign policies are indeed interconnected, the West's response to his "New Thinking" could have an impact on *perestroika*. But what should this response be? Would Gorbachev's proposal lead to a safer and more secure world? Before we attempt to answer these questions, let us first examine the historical record of the Soviet Union's involvement in world affairs.

## HISTORICAL BACKGROUND

Russia entered the arena of European politics at the beginning of the eighteenth century, after Peter the Great had thoroughly modernized its armed forces. During the next hundred years, Russia participated in every major conflict, intrigue, and deal that affected Europe's political map and balance of power. Russia's own chief objective in Europe was to gain access to the open seas and to achieve limited territorial expansion. At the same time, Russian diplomats and warriors pursued, with varying degrees of success, an active policy in Asia, where the growing Russian Empire came face to face with Turkey, Persia (Iran), China, and Great Britain, which was developing an interest in the same parts of Asia.

Russian foreign policy achieved its greatest success around the turn of the next century. After its victory over the invading armies of Napoleon (1812), Russia temporarily became the dominant power and a guardian of the status quo in continental Europe, earning the nickname of "Europe's Gendarme." The advent of industrialization, which Russia was slow to embrace, began to change the balance of power against it. In the mid-1850s, the Russian Empire suffered its first major military setback at the hands of England, France, and Turkey,[1] which landed troops in the Crimea and eventually captured Sevastopol, the main base of the Russian navy in the Black Sea. For the remainder of the nineteenth century, Russia's active foreign policy was limited to the Balkans, Central Asia, and the Far East.

The beginning of the twentieth century struck another serious blow to the international image of the Russian Empire, which was beset by severe economic and political problems. From 1904 to 1905, Russia was militarily humiliated once again, this time by Japan, with which it fought a bloody war in the northern provinces of China. Less than ten years later, Russia became hopelessly embroiled in a new European power game that eventually led to World War I. Russia sided with Britain and France, forming the Triple Entente. The eventual victory of the Triple Entente over the Central Powers[2] was supposed to give Russia a piece of Turkish territory around the Bosporus and Dardanelles Straits, which connect the Black Sea with the Mediterranean. However, the war did not go well for Russia. In 1917, a series of military defeats combined with economic woes first toppled the monarchy and then triggered the October Revolution. In a very real sense, the immediate cause of the fall of the Russian Empire was the failure of its foreign policy on the eve of and during World War I, which set into motion an irreversible chain

---

[1] The Kingdom of Sardinia, a part of Italy, also participated in the war on the side of Britain, France, and Turkey.

[2] The term "Central Powers" was used to refer to Germany, Austria-Hungary, and their allies in World War I. They were opposed by the forces of the Entente, whose main participants were Britain, France, and Russia. The United States sided with the Entente.

reaction at home. The Revolution, in turn, had a tremendous impact on Russia's international position.

## WORLD REVOLUTION

For seven decades, ideas and actions generated by the 1917 October Revolution have kept the world in turmoil. From the very start, the Lenin regime saw itself as the "advanced detachment" of the world revolution that promised to follow the events in Russia. According to Lenin, Russia represented the weakest link and, therefore, the first to be broken in the chain of capitalist nations, all of which were about to undergo revolutionary transformations. Speaking over the heads of official governments, Lenin addressed passionate appeals to the masses on both sides of the trench war in Europe to rise and do away with the old order of things. New Russia's first actions on the diplomatic stage were just as unorthodox and startling: Lenin opened negotiations with Germany for an immediate separate peace without "annexations and indemnities."

Alarmed, if not outrightly frightened, Russia's former partners in war—Great Britain, France, and the United States—responded first by not recognizing the Soviet government and then by providing aid and comfort to the anti-government side, the White Movement, in the civil war that ensued. The commitment of troops, token in the case of the United States, to fight on the anti-government side was the next, seemingly logical, step. Lenin's response to foreign intervention in the civil war was to create in Moscow a formal headquarters for the promotion of world revolution. Established in March 1919, it was called the Communist International, or Comintern.

The Comintern was presided over by high Soviet officials[3] and funded by Soviet money. Functioning as a tool of Soviet Russia's foreign policy, it overshadowed, for the time being, the official Ministry of Foreign Affairs.[4] The Comintern's agents were sent clandestinely to various countries to help organize foreign Communist parties, incite revolts, and generally create trouble for established governments. In Europe, exaggerated stories about the Comintern's exploits gave the impression that the world revolution, spearheaded by the Red Army, was indeed imminent. In retrospect, it is clear that much of this early "red scare" had no basis in fact, because Soviet Russia was simply too weak to mount any kind of offensive war. In other words, Moscow's bark was considerably worse than its bite. The talk about world revolution was mainly an excuse for the revolution in Russia. But at the time, Russia's neighbors were sufficiently impressed to seek accommodation with Moscow.

---

[3]The first head of the Comintern was Grigori Zinovyev, a close associate of Lenin.

[4]At first it was known as the People's Commissariat for Foreign Affairs.

**BOX 12–2**   *An Excerpt from the Manifesto of the Communist International (Comintern) Issued by Its First Congress in March 1919 in Moscow*

---

...We Communists, the representatives of the revolutionary proletariat of various countries of Europe, America and Asia, who have gathered in Soviet Moscow, feel and consider ourselves to be the heirs and executors of the cause whose programme was announced seventy-two years ago. Our task is to generalize the revolutionary experience of the working class, to cleanse the movement of the disintegrating admixtures of opportunism and social-patriotism, to mobilize the forces of all genuinely revolutionary parties of the world proletariat and thereby facilitate and hasten the victory of the Communist revolution throughout the world....

English translation by Jane Degras; quoted in Robert V. Daniels, *A Documentary History of Communism* (New York: Vintage Press, 1962), vol. 2, p. 88.

---

Thus, the Comintern's revolutionary rhetoric may even have helped the Soviet Union to secure normalization of relations with other countries during the 1920s. While the Comintern was engaged in its impotent daydreaming about world revolution, Soviet leaders tried more conventional foreign policies based on geopolitical considerations. Their vehicle for this was the Ministry of Foreign Affairs. Soviet diplomats began to appear in European capitals. The seeming dichotomy between the two approaches was used in most cases to Soviet advantage, although at the beginning there were probably instances of crossed purposes and confused signals. By the end of the 1920s, the Soviet Union had formal diplomatic relations with all major nations except the United States and with most of its neighbors in both Europe and Asia. Gradually, conventional diplomacy gained the upper hand, and talk about world revolution ceased. In the early 1930s, the Comintern was relegated by Stalin to the status of a guest house and spy school for foreign Communists. The Comintern was formally disbanded in 1943 to please the USSR's wartime allies, but its functions had already been transferred much earlier to a special section of the Central Committee of the CPSU, making the two-level approach to the outside world a permanent feature of Soviet foreign policy.

## CAPITALIST ENCIRCLEMENT

Normalization of relations did not mean the establishment of friendly ties with the outside world. On the contrary, the way Stalin saw it, the Soviet Union was surrounded by permanently hostile countries. He called this the "capitalist encirclement" and argued that the USSR must industrialize or perish. It was not just a pretext to make guns instead of butter, but a real fear.

The main goal of Soviet foreign policy shifted to finding weak spots and openings in the encirclement and thereby preventing it from becoming complete. With this in mind, the Soviet Union joined the League of Nations in 1934 and promoted the concept of collective security against the rising threats from Germany and Japan. From Moscow's own point of view, nothing could be worse than a two-front war in Europe and Asia, especially because in the early and mid-1930s, the Soviet Union was militarily and economically much weaker than either Germany or Japan. Yet such a war was a distinct possibility during the 1930s.

Against this menacing backdrop, the recognition of the Soviet Union by the United States in 1933 was perceived in Moscow as an important diplomatic victory, a break in the encirclement. The threat of a two-front war, however, remained, compounded by the not-too-far-fetched suspicion that Great Britain and France could easily attempt to make a deal with Hitler at the expense of the Soviet Union. Soviet diplomacy was doing its best not to allow such collusion to take place. However, there were not many levers that Soviet diplomats could pull, given the weak position of their country.

Stalin tried to do something else to postpone, if not to prevent, an attack on the Soviet Union. He tried to impress potential enemies with growing Soviet military might. The first such attempt, which pitted Soviet military planes and advisors against their German counterparts in the civil war in Spain (1936–1939), failed. The victorious Germans were not impressed, let alone intimidated, by what they saw of the Soviet military hardware and personnel in Spain. The second effort, much more costly to the Soviet Union, was a success. It consisted of two separate border wars with Japan. In August 1938, Soviet troops repelled a limited Japanese invasion near Khasan Lake on the Soviet-Chinese border. The next year (May 1939) the same scenerio was repeated, but on a larger scale, near Khalkin-Gol in Mongolia.[5] This double-barreled lesson probably contributed to Japan's decision in the early 1940s not to venture into an all-out war with the Soviet Union, thus saving it from fighting simultaneously on two fronts.

If the high point in Soviet foreign policy of that period was reached in 1933, when the United States recognized the Soviet Union, its bottom was hit in 1938, when Chamberlain and Hitler met in Munich. The Munich Agreement marked the worst possible shift in the European situation, a shift away from the concept of collective security that the Soviet Union had been vigorously promoting. In fact, Moscow saw this agreement as a green light for Hitler to direct his drive for *Lebensraum* (living space) eastward, toward the Soviet Union. Now Moscow decided that it, too, should look for a private deal with Berlin. In August 1939, while still negotiating without much

---

[5]It was a sizable military operation involving several infantry divisions, tanks, and airplanes on both sides. The Soviet troops were led by Georgi Zhukov.

progress or hope with the British and French about collective security, the Soviet Union concluded a nonaggression treaty with Nazi Germany. This was the infamous Molotov-Ribbentrop treaty that did to Poland what the Chamberlain-Hitler treaty had done earlier to Czechoslovakia. Unlike Czechoslovakia, Poland decided to fight for its existence. World War II began, but for a time the USSR was not directly involved in it. Moscow had reason to be satisfied with its foreign policy.

The understanding that was reached between Nazi Germany and the Soviet Union had some historic roots and a recent precedent. The roots went back to the Versailles Peace Conference[6] at which neither Germany, the vanquished villain, nor Russia, the unreliable ally, had anything to say about the revised map of Europe. The precedent occurred in 1922 in the form of the Rapallo Treaty by means of which the two European outcast nations tried to assert themselves.

## WORLD WAR II

According to Soviet historians, Moscow never deceived itself about the chances of staying out of the expanding European conflict altogether. They claim that, by signing the nonaggression pact with Hitler, Stalin merely hoped to gain additional time to better prepare his country for what was coming. Between September 1939 and June 1941, the Soviet Union did indeed improve its position by modernizing the armed forces and moving its border in Europe farther west. The latter accomplishment was achieved with Germany's consent and at the expense of Poland, Romania, and the three Baltic republics—Estonia, Latvia, and Lithuania—between 1939 and 1940. During the winter of 1940 and 1941, the USSR, acting on its own, forced a bloody war on Finland and, as a result, pushed its border farther away from Leningrad.

How much all of this actually helped the USSR is not certain, because in June 1941, when the Nazi attack finally came, Germany was also much stronger than it had been two years earlier. Another uncertainty surrounds the question of why the German attack took Stalin so much by surprise. Perhaps he was too suspicious by nature to heed numerous warnings that came from various sources. Or maybe too many false alarms had reached him earlier. In any case, the massive attack that came early in the morning of June 22, 1941, caught the USSR poorly prepared.

The first year and a half of the war resulted in the German armies' advancing to Leningrad, Moscow, and Stalingrad (Volgograd), and reaching the main range of the Caucasian Mountains. The turning point came late in

---

[6]The Versailles Peace Conference (Paris) conducted its business in 1919. The Peace Treaty was signed in January 1920.

**BOX 12-3**    *Lenin's Thoughts on Tactical Flexibility*

To carry out a war for the overthrow of the international bourgeoisie, a war which is a hundred times more difficult, prolonged and complicated than the most stubborn of ordinary wars between states, and to refuse beforehand to maneuver, to utilize the conflict of interests (even though temporary) among one's enemies, to refuse to temporize and compromise with possible (even though transient, unstable, vacillating and conditional) allies—is not this ridiculous in the extreme? Is it not as though, in a difficult ascent of an unexplored and heretofore inaccessible mountain, we were to renounce beforehand the idea that at times we might have to go in zigzags, sometimes retracing our own steps, sometimes abandoning the course already selected and trying out various others?

V. I. Lenin, *Selected Works* (New York: International Publishers, 1960), vol. 10, pp. 111–112.

1942, in the great battle of Stalingrad. But it took the Red Army[7] almost two and a half years to reach Berlin. Thus, for several years, much of the European USSR was the theater of giant battles involving millions of people, both military and civilian, and thousands of tanks, airplanes, cannons, and other instruments of death and destruction.

In the course of the war, the USSR established close ties with the Western allies, Britain and the United States. The latter supported the Soviet war effort with large quantities of economic and military aid. However, frictions, mutual suspicions, and misunderstandings also marred the "Great Alliance" from the very beginning. They became aggravated and were compounded as the war progressed. The Soviet side, for example, took a dim view of the slow pace of its allies' efforts to open a second front in Europe. The Western side had uneasy premonitions about the future status of eastern Europe.

Three major summit conferences involved the leaders of the Western allies and the Soviet Union: Teheran (1943), Yalta (February 1945), and Potsdam (July 1945). In a continuing controversy, these conferences are credited or blamed for having shaped the map of the postwar world. Actually, more history was recorded than made at the conference table. The reshaping of the political map of Asia and Europe was done by victorious armies on battlefields, proving that possession is nine tenths of the law. By the time the war was over, the Red Army physically occupied most of east and central Europe and the northern provinces of China and Korea. In Austria, Germany, and Korea, areas agreed upon in advance were occupied by the armies of the Western powers.

[7]The name "Red Army" was officially changed to "Soviet Army" in 1946.

## COLD WAR

It would have been a miracle if all the changes that occurred in the wake of World War II had not produced a great amount of tension between the Soviet Union and the West, no longer united by fear of a common enemy. They, of course, had never had anything else in common. The miracle did not happen, and the ensuing decade of painful adjustment to the new and still fluctuating balance of power became known as the Cold War, for which each side blamed the other.

In retrospect, it is clear that the initiative for the Cold War came from the West, mainly for the following two reasons: First, in the West, and particularly in the United States, the wartime marriage of convenience had been glorified and celebrated as a great love affair. Afterward, the inevitable disappointment and embarrassment set in. Second, the West's monopoly on atomic weapons offered too much of a temptation not to try to roll back, "destabilize," or at least stop the "red tide." Crude actions and moves by Stalin contributed to, or at least justified, the quick change from friendly relations to open hostilities toward Moscow.

During the Cold War, every Soviet move in international politics was alleged to promote "world peace." And every countermove by the West was supposed to protect the world from the "Communist threat." From the Soviet point of view, the early years of the Cold War were the worst because of the chaotic state of the USSR's economy and America's monopoly on atomic weapons. The Truman Doctrine[8] and the "policy of containment,"[9] which surrounded the USSR with American bases, were seen by Moscow as a new kind of "capitalist encirclement." For its part, the West suspected the Soviet Union of being behind every trouble this side of the "Iron Curtain."[10]

The term "Iron Curtain" defined the main battle line of the Cold War—the boundary dividing East and West Europe. Its counterpart in Asia was promptly nicknamed the "Bamboo Curtain." After the Communist victory in China (1949), more than one third of humanity and almost as large a portion of the globe were enclosed inside the Iron and Bamboo Curtains, forming a giant Communist empire governed and run from Moscow. But it was a giant on clay feet—a fact that no amount of Communist propaganda could conceal and that was manifest in Soviet foreign policy, no matter how aggressive it seemed on occasion. Stalin's stance in international affairs was that of a commander of a besieged fortress surrounded on all sides by

[8]The Truman Doctrine committed the United States to come to the aid of countries threatened by Communism from without or within.

[9]The "policy of containment" was first expounded in an article which appeared in 1947 in *Foreign Affairs*. The article, signed "Mr. X," was written by George Kennan, a high-ranking American diplomat.

[10]The expression "Iron Curtain" was made famous by Winston Churchill in his speech at Westminster College in Fulton, Missouri, in 1946.

superior enemy forces. The Soviet Union was weak and on the defensive, but its leaders used occasional diversions to create the impression of strength. Stalin's method of concealing the fear of the West's nuclear superiority was to maintain publicly that a global nuclear war would destroy only the capitalist part of the world. Lenin was generously quoted to point out the inevitability of such a war, or wars, in the future. Stalin fully shared Lenin's prophecies.

What is often forgotten is that, in all probability, Stalin's conviction that war between the Soviet Union and the West was inevitable stemmed not from his belligerency, but from his fear. Like Lenin before him, Stalin was inclined to overestimate the will of the capitalist world to wipe out its challenger, the Soviet Union, while it was weak. The capitalist world, for its part, seemed to greatly overestimate the strength of the Soviet Union, which was badly crippled by World War II. If there ever was an Iron Curtain, its purpose must have been to conceal the Soviet Union's relative weakness, not its strength. It was a defensive overreaction born of Stalin's insecurity.

The balance of power in the postwar world, however, was changing in favor of the Soviet Union. By itself, Europe—emasculated and ravaged by war—was no longer a match for the Soviet Union. The West's global position was being undermined by the rapid disintegration of the old colonial empires in Asia and Africa. In the late 1940s, the USSR began to build its own nuclear arsenal, and thus ended America's short-lived monopoly on the new weapons of mass destruction. This marked an important watershed in East-West relations.

## "PEACEFUL COEXISTENCE"

There was a significant change in Soviet foreign policy soon after Stalin's death (March 1953). The concept of a besieged fortress was replaced by a new vision of the world consisting of three parts: (1) the camp of the Socialist nations led by the USSR; (2) the camp of the capitalist nations headed by the United States; and (3) a large and expanding pool of uncommitted developing nations, the Third World. Also new was the Soviet thesis that a nuclear war would be equally destructive for both sides and must, therefore, be prevented. Embroidered with appropriate quotations from Lenin, taken out of context, this became known as the policy of "peaceful coexistence."

During the next twenty years, the concept of peaceful coexistence was thoroughly tested in application to a large number of different international situations: truce in Korea, recurring crises over Berlin, Soviet repressions of unrest in east Europe, the Cuban missile crisis, and Soviet moves in Africa and Asia. Peaceful coexistence also guided Soviet foreign policy in such major international events as America's military involvement in Indochina. During the Vietnam War, Moscow showed remarkable restraint and flexi-

**BOX 12–4**   *Khrushchev on Peaceful Coexistence (1959)*

---

In the West they say that we have issued a "challenge." Well, if they like the word, let us consider that we have. But it is a challenge to *compete in peaceful economic development and in raising people's living standard.*

Quoted in Arthur E. Adams (ed.), *Soviet Foreign Policy* (Boston: D.C. Heath, 1961), p. 394. (emphasis in the original)

---

bility, and it managed to combine moral and material support for its Communist ally with an actual improvement of relations with Washington.

The declaration of peaceful coexistence also made Soviet foreign policy much more active all over the world. Stalin's heirs began to travel abroad, receive foreign leaders in Moscow, arrange summit conferences, and mend fences and build bridges of international understanding. As far as they were concerned, the long siege of the "fortress of Socialism" was lifted. Behind this major change was the massive buildup of the Soviet national economy and its military potential. It was peaceful coexistence through strength—the strength of the Soviet Union, of course. Peaceful coexistence was going to give Soviet leaders the time needed to make the Soviet Union even stronger.

The broad area within which the Soviet policy of peaceful coexistence was conducted had clearly defined limits: On one side, a global nuclear war was an unacceptable risk because it threatened mutual destruction; and on the other side, a genuinely peaceful and lasting accommodation with the West was just as unacceptable on ideological grounds.

During this period, the upper reach and the lower limit of the growing Soviet power were symbolized by the Hungarian Revolt and Cuban missile crisis, respectively. In 1956, by not challenging Moscow's brutal suppression of a mass uprising in Hungary, the West recognized, by default, Soviet hegemony in East Europe. In 1962, by forcing the withdrawal of Soviet missiles from Cuba, the West rejected Moscow's premature claim to strategic parity.

## DÉTENTE

At the beginning of the 1970s, Soviet foreign policy again shifted into a higher gear. In Russian, it was called *razryadka napryazheniya*, which means a "lessening (or relaxing) of tension." This became known in the West as *détente*, a French word that seemed to convey a somewhat more positive meaning.

The promised lessening of tension reflected diminishing fears on the part of Soviet leaders, who had begun to overcome their traditional inferiority complex vis-à-vis the West—thanks to a new, and, in their opinion, decisively favorable change in the configuration of forces in the world. As perceived by Moscow, détente called for ambitious, and presumably mutually beneficial, cooperation between the East and West on the basis of full equality. It also implied that competition between the two sides would continue, but strictly within the framework of peaceful coexistence. Cooperation would make competition safer and less costly for both sides.

There were two high points of détente. The first came in 1972 with the signing in Moscow of a formal American-Soviet agreement explicitly recognizing the existence of strategic parity, accepting it as a basis for East-West relations, and thus bestowing on the Soviet Union the status of a superpower. An earlier bid for the latter had been rejected during the Cuban missile crisis.

The second high point, reached in 1975, and known as the Helsinki Final Act, was a logical consequence of the first one. Its chief accomplishment, as viewed from Moscow, was the reconfirmation of the postwar status quo in Europe, divided between the East and West. But it also contained the Third Basket, promising respect for human rights, which was considered in the West to be an important additional proviso for peaceful coexistence.

Détente brought about a sharp increase in East-West trade, business deals, and various contacts and exchanges. But not everybody in the West agreed with détente's main assumption: Strategic parity between the two camps is a good basis for international relations. This opposition gained strength in the early 1980s, in the wake of the crises in Afghanistan and Poland. In fact, President Carter declared détente dead, and President Reagan later sought to bury it under a heap of anti-Soviet rhetoric reminiscent of the worst days of the Cold War. The Korean airliner incident (September 1983) seemed to be the last straw; the USSR again became "the evil empire."

To the extent that détente was a deal between the superpowers, agreed upon by their two top leaders, it could be unilaterally canceled by either side. In the Soviet perception, however, détente was much more than that, because it reflected "objective factors" and "qualitative changes" in the configuration of forces in the world. In Moscow's view, détente stands for a phase in the historical process that cannot be reversed. Because of the cataclysmic nature of modern arms possessed by both sides, Moscow insists there is no rational alternative to this approach to international relations.

**BOX 12–5**   *Yuri Andropov on Détente (In an Address to the Central Committee)*

"No, the policy of détente is by no means a finished phase. The future belongs to it."

*Pravda*, November 23, 1982, p. 2.

Encouraged by support from a large segment of public opinion in Europe and elsewhere, Moscow held fast in its position, and eventually forced Washington's most conservative administration since World War II to seek high-level talks. According to the Soviet assessment, the Gorbachev-Reagan meeting in Geneva in November 1985 proved that détente, based on equality between the two superpowers, is an imperative for mutual survival in the nuclear age. The point was reiterated by summit meetings that followed.

It is this view of recent developments that gives the Soviet leaders reason to believe that their country has come a long way in asserting its rightful place in the world. But they are also aware of many problems and adversaries facing them in the international arena.

## ADVERSARIES

Probably like all other nations, the Soviet Union had found many adversaries in the international arena long before it made any friends. Chronologically, the first of its main adversaries was Britain. For more than ten years following the 1917 Revolution, Britain organized and led numerous attempts to overthrow the Communist regime in Moscow. During Russia's civil war, the British actively supported White Russian armies and various separatist ethnic forces with material and combat personnel. Later, during the 1920s, the two countries found themselves on the brink of war over a number of issues, several of which were reinforced by the traditional Anglo-Russian rivalries of the pre-revolutionary era.

From the early 1930s until the end of World War II, Germany replaced Britain as Moscow's number-one enemy. The well-founded fear and suspicion of Nazi intentions did not disappear even during the short period of the Molotov-Ribbentrop rapprochement. In the course of the German-Soviet war (Great Patriotic War), anti-German feelings rose high because of the atrocities committed by the Nazis on Soviet soil. Emotionally, the war was an unprecedented struggle for the Soviet Union's national survival.

Immediately after World War II, the United States became, in Moscow's view, the main opponent and potentially the ultimate enemy of the "camp of Socialism." In the new bipolar world, which seemed to come almost straight out of a Marxist textbook, the United States epitomized the modern version of capitalism-imperialism with its global interests and commitments. Starting with the Truman Doctrine, which sought to check Soviet advances in the aftermath of World War II, and the Marshall Plan and other measures that helped to rebuild the economic power of western Europe, the United States has been leading a worldwide crusade against the USSR and its allies. American involvement in wars in Korea and Vietnam, as well as its lesser confrontations in other parts of the world, were seen by Moscow as skirmishes designed to test and provoke the Soviet Union. In the Soviet mass media, the United States has been depicted as the last stronghold of capitalism, a doomed society without a future, but nevertheless a dangerous foe. Soviet leaders are well aware of the tremendous military and economic might of the United States, which they regard with a mixture of awe, hate, and admiration.

Japan and several other countries on the perimeter of the Soviet Union (Finland, Poland, and Romania) have been episodic adversaries, dangerous not in themselves, but in combination with one of the two historical archenemies, Britain and Germany. China probably belonged to the same category during the 1960s and 1970s, except that its potential danger was seen in terms of the overall balance of power between the Soviet Union and the United States together with western Europe.

The historical adversary, however, is the United States. From the Soviet leaders' vantage point, only America still possesses the potential to threaten the existence of the Soviet Union. From an ideological point of view, the American-Soviet rivalry is supposed to be, in the words of the Internationale (the Communist anthem), "the last—and decisive—battle" between capitalism and Communism. Moscow's problem is how to win this ultimate competition without risking global holocaust. What makes the United States especially dangerous at this time is its unwillingness to accept the "historically inevitable" (and, therefore, irreversible) loss of absolute superiority. Here is how the United States is described in the CPSU's new program:

> The citadel of international reaction is U.S. imperialism. The threat of war comes chiefly from it. Claiming world domination, it arbitrarily declares whole countries zones of its "vital interest."

## USA-USSR CONFRONTATION

This worst-case scenario is a mirror image of the "red danger," the spectre of which has been haunting the United States for much of the Soviet era. At the beginning of this era, there was a brief and halfhearted U.S. intervention in the civil war in Russia on the side of counterrevolution. It was followed by almost fifteen years of nonrecognition of the Soviet regime by Washington. The next fifteen years, from the establishment of diplomatic relations in 1933 to the onset of the Cold War in 1947, included some four years of close wartime alliance forced on the two nations by their fear of common enemies—Germany and Japan. Then a new period of relations between Moscow and Washington set in: a period of more than four decades characterized by mutual fear and mistrust about each other's intentions.

Since intentions alone could not cause much harm, during the first half of this period only the Soviet Union had real reason to fear the other side—the militarily superior United States. In the late 1960s, the inferior-superior relationship between the USSR and USA began to change and was ultimately replaced by a dangerous kind of strategic equality aptly called MAD (Mutual Assured Destruction). At that point, the intentions of both sides—at least their rational intentions—should have become completely irrelevant. However, for the next two decades both sides continued to profess fear of each other's intentions and make efforts to achieve—or in the case of the United States, to restore—a usable superiority over the other.

It was left to Gorbachev to declare dramatically that Soviet-American relations were hopelessly stalemated and to call for joint efforts to defuse this dangerous impasse. At the same time and in spite of a great amount of publicity generated by the numerous Soviet-American summit meetings, Gorbachev actually began to downgrade the relative importance of relations between the two superpowers. He has done this by opening up more to western Europe, Japan, and the PRC (China), thus shifting the overall balance of Soviet foreign policy away from its traditional fixation on the United States. So far, Gorbachev's pragmatic approach to Soviet-American relations has not changed the assessment of the United States contained in the 1986 edition of the CPSU Program. Was it because Moscow was still awaiting a reciprocal move from Washington? Will it be changed now that President George Bush has responded to Gorbachev's initiatives?

## ALLIES

It has been much more difficult for the Soviet Union to make friends than to make enemies. The first generation of Soviet allies had to be literally created by the Soviet Union using the political, military, and economic means at its disposal. Mongolia was the first, and for almost twenty years, the only ally to be established in this manner in the exact image of the Soviet Union. In the early 1920s, Mongolia, a large and sparsely populated area on the Sino-Soviet border, emerged as the second Communist (Socialist) nation in the world.[11] After World War II, Communist regimes were installed in several, but not all, East European countries occupied by the Red Army: Poland, Czechoslovakia, Hungary, Romania, Bulgaria, and the eastern part of Germany (East Germany). In the two other East European countries, Yugoslavia and Albania, local Communists came to power almost without direct aid from the Red Army. But this "osmosis" would not have occurred had it not been for the Soviet presence in the neighboring countries.

[11]The Mongolian People's Democratic Republic was formally founded in 1924.

**TABLE 12–1** Russo-American Relations

| | |
|---|---|
| 1781 | First U.S. envoy, Francis Dana, sent to St. Petersburg; Russia unofficially supports the American Revolution. |
| 1809 | Russia recognizes the U.S.; John Quincy Adams becomes first minister to Petersburg. |
| 1832 | Russia-U.S. commercial treaty. |
| 1863 | Russian navy ships show flag in New York and San Francisco demonstrating Russia's support for the North in the Civil War. |
| 1867 | U.S. purchase of Alaska from Russia. |
| 1890s | Russian-U.S. frictions in the Far East over China and Korea. |
| 1904–05 | U.S. mediation in the Russo-Japanese War; U.S. gives unofficial support to Japan. |
| 1914–17 | Sharp increase of American trade with Russia during WWI; military alliance; U.S. support of the Provisional Government. |
| 1918–20 | U.S. armed intervention in Russia's Civil War (on the Whites' side); break of diplomatic relations. |
| 1920s | Limited trade and business contracts. |
| 1933 | U.S. recognition of the Soviet Union; modest increase in commercial relations. |
| 1941–45 | World War II: military alliance; U.S. military and economic aid to Russia; diplomatic negotiations, conferences, and agreements. |
| 1945–56 | The Cold War; "policy of containment" and Truman Doctrine (1947); Berlin Blockade, NATO (1949); Korean War (1950–53); Warsaw Pact (1955); Hungarian Revolt (1956). |
| 1956–70 | The Cool War: Soviet policy of "peaceful coexistence"; Khrushchev's visits to the U.S.; Berlin Wall (1961); Cuba Crisis (1962); "Hot Line" (1963); Czechoslovakian Crisis (1968). |
| 1970–79 | Détente: SALT I (1972); Helsinki Accords (1975); increased cultural and scientific cooperation; problems with trade; human rights; SALT II; Afghanistan Crisis; grain embargo; Olympics boycott (Moscow 1980). |
| 1980–84 | American-Soviet tensions over Poland, Central America, European Missiles; natural gas pipeline controversy; Olympics boycott (Los Angeles); SDI ("Star Wars"). |
| 1985–88 | Reagan-Gorbachev meetings; INF Treaty; Lessening of tensions. |
| 1989– | Bush-Gorbachev meeting in Malta; relations continue to improve. |

*Source:* Compiled by the author.

In Asia, the Red Army bodily installed a Communist regime in the northern half of Korea (North Korea) immediately after the collapse of the Japanese Empire. The Soviet Union then proceeded to help the Chinese Communists achieve victory over the Nationalist forces, which were supported by the United States. Mainland China became a Communist nation in 1949, and during the first ten years of its existence it was a staunch ally of the Soviet Union.

The emergence of three other Communist nations in Asia—Vietnam, Cambodia, and Laos—was the result of a combination of heavy-handed French and American military interference and both moral and material support from the Soviet Union and China. A similar mishandling, this time by the United States alone, of an erstwhile nationalist revolution in Cuba led to the creation of the first Communist nation in the western hemisphere. Among the few Communist or pro-Communist regimes of more recent vintage in Africa, Asia, and the Middle East are Angola, Ethiopia, Afghanistan, and South Yemen. Serving as an arm of Soviet foreign policy, Cuba has been helping to set up and maintain pro-Communist regimes in other Third World countries. In all, approximately one third of humankind, in some twenty different countries scattered over the entire globe, came to live under Communism (Socialism). Every Communist regime in the world, including China and Yugoslavia, suspected that its existence would not be possible without the continuing support, direct or indirect, from the Soviet Union. The dramatic events of 1990 in eastern Europe fully confirmed this suspicion. In a major demonstration designed to prove that his "New Thinking" was for real, Gorbachev, whom *Time* called the "impresario of calculated disorder,"[12] withdrew Soviet support from the Communist regimes in Bulgaria, Czechoslovakia, East Germany, Hungary, Poland, and Rumania, causing them to collapse under their own weight. Of course, this brought about a drastic change in Soviet relations with these countries.

The Soviet Union is still tied to its former satellites by multinational and bilateral agreements. The two main multinational instruments are the Warsaw Pact (1955)[13] and the Comecon (1949), the latter of which we have already mentioned. The east European nations have another "organic" link with the Soviet Union over which they have little control: geography. They all live in the Soviet shadow. This is also true of Yugoslavia, over which the shadow appears to be darkening, because of her internal ethnic strife.

Even while technically continuing to be allied with the Soviet Union, the East European countries are enjoying as much sovereignty and independence as they have ever had, and definitely much more than they were allotted during the last forty years when they had to abide by the so-called Brezhnev Doctrine.

## BREZHNEV DOCTRINE

Member countries of the Soviet bloc were expected to adhere to a set of three principles: (1) maintaining the commanding position of the ruling Communist Party; (2) continuing to "build Socialism;" and (3) demonstrating loyalty to Moscow. Individual regimes had certain leeway on each of these points, reflecting the peculiarities of their domestic conditions, cultural traditions, and geopolitical factors. They all knew, however, that a serious departure

[12]*Time*, January 1, 1990, p. 2.

[13]The Warsaw Pact (Warsaw Treaty Organization) was launched in 1955 in response to the admission of West Germany (FRG) to the NATO (North Atlantic Treaty Organization). At present, it has seven member-countries: Bulgaria, Czechoslovakia, East Germany (GDR), Hungary, Poland, Romania, and the USSR.

from any one of these three points would activate a control mechanism that has been nicknamed in the West the "Brezhnev Doctrine." In theory, this doctrine proclaimed that the "new and superior" international order governing relations within the Soviet bloc is based on the principle of limited sovereignty, making it obligatory for every member-nation to safeguard the status quo of all the other members (just as individual citizens in a Socialist society are supposed to be each other's keepers).

In practice, Moscow decided when and how to use the Brezhnev Doctrine. Its actual application varied. In 1956 (before the term "Brezhnev Doctrine" was coined), Soviet tanks put a bloody end to a short-lived anti-Communist revolution in Hungary. In 1968, a Soviet-led invasion of Czechoslovakia forced the resignation of a liberal Marxist regime. In 1979, a large contingent of Soviet troops entered Afghanistan to oust one and install and keep in power another Communist government. And in the early 1980s, Moscow managed, by remote control, to bring to heel mass labor unrest in Poland.

It is rather obvious that there was an analogy between the Brezhnev Doctrine of limited sovereignty and the "National in form, Socialist in content" formula. In fact, they could be seen as the initial and concluding stages, respectively, of the same process of denationalization by Marxism-Leninism. Thus, there is reason to believe that Gorbachev's decision to let go of eastern Europe represents not only a cost-benefit calculation and a political concession, but also an ideological retreat. Now his problem is how to stop the domino effect of this decision from crossing Soviet borders and affecting the ethnic republics of the USSR itself. Gorbachev's "New Thinking" has canceled, or at least seriously modified, the "Brezhnev Doctrine."

## NEUTRALS

Philosophically, the notion of neutrality or a third position does not fit the ideology of Marxism-Leninism. But even in the black-or-white world of Stalin, based on the maxim, "He who is not with me is against me," there was always some margin of tolerance for such countries as Austria, Finland, and Switzerland. It was, however, left to Stalin's heirs to change Soviet policy to something closer to "He who is not against me is with me," and to give the status of neutrality in international relations official respectability. On the theoretical level, this has been done without causing violence to Marxism-Leninism by simply treating the condition of neutrality as a transitional phenomenon and a product of the decomposition of colonial empires. The Marxist term for it, coined by Lenin many years ago, is the "struggle for national liberation." This applies mostly to former colonies.

On the practical level, Soviet foreign policy changed dramatically during the mid-1950s when Khrushchev began to openly court the favor of

**BOX 12–6** *The USSR Constitution on Soviet Foreign Policy*

Article 28: "Leninist policy of peace" in dealing with capiltaist nations.
Article 29: "Supporting the struggle of peoples for national liberation" in the
Third World.
Article 30: "Socialist internationalism" as a basis for relations with Socialist
states.

such countries as India and Egypt. Ever since that time, the Soviet Union has been pursuing a policy of active involvement with developing countries on all continents. This includes limited economic and military aid and unlimited political support without any visible strings attached. Invisible strings, which do not seem to bother the recipients of Soviet aid and support, merely imply that the developing countries must strive to reduce their dependence on the capitalist West. For several decades, the basis of Soviet policy toward neutrals was to find ways to weaken the West by hurting its vested political and economic interests in the Third World countries. The cost effectiveness of any given Soviet policy in the Third World—for example, the dispatch of Cuban "volunteers" to Angola—was figured on the basis of the expected losses to the other side. It was primarily this consideration that has motivated Soviet military aid to the Arab countries opposing pro-American Israel. Another consideration was the probability of a desirable chain reaction. For instance, Soviet support—mostly verbal—for revolutionary movements in small Central American countries was aimed at destabilizing Latin America as a whole.

Gorbachev's "New Thinking" calls for a more sophisticated approach to the developing countries, which are now treated as full members of the interdependent international community, rather than as pawns in Soviet relations with the West. This implies a more cautious attitude toward the "national liberation movements." As a sign of this change, there has been an improvement in Soviet-Israeli relations.

As we have seen, Gorbachev's most dramatic move so far has been in Europe, where an entirely different model for neutrality is being promoted by Soviet foreign policy. Its best known example is Finland, which has given it the name "Finlandization." In its extreme form, Finlandization means completely orienting and tying the economy of a nation to the Soviet national economy. Although Finland's present economic cooperation with the Soviet Union involves several levels and kinds of bilateral transactions, the basic idea is the opposite of the traditional relationship between a colonial power and its colonies. The Soviet Union supplies raw materials and uses Finland as a country workshop for its needs. Economically, Finland benefits from this dependency and enjoys living standards higher than those of the Soviet

Union. Politically, it has been expected to maintain neutrality with a pro-Soviet tilt. As a long-range goal, Moscow appears to be ready to extend Finlandization to other neighboring European countries. Could it be that Gorbachev has decided that in the long run a self-interested trading partner is more valuable than a make-believe ally? (Just as he had concluded earlier that to run his country, a real majority of 51 percent was preferable to a phony majority of 99 percent.)

Regardless of gradations and shades, the concept of neutrality is now acceptable to Moscow, also as a means for changing former adversaries into business partners and even friends. Soviet foreign policy strives to accelerate the transition. Soviet influence among the so-called nonaligned nations appears to be growing. In fact, it is this large group of mostly underdeveloped countries that can perform a useful function, in Moscow's eyes, in various international organizations, including the United Nations, by giving support to Soviet proposals and resolutions.

## THE USSR AND THE U.N.

The Soviet Union is one of the founding members of the United Nations (U.N.). With the other four great powers (United States, China, Britain, and France), the USSR has a permanent seat and veto power in the U.N. Security Council. As we already know, Soviet membership in the U.N. has another peculiar feature, not shared by any other member: The USSR is the only nation that has three delegations, instead of one, at the U.N.: One delegation represents the country as a whole, while the other two represent its two component republics, Byelorussia and the Ukraine.[14] This triple representation, which is duly reflected in all permanent bodies of the U.N., was granted to the Soviet Union, not in recognition of its enormous size or ethnic diversity, but rather as a private compromise between Roosevelt and Stalin. Because Stalin at first demanded that all the Soviet Union's republics should have votes in the U.N., his eventual acquiescence to the total of only three delegations for the Soviet Union was hailed in the West as a real concession. It seemed so important, especially for the United States, to secure Soviet participation in the prototype of a world government that Stalin probably could have held out for an even higher price.

As we know, numbers of votes or any other concepts of formal democracy are not very important to Marxist-Leninist ideology. Lenin used to say that a majority is not a matter of arithmetic but of politics. Besides, as seen by Soviet leaders, from Stalin to the current ones, the arithmetic of the U.N. is quite simple: On any important issue there are just two sides, Socialism

---

[14]In an ironic twist of ethnic politics, some nationalistic groups in the Soviet Baltic republics are now demanding separate membership seats in the U.N. for the Estonian, Latvian, and Lithuanian SSR's.

and capitalism. The more the capitalist side can be divided and fragmented, the better it is for Soviet propaganda. But in the final analysis, the real count remains one against one, right against wrong. The position of the Communist "right" is not negotiable. Nothing can be more removed from Marxist-Leninist ideology than the notion of a world government or even its forerunner, such as the U.N., unless it can be completely dominated by the Communist side.

But Soviet leaders have always been ready and willing to use the U.N. for their propaganda purposes. During the 1940s and 1950s, this meant being constantly outvoted and resorting to their veto power. But in the 1960s the situation began to change, mostly because many newly established nations, former colonies, could not resist the temptation of voting against their former Western overlords. Since the early 1970s, the Soviet bloc and the Third World nations often found themselves on the same side of an issue also because of more positive political and economic considerations. Generally speaking, the West tends to be supportive of the status quo on various international problems before U.N. committees and branches. The Soviet bloc and the Third World nations, on the other hand, find it more in their common interest to seek and promote changes.

As a result, during the last two decades, the Western great powers—Britain, France, and the United States—resorted to the veto power in the Security Council five times more frequently than did the Soviet Union. Moscow, of course, was delighted by this. It must have give Soviet leaders a special kind of satisfaction to use formal democracy, for which they have so much contempt, against the West in various U.N. forums in which the number of passed Soviet-sponsored resolutions grew, thanks to the support of the Third World nations. Predictably, votes in various U.N. forums that favored the Soviet side were hailed in Moscow as great victories of Marxist-Leninist ideas. But votes that rebuked the USSR were dismissed by Soviet propaganda as results of imperialist ploys and conspiracies.

Given the changing arithmetics of world politics, it is logical for Gorbachev to emphasize in his "New Thinking" the role of the U.N. as an international arbitrator. The U.N. and its many branches provide Moscow with a means to influence the world's public opinion, thus putting considerable pressure on the West's democratic governments.

## FOREIGN SERVICE

Important foreign policy decisions are made in the highest party councils in charge of specific moves and countermoves on the international stage. Usually, one of the members of the top party leadership has the title of foreign minister. Since 1917, only eight persons have held this office: Lev Trotsky (1917–1918), Georgi Chicherin (1918–1930), Maxim Litvinov (1930–

1939), Vyacheslav Molotov (1939–1949 and 1953–1956), Andrei Vyshinsky (1949–1953), Dmitri Shepilov (1956), Andrei Gromyko (1957–1985), and Eduard Shevardnadze (since 1985).

The USSR Ministry of Foreign Affairs is a union-republic bureaucracy, which means that, in addition to Moscow, every union republic has its own ministry of foreign affairs. It is not clear what such ministries do, because none of the union republics maintains its own foreign relations or receives and posts ambassadors.[15] The USSR Ministry of Foreign Affairs is structured along conventional lines. It is headed by the minister, who is a full member of the Politburo, and his eight to ten deputies. Its table of organization divides the world first of all into three blocs—Socialist, developing, and capitalist—and then into major geographic regions that are further subdivided into desks in charge of individual countries or groups of small neighboring countries. Altogether, there are seventeen area-country departments at this time. Periodic changes in the structure of the Ministry and posting of ambassadors reflect the shifting priorities in Soviet foreign policy. Another grid provides a functional division: political, economic, protocol, legal, consular, and others. The ministry has its own research facilities and a training institution for professional diplomats, called the academy. The ministry is also responsible, along with the State Committee on Public Education, for a prestigious college-level school, the Moscow Institute of International Relations, which is the main supplier of young foreign service officers.

Soviet embassies, missions, and consulates are found in more than 100 countries. They are staffed with thousands of diplomats and support personnel who reside abroad, usually accompanied by wives and children. As a rule, wives hold various clerical jobs or teach in embassy schools. Abroad, Soviet families are often housed in special compounds or apartment houses rented for this purpose. They keep to themselves as much as possible and avoid contacts with local people and other diplomats. Soviet personnel are paid in local currencies and receive differentials that bring their incomes closer to those of their Western counterparts. Being abroad, particularly in the West, gives Soviet diplomats and employees an opportunity to buy better-quality foreign goods, which is a rare privilege.

Because their profession also exposes them to foreign life, Soviet diplomats are selected with the utmost care and thoroughness. For example, it takes the approval of the Central Committee of the CPSU to be stationed in the United States. About a dozen of the most important ambassadors belong to the Central Committee. All Soviet diplomats are members of the Communist Party or the Komsomol. In a typical embassy, a majority of the officers comes from the Ministry of Foreign Affairs; some represent the Ministry of Foreign Trade, the Ministry of Culture, or other central bureaucracies. The

---

[15]The Ukraine and Byelorussia have their "own" ambassadors to the United Nations.

Soviet military establishment is officially represented by attachés in all major countries of the world. So is the KGB, although, of course, not as openly.

The use, or rather misuse, of diplomatic cover for espionage appears to be widespread in the Soviet foreign service, judging by the number of Soviet operatives caught, accused, and expelled from various countries. Another impressive statistic, which is just as embarrassing for the Soviet leaders, is the number of defections among Soviet diplomats.

## FOREIGN COMMUNISTS

As we already know, right from the start there has been a second channel for Soviet foreign relations conducted on the Communist Party level. Currently, this important function is performed directly by the Central Committee of the CPSU through an office headed by a senior member of the Secretariat and the Politburo. It involves the relations between the CPSU and all foreign Communist and "workers'" parties. Little is known about the actual operation of this office, as it prefers to conduct its quasi-diplomatic business in secret. Public announcements detail only visits by CPSU delegations abroad, trips by foreign Communist leaders to Moscow, and large international Communist forums, such as the Moscow Conferences of 1957, 1960, and 1969. In the past, Soviet leaders were quite open, and even boastful, about their ability to control foreign Communist parties through the Comintern, and later, in Europe, through the Cominform (Communist Information Bureau, 1947–1956).[16] Since the death of Stalin, however, the official position of the CPSU has been that all foreign Communist parties, in or out of power, handle their own business independently and operate in accordance with local conditions. They are, however, expected to adhere to the principle of "proletarian internationalism" and to the motto: "Proletarians of all countries, unite!" In the semantics of Communism, to swear allegiance to "proletarian internationalism" means to recognize the leading international role of the CPSU.

It appears that we are dealing here with one more Marxist-Leninist "unity of contradictions": Foreign Communist parties are supposed to act as if they were independent so as not to embarrass the Soviet Union; but at the same time, they are fully expected to show complete solidarity with the CPSU. Such ambiguity is not new in the history of Marxism-Leninism. Recurring division and unification have been two common phases of its development from the very beginning. As Lenin put it on the eve of the famous Second Party Congress in 1903: "Before we unite, we must separate." In more recent times, Yugoslavia, Albania, and China have successfully

[16]The Cominform had its headquarters originally in Belgrade, Yugoslavia (1947). In 1948, Yugoslavia was expelled from the organization, and the headquarters was moved to Prague, Czechoslovakia. It was disbanded in 1956.

demonstrated that Moscow's claim to hegemony within the international Communist movement can be challenged. Other foreign Communist parties, however, have tried and failed to break away from Moscow. This apparently included so-called Eurocommunism,[17] a recent effort on the part of the French, Spanish, and Italian Communist parties to give the Marxist-Leninist ideology a "human face" in contrast to the Soviet model. The idea was to show the voters in these countries that Marxism-Leninism can be independent of Moscow and function within a democratic context. Now, of course, the new Soviet leaders are themselves championing this idea. Gorbachev and his team are also promoting friendly relations with practically all Socialist parties, especially the Social Democratic parties (Marxists).

It is difficult to tell how much of this fluctuation to and from Moscow is actually caused and controlled by Soviet leaders. We do know, however, that on several occasions in the past, local Communist parties have, on orders from Moscow, obediently sacrificed their own interests for the sake of the major goals of Soviet foreign policy.[18]

## TOTAL EFFORT

Besides the USSR Ministry of Foreign Affairs and the foreign department of the Central Committee of the CPSU, Soviet foreign policy flows through several other channels, which were mentioned in previous chapters. Here we simply review them together to get a fuller picture of the Soviet Union's growing impact on world affairs.

Foreign trade and economic relations function not only as means to prop up the Soviet national economy, but also as tools to influence other nations: allies, neutrals, and potential adversaries. Commercial and business deals offered by Moscow carry increasingly heavy political weight with many nations.

Soviet ability to deliver modern armaments provides another important channel for controlling allies and influencing countries of the Third World. Various military, technical, and economic assistance projects give Moscow more leverage with the developing nations.

The Soviet Union participates in a large number of international events and exchanges involving science, culture, education, sports, and other traditionally nonpolitical activities. Given the climate of the East-West competition, many such activities tend to assume symbolic meaning that helps the Soviet Union's public image.

[17]Eurocommunism (European Communism) had a precursor, called "polycentrism," which came into being in the wake of the Twentieth Party Congress. It meant a degree of autonomy for various Communist parties.

[18]For example, in the 1920s, Moscow ordered the Chinese Communists to cooperate with the Nationalists. The outcome of this cooperation was an almost complete destruction of the Chinese Communist Party. In the 1930s, on Stalin's order, the Polish Communist Party destroyed itself.

Soviet efforts to influence the world's public opinion employ all kinds of propaganda, including multilingual publications and radio broadcasts, sponsorship of various campaigns and movements, and disinformation ploys.

The Soviet Union's formidable military might casts a long shadow that reaches far beyond its borders. Soviet troops are stationed in several east European and Asian countries, Soviet military advisors are found in many more countries around the globe, Soviet "blue water" navy ships are present in all oceans, and Soviet rockets can presumably reach any corner of the world.

Last, but not least, are the Soviet intelligence-gathering operations abroad. In addition to the KGB, the Soviet military intelligence network (called in Russian the *GRU*—Chief Intelligence Administration) is known to be engaged in extensive cloak-and-dagger activities.

Similar instruments of foreign policy are used today by practically all major nations. Moreover, in every single endeavor, taken by itself, the Soviet Union probably still lacks the quality, sophistication, and resources of its combined opponents. But what distinguishes the Soviet Union's performance in the world arena is its proven ability to totally consolidate all its efforts. In comparison with pluralistic Western nations, the Soviet Union has the advantage of a clenched fist over an open hand in promoting its foreign policy goals.

But under *glasnost*, Soviet foreign policy has become open for public discussion and even sharp criticism, forcing Kremlin leaders to admit earlier mistakes such as the Soviet invasion of Afghanistan in 1979.

## MAJOR GOALS

In the twilight just before World War II, Winston Churchill referred to Soviet foreign policy in these eloquent words: "I cannot forecast for you the action of Russia. It is a riddle wrapped in a mystery inside an enigma."[19] The second part of this fancy metaphor, which dates back to 1939, has often been used to support assertions of the allegedly "mysterious nature" of the Soviet Union and its foreign policy. Actually, there was very little mystery in Soviet foreign policy under Stalin and his immediate successors. Like a steamroller, the Soviet Union moved toward its goals slowly and not very gracefully, but steadfastly, while the West debated what to do about it. To paraphrase Winston Churchill, the West's policy in regard to Russia was, more often than not, an illusion wrapped in wishful thinking inside a fantasy. Western observers saw the Soviet Union as either coming (about to attack with its missiles, tanks, and hordes of soldiers) or going (about to collapse, disintegrate, or self-destruct). Some of this self-deception continues.

There is definitely nothing mysterious about Soviet foreign policy today. Besides having an obvious desire to avoid an all-destructive nuclear

[19]The text of the speech is contained in Churchill's *Blood, Sweat, and Tears* (New York: G. P. Putnam, 1941).

**BOX 12–7**    *Excerpt from the Current CPSU Program*

The young forward-looking world of Socialism is opposed by the exploiter world of capitalism which is still strong and dangerous but which has already passed its peak. *The general crisis of capitalism is deepening.* The sphere of its domination is shrinking inevitably, its historical doom becoming even more obvious.

*Program of the Communist Party of the Soviet Union* (Moscow: Politizdat, 1986) p. 16.

holocaust, the Soviet Union is currently pursuing three major geopolitical goals. The most urgent task is to nullify the lingering fear of a "Soviet Threat" and improve USSR's image in the world. Just as important is the need to stabilize the new situation in Europe created by the collapse of those communist regimes, troops withdrawals, and prospects for a German reunification. And the third major goal is to complete the process of neutralizing and isolating the countries along the Soviet border in the south. To Moscow, these goals are peaceful and defensive.

Direct and indirect means of promoting these goals include various types of traditional diplomacy. In the Far East, the Soviet Union is rebuilding and expanding relations with China, offering attractive economic deals to Japan, and, concurrently, actively seeking ways to come to terms with such countries as South Korea.

In Europe, Soviet foreign policy is promoting the idea of a "Common European Home," and playing down its implied anti-American overtones. Moscow's strategic long-rang objective however, is to persuade the western European nations to trade their dependence on the United States for attractive economic and business deals with the Soviet Union.

At the same time, Moscow seeks to improve relations with the United States on a number of important issues: arms control, troop reductions, regional conflicts, German reunification, trade, environmental concerns, and various bilateral exchanges. As before, personal diplomacy is playing a major role in these efforts.

South of the border, Soviet foreign policy is cautiously trying to deal with the uncertain situation that has developed in Iran after the death of Ayatollah Khomeini. Turkey finds itself under growing pressure from its northern neighbor to move away from the West. In Afghanistan, where Moscow has installed a Marxist regime dependent on its support, the current limited goal is to hold the line. And traditionally friendly relations with India continue.

Most of the Soviet moves and countermoves elsewhere in the world are supportive of one or more major goals. In the Third World, rather than following a carefully drawn master plan, Soviet foreign policy is committed to supporting political change in the hope that it would favor socialism. Soviet foreign policy is rarely hampered by considerations of vested economic interests, mainly because the USSR is not very involved in international business and does not depend on imported oil or other raw materials.

As noted, the ongoing domestic reforms of *perestroika* and *glasnost* are being used by Gorbachev as "collateral" in his effort to improve the Soviet image abroad and promote other objectives of Soviet foreign policy. A reverse relationship is also at play here: Gorbachev's perceived successes in world affairs strengthen his position at home and buy more time for the reforms.

## NUCLEAR THREAT

It has been suggested that, during the angry years of the Cold War, the United States could but would not, and the Soviet Union would but could not, annihilate the other side. We know the first part of this supposition to be true: For several years the United States was in a position to destroy the Soviet Union without fear of nuclear retaliation. Because history cannot be rewritten in the subjunctive, we will never know for sure what would have happened if the imbalance of nuclear power during the Cold War had been reversed. Would Stalin have shown as much restraint as Truman did? We will never know for certain.

Soviet leaders proudly say that in developing their arsenal of nuclear weapons and delivery systems they had always followed the West, responding to initiatives of the other side. The historic record bears this out. Perhaps all it really proves is the well-known fact that, until quite recently Soviet military technology was lagging behind that of the West. However, it does give the Soviet side a certain propaganda advantage, especially because Moscow has never threatened to use nuclear weapons first. All post-Stalin Soviet leaders have held consistently realistic and rational views on the consequences of nuclear war. According to these views, should such a war be started by either side, there would be no way to limit, win, or even survive it. This consistent public position has enabled them to claim that Moscow is more willing and ready than its opponents to conduct nuclear disarmament negotiations without any preconditions or reservations. In June 1982, the Soviet Union unilaterally declared that it will not be the first to use nuclear weapons. More recently, Gorbachev has come up with several concrete initiatives and formal proposals dealing with the nuclear threat.

Gorbachev's "peace offensive" unlike those of his predecessors, is being taken seriously, because it is back up by concrete deeds. He and his aides may or may not believe that nuclear war is winnable, but they most certainly believe that the propaganda war about this issue is. The CPSU Program insists that any thought of starting nuclear war would do violence to the principles of Marxism-Leninism. If this is true, it is not because the Marxist ideology has suddenly turned pacifist, but rather because its emphasis on the inevitability of the historical process, which is seen as a "one-way street," discourages taking high risks in foreign affairs.

Former President Ronald Reagan is credited with stating that "nuclear arms are immoral," but it is Mikhail Gorbachev who took the high moral ground on this issue, while the West is still not sure if it can do without "nukes."

## FOREIGN POLICY AND IDEOLOGY

From the point of view of Marxism-Leninism, Soviet foreign policy is an important instrument in "building Communism," the first condition for which is the security of the Soviet Union. The ultimate goal, of course, has always been "world revolution," meaning Communist takeovers by whatever means, and with or without Soviet support, in every part of the planet.

The long-range strategic priorities in the realm of international relations are determined by Soviet leaders on the basis of a number of ideological assumptions about the course of human history. The main assumptions are as follows: (1) humanity is converging into one and will eventually function as a global society; (2) this global future belongs to Communism, which will ultimately triumph everywhere in the world; (3) its chief opponent, capitalism, is doomed by its own internal contradictions; (4) the contest between Communism and capitalism is rooted in economics; (5) all Communist parties, both in and out of power, must strive to expedite the "inevitable" collapse of capitalism; (6) temporary alliances with and support of national liberation movements should be promoted to deepen the crisis of capitalism; and (7) it should, however, always be remembered that Lenin urged caution against premature moves and unnecessary risks. Gorbachev's "New Thinking" underscores this last point by placing "global survival" in the nuclear-armed world above "class struggle." It calls for international cooperation instead of confrontation, and no longer insists that capitalism is undergoing a "global crisis." Gorbachev's "New Thinking," however does not cancel competition between the two systems.

The ideological scenario provides a source of continuity for Soviet foreign policy in its pursuit of long-range strategic goals. The ideology gives Soviet foreign policy a global vision. At the same time, Marxism-Leninism is used by Soviet foreign policy as one of its tactical weapons. This is done by direct propaganda efforts that precede or accompany Soviet diplomatic moves, and through various indirect channels, such as foreign Communist parties, "popular fronts," "peace movements," and "friendship societies." On the other hand, ideology has never been an impediment to the exercise of the tactical flexibility enjoyed by Soviet foreign policy. In Lenin's words,

BOX 12–8    *Mikhail Gorbachev on International Competition*

Socialism, as Lenin has taught, will prove its superiority, but it will do so not by force of arms, but by example in all spheres of society's life, economic, political, and moral.

*Pravda*, March 15, 1985, p. 1.

"at times we might have to go in zigzags, sometimes retracing our steps, sometimes abandoning the course already selected and trying out various others" (see Box 12–3). The road that is supposed to lead the Soviet Union to its promised rendezvous with history has indeed been full of zigzags and detours, but its main direction, determined by ideology, remains the same.

Do the national interests of the Soviet Union and ideological principles ever collide? Is Soviet foreign policy ever faced with the choice between the ideology and *realpolitik*?[20] As far as Soviet leaders are concerned, such problems simply do not exist: What is good for Marxism-Leninism is also good for the Soviet Union, and vice versa.

Viewed dialectically, ideological ambitions and geopolitical considerations both oppose and complement each other in Soviet foreign policy. The opposition stems from an obvious discrepancy between the ultimate goal of "world revolution" and the actual state of international affairs. As long as Soviet leaders perceive the balance of power as being still unfavorable to them, the Soviet Union will keep its global mission on a back burner, while continuing to exploit and amplify various crises, tensions, troubles, and conflicts originating elsewhere. But if and when this perception should give way to a feeling of superiority, the international role of the Soviet Union is likely to become much more active because of its commitment to an ideology that does not tolerate a power vacuum and demands complete victory for its causes in the end. Soviet leaders believe, or at least profess to believe, that this is the only sure way to secure world peace. Former Secretary of State Henry Kissinger summarized his thoughts on the ideological roots of Soviet foreign policy as follows:

Permanent peace, according to Communist theory, can be...achieved...only by a Communist victory. Hence, any Soviet move, no matter how belligerent, advances the cause of peace, while any capitalist policy, no matter how conciliatory, serves the ends of war....[21]

[20]*Realpolitik* (German) means a pragmatic foreign policy based on geopolitical considerations.
[21]Henry A. Kissinger, *White House Years* (Boston: Little, Brown, 1979), p. 116.

To do justice to Marxism-Leninism, we should remember that this ideology not only rationalizes every Soviet move as contributing to world peace, but also cautions Soviet leaders against making rash moves. According to Mikhail Gorbachev, Communism will triumph by peaceful means (Box 12–8). The CPSU Program echoes this optimistic view of the future:

> The CPSU proceeds from the belief that the historical dispute between the two opposing social systems, into which the world is divided today, can and must be settled by peaceful means.

After all, the promise or threat of the forthcoming advent of world Communism is relevant only if one accepts Marx's theory about preordained development of history, which is largely an article of faith rather than empirical evidence. The so-called "world revolution" is not so much a question of "when," but of "if."

### GLOSSARY

**Brezhnev Doctrine:** USSR's pledge to protect Communist regimes in all Socialist nations.
**Capitalist Encirclement:** USSR surrounded by capitalist enemies (before World War II).
**Cominform:** Communist Information Bureau (for eastern Europe, 1947–1956).
**Comintern:** Communist International (1919–1943).
**Containment Policy:** United States commitment to contain Soviet expansion.
**Coup d'etat:** Unexpected move; sudden change of government.
**Détente:** Lessening East-West tension.
**Eurocommunism:** Communist movements in western Europe.
**Helsinki Accord:** Recognition of status quo in all of Europe; human rights accord (1975).
**Lebensraum:** Living space (German); territorial expansion.
**Linkage:** Linking trade and technical cooperation to the Soviet's "good behavior."
**Munich Agreements:** Appeasement of Hitler by England and France (1938).
**Peaceful Coexistence:** Prevention of major East-West military confrontations.
**Potsdam Agreements:** 1945 agreements on postwar Germany.
**Realpolitik:** Pragmatic foreign policy based on geopolitical considerations (German term).
**Truman Doctrine:** Decision to resist further Soviet expansion (Turkey, Iran, Greece) after World War II (1947).
**Warsaw Pact:** Warsaw Treaty Organization (WTO), established in 1955.
**World Revolution:** Change to Communism in all countries of the world.
**Yalta Agreements:** Agreements concerning the postwar status of east Europe and the Far East (1945).

### RECOMMENDED READINGS

GORBACHEV, MIKHAIL S., *Perestroika: New Thinking for our Country and the World.* New York: Harper & Row, 1988.
KENNAN, GEORGE, *Russia and the West under Lenin and Stalin.* Boston: Little, Brown, 1960.
RUBINSTEIN, ALVIN Z., *Soviet Foreign Policy since World War II.* Boston: Little, Brown, 1989.

# CONSTITUTION (FUNDAMENTAL LAW) OF THE UNION OF SOVIET SOCIALIST REPUBLICS

(Adopted on October 7, 1977; Amended on December 1, 1988)

The Great October Socialist Revolution, made by the workers and peasants of Russia under the leadership of the Communist Party headed by Lenin, overthrew capitalist and landowner rule, broke the fetters of oppression, established the dictatorship of the proletariat, and created the Soviet state, a new type of state, the basic instrument for defending the gains of the revolution and for building socialism and communism. Humanity thereby began the epochmaking turn from capitalism to socialism.

After achieving victory in the Civil War and repulsing imperialist intervention, the Soviet government carried through far-reaching social and economic transformations, and put an end once and for all to exploitation of man by man, antagonisms between classes, and strife between nationalities. The unification of the Soviet Republics in the Union of Soviet Socialist Republics multiplied the forces and opportunities of the peoples of the country in the building of socialism. Social ownership of the means of production and genuine democracy for the working masses were established. For the first time in the history of mankind a socialist society was created.

The strength of socialism was vividly demonstrated by the immortal feat of the Soviet people and their Armed Forces in achieving their historic victory in the Great Patriotic War. This victory consolidated the influence and international standing of the Soviet Union and created new opportunities for growth of the forces of socialism, national liberation, democracy, and peace throughout the world.

Continuing their creative endeavors, the working people of the Soviet Union have ensured rapid, all-round development of the country and steady improvement of the socialist system. They have consolidated the alliance of the working class, collective-farm peasantry, and people's intelligentsia, and friendship of the nations and nationalities of the USSR. Sociopolitical and ideological unity of Soviet society, in which the working class is the leading force, has been achieved. The aims of the dictatorship of the proletariat having been fulfilled, the Soviet state has become a state of the whole people. The leading role of the Communist Party, the vanguard of all the people, has grown.

In the USSR a developed socialist society has been built. At this stage, when socialism is developing on its own foundations, the creative forces of the new system and the advantages of the socialist way of life are becoming increasingly evident, and the working people are more and more widely enjoying the fruits of their great revolutionary gains.

It is a society in which powerful productive forces and progressive science and culture have been created, in which the well-being of the people is constantly rising, and more and more favourable conditions are being provided for the all-round development of the individual.

It is a society of mature socialist social relations, in which, on the basis of the drawing together of all classes and social strata and of the juridical and factual equality of all its nations and nationalities and their fraternal co-operation, a new historical community of people has been formed—the Soviet people.

It is a society of high organisational capacity, ideological commitment, and consciousness of the working people, who are patriots and internationalists.

It is a society in which the law of life is concern of all for the good of each and concern of each for the good of all.

It is a society of true democracy, the political system of which ensures effective management of all public affairs, ever more active participation of the working people in running the state, and the combining of citizens' real rights and freedoms with their obligations and responsibility to society.

Developed socialist society is a natural, logical stage on the road to communism.

The supreme goal of the Soviet state is the building of a classless communist society in which there will be public, communist self-government. The main aims of the people's socialist state are: to lay the material and technical foundation of communism, to perfect socialist social relations and transform them into communist relations, to mould the citizen of communist society, to raise the people's living and cultural standards, to safeguard the country's security, and to further the consolidation of peace and development of international co-operation.

The Soviet people,

guided by the ideas of scientific communism and true to their revolutionary traditions,

relying on the great social, economic, and political gains of socialism,

striving for the further development of socialist democracy,

taking into account the international position of the USSR as part of the world system of socialism, and conscious of their internationalist responsibility,

preserving continuity of the ideas and principles of the first Soviet Constitution of 1918, the 1924 Constitution of the USSR and the 1936 Constitution of the USSR,

hereby affirm the principles of the social structure and policy of the USSR, and define the rights, freedoms and obligations of citizens, and the principles of the organisation of the socialist state of the whole people, and its aims, and proclaim these in this Constitution.

## I. PRINCIPLES OF THE SOCIAL STRUCTURE AND POLICY OF THE USSR

### Chapter 1   The Political System

*Article 1.* The Union of Soviet Socialist Republics is a socialist state of the whole people, expressing the will and interests of the workers, peasants, and intelligentsia, the working people of all the nations and nationalities of the country.

*Article 2.* All power in the USSR belongs to the people.

The people exercise state power through Soviets of People's Deputies, which constitute the political foundation of the USSR.

All other state bodies are under the control of, and accountable to, the Soviets of People's Deputies.

*Article 3.* The Soviet state is organised and functions on the principle of democratic centralism, namely the electiveness of all bodies of state authority from the lowest to the highest, their accountability to the people, and the obligation of lower bodies to observe the decisions of higher ones. Democratic centralism combines central leadership with local initiative and creative activity and with the responsibility of each state body and official for the work entrusted to them.

*Article 4.* The Soviet state and all its bodies function on the basis of the socialist law, ensure the maintenance of law and order, and safeguard the interests of society and the rights and freedoms of citizens.

State organisations, public organisations, and officials shall observe the Constitution of the USSR and Soviet laws.

*Article 5.* Major matters of state shall be submitted to nationwide discussion and put to a popular vote (referendum).

*Article 6.* The leading and guiding force of Soviet society and the nucleus of its political system, of all state organisations and public organisations, is the Communist Party of the Soviet Union. The CPSU exists for the people and serves the people.

The Communist Party, armed with Marxism-Leninism, determines the general perspectives of the development of society and the course of the home and foreign policy of the USSR, directs the great constructive work of the Soviet people, and imparts a planned, systematic, and theoretically substantiated character to their struggle for the victory of communism.

All party organisations shall function within the framework of the Constitution of the USSR.

*Article 7.* Trade unions, the All-Union Leninist Young Communist League, cooperatives, and other public organisations, participate, in accordance with the aims laid down in their rules, in managing state and public affairs, and in deciding political, economic, and social and cultural matters.

*Article 8.* Work collectives take part in discussing and deciding state and public affairs, in planning production and social development, in training and placing personnel, and in discussing and deciding matters pertaining to the management of enterprises and institutions, the improvement of working and living conditions, and the use of funds allocated both for developing production and for social and cultural purposes and financial incentives.

Work collectives promote socialist emulation, the spread of progressive methods of work, and the strengthening of production discipline, educate their members in the spirit of communist morality, and strive to enhance their political consciousness and raise their cultural level and skills and qualifications.

*Article 9.* The principal direction in the development of the political system of Soviet society is the extension of socialist democracy, namely ever broader participation of citizens in managing the affairs of society and the state, continuous improvement of the machinery of state, heightening of the activity of public organisations, strengthening of the system of people's control, consolidation of the legal foundations of the functioning of the state and of public life, greater openness and publicity, and constant responsiveness to public opinion.

## Chapter 2 The Economic System

*Article 10.* The foundation of the economic system of the USSR is socialist ownership of the means of production in the form of state property (belonging to all the people), and collective farm-and-co-operative property.

Socialist ownership also embraces the property of trade unions and other public organisations which they require to carry out their purposes under their rules.

The state protects socialist property and provides conditions for its growth.

No one has the right to use socialist property for personal gain or other selfish ends.

*Article 11.* State property, i.e. the common property of the Soviet people, is the principal form of socialist property.

The land, its minerals, waters, and forests are the exclusive property of the state. The state owns the basic means of production in industry, construction, and agriculture; means of transport and communication; the banks; the property of state-run trade organisations and public utilities, and other state-run undertakings; most urban housing; and other property necessary for state purposes.

*Article 12.* The property of collective farms and other co-operative organisations, and of their joint undertakings, comprises the means of production and other assets which they require for the purposes laid down in their rules.

The land held by collective farms is secured to them for their free use in perpetuity.

The state promotes development of collective farm-and-co-operative property and its approximation to state property.

Collective farms, like other land users, are obliged to make effective and thrifty use of the land and to increase its fertility.

*Article 13.* Earned income forms the basis of the personal property of Soviet citizens. The personal property of citizens of the USSR may include articles of everyday use, personal consumption and convenience, the implements and other objects of a small-holding, a house, and earned savings. The personal property of citizens and the right to inherit it are protected by the state.

Citizens may be granted the use of plots of land, in the manner prescribed by law, for a subsidiary small-holding (including the keeping of livestock and poultry), for fruit and vegetable growing, or for building an individual dwelling. Citizens are required to make rational use of the land allotted to them. The state and collective farms provide assistance to citizens in working their small-holdings.

Property owned or used by citizens shall not serve as a means of deriving unearned income or be employed to the detriment of the interests of society.

*Article 14.* The source of the growth of social wealth and of the well-being of the people, and of each individual, is the labour, free from exploitation, of Soviet people.

The state exercises control over the measure of labour and consumption in accordance with the principle of socialism: "From each according to his ability, to each according to his work." It fixes the rate of taxation on taxable income.

Socially useful work and its results determine a person's status in society. By combining material and moral incentives and encouraging innovation and a creative attitude to work, the state helps transform labour into the prime vital need of every Soviet citizen.

*Article 15.* The supreme goal of social production under socialism is the fullest possible satisfaction of the people's growing material, and cultural and intellectual requirements.

Relying on the creative initiative of the working people, socialist emulation, and scientific and technological progress, and by improving the forms and methods of economic management, the state ensures growth of the productivity of labour, raising of the efficiency of production and of the quality of work, and dynamic, planned, proportionate development of the economy.

*Article 16.* The economy of the USSR is an integral economic complex comprising all the elements of social production, distribution, and exchange on its territory.

The economy is managed on the basis of state plans for economic and social development, with due account of the sectoral and territorial principles, and by combining centralised direction with the managerial independence and initiative of individual and amalgamated enterprises and other organisations, for which active use is made of management accounting, profit, cost, and other economic levers and incentives.

*Article 17.* In the USSR, the law permits individual labour in handicrafts, farming, the provision of services for the public, and other forms of activity based exclusively on the personal work of individual citizens and members of their families. The state makes regulations for such work to ensure that it serves the interest of society.

*Article 18.* In the interests of the present and future generations, the necessary steps are taken in the USSR to protect and make scientific, rational use of the land and its mineral and water resources, and the plant and animal kingdoms; to preserve the purity of air and water, ensure reproduction of natural wealth, and improve the human environment.

## Chapter 3   Social Development and Culture

*Article 19.* The social basis of the USSR is the unbreakable alliance of the workers, peasants, and intelligentsia.

The state helps enhance the social homogeneity of society, namely the elimination of class differences and of the essential distinctions between town and country and between mental and physical labour, and the all-round development and drawing together of all the nations and nationalities of the USSR.

*Article 20.* In accordance with the communist ideal—"The free development of each is the condition of the free development of all"—the state pursues the aim of giving citizens more and more real opportunities to apply their creative energies, abilities, and talents, and to develop their personalities in every way.

*Article 21.* The state concerns itself with improving working conditions, safety and labour protection, and the scientific organisation of work, and with reducing and ultimately eliminating all arduous physical labour through comprehensive mechanisation and automation of production processes in all branches of the economy.

*Article 22.* A programme is being consistently implemented in the USSR to convert agricultural work into a variety of industrial work, to extend the network of educational, cultural, and medical institutions, and of trade, public catering, service and public utility facilities in rural localities, and transform hamlets and villages into well-planned and well-appointed settlements.

*Article 23.* The state pursues a steady policy of raising people's pay levels and real incomes through increase in productivity.

In order to satisfy the needs of Soviet people more fully social consumption funds are created. The state, with the broad participation of public organisations and work collectives, ensures the growth and just distribution of these funds.

*Article 24.* In the USSR, state systems of health protection, social security, trade and public catering, communal services and amenities, and public utilities, operate and are being extended.

The state encourages co-operatives and other public organisations to provide all types of services for the population. It encourages the development of mass physical culture and sport.

*Article 25.* In the USSR there is a uniform system of public education, which is being constantly improved, that provides general education and vocational training for citizens, serves the communist education and intellectual and physical development of the youth, and trains them for work and social activity.

*Article 26.* In accordance with society's needs the state provides for planned development of science and the training and scientific personnel and organises introduction of the results of research in the economy and other spheres of life.

*Article 27.* The state concerns itself with protecting, augmenting and making extensive use of society's cultural wealth for the moral and aesthetic education of the Soviet people, for raising their cultural level.

In the USSR development of the professional, amateur, and folk arts is encouraged in every way.

### Chapter 4    Foreign Policy

*Article 28.* The USSR steadfastly pursues a Leninist policy of peace and stands for strengthening of the security of nations and broad international co-operation.

The foreign policy of the USSR is aimed at ensuring international conditions favourable for building communism in the USSR, safeguarding the state interests of the Soviet Union, consolidating the positions of world socialism, supporting the struggle of peoples for national liberation and social progress, preventing wars of aggression, achieving universal and complete disarmament, and consistently implementing the principle of the peaceful coexistence of states with different social systems.

In the USSR war propaganda is banned.

*Article 29.* The USSR's relations with other states are based on observance of the following principles: sovereign equality; mutual renunciation of the use or threat of force; inviolability of frontiers; territorial integrity of states; peaceful settlement of disputes; non-intervention in internal affairs; respect for human rights and fundamental freedoms; the equal rights of peoples and their right to decide their own destiny; co-operation among states; and fulfilment in good faith of obligations arising from the generally recognised principles and rules of international law, and from the international treaties signed by the USSR.

*Article 30.* The USSR, as part of the world system of socialism and of the socialist community, promotes and strengthens friendship, co-operation, and comradely mutual assistance with other socialist countries on the basis of the principle of socialist internationalism, and takes an active part in socialist economic integration and the socialist international division of labour.

### Chapter 5    Defense of the Socialist Motherland

*Article 31.* Defense of the Socialist Motherland is one of the most important functions of the state, and is the concern of the whole people.

In order to defend the gains of socialism, the peaceful labour of the Soviet people, and the sovereignty and territorial integrity of the state, the USSR maintains armed forces and has instituted universal military services.

The duty of the Armed Forces of the USSR to the people is to provide reliable defence of the Socialist Motherland and to be in constant combat readiness, guaranteeing that any aggressor is instantly repulsed.

*Article 32.* The state ensures the security and defense capability of the country, and supplies the Armed Forces of the USSR with everything necessary for that purpose.

The duties of state bodies, public organisations, officials, and citizens in regard to safeguarding the country's security and strengthening its defence capacity are defined by the legislation of the USSR.

## II. THE STATE AND THE INDIVIDUAL

### Chapter 6    Citizenship of the USSR;
### Equality of Citizens' Rights

*Article 33.* Uniform federal citizenship is established for the USSR. Every citizen of a Union Republic is a citizen of the USSR.

The grounds and procedure for acquiring or forfeiting Soviet citizenship are defined by the Law on Citizenship of the USSR.

When abroad, citizens of the USSR enjoy the protection and assistance of the Soviet state.

*Article 34.* Citizens of the USSR are equal before the law, without distinction of origin, social or property status, race or nationality, sex, education, language, attitude to religion, type and nature of occupation, domicile, or other status.

The equal rights of citizens of the USSR are guaranteed in all fields of economic, political, social, and cultural life.

*Article 35.* Women and men have equal rights in the USSR.

Exercise of these rights is ensured by according women equal access with men to education and vocational and professional training, equal opportunities in employment, remuneration, and promotion, and in social and political, and cultural activity, and by special labour and health protection measures for women; by providing conditions enabling mothers to work; by legal protection, and material and moral support for mothers and children, including paid leaves and other benefits for expectant mothers and mothers, and gradual reduction of working time for mothers with small children.

*Article 36.* Citizens of the USSR of different races and nationalities have equal rights.

Exercise of these rights is ensured by a policy of all-round development and drawing together of all the nations and nationalities of the USSR, by educating citizens in the spirit of Soviet patriotism and socialist internationalism, and by the possibility to use their native language and the languages of other peoples of the USSR.

Any direct or indirect limitation of the rights of citizens or establishment of direct or indirect privileges on grounds of race or nationality, and any advocacy of racial or national exclusiveness, hostility, or contempt, are punishable by law.

*Article 37.* Citizens of other countries and stateless persons in the USSR are guaranteed the rights and freedoms provided by law, including the right to apply to a court and other state bodies for the protection of their personal, property, family, and other rights.

Citizens of other countries and stateless persons, when in the USSR, are obliged to respect the Constitution of the USSR and observe Soviet laws.

*Article 38.* The USSR grants the right of asylum to foreigners persecuted for defending the interests of the working people and the cause of peace, or for participation in the revolutionary and national-liberation movement, or for progressive social and political, scientific, or other creative activity.

## Chapter 7   The Basic Rights, Freedoms, and Duties of Citizens of the USSR

*Article 39.* Citizens of the USSR enjoy in full the social, economic, political, and personal rights and freedoms proclaimed and guaranteed by the Constitution of the USSR and by Soviet laws. The socialist system ensures enlargement of the rights and freedoms of citizens and continuous improvement of their living standards as social, economic, and cultural development programmes are fulfilled.

Enjoyment by citizens of their rights and freedoms must not be to the detriment of the interests of society or the state, or infringe the rights of other citizens.

*Article 40.* Citizens of the USSR have the right to work (that is, to guaranteed employment and pay in accordance with the quantity and quality of their work, and not below the state-established minimum), including the right to choose their trade or profession, type of job and work in accordance with their inclinations, abilities, training, and education, with due account of the needs of society.

This right is ensured by the socialist economic system, steady growth of the productive forces, free vocational and professional training, improvement of skills, training in new trades or professions, and development of the systems of vocational guidance and job placement.

*Article 41.* Citizens of the USSR have the right to rest and leisure.

This right is ensured by the establishment of a working week not exceeding 41 hours, for workers and other employees, a shorter working day in a number of trades and industries, and shorter hours for night work; by the provision of paid annual holidays, weekly days of rest, extension of the network of cultural, educational and health-building institutions, and the development on a mass scale of sport, physical culture, and camping and tourism; by the provision of neighbourhood recreational facilities, and of other opportunities for rational use of free time.

The length of collective farmers' working and leisure time is established by their collective farms.

*Article 42.* Citizens of the USSR have the right to health protection.

This right is ensured by free, qualified medical care provided by state health institutions; by extension of the network of therapeutic and health-building institutions; by the development and improvement of safety and hygiene in industry; by carrying out broad prophylactic measures; by measures to improve the environment; by special care for the health of the rising generation, including prohibition of child labour, excluding the work done by children as part of the school curriculum; and by developing research to prevent and reduce the incidence of disease and ensure citizens a long and active life.

*Article 43.* Citizens of the USSR have the right to maintenance in old age, in sickness, and in the event of complete or partial disability or loss of the breadwinner.

This right is guaranteed by social insurance of workers and other employees and collective farmers; by allowances for temporary disability; by the provision by the state or by collective farms of retirement pensions, disability pensions, and pensions for loss of the breadwinner; by providing employment for the partially disabled; by care for the elderly and the disabled; and by other forms of social security.

*Article 44.* Citizens of the USSR have the right to housing.

This right is ensured by the development and upkeep of state and socially-owned housing; by assistance for co-operative and individual house building; by fair distribution, under public control, of the housing that becomes available through fulfilment of the programme of building well-appointed dwellings, and by low rents and low charges for utility services. Citizens of the USSR shall take good care of the housing allocated to them.

*Article 45.* Citizens of the USSR have the right to education.

This right is ensured by free provision of all forms of education, by the institution of universal, compulsory secondary education, and broad development of vocational, specialised secondary, and higher education, in which instruction is oriented toward practical activity and production; by the development of extramural, correspondence and evening courses; by the provision of state scholarships and grants and privileges for students; by the free issue of school textbooks; by the opportunity to attend a school where teaching is in the native language; and by the provision of facilities for self-education.

*Article 46.* Citizens of the USSR have the right to enjoy cultural benefits.

This right is ensured by broad access to the cultural treasures of their own land and of the world that are preserved in state and other public collections; by the development and fair distribution of cultural and educational institutions throughout the country; by developing television and radio broadcasting and the publishing of books, newspapers, and periodicals, and by extending the free library service; and by expanding cultural exchanges with other countries.

*Article 47.* Citizens of the USSR, in accordance with the aims of building communism, are guaranteed freedom of scientific, technical, and artistic work. This freedom is ensured by broadening scientific research, encouraging invention and innovation, and developing literature and the arts. The state provides the necessary material conditions for this and support for voluntary societies and unions of workers in the arts, organises introduction of inventions and innovations in production and other spheres of activity.

The rights of authors, inventors, and innovators are protected by the state.

*Article 48.* Citizens of the USSR have the right to take part in the management and administration of state and public affairs and in the discussion and adoption of laws and measures of All-Union and local significance.

This right is ensured by the opportunity to vote and to be elected to Soviets of People's Deputies and other elective state bodies, to take part in nationwide discussions and referendums, in people's control, in the work of state bodies, public organisations, and local community groups, and in meetings at places of work or residence.

*Article 49.* Every citizen of the USSR has the right to submit proposals to state bodies and public organisations for improving their activity, and to criticise short-comings in their work.

Officials are obliged, within established time-limits, to examine citizens' proposals and requests, to reply to them, and to take appropriate action.

Persecution for criticism is prohibited. Persons guilty of such persecution shall be called to account.

*Article 50.* In accordance with the interests of the people and in order to strengthen and develop the socialist system, citizens of the USSR are guaranteed freedom of speech, of the press, and of assembly, meetings, street processions, and demonstrations.

Exercise of these political freedoms is ensured by putting public buildings, streets, and squares at the disposal of the working people and their organisations, by broad dissemination of information, and by the opportunity to use the press, television, and radio.

*Article 51.* In accordance with the aims of building communism, citizens of the USSR have the right to associate in public organisations that promote their political activity and initiative and satisfaction of their various interests.

Public organisations are guaranteed conditions for successfully performing the functions defined in their rules.

*Article 52.* Citizens of the USSR are guaranteed freedom of conscience, that is, the right to profess or not to profess any religion, and to conduct religious worship or atheistic propaganda. Incitement of hostility or hatred on religious grounds is prohibited.

In the USSR, the church is separated from the state, and the school from the church.

*Article 53.* The family enjoys the protection of the state.

Marriage is based on the free consent of the woman and the man; the spouses are completely equal in their family relations.

The state helps the family by providing and developing a broad system of child-care institutions, by organising and improving communal services and public catering, and by paying grants on the birth of a child, by providing children's allowances and benefits for large families, and other forms of family allowances and assistance.

*Article 54.* Citizens of the USSR are guaranteed inviolability of the person. No one may be arrested except by a court decision or on the warrant of a procurator.

*Article 55.* Citizens of the USSR are guaranteed inviolability of the home. No one may, without lawful grounds, enter a home against the will of those residing in it.

*Article 56.* The privacy of citizens, and of their correspondence, telephone conversations, and telegraphic communications is protected by law.

*Article 57.* Respect for the individual and protection of the rights and freedoms of citizens are the duty of all state bodies, public organisations, and officials.

Citizens of the USSR have the right to protection by the courts against encroachments on their honour and reputation, life and health, and personal freedom and property.

*Article 58.* Citizens of the USSR have the right to lodge a complaint against the actions of officials, state bodies, and public bodies. Complaints shall be examined according to the procedure and within the time-limit established by law.

Actions by officials that contravene the law or exceed their powers, and infringe the rights of citizens, may be appealed against in a court in the manner prescribed by law.

Citizens of the USSR have the right to compensation for damage resulting from unlawful actions by state organisations and public organisations, or by officials in the performance of their duties.

*Article 59.* Citizens' exercise of their rights and freedoms is inseparable from the performance of their duties and obligations.

Citizens of the USSR are obliged to observe the Constitution of the USSR and Soviet laws, comply with the standards of socialist conduct, and uphold the honour and dignity of Soviet citizenship.

*Article 60.* It is the duty of, and a matter of honour for, every able-bodied citizen of the USSR to work conscientiously in his chosen, socially useful occupation, and strictly to observe labour discipline. Evasion of socially useful work is incompatible with the principles of socialist society.

*Article 61.* Citizens of the USSR are obliged to preserve and protect socialist property. It is the duty of a citizen of the USSR to combat misappropriation and squandering of state and socially-owned property and to make thrifty use of the people's wealth.

Persons encroaching in any way on socialist property shall be punished according to the law.

*Article 62.* Citizens of the USSR are obliged to safeguard the interests of the Soviet state, and to enhance its power and prestige.

Defence of the Socialist Motherland is the sacred duty of every citizen of the USSR.

Betrayal of the Motherland is the gravest of crimes against the people.

*Article 63.* Military service in the ranks of the Armed Forces of the USSR is an honourable duty of Soviet citizens.

*Article 64.* It is the duty of every citizen of the USSR to respect the national dignity of other citizens, and to strengthen friendship of the nations and nationalities of the multinational Soviet state.

*Article 65.* A citizen of the USSR is obliged to respect the rights and lawful interests of other persons, to be uncompromising toward anti-social behaviour, and to help maintain public order.

*Article 66.* Citizens of the USSR are obliged to concern themselves with the upbringing of children, to train them for socially useful work, and to raise them as worthy members of socialist society. Children are obliged to care for their parents and help them.

*Article 67.*   Citizens of the USSR are obliged to protect nature and conserve its riches.

*Article 68.*   Concern for the preservation of historical monuments and other cultural values is a duty and obligation of citizens of the USSR.

*Article 69.*   It is the internationalist duty of citizens of the USSR to promote friendship and co-operation with peoples of other lands and help maintain and strengthen world peace.

## III. THE NATIONAL-STATE STRUCTURE OF THE USSR

### Chapter 8   The USSR—A Federal State

*Article 70.*   The Union of Soviet Socialist Republics is an integral, federal, multinational state formed on the principle of socialist federalism as a result of the free self-determination of nations and the voluntary association of equal Soviet Socialist Republics.

The USSR embodies the state unity of the Soviet people and draws all its nations and nationalities together for the purpose of jointly building communism.

*Article 71.*   The Union of Soviet Socialist Republics unites:
the Russian Soviet Federative Socialist Republic,
the Ukrainian Soviet Socialist Republic,
the Byelorussian Soviet Socialist Republic,
the Uzbek Soviet Socialist Republic,
the Kazakh Soviet Socialist Republic,
the Georgian Soviet Socialist Republic,
the Azerbaijan Soviet Socialist Republic,
the Lithuanian Soviet Socialist Republic,
the Moldavian Soviet Socialist Republic,
the Latvian Soviet Socialist Republic,
the Kirghiz Soviet Socialist Republic,
the Tajik Soviet Socialist Republic,
the Armenian Soviet Socialist Republic,
the Turkmen Soviet Socialist Republic,
the Estonian Soviet Socialist Republic.

*Article 72.*   Each Union Republic shall retain the right freely to secede from the USSR.

*Article 73.*   The jurisdiction of the Union of Soviet Socialist Republics, as represented by its highest bodies of state authority and administration, shall cover:

1. the admission of new republics to the USSR; endorsement of the formation of new autonomous republics and autonomous regions within Union Republics;

2. determination of the state boundaries of the USSR and approval of changes in the boundaries between Union Republics;

3. establishment of the general principles for the organisation and functioning of republican and local bodies of state authority and administration;

4. the ensurance of uniformity of legislative norms throughout the USSR and establishment of the fundamentals of the legislation of the Union of Soviet Socialist Republics and Union Republics;

5. pursuance of a uniform social and economic policy; direction of the country's economy; determination of the main lines of scientific and technological progress and the general measures for rational exploitation and conservation of

natural resources; the drafting and approval of state plans for the economic and social development of the USSR,and endorsement of reports on their fulfilment;

6. the drafting and approval for the consolidated Budget of the USSR, and endorsement of the report on its execution; management of a single monetary and credit system; determination of the taxes and revenues forming the Budget of the USSR; and the formulation of prices and wages policy;

7. direction of the sectors of the economy, and of enterprises and amalgamations under Union jurisdiction, and general direction of industries under Union-Republican jurisdiction;

8. issues of war and peace, defence of the sovereignty of the USSR and safeguarding of its frontiers and territory, and organisation of defence; direction of the Armed Forces of the USSR;

9. state security;

10. representation of the USSR in international relations; the USSR's relations with other states and with international organisations; establishment of the general procedure for, and co-ordination of, the relations of Union Republics with other states and with international organisations; foreign trade and other forms of external economic activity on the basis of state monopoly;

11. control over observance of the Constitution of the USSR, and ensurance of conformity of the Constitutions of Union Republics to the Constitution of the USSR;

12. and settlement of other matters of All-Union importance.

*Article 74.* The laws of the USSR shall have the same force in all Union Republics. In the event of a discrepancy between a Union-Republic law and an All-Union law, the law of the USSR shall prevail.

*Article 75.* The territory of the Union of Soviet Socialist Republics is a single entity and comprises the territories of the Union Republics.

The sovereignty of the USSR extends throughout its territory.

### Chapter 9    The Union Soviet Socialist Republic

*Article 76.* A Union Republic is a sovereign Soviet socialist state that has united with other Soviet Republics in the Union of Soviet Socialist Republics.

Outside the spheres listed in Article 73 of the Constitution of the USSR, a Union Republic exercises independent authority on its territory.

A Union Republic shall have its own Constitution conforming to the Constitution of the USSR with the specific features of the Republic being taken into account.

*Article 77.* Union Republics take part in decision-making in the Supreme Soviet of the USSR, the Presidium of the Supreme Soviet of the USSR, the Government of the USSR, and other bodies of the Union of Soviet Socialist Republics in matters that come within the jurisdiction of the Union of Soviet Socialist Republics at the Congress of People's Deputies of the USSR.

A Union Republic shall ensure comprehensive economic and social development on its territory, facilitate exercise of the powers of the USSR on its territory, and implement the decisions of the highest bodies of state authority and administration of the USSR.

In matters that come within its jurisdiction, a Union Republic shall co-ordinate and control the activity of enterprises, institutions, and organisations subordinate to the Union.

*Article 78.* The territory of a Union Republic may not be altered without its consent. The boundaries between Union Republics may be altered by mutual agreement of the Republics concerned, subject to ratification by the Union of Soviet Socialist Republics.

*Article 79.* A Union Republic shall determine its division into territories, regions, areas, and districts, and decide other matters relating to its administrative and territorial structure.

*Article 80.* A Union Republic has the right to enter into relations with other states, conclude treaties with them, exchange diplomatic and consular representatives, and take part in the work of international organisations.

*Article 81.* The sovereign rights of Union Republics shall be safeguarded by the USSR.

## Chapter 10   The Autonomous Soviet Socialist Republic

*Article 82.* An Autonomous Republic is a constituent part of a Union Republic.

In spheres not within the jurisdiction of the Union of Soviet Socialist Republics and the Union Republic, an Autonomous Republic shall deal independently with matters within its jurisdiction.

An Autonomous Republic shall have its own Constitution conforming to the Constitutions of the USSR and the Union Republic with the specific features of the Autonomous Republic being taken into account.

*Article 83.* An Autonomous Republic takes part in decision-making through the highest bodies of state authority and administration of the USSR and of the Union Republic respectively, in matters that come within the jurisdiction of the USSR and the Union Republic.

An Autonomous Republic shall ensure comprehensive economic and social development on its territory, facilitate exercise of the powers of the USSR and the Union Republic on its territory, and implement decisions of the highest bodies of state authority and administration of the USSR and the Union Republic.

In matters within its jurisdiction, an Autonomous Republic shall co-ordinate and control the activity of enterprises, institutions, and organisations subordinate to the Union or the Union Republic.

*Article 84.* The territory of an Autonomous Republic may not be altered without its consent.

*Article 85.* The Russian Soviet Federative Socialist. Republic includes the Bashkir, Buryat, Daghestan, Kabardin-Balker, Kalmyk, Karelian, Komi, Mari, Mordovian, North Ossetian, Tatar, Tuva, Udmurt, Chechen-Ingush, Chuvash, and Yakut Autonomous Soviet Socialist Republics.

The Uzbek Soviet Socialist Republic includes the Kara-Kalpak Autonomous Soviet Socialist Republic.

The Georgian Soviet Republic includes the Abkhasian and Adzhar Autonomous Soviet Socialist Republics.

The Azerbaijan Soviet Socialist Republic includes the Nakhichevan Autonomous Soviet Socialist Republic.

## Chapter 11   The Autonomous Region and Autonomous Area

*Article 86.* An Autonomous Region is a constituent part of a Union Republic or Territory. The Law of an Autonomous Region, upon submission by the Soviet of People's Deputies of the Autonomous Region concerned, shall be adopted by the Supreme Soviet of the Union Republic.

*Article 87.* The Russian Soviet Federative Socialist Republic includes the Adygei, Gorno-Altai, Jewish, Karachai-Circassian, and Khakass Autonomous Regions.

The Georgian Soviet Socialist Republic includes the South Ossetian Autonomous Region.

The Azerbaijan Soviet Socialist Republic includes the Nagorno-Karabakh Autonomous Region.

The Tajik Soviet Socialist Republic includes the Gorno-Badakhshan Autonomous Region.

*Article 88.* An Autonomous Area is a constituent part of a Territory or Region. The Law of an Autonomous Area shall be adopted by the Supreme Soviet of the Union Republic concerned.

## IV. SOVIETS OF PEOPLE'S DEPUTIES AND ELECTORAL PROCEDURE

### Chapter 12   The System and the Principles Governing the Work of the Soviets of People's Deputies

*Article 89.* The Soviets of People's Deputies, i.e. the Congress of People's Deputies and the Supreme Soviet of the USSR, the Congresses of People's Deputies and Supreme Soviets of the Union and Autonomous Republics, and the local Soviets of People's Deputies—of the Territories, Regions, Autonomous Regions, Autonomous Areas, districts, cities, city districts, settlements and villages—shall constitute a single system of representative bodies of state authority.

*Article 90.* The term of the Soviets of People's Deputies shall be five years.

Elections to Soviets of People's Deputies shall be called not later than four months before the expiry of the term of the corresponding bodies of state authority.

*Article 91.* The Congresses of People's Deputies and sessions of the Supreme Soviets and local Soviets shall settle the most important matters of national, republican and local significance or call a referendum.

Congresses of People's Deputies shall elect the Supreme Soviets and Chairmen of the Supreme Soviets. The local Soviets of People's Deputies shall elect Chairmen of the Soviets. The Supreme Soviets and local Soviets of People's Deputies, except the city (district subordination), settlement and village Soviets, shall form their own presidiums.

Soviets of People's Deputies shall set up standing commissions and form executive-administrative and other bodies accountable to them.

Officials elected or appointed by Soviets of People's Deputies cannot hold their posts for more than two consecutive terms.

Any official guilty of the poor performance of his job can be released from his post before the expiry of his term.

*Article 92.* Soviets of People's Deputies shall form people's control bodies combining state control with public control by the working people at enterprises, institutions, and organisations.

People's control bodies shall check on the compliance with the law and on the fulfilment of state programmes and assignments, combat breaches of state discipline, localistic tendencies, narrow departmental attitudes, mismanagement, wastefulness, red tape and bureaucracy; they shall coordinate the work of other control bodies and help improve the structure and working of the state apparatus.

*Article 93.* Soviets of People's Deputies shall direct all sectors of state, economic, and social and cultural development, either directly or through bodies instituted by them, take decisions and ensure their execution, and verify their implementation.

*Article 94.* Soviets of People's Deputies shall function on the basis of collective, free and constructive discussion and decision-making, of glasnost, of systematic reporting back to them and the people by their executive-administrative and other bodies set up by the Soviets, and of involving citizens on a broad scale in their work.

Soviets of People's Deputies and the bodies set up by them shall take into account public opinion, submit for public discussion major questions of national and local importance and systematically inform the citizens about their work and the decisions taken by them.

## Chapter 13   The Electoral System

*Article 95.* People's Deputies shall be elected in one-candidate and multi-candidate electoral districts on the basis of universal, equal and direct suffrage by secret ballot. To ensure the representation of public organisations, in accordance with the quotas established by the laws of the USSR and the union and Autonomous Republics, one-third of the People's Deputies of the USSR and People's Deputies of the Union and Autonomous Republics shall be elected from public organisations, such as the Communist Party of the Soviet Union, trade unions, co-operative organisations, the All-Union Leninist Young Communist League, organisations of women, war veterans, retired workers, and of scientists, creative unions and other organisations formed in accordance with the law and having all-Union or republican organs. Elections of People's Deputies nominated by public organisations shall be held at their congresses or conferences, or plenary meetings of their all-Union or republican bodies.

*Article 96.* Elections of People's Deputies from electoral districts shall be universal: citizens of the USSR who have reached the age of 18 shall have the right to vote. The right to elect deputies from public organisations shall be granted to all delegates to their congresses or conferences, or participants in the plenary meetings of their all-Union or republican bodies.

To be eligible for election as People's Deputy a citizen of the USSR must have reached the age of 18 and as People's Deputy of the USSR, the age of 21.

A citizen of the USSR cannot simultaneously be a People's Deputy to more than two Soviets of People's Deputies.

Members of the Council of Ministers of the USSR, Councils of Ministers of the Union and Autonomous Republics and executive committees of the local Soviets of People's Deputies, with the exception of chairmen of these bodies, and also heads of departments, sectors and administrations of the executive committees of the local Soviets, judges and state arbitrators cannot be elected deputies to the Soviet which appoints or elects them.

The mentally ill, pronounced not *sui juris* by a court of law and those serving a term of imprisonment or sent by a court of law to undergo compulsory treatment shall not participate in elections.

*Article 97.* Elections of People's Deputies from electoral districts shall be equal: in every electoral district each voter shall have one vote; all voters shall exercise the franchise on an equal footing.

In the elections of People's Deputies from a public organisation each delegate to its congress or conference and each participant in the plenary meeting shall have one vote and they all shall exercise the franchise on an equal footing.

*Article 98.* Elections of People's Deputies from electoral districts shall be direct: People's Deputies shall be elected by citizens by direct vote.

People's Deputies from public organisations shall be elected by direct vote by the delegates to their congresses or conferences or by the participants in the plenary meetings of their all-Union or republican bodies.

*Article 99.* Voting at the elections of People's Deputies shall be secret: control over the voters' exercise of the franchise is inadmissible.

*Article 100.* The following shall have the right to nominate candidates for election as People's Deputies from electoral districts: work collectives, public organisations, meetings of voters in their places of residence and meetings of servicemen in their military units; the following shall have the right to nominate candidates for election as People's Deputies from public organisations: their all-Union or republican bodies, which shall take into account the proposals concerning candidates of local bodies, grass-root work collectives and members of these organisations.

The number of candidates nominated for election shall not be limited. Each participant in the election meeting can propose for discussion any candidacies, including his or her own.

Ballots can carry the names of any number of candidates.

Elections of People's Deputies from electoral districts may be preceded by district election meetings for discussing candidates nominated for election as deputies from the electoral district, and for taking decisions on the presentation of candidates for registration with a corresponding electoral commission.

The expenses involved in the preparation and holding of the elections of People's Deputies shall be met by the state.

*Article 101.* Preparations for the election of People's Deputies shall be made openly and publicly.

The holding of the elections shall be ensured by electoral commissions, which shall be composed of representatives of work collectives, public organisations, meetings of voters at their places of residence and servicemen in their military units.

Citizens of the USSR, work collectives and public organisations shall be guaranteed the possibility of free and all-round discussion of the political, professional and personal qualities of candidates to People's Deputies as well as the right to campaign for or against a candidate at meetings, in the press and on television and radio.

The order of holding elections of People's Deputies is determined by the laws of the Union of Soviet Socialist Republics and Union and Autonomous Republics.

*Article 102.* Voters and public organisations shall give mandates to their deputies.

The appropriate Soviets of People's Deputies shall examine electors' mandates, take them into account in drafting economic and social development plans and in drawing up the budget, organise the implementation of the mandates, and inform citizens about it.

## Chapter 14  People's Deputies

*Article 103.* Deputies are the plenipotentiary representatives of the people in the Soviets of People's Deputies.

In the Soviets, Deputies deal with matters relating to state, economic, and social and cultural development, organise implementation of the decisions of the Soviets, and exercise control over the work of state bodies, enterprises, institutions, and organisations.

Deputies shall be guided in their activities by the interests of the state as a whole, take the needs of their constituents and the interests of the public organisations that have elected them into account, and work to implement the mandates they have received from their voters and public organisations.

*Article 104.* Deputies shall exercise their powers, as a rule, without discontinuing their regular employment or duties.

During meetings of Congresses of People's Deputies, sessions of Supreme Soviets or local Soviets of People's Deputies, and so as to exercise their deputy's powers in other cases stipulated by law, deputies shall be released from their regular employment or duties and compensated from the appropriate state or local budget for the expenses connected with their work as deputies.

*Article 105.* Deputies have the right to address inquiries to the appropriate state bodies and officials, who are obliged to reply to them at a Congress of People's Deputies or a session of a Supreme Soviet or a local Soviet of People's Deputies.

Deputies have the right to approach any state or public body, enterprise, institution, or organisation on matters arising from their work as Deputies and to take part in considering the questions raised by them. The heads of the state or public bodies, enterprises, institutions, or organisations concerned are obliged to receive Deputies without delay and to consider their proposals within the time-limit established by law.

*Article 106.* Deputies shall be ensured conditions for the unhampered and effective exercise of their rights and duties.

The immunity of Deputies, and other guarantees of their activity as Deputies, are defined in the Law on the Status of Deputies and other legislative acts of the USSR and of Union and Autonomous Republics.

*Article 107.* Deputies shall report on their work and on that of a Congress of People's Deputies, a Supreme Soviet or a local Soviet of People's Deputies to their constituents, work collectives and public organisations that nominated them or to the public organisations that elected them.

Deputies who have not justified the confidence of their constituents or public organisations may be recalled at any time, by decision of a majority of the voters or the public organisations that elected them, in accordance with the procedure established by law.

## V. HIGHER BODIES OF STATE AUTHORITY AND ADMINISTRATION OF THE USSR

### Chapter 15   The Congress of People's Deputies of the USSR and the Supreme Soviet of the USSR

*Article 108.* The highest body of state authority of the USSR shall be the Congress of People's Deputies of the USSR.

The Congress of People's Deputies of the USSR is empowered to consider and resolve any issue within the jurisdiction of the Union of Soviet Socialist Republics.

The exclusive prerogative of the Congress of People's Deputies of the USSR shall be:

1) the adoption and amendment of the Constitution of the USSR;

2) decision-making on questions of the national and state structure of the USSR within the jurisdiction of the Union of Soviet Socialist Republics;

3) the determination of the state borders of the USSR; endorsement of border changes between the Union Republics;

4) the definition of guidelines for the home and foreign policies of the USSR;

5) the approval of long-term state plans and most important national programmes for the economic and social development of the USSR;

6) the election of the Supreme Soviet of the USSR;

7) the election of the Chairman of the Supreme Soviet of the USSR;

8) the election of the First Vice-Chairman of the Supreme Soviet of the USSR;

9) the endorsement of the Chairman of the Council of Ministers of the USSR;

10) the endorsement of the Chairman of the People's Control Committee of the USSR, the Chairman of the Supreme Court of the USSR, the Procurator-General of the USSR, and the Chief State Arbitrator of the USSR;

11) the election of the Committee for Constitutional Supervision of the USSR;

12) the revocation of legislative acts passed by the Supreme Soviet of the USSR;

13) decision-making on holding a nationwide vote (referendum).

The Congress of People's Deputies of the USSR shall adopt laws of the USSR and decrees by a majority vote of People's Deputies of the USSR.

*Article 109.*  The Congress of People's Deputies of the USSR shall consist of 2,250 deputies, to be elected in the following order:

750 deputies from territorial electoral districts with equal numbers of voters;

750 deputies from national-territorial electoral districts on the basis of the following representation: 32 deputies from each Union Republic, 11 deputies from each Autonomous Republic, 5 deputies from each Autonomous Region and one deputy from each Autonomous Area;

750 deputies from all-Union public organisations on the basis of the representation established by the Law on the Election of People's Deputies of the USSR.

*Article 110.*  The Congress of People's Deputies of the USSR shall meet in its first session not later than two months after the elections.

The Congress of People's Deputies of the USSR, upon recommendation of the Credentials Commission elected by it, shall decide on the eligibility of deputies, and, in cases where the election law has been violated, shall declare the election of the deputies concerned null and void.

The Congress of People's Deputies of the USSR is called by the Supreme Soviet of the USSR.

Regular sessions of the Congress of People's Deputies of the USSR shall be held once a year. Special sessions shall be called upon the initiative of the Supreme Soviet of the USSR, on the proposal of one of the Chambers of the Supreme Soviet of the USSR, the Presidium of the Supreme Soviet of the USSR, the Chairman of the Supreme Soviet of the USSR, at least one-fifth of the People's Deputies of the USSR, or upon the initiative of a Union Republic as represented by its highest body of state authority.

The first post-election session of the Congress of People's Deputies of the USSR shall be chaired by the Chairman of the Central Electoral Commission for Election of People's Deputies of the USSR, and subsequent ones by the Chairman of the Supreme Soviet of the USSR or his deputy.

*Article 111.*  The Supreme Soviet of the USSR shall be the permanent legislative, administrative and control body of state authority of the USSR.

The Supreme Soviet of the USSR shall be elected by secret ballot from among the People's Deputies of the USSR at the Congress of People's Deputies of the USSR and shall be accountable to it.

The Supreme Soviet of the USSR shall consist of two Chambers: the Soviet of the Union and the Soviet of Nationalities, both having equal numbers of deputies. The Chambers of the Supreme Soviet of the USSR shall have equal rights.

The Chambers shall be elected at the Congress of People's Deputies of the USSR by general ballot. The Soviet of the Union shall be elected from among the People's Deputies of the USSR representing territorial electoral districts and the People's Deputies of the USSR representing public organisations, taking into account the size of the electorate in a Union Republic or region. The Soviet of Nationalities shall be elected from among the People's Deputies of the USSR representing national-territorial electoral districts and the People's Deputies of the USSR representing public organisations on the basis of the following representation: 11 deputies from each Union Republic, 4 deputies from each Autonomous Republic, 2 deputies from each Autonomous Region and one deputy from each Autonomous Area.

The Congress of People's Deputies shall annually re-elect one-fifth of the deputies to the Soviet of the Union and the Soviet of Nationalities.

Each Chamber of the Supreme Soviet of the USSR shall elect a Chairman and two Deputy-Chairmen. The Chairmen of the Soviet of the Union and of the Soviet of Nationalities shall preside over the sittings of their respective chambers and conduct their affairs.

Joint sittings of the Chambers shall be presided over by the Chairman of the Supreme Soviet of the USSR or his First Deputy, or alternately by the Chairman of the Soviet of the Union and the Chairman of the Soviet of Nationalities.

*Article 112.* The Supreme Soviet of the USSR shall be convened annually by the Presidium of the Supreme Soviet of the USSR for its recurrent spring and autumn sessions to last, as a rule, three to four months each.

Special sessions shall be convened by the Presidium of the Supreme Soviet of the USSR at its discretion or on the proposal of the Chairman of the Supreme Soviet of the USSR, or of a Union Republic in the form of its supreme body of state authority, or of not less than one-third of the deputies of one of the Chambers of the Supreme Soviet of the USSR.

A session of the Supreme Soviet of the USSR shall consist of separate and joint sittings of the Chambers, and of meetings of the standing commissions of the Chambers and committees of the Supreme Soviet of the USSR held between the sittings of the Chambers. A session may be opened or closed at either separate or joint sittings of the Chambers.

Upon the expiry of the mandate of the Congress of People's Deputies of the USSR, the Supreme Soviet of the USSR shall retain its mandate until the formation by a newly-elected Congress of People's Deputies of the USSR of a new Supreme Soviet of the USSR.

*Article 113.* The Supreme Soviet of the USSR shall:

1) name the date of elections of People's Deputies of the USSR and approve the composition of the Central Electoral Commission for Election of People's Deputies of the USSR;

2) appoint the Chairman of the Council of Ministers of the USSR, on his proposal approve the composition of the Council of Ministers of the USSR and make changes in it, and form and abolish Ministries and State Committees of the USSR on the proposal of the Council of Ministers of the USSR;

3) form the Council of Defence of the USSR and confirm its composition; appoint and dismiss the high command of the Armed Forces of the USSR;

4) elect the Committee of Public Inspection of the USSR and the Supreme Court of the USSR, appoint the Procurator-General of the USSR and the Chief State Arbitrator of the USSR; and approve the composition of the Board of the Procurator's Office of the USSR and the Board of State Arbitration of the USSR;

5) regularly hear the reports of the bodies which it forms or elects and of the officials whom it appoints or elects;

6) ensure uniformity of legislative regulation on the whole territory of the USSR and establish the fundamentals of legislation of the USSR and the Union Republics;

7) carry out legislative regulation of relations of ownership, organisation of management of the national economy and social and cultural development, the budget and financial system, work remuneration and price formation, taxation, protection of the environment and use of natural resources, and exercise of the constitutional rights, freedoms and duties of citizens, and other relations the regulation of which is within the competence of the USSR;

8) interpret laws of the USSR;

9) establish the general principles of the organisation and the activity of republican and local bodies of state authority and administration, and determine the fundamentals of the legal status of public organisations;

10) submit the drafts of long-term state plans and the most important all-Union programmes of economic and social development of the USSR for endorsement by the Congress of People's Deputies of the USSR; approve state plans for economic and social development of the USSR and the State Budget of the USSR; exercise control over the course of the fulfilment of the plan and budget; approve the reports on their fulfilment; in case of necessity make changes in the plan and the budget;

11) ratify and renounce international treaties of the USSR;

12) exercise control over granting loans, rendering economic and other assistance to foreign states, and concluding agreements on state loans and credits received from sources abroad;

13) determine the main measures in the sphere of defence and ensurance of state security; order general or partial mobilisation; proclaim a state of war in the event of an armed attack on the USSR or when it is necessary to meet international treaty obligations relating to mutual defence against aggression;

14) adopt decisions on using contingents of the Armed Forces of the USSR when it is necessary to meet international treaty obligations relating to maintenance of peace and security;

15) institute military and diplomatic ranks and other special titles;

16) institute orders and medals of the USSR, and honorific titles of the USSR;

17) issue all-Union acts of amnesty;

18) have the right to revoke Decrees and decisions of the Presidium of the Supreme Soviet of the USSR, directives of the Chairman of the Supreme Soviet of the USSR, and decisions and directives of the Council of Ministers of the USSR;

19) revoke decisions and directives of the Councils of Ministers of the Union Republics should they fail to conform to the Constitution and laws of the USSR;

20) resolve other questions within the competence of the USSR except those which are within the exclusive competence of the Congress of People's Deputies of the USSR.

The Supreme Soviet of the USSR adopts laws of the USSR and decisions.

The laws and decisions, adopted by the Supreme Soviet of the USSR, may not contradict the laws and other acts adopted by the Congress of People's Deputies of the USSR.

*Article 114.* The right to initiate legislation at the Congress of People's Deputies of the USSR and in the Supreme Soviet of the USSR is vested in People's Deputies of the USSR, the Soviet of the Union, the Soviet of Nationalities, the Presidium of the Supreme Soviet of the USSR, the Chairman of the Supreme Soviet of the USSR, the Constitutional Inspection Committee of the USSR, the Council of Ministers of the USSR, the Union Republics through their highest bodies of state authority, the committees of the Supreme Soviet of the USSR and the standing commissions of its Chambers, the Committee of Public Inspection of the USSR, the Supreme Court of the USSR, the Procurator-General of the USSR, and the Chief State Arbitrator of the USSR.

The right to initiate legislation is also vested in public organisations through their all-Union bodies and in the Academy of Sciences of the USSR.

*Article 115.* Draft laws submitted for consideration by the USSR Supreme Soviet shall be debated by its Chambers at separate or joint sittings.

A law of the USSR shall be deemed adopted when a majority of the deputies have voted for it in each Chamber.

Draft laws and other major matters of state may be submitted for nationwide debate by a decision of the USSR Supreme Soviet taken on its own initiative or on the proposal of a Union Republic through its highest body of state authority.

*Article 116.* Each Chamber of the Supreme Soviet of the USSR has the right to consider any question within the competence of the Supreme Soviet of the USSR.

Questions of social and economic development and of the development of the state, which are of common significance to the whole country, of the rights, freedoms and duties of citizens of the USSR, of foreign policy, and of defence and state security of the USSR are subject to consideration, above all, in the Soviet of the Union.

Questions of ensurance of national equality and interests of nationalities and ethnic groups in combination with the common interests and requirements of the Soviet multinational state, and perfection of the legislation regulating interethnic relations are subject, above all, to consideration in the Soviet of Nationalities.

Each Chamber adopts decisions within its competence.

A decision adopted by one of the Chambers shall, if necessary, be submitted to the other Chamber and in the event of approval by it shall acquire the force of a decision of the Supreme Soviet of the USSR.

*Article 117.* In the event of disagreement between the Soviet of the Union and the Soviet of Nationalities, the matter at issue shall be referred for settlement to a Conciliation Commission formed by the Chambers on a parity basis, after which it shall be considered for a second time by the Soviet of the Union and the Soviet of Nationalities at a joint sitting. If agreement is again not reached, the matter shall be submitted for consideration by the Congress of People's Deputies of the USSR.

*Article 118.* The Presidium of the USSR Supreme Soviet is a body which is accountable to the Supreme Soviet of the USSR, ensures organisation of the work of the Congress of People's Deputies of the USSR and the Supreme Soviet of the USSR, and exercises other powers vested in it by the Constitution and laws of the USSR.

The Presidium of the Supreme Soviet of the USSR includes the Chairman of the Supreme Soviet of the USSR, the First Vice-Chairman of the Supreme Soviet of the USSR, fifteen Vice-Chairmen—the Chairmen of the Supreme Soviets of the Union Republics, the Chairmen of the Soviet of the Union and the Soviet of Nationalities, the Chairman of the Committee of Public Inspection of the USSR, and the Chairmen of the standing commissions of the Chambers and committees of the Supreme Soviet of the USSR.

The Presidium of the Supreme Soviet of the USSR is headed by the Chairman of the Supreme Soviet of the USSR.

*Article 119.*  The Presidium of the Supreme Soviet of the USSR shall:

1) convene sessions of the Supreme Soviet of the USSR;

2) organise preparation of sittings of the Congress of People's Deputies of the USSR and sessions of the Supreme Soviet of the USSR;

3) coordinate the activity of the standing commissions of the Chambers and committees of the Supreme Soviet of the USSR;

4) give assistance to the People's Deputies of the USSR in exercising their powers and provide necessary information to them;

5) exercise control over the observance of the Constitution of the USSR and ensure correspondence of the Constitutions and laws of the Union Republics to the Constitution and laws of the USSR;

6) organise preparation and holding of nationwide votes (referendums), as well as nationwide discussions of draft laws of the USSR and other most important matters of state;

7) confer the highest military and diplomatic ranks and other special titles;

8) award orders and medals of the USSR and confer honorific titles of the USSR;

9) grant citizenship of the USSR, and rule on matters of the renunciation or deprivation of citizenship of the USSR and of granting asylum;

10) exercise the right of pardon;

11) appoint and recall diplomatic representatives of the USSR to other countries and to international organisations;

12) receive the letters of credence and recall of the diplomatic representatives of foreign states accredited to it;

13) between sessions of the Supreme Soviet of the USSR order general or partial mobilisation, proclaim a state of war in the event of an armed attack on the USSR, or when it is necessary to meet international treaty obligations relating to mutual defence against aggression;

14) in the interests of defence of the USSR and security of its citizens proclaim martial law or a state of emergency throughout the country or in particular localities, provided that the issue is considered with the Presidium of the Supreme Soviet of the relevant Union Republic; may introduce in the above cases special forms of government run by the state bodies of the USSR and the Union Republics;

15) publish laws of the USSR and other acts approved by the Congress of People's Deputies of the USSR, the Supreme Soviet of the USSR, its Chambers, the Presidium of the Supreme Soviet of the USSR, and the Chairman of the Supreme Soviet of the USSR in the languages of the Union Republics.

The Presidium of the Supreme Soviet of the USSR issues Decrees and adopts decisions.

*Article 120.*  The Chairman of the Supreme Soviet of the USSR shall be the highest-ranking official in the Soviet state and represent the Union of Soviet Socialist Republics inside the country and in international relations.

The Chairman of the Supreme Soviet of the USSR shall be elected by the Congress of People's Deputies of the USSR from among the People's Deputies of the USSR by secret ballot for a term of five years and not more than for two consecutive terms. He may be recalled at any time by secret ballot by the Congress of People's Deputies of the USSR.

The Chairman of the Supreme Soviet of the USSR shall be accountable to the Congress of People's Deputies of the USSR and to the Supreme Soviet of the USSR.

*Article 121.*  The Chairman of the Supreme Soviet of the USSR shall:

1) implement general guidance over the preparation of questions to be examined by the Congress of People's Deputies of the USSR and the Supreme Soviet of the USSR; sign laws of the USSR and other acts adopted by the Congress of People's

Deputies of the USSR, the Supreme Soviet of the USSR, and the Presidium of the Supreme Soviet of the USSR;

2) submit to the Congress of People's Deputies of the USSR and the Supreme Soviet of the USSR reports on the state of the country and on important issues of Soviet domestic and foreign policy and of safeguarding the USSR's defence capability and security;

3) suggest to the Congress of People's Deputies of the USSR a nominee for election as First Vice-Chairman of the Supreme Soviet of the USSR, and also proposals on the personal composition of the Constitutional Inspection Committee of the USSR;

4) suggest to the Supreme Soviet of the USSR candidates for appointment as Chairman of the USSR Council of Ministers, Chairman of the Public Inspection Committee of the USSR, Chairman of the Supreme Court of the USSR, Procurator-General of the USSR, Chief State Arbitrator of the USSR, and then present those officials to the Congress of People's Deputies of the USSR for approval;

5) head the Defence Council of the USSR;

6) conduct negotiations and sign international treaties of the USSR.

The Chairman of the Supreme Soviet of the USSR shall issue directives.

The First Vice-Chairman of the Supreme Soviet of the USSR and the other Vice-Chairmen shall carry out at the Chairman's instructions some of his functions, and stand in for the Chairman when the latter is absent, or unable to perform his duties.

*Article 122.* The Soviet of the Union and the Soviet of Nationalities shall elect from among the members of the Supreme Soviet of the USSR and other People's Deputies of the USSR standing commissions of their Chambers to perform legislative work and to make a preliminary review of matters coming within the jurisdiction of the USSR Supreme Soviet, to promote the implementation of laws of the USSR and other decisions adopted by the Congress of People's Deputies of the USSR and the Supreme Soviet of the USSR, and to supervise the performance of state bodies and organisations.

With the same aims the Chambers of the Supreme Soviet of the USSR can set up committees of the Supreme Soviet of the USSR on the parity basis.

The Supreme Soviet of the USSR, including both its Chambers, can set up, when they find it necessary, commissions of inquiry and audit, and commissions on any other matter.

The standing commissions of the Chambers and the committees of the Supreme Soviet of the USSR shall annually replace one-fifth of their members.

*Article 123.* The laws and other decisions of the Congress of People's Deputies of the USSR and the Supreme Soviet of the USSR, and resolutions of its Chambers shall be adopted, as a rule, after a preliminary review of the drafts by the corresponding standing commissions of the Chambers or committees of the Supreme Soviet of the USSR.

The appointment and election of officials to the USSR Council of Ministers, the Public Inspection Committee of the USSR and also the collegiums of the Procurator's Office of the USSR and of the State Arbitration of the USSR shall be done on conclusions by the respective standing commissions of the Chambers or committees of the Supreme Soviet of the USSR.

All state and public bodies, organisations and officials must abide by the demands of the commissions of the Chambers and commissions and committees of the Supreme Soviet of the USSR and provide them with necessary materials and documents.

The recommendations of the commissions and committees shall be necessarily considered by state and public bodies, institutions and organisations. The results of such examination and the measures adopted shall be reported to the commissions and committees within the terms set by them.

*Article 124.* A People's Deputy of the USSR has the right, at meetings of the Congress of People's Deputies of the USSR and at sessions of the Supreme Soviet of the USSR, to make an inquiry to the Chairman of the Supreme Soviet of the USSR, to the Council of Ministers of the USSR and to the heads of other organs formed or elected by the Congress of People's Deputies of the USSR and by the Supreme Soviet of the USSR. The organ or the official to whom the inquiry is addressed must give an oral or written answer at the very same meeting of the Congress or the session of the Supreme Soviet of the USSR within three days at the most.

The People's Deputies of the USSR shall be released from their employment or production duties for the appropriate term, to exercise their deputies' duties in the Congress of People's Deputies of the USSR, in the Supreme Soviet of the USSR, in its Chambers, commissions and committees, and also among the population. People's Deputies of the USSR elected to the Supreme Soviet of the USSR shall be released from their employment or production duties for the whole duration of their term of office in the Supreme Soviet of the USSR.

A People's Deputy of the USSR cannot be criminally prosecuted, arrested or subjected to measures of administrative punishment imposed by court orders without the consent of the Supreme Soviet of the USSR, and in the period between its sessions, without the consent of the Presidium of the Supreme Soviet of the USSR.

*Article 125.* The Constitutional Inspection Committee of the USSR shall be elected by the Congress of People's Deputies of the USSR from among specialists in politics and law, and shall consist of a Chairman, Vice-Chairman and 21 committee members, including representatives of every Union Republic, elected for a ten-year term.

People elected to the Constitutional Inspection Committee of the USSR cannot simultaneously be members of organs whose acts are subject to inspection by the Committee.

In performing their duties, those elected to the Constitutional Inspection Committee of the USSR are independent and obey only the Constitution of the USSR.

The Constitutional Inspection Committee of the USSR shall:

1) at its own initiative or on the instructions of the Congress of People's Deputies of the USSR submit to the Congress conclusions on the conformity of draft laws of the USSR to be examined by the Congress to the Constitution of the USSR;

2) at its own initiative, on the instructions of the Congress of People's Deputies of the USSR, or at the suggestion of the Supreme Soviet of the USSR or the highest bodies of state authority of the Union Republics submit to the Supreme Soviet of the USSR conclusions on the conformity of acts of the Supreme Soviet of the USSR and of its Chambers, and of the draft acts by those bodies with the Constitution of the USSR and with the laws of the USSR adopted by the Congress of People's Deputies of the USSR;

3) see to it that the Constitutions and laws of the Union Republics and the Decrees of the Council of Ministers of the USSR and of the Councils of Ministers of the Union Republics conform to the Constitution and laws of the USSR;

4) provide conclusions, at its own initiative, on the instructions of the Congress of People's Deputies of the USSR or at the suggestion of the Supreme Soviet of the USSR or its Chambers, the Presidium of the Supreme Soviet of the USSR, the Chairman of the Supreme Soviet of the USSR, or the standing commissions of the Chambers and committees of the Supreme Soviet of the USSR, the Council of Ministers of the USSR, or the highest bodies of state authority of Union Republics, on

the conformity of the acts of other state bodies and public organisations with the Constitution and laws of the USSR.

Upon discovering contradictions between an act or its individual provisions and the Constitution or laws of the USSR, the Constitutional Inspection Committee of the USSR shall direct its conclusion to the organ which has issued that act, to correct the violation. The dispatch of such a conclusion by the Committee suspends the effect of the act or its individual provisions contradicting the Constitution or laws of the USSR.

The Constitutional Inspection Committee of the USSR has the right to table motions in the Congress of People's Deputies of the USSR, the Supreme Soviet or the Council of Ministers of the USSR on the revocation of acts by organs, or officials accountable to them, which contradict the Constitution or laws of the USSR.

The organisation and procedure of the performance of the Constitutional Inspection Committee of the USSR are stipulated by the Law on Constitutional Inspection in the USSR.

*Article 126.* The Congress of People's Deputies of the USSR and the Supreme Soviet of the USSR shall exercise control over the performance of all state bodies accountable to them.

The Supreme Soviet of the USSR shall guide the performance by the Public Inspection Committee of the USSR which presides over the system of public inspection bodies.

The organisation and procedure of the performance of public inspection bodies are stipulated by the Law on Public Inspection in the USSR.

*Article 127.* The order of performance of the Congress of People's Deputies of the USSR, of the Supreme Soviet of the USSR and of their organs is stipulated by the Operating Procedure of the Congress of People's Deputies of the USSR and the Supreme Soviet of the USSR and by other laws of the USSR issued on the basis of the Constitution of the USSR.

*Article 125.* The Soviet of the Union and the Soviet of Nationalities shall elect standing commissions from among the Deputies to make a preliminary review of matters coming within the jurisdiction of the Supreme Soviet of the USSR, to promote execution of the laws of the USSR and other acts of the Supreme Soviet of the USSR and its Presidium, and to check on the work of state bodies and organisations. The chambers of the Supreme Soviet of the USSR may also set up joint commissions on a parity basis.

When it deems it necessary, the Supreme Soviet of the USSR sets up commissions of inquiry and audit, and commissions on any other matter.

All state and public bodies, organisations and officials are obliged to meet the requests of the commissions of the Supreme Soviet of the USSR and of its chambers, and submit the requisite materials and documents to them.

The commissions' recommendations shall be subject to consideration by state and public bodies, institutions and organisations. The commissions shall be informed, within the prescribed time limit, of the results of such consideration or of the action taken.

*Article 126.* The Supreme Soviet of the USSR shall supervise the work of all state bodies accountable to it.

The Supreme Soviet of the USSR shall form a Committee of People's Control of the USSR to head the system of people's control.

The organisation and procedure of people's control bodies are defined by the Law on People's Control in the USSR.

*Article 127.*  The procedure of the Supreme Soviet of the USSR and of its bodies shall be defined in the Rules and Regulations of the Supreme Soviet of the USSR and other laws of the USSR enacted on the basis of the Constitution of the USSR.

## Chapter 16    The Council of Ministers of the USSR

*Article 128.*  The Council of Ministers of the USSR, i.e. the Government of the USSR, is the highest executive and administrative body of state authority of the USSR.

*Article 129.*  The Council of Ministers of the USSR shall be formed by the Supreme Soviet of the USSR at a joint sitting of the Soviet of the Union and the Soviet of Nationalities, and shall consist of the Chairman of the Council of Ministers of the USSR, First Vice Chairmen and Vice Chairmen, Ministers of the USSR, and Chairmen of State Committees of the USSR.

The Chairmen of the Councils of Ministers of Union Republics shall be *ex officio* members of the Council of Ministers of the USSR.

The Supreme Soviet of the USSR, on the recommendation of the Chairman of the Council of Ministers of the USSR, may include in the Government of the USSR the heads of other bodies and organisations of the USSR.

The Council of Ministers of the USSR shall tender its resignation to a newly elected Supreme Soviet of the USSR at its first session.

*Article 130.*  The Council of Ministers of the USSR shall be responsible and accountable to the Congress of People's Deputies of the USSR and the Supreme Soviet of the USSR.

A new Council of Ministers of the USSR shall submit a programme of activities for its term of office to the Supreme Soviet of the USSR.

The Council of Ministers of the USSR shall report at least once a year on its work to the Supreme Soviet of the USSR.

*Article 131.*  The Council of Ministers of the USSR is empowered to deal with all matters of state administration within the jurisdiction of the Union of Soviet Socialist Republics insofar as, under the Constitution of the USSR, they do not come within the competence of the Congress of People's Deputies of the USSR, the Supreme Soviet of the USSR and its Presidium, or the Chairman of the Supreme Soviet of the USSR.

Within its powers the Council of Ministers of the USSR shall:

1. ensure direction of economic, social, and cultural development; draft and implement measures to promote the well-being and cultural development of the people; to develop science and engineering, to ensure rational exploitation and conservation of natural resources, to consolidate the monetary and credit system, to pursue a uniform prices, wages, and social security policy, and to organise state insurance and a uniform system of accounting and statistics; and organise the management of industrial, constructional, and agricultural enterprises and amalgamations, transport and communications undertakings, banks, and other organisations and institutions of All-Union subordination;

2. draft current and long-term state plans for the economic and social development of the USSR and the Budget of the USSR, and submit them to the Supreme Soviet of the USSR; take measures to execute the state plans and Budget; and report to the Supreme Soviet of the USSR on the implementation of the plans and Budget;

3. implement measures to defend the interests of the state, protect socialist property, and maintain public order, and guarantee and protect citizens' rights and freedoms;

4. take measures to ensure state security;

5. exercise general direction of the development of the Armed Forces of the USSR, and determine the annual contingent of citizens to be called up for active military service;

6. provide general direction in regard to relations with other states, foreign trade, and economic, scientific, technical, and cultural co-operation of the USSR with other countries; take measures to ensure fulfilment of the USSR's international treaties; and ratify and denounce intergovernmental international agreements;

7. and when necessary, form committees, central boards, and other departments under the Council of Ministers of the USSR to deal with matters of economic, social and cultural development, and defence.

*Article 132.* A Presidium of the Council of Ministers of the USSR, consisting of the Chairman, the First Vice Chairmen, and Vice Chairmen of the Council of Ministers of the USSR, shall function as a standing body of the Council of Ministers of the USSR to deal with questions relating to guidance of the economy, and with other matters of state administration.

*Article 133.* On the basis of, and in execution of, the laws of the USSR and other decisions by the Congress of People's Deputies of the USSR and the Supreme Soviet of the USSR, the Council of Ministers of the USSR shall issue decisions and ordinances and check on their fulfilment. Decisions and instructions by the Council of Ministers of the USSR shall be binding throughout the entire territory of the USSR.

*Article 134.* The Council of Ministers of the USSR has the right, in matters within the jurisdiction of the Union of Soviet Socialist Republics, to suspend execution of decisions and ordinances of the Councils of Ministers of Union Republics, and to rescind acts of ministries and state committees of the USSR, and of other bodies subordinate to it.

*Article 135.* The Council of Ministers of the USSR shall co-ordinate and direct the work of All-Union and Union-Republican ministries, state committees of the USSR, and other bodies subordinate to it.

All-Union ministries and state committees of the USSR shall direct the work of the branches of administration entrusted to them, or exercise inter-branch administration, throughout the territory of the USSR directly or through bodies set up by them.

Union-Republican ministries and state committees of the USSR direct the work of the branches of administration entrusted to them, or exercise inter-branch administration, as a rule, through the corresponding ministries and state committees, and other bodies of Union Republics, and directly administer individual enterprises and amalgamations of Union subordination.

Ministries and state committees of the USSR shall be responsible for the condition and development of the spheres of administration entrusted to them; within their competence, they issue orders and other acts on the basis of, and in execution of, the laws of the USSR and other decisions of the Congress of the People's Deputies of the USSR and the Supreme Soviet of the USSR and of decisions and ordinances of the Council of Ministers of the USSR, and organise and verify their implementation.

*Article 136.* The competence of the Council of Ministers of the USSR and its Presidium, the procedure for their work, relationships between the Council of Ministers and other state bodies, and the list of All-Union and Union-Republican ministries and state committees of the USSR are defined, on the basis of the Constitution, in the Law on the Council of Ministers of the USSR.

## VI. BASIC PRINCIPLES OF THE STRUCTURE
## OF THE BODIES OF STATE AUTHORITY
## AND ADMINISTRATION IN UNION REPUBLICS

### Chapter 17   Higher Bodies of State Authority
### and Administration of A Union Republic

*Article 137.*   The highest body of state authority of a Union Republic shall be the Congress of People's Deputies of that Republic.

The powers of the Congress of People's Deputies of a Union Republic shall be defined by the Constitution of the Republic.

*Article 138.*   The Supreme Soviet of a Union Republic is the standing legislative, administrative and control body of state authority of that Republic. The Supreme Soviet of a Union Republic shall be accountable to the Congress of People's Deputies of the Republic.

The Chairman of the Supreme Soviet of a Union Republic shall be accountable to the Congress of People's Deputies and the Supreme Soviet of the Republic.

The powers of the Supreme Soviet of a Union Republic, its Presidium and the Republic's Chairman of the Supreme Soviet shall be defined by the Constitution of the Republic.

*Article 139.*   The Supreme Soviet of a Union Republic shall form a Council of Ministers of the Union Republic, i.e. the Government of that Republic, which shall be the highest executive and administrative body of state authority in the Republic.

The Council of Ministers of a Union Republic shall be responsible and accountable to the Congress of People's Deputies and the Supreme Soviet of that Republic.

*Article 140.*   The Council of Ministers of a Union Republic issues decisions and ordinances on the basis of, and in pursuance of, the legislative acts of the USSR and of the Union Republic, and of decisions and ordinances of the Council of Ministers of the USSR, and shall organise and verify their execution.

*Article 141.*   The Council of Ministers of a Union Republic has the right to suspend the execution of decisions and ordinances of the Councils of Ministers of Autonomous Republics, to rescind the decisions and orders of the Executive Committees of Soviets of People's Deputies of Territories, Regions, and cities (i.e. cities under Republic jurisdiction) and of Autonomous Regions, and in Union Republics not divided into regions, of the Executive Committees of district and corresponding city Soviets of People's Deputies.

*Article 142.*   The Council of Ministers of a Union Republic shall co-ordinate and direct the work of the Union-Republican and Republican ministries and of state committees of the Union Republic, and other bodies under its jurisdiction.

The Union-Republican ministries and state committees of a Union Republic shall direct the branches of administration entrusted to them, or exercise inter-branch control, and shall be subordinate to both the Council of Ministers of the Union Republic and the corresponding Union-Republican ministry or state committee of the USSR.

Republican ministries and state committees shall direct the branches of administration entrusted to them, or exercise inter-branch control, and shall be subordinate to the Council of Ministers of the Union Republic.

## Chapter 18 Higher Bodies of State Authority and Administration of an Autonomous Republic

*Article 143.* The highest body of state authority of an Autonomous Republic shall be the Congress of People's Deputies of that Republic.

*Article 144.* The Supreme Soviet of an Autonomous Republic is the standing legislative, administrative and control body of state authority of that Republic. The Supreme Soviet of an Autonomous Republic shall be accountable to the Congress of People's Deputies of the Republic.

The Chairman of the Supreme Soviet of an Autonomous Republic shall be accountable to the Congress of People's Deputies and the Supreme Soviet of the Republic.

The Council of Ministers of an Autonomous Republic shall be responsible and accountable to the Congress of People's Deputies and the Supreme Soviet of the Republic.

## Chapter 19 Local Bodies of State Authority and Administration

*Article 145.* The bodies of state authority in Territories, Regions, Autonomous Regions, Autonomous Areas, districts, cities, city districts, settlements, and rural communities shall be the corresponding Soviets of People's Deputies.

*Article 146.* Local Soviets of People's Deputies shall deal with all matters of local significance in accordance with the interests of the whole state and of the citizens residing in the area under their jurisdiction, implement decisions of higher bodies of state authority, guide the work of lower Soviets of People's Deputies, take part in the discussion of matters of Republican and All-Union significance, and submit their proposals concerning them.

Local Soviets of People's Deputies shall direct state, economic, social, and cultural development within their territory; endorse plans for economic and social development and the local budget; exercise general guidance over state bodies, enterprises, institutions, and organisations subordinate to them; ensure observance of the laws, maintenance of law and order, and protection of citizens' rights; and help strengthen the country's defence capacity.

*Article 147.* Within their powers, local Soviets of People's Deputies shall ensure the comprehensive, all-round economic and social development of their area; exercise control over the observance of legislation by enterprises, institutions, and organisations subordinate to higher authorities and located in their area; and co-ordinate and supervise their activity as regards land use, nature conservation, building, employment of manpower, production of consumer goods, and social, cultural, communal, and other services and amenities for the public.

*Article 148.* Local Soviets of People's Deputies shall decide matters within the powers accorded them by the legislation of the USSR and of the appropriate Union Republic and Autonomous Republic. Their decisions shall be binding on all enterprises, institutions, and organisations located in their area and on officials and citizens.

*Article 149.* The work of the territorial, regional, Autonomous Region and Area, district, city and city district Soviets of People's Deputies shall be organised by their Presidiums with Soviets' Chairmen at the head, and of city (district subordination), settlement and village Soviets by their Chairmen.

*Article 150.* The executive and administrative bodies of the local Soviets of People's Deputies shall be the Executive Committees they elect.

Executive Committees shall report on their work at least once a year to the Soviets that elected them and to meetings of work collectives and neighbourhoods.

The Executive Committees of local Soviets shall be directly accountable to the Soviets that elected them and to the higher executive and administrative body.

## VII. JUSTICE, ARBITRATION, AND PROCURATOR'S SUPERVISION

### Chapter 20    Courts ana Arbitration

*Article 151.* In the USSR justice is administered only by the courts.

In the USSR there are the following courts: the Supreme Court of the USSR, the Supreme Courts of Union Republics, the Supreme Courts of Autonomous Republics, Territorial, Regional, and city courts, courts of Autonomous Regions, courts of Autonomous Areas, district (city) people's courts, and military tribunals in the Armed Forces.

*Article 152.* All courts in the USSR shall be formed on the principle of the election of judges and people's assessors.

People's judges of people's district (city) courts and judges of territorial, regional and city courts shall be elected by the corresponding higher Soviets of People's Deputies.

The judges of the Supreme Court of the USSR, Supreme Courts of Union and Autonomous Republics, courts of Autonomous Regions and Areas shall be elected respectively by the Supreme Soviet of the USSR, Supreme Soviets of Union and Autonomous Republics, Soviets of People's Deputies of Autonomous Regions and Areas.

People's assessors of people's district (city) courts shall be elected at meetings of citizens at their places of residence of work by a show of hands and people's assessors of higher courts by respective Soviets of People's Deputies.

The judges of military tribunals shall be elected by an open vote by the Presidium of the Supreme Soviet of the USSR and people's assessors by meetings of servicemen.

The judges of all courts shall be elected for a term of ten years. The people's assessors of all courts shall be elected for a term of five years.

The judges and people's assessors are responsible and accountable to the bodies that elected them or to their electors and may be recalled by them in the manner prescribed by law.

*Article 153.* The Supreme Court of the USSR is the highest judicial body in the USSR and supervises the administration of justice by the courts of the USSR and Union Republics within the limits established by law.

The Supreme Court of the USSR shall consist of a Chairman, Vice-Chairmen, members and people's assessors. The Chairmen of the Supreme Courts of Union Republics are *ex officio* members of the Supreme Court of the USSR.

The organisation and procedures of the Supreme Court of the USSR are defined in the Law of the Supreme Court of the USSR.

*Article 154.* The hearing of civil and criminal cases in all courts is collegial; in courts of first instance cases are heard with the participation of people's assessors. In the administration of justice people's assessors have all the rights of a judge.

*Article 155.* Judges and people's assessors are independent and subject only to the law.

Judges and people's assessors shall be ensured conditions for the free and effective discharge of their rights and duties. Any interference in the administration of justice by judges and people's assessors is impermissible and punishable by law.

The inviolability of judges and people's assessors and other guarantees of their independence are established by the Law on the Status of Judges in the USSR and other legislative acts of the USSR and Union Republics.

*Article 156.* Justice is administered in the USSR on the principle of the equality of citizens before the law and the court.

*Article 157.* Proceedings in all courts shall be open to the public. Hearings *in camera* are only allowed in cases provided for by law, with observance of all the rules of judicial procedure.

*Article 158.* A defendant in a criminal action is guaranteed the right to legal assistance.

*Article 159.* Judicial proceedings shall be conducted in the language of the Union Republic, Autonomous Republic, Autonomous Region, or Autonomous Area, or in the language spoken by the majority of the people in the locality. Persons participating in court proceedings, who do not know the language in which they are being conducted, shall be ensured the right to become fully acquainted with the materials in the case; the services of an interpreter during the proceedings; and the right to address the court in their own language.

*Article 160.* No one may be adjudged guilty of a crime and subjected to punishment as a criminal except by the sentence of a court and in conformity with the law.

*Article 161.* Colleges of advocates are available to give legal assistance to citizens and organisations. In cases provided for by legislation citizens shall be given legal assistance free of charge.

The organisation and procedure of the bar are determined by legislation of the USSR and Union Republics.

*Article 162.* Representatives of public organisations and of work collectives may take part in civil and criminal proceedings.

*Article 163.* Economic disputes between enterprises, institutions, and organisations are settled by state arbitration bodies within the limits of their jurisdiction.

The organisation and manner of functioning of state arbitration bodies are defined in the Law on State Arbitration in the USSR.

## Chapter 21   The Procurator's Office

*Article 164.* Supreme power of supervision over the strict and uniform observance of laws by all ministries, state committees and department, enterprises, institutions and organisations, executive-administrative bodies of local Soviets of People's Deputies, collective farms, cooperatives and other public organisations, officials, and citizens is vested in the Procurator-General of the USSR and procurators subordinate to him.

*Article 165.* The Procurator-General of the USSR is responsible and accountable to the Congress of People's Deputies of the USSR and the Supreme Soviet of the USSR.

*Article 166.* The procurators of Union Republics, Autonomous Republics, Territories, Regions, and Autonomous Regions are appointed by the Procurator-General of the USSR. The procurators of Autonomous Areas and district and city procurators are appointed by the Procurators of Union Republics, subject to confirmation by the Procurator-General of the USSR.

*Article 167.* The term of office of the Procurator-General of the USSR and all lower-ranking procurators shall be five years.

*Article 168.* The agencies of the Procurator's Office exercise their powers independently of any local bodies whatsoever, and are subordinate solely to the Procurator-General of the USSR.

The organisation and procedure of the agencies of the Procurator's Office are defined in the Law on the Procurator's Office of the USSR.

## VIII. THE EMBLEM, FLAG, ANTHEM, AND CAPITAL OF THE USSR

*Article 169.* The State Emblem of the Union of Soviet Socialist Republics is a hammer and sickle on a globe depicted in the rays of the sun and framed by ears of wheat, with the inscription "Workers of All Countries, Unite!" in the languages of the Union Republics. At the top of the Emblem is a five-pointed star.

*Article 170.* The State Flag of the Union of the Soviet Socialist Republics is a rectangle of red cloth with a hammer and sickle depicted in gold in the upper corner next to the staff and with a five-pointed red star edged in gold above them. The ratio of the width of the flag to its length is 1:2.

*Article 171.* The State Anthem of the Union of Soviet Socialist Republics is confirmed by the Presidium of the Supreme Soviet of the USSR.

*Article 172.* The Capital of the Union of Soviet Socialist Republics is the city of Moscow.

## IX. THE LEGAL FORCE OF THE CONSTITUTION OF THE USSR AND PROCEDURE FOR AMENDING THE CONSTITUTION

*Article 173.* The Constitution of the USSR shall have supreme legal force. All laws and other acts of state bodies shall be promulgated on the basis of and in conformity with it.

*Article 174.* The Constitution of the USSR may be amended by a decision of the Congress of People's Deputies of the USSR, adopted by a majority of not less than two-thirds of the total number of People's Deputies of the USSR.

# RUSSIAN HISTORY CHRONOLOGY

## THE BEGINNINGS

| | |
|---|---|
| 862 | Rus established as a political entity (Novgorod, later Kiev) |
| 988 | Conversion to Christianity |
| 1223 | Beginning of Mongol (Tatar) invasion (Battle of Kalka) |
| 1240–42 | Alexander "Nevsky" defeats Swedes and Germans |
| 1300s | Rise of Moscow |
| 1380 | Dmitri "Donskoy" defeats Tatars (Battle of Kulikovo) |
| 1472 | Ivan III's marriage to Sophia (Moscow—"the Third Rome") |
| 1480 | End of Tatar rule over Russia |

## 16th CENTURY

| | |
|---|---|
| 1533 | Accession of Ivan IV ("the Terrible") |
| 1547 | Ivan IV crowned czar |
| 1552 | Annexation of Kazan |
| 1556 | Annexation of Astrakhan |
| 1565 | Founding of *oprichnina* (political police) |
| 1582 | Beginning of the conquest of Siberia |
| 1584 | Death of Ivan; reign of Fyodr, 1584–1598 |

## "TIME OF TROUBLES"

| | |
|---|---|
| 1598 | End of first ("Ryurik") dynasty; Boris Godunov becomes czar |
| 1604 | "False Dmitri" challenges Godunov |
| 1605 | Godunov dies; "False Dmitri" becomes czar |
| 1606 | "False Dmitri" murdered; Vasilii Shuisky becomes czar |
| 1606–08 | Bolotnikov's uprising (peasant war) |
| 1610–13 | Poles occupy Moscow |
| 1612 | Minin and Pozharsky lead war of national liberation |
| 1613 | Romanov dynasty established |

## 17th CENTURY

| | |
|---|---|
| 1613 | Czar Mikhail (1613–1645) |
| 1637 | Russians reach Pacific Ocean |
| 1645 | Czar Alexis (1645–1676) |

| | |
|---|---|
| 1654 | "Reunification" with Ukraine |
| 1650's–60's | Religious schism |
| 1670–71 | Razin's uprising (peasant war) |
| 1676 | Czar Fyodr (1676–1682) |
| 1682 | Czars Peter and Ivan; Sophia's regency (1682–1689) |
| 1689 | Nerchinsk treaty with China |

## PETER THE GREAT'S REIGN

| | |
|---|---|
| 1689 | Accession of Peter as ruler |
| 1696 | Conquest of Azov |
| 1700 | Calendar reform |
| 1703 | Petersburg founded |
| 1708 | Administrative reforms |
| 1709 | Victory over Swedes (Battle of Poltava) |
| 1713 | Petersburg becomes capital |
| 1724 | Academy of Sciences founded |
| 1725 | Death of Peter |

## 18th CENTURY

| | |
|---|---|
| 1725–27 | Catherine I |
| 1727–30 | Peter II |
| 1730–40 | Anna |
| 1740–41 | Ivan VI |
| 1741 | Accession of Elizabeth (Peter's daughter) |
| 1755 | University of Moscow founded |
| 1762 | Death of Elizabeth; Peter III |
| 1762 | Catherine II ("the Great") |
| 1773–74 | Pugachev's uprising (peasant war) |
| 1796 | Death of Catherine II; Paul (1796–1801) |

## 19th CENTURY

| | |
|---|---|
| 1801 | Alexander I (1801–1825); beginning of the conquest of the Caucasus |
| 1809 | Annexation of Finland |
| 1812 | Napoleon occupies Moscow; Russian victory |
| 1825 | Decembrist Uprising; Nikolai I (1825–1855) |
| 1853–56 | Crimean War |
| 1855 | Alexander II (1855–1881) |
| 1861 | Emancipation of serfs |
| 1864 | Judicial reforms |
| 1870 | Local government reform |
| 1874 | Army reform |
| 1881 | Assassination of Alexander II; Alexander III (1881–1894) |

| | |
|---|---|
| 1894 | Nikolai II (1894–1917) |
| 1898 | First (founding) Congress of RSDWP (Russian Social Democratic Workers' Party) |

## 20th CENTURY

| | |
|---|---|
| 1903 | Second Party Congress (Bolshevik-Menshevik split) |
| 1904–05 | Russo-Japanese War |
| 1905 | "Bloody Sunday," abortive revolution; October "manifesto" |
| 1906 | Duma (parliament) elected |
| 1914 | World War; military setbacks |

## RUSSIAN REVOLUTION, 1917

| | |
|---|---|
| March | Demonstrations and riots; formation of Provisional Government; abdication of Nikolai II; Lvov becomes Prime Minister |
| April | Lenin returns to Russia; Russia to continue war |
| May | Coalition Provisional Government |
| June | First Congress of Soviets |
| July | Bolshevik abortive uprising; Kerensky becomes Prime Minister |
| August | Sixth Party Congress |
| September | Kornilov attempts to seize power |
| October | Bolsheviks gain power in *soviets* |
| November | Bolshevik Revolution (November 7); Soviet government |
| December | Left SRs (Social Revolutionaries) join government |

## SOVIET ERA

| | |
|---|---|
| 1918 | Government moves to Moscow; Left SRs quit government; attempt on Lenin's life; beginning of civil war and foreign intervention; Seventh Party Congress |
| 1919 | "White" armies advance toward Moscow; founding of Comintern; Eighth Party Congress |
| 1920 | "Whites" defeated; end of civil war; Ninth Party Congress |
| 1921 | Tenth Party Congress; Kronstadt uprising; beginning of NEP |
| 1922 | Eleventh Party Congress; Stalin becomes secretary general; USSR founded (December 30); Lenin's illness |
| 1923 | Twelfth Party Congress; power struggle begins |
| 1924 | Lenin dies ( January 21); Thirteenth Party Congress; power struggle continues; first USSR Constitution (December 31) |
| 1925 | Fourteenth Party Congress; Trotsky loses power |
| 1926 | Kamenyev, Zinovyev, Trotsky ousted from Politburo |
| 1927 | Fifteenth Party Congress; Trotsky expelled from Party |
| 1928 | End of NEP; Commission of First Five-Year Plan |

| 1929 | Mass collectivization begins; Trotsky expelled from USSR; Bukharin ousted from Politburo |
| 1930 | Continuation of mass collectivization; Sixteenth Party Congress; Rykov ousted from Politburo |
| 1931 | Rapid industrialization; mass famine |
| 1932 | Consolidation of all writers' groups |
| 1933 | Recognition by United States |
| 1934 | Seventeenth Party Congress; First Congress of Writers' Union; assassination of Kirov (December 1); beginning of mass terror |
| 1935 | Comintern supports "popular fronts"; Stakhanov movement begins (overfulfillment of production quotas) |
| 1936 | "Stalin" Constitution (December 6); "Show trials" |
| 1937 | Ordzhonikidze commits suicide; arrests of military leaders |
| 1938 | Beria becomes head of security |
| 1939 | Soviet-Nazi pact; annexation of west Byelorussia and west Ukraine; Eighteenth Party Congress |
| 1940 | Annexation of Baltic republics and Bessarabia; Soviet-Finnish War |

## WORLD WAR II (GREAT PATRIOTIC WAR)

| 1941 | Germany attacks (June 22); major military setbacks; Red Army in retreat; Germans take Kiev and approach Moscow and Leningrad; Red Army repels offensive against Moscow |
| 1942 | Germans advance to Volga and north Caucasus; Battle of Stalingrad; Red Army begins its counteroffensive |
| 1943 | Battle of Kursk; liberation of most of Soviet territory; Teheran Conference |
| 1944 | Red Army enters east Europe: Romania, Bulgaria, Poland, Czechoslovakia, Hungary |
| 1945 | Battle of Berlin (April, May); Germany surrenders (May 9); Yalta and Potsdam Conferences; War against Japan (August 8); occupation of Manchuria and North Korea |

## POSTWAR ERA

| 1946 | Reconstitution of economy begins, Zhdanov attacks writers |
| 1947 | Truman Doctrine; Cominform established |
| 1948 | Berlin blockade; break with Tito |
| 1949 | First Soviet atomic bomb tested; Communists take over China; Comecon founded |
| 1950 | Korean War begins |
| 1952 | Nineteenth Party Congress |
| 1953 | Stalin dies (March 5); Beria-Malenkov-Molotov takeover; Beria falls (June); Khrushchev becomes head of Party; Soviet H-bomb developed |

| 1954 | Literary "thaw" begins; Khrushchev visits China |
|------|------|
| 1955 | Malenkov resigns; Warsaw Pact formed |
| 1956 | Twentieth Party Congress; "De-Stalinization" begins; Hungarian Revolt |
| 1957 | Ouster of "anti-Party group" (Malenkov, Molotov, and others); first *sputnik* launched |
| 1958 | Khrushchev assumes dual leadership (party-government) |
| 1959 | Twenty-first Party Congress; Khrushchev visits the United States and China |
| 1960 | USSR-China quarrel begins |
| 1961 | Twenty-second Party Congress; Gagarin becomes the first man in space |
| 1962 | Cuban missile crisis |
| 1964 | Khrushchev forced to retire; Brezhnev takes over as General Secretary |
| 1966 | Twenty-third Party Congress |
| 1968 | Intervention in Czechoslovakia |
| 1971 | Twenty-fourth Party Congress; Khrushchev dies (September) |
| 1972 | SALT I; Brezhnev-Nixon meeting in Moscow; "détente" |
| 1973 | Brezhnev visits Washington |
| 1974 | Vladivostok meeting (Brezhnev-Ford); Solzhenitsyn expelled from USSR |
| 1975 | Helsinki Accord (European Security Conference) |
| 1976 | Twenty-fifth Party Congress; Tenth Five-Year Plan begins |
| 1977 | "Brezhnev" Constitution; Brezhnev becomes chief of state |
| 1979 | SALT II (Brezhnev-Carter meeting); Afghanistan crisis |
| 1980 | American-Soviet tensions, Moscow Olympics, Polish crisis |
| 1981 | Reagan's economic sanctions, Twenty-sixth Party Congress, Eleventh Five-Year Plan begins |
| 1982 | Gas pipeline controversy, START; Andropov succeeds Brezhnev as General Secretary after Brezhnev's death (November 10). |
| 1983 | Andropov's "anticorruption" campaign begins; Andropov becomes chief of state; Korean airliner shot down over Sakhalin (September 1) |
| 1984 | Andropov dies (February 9) and is succeeded as General Secretary by Chernenko. |
| 1985 | Chernenko dies (March 10) and Gorbachev becomes General Secretary; Gorbachev meets Reagan in Geneva (November) |
| 1986 | Twenty-seventh Party Congress (February-March); Twelfth Five-Year Plan begins; Chernobyl nuclear disaster (April-May); Gorbachev-Reagan meeting in Reykjavik (October); ethnic riots in Alma-Ata (December) |
| 1987 | Gorbachev-Reagan meeting in Washington; INF Treaty (December) |
| 1988 | Armenian-Azerbaijan clashes; Gorbachev-Reagan meeting in Moscow (May-June); Twentieth All-Union Party |

Conference (July-August); Gorbachev becomes chief of
state (October); Soviet Constitution amended; Gorbachev
speaks at the U.N. in New York; earthquake in Armenia
(December).

1989    Violent repression of nationalist demonstrations in Georgia
(April); multi-candidate elections of People's Deputies
(April-May); Gorbachev's visit to China (May); ethnic
clashes in Uzbekistan (June); ethnic strife between Armenia
and Azerbaijan; Lithuanian bid for independce (October-
December); Gorbachev-Bush meeting in Malta (December).

# MIKHAIL SERGEYEVICH GORBACHEV
## (A SHORT BIOGRAPHY)

Mikhail Sergeyevich Gorbachev was born on March 2, 1931, in a village called Privolnoye near the city of Stavropol in the northern part of the Caucasus, some 800 miles south of Moscow. His parents and grandparents were peasants. An only child, the boy had to start earning his keep at age 14, combining a summer job as an apprentice field mechanic with his schooling the rest of the year.

There were several unusual circumstances related to Gorbachev's early years which distinguish him from his predecessors in the top Kremlin position: Both his father and grandfather on the paternal side were card-carrying party members. Gorbachev was born and grew up during the third and fourth postrevolution decades, i.e. the Stalin era. As an 11-year-old boy, he lived for several months under the Nazi occupation of his native village. At the early age of 18 (1949), Gorbachev was awarded the Order of the Labor Red Banner for his summer work on the collective farm. And the next year (1950) he applied for admission to the CPSU. He became a full member shortly after his twentieth birthday, thus continuing his family's tradition.

By that time (1952), Gorbachev distinguished himself in two more ways: He succeeded against formidable odds to be admitted to the prestigious Moscow State University, and he chose law as his academic specialization over other majors seemingly more promising and consistent with his background.

Perhaps more predictable was Gorbachev's active involvement in party and Komsomol work while pursuing his legal studies. Still, he managed to maintain a high grade average.

After graduating as a lawyer in 1955, he was offered and accepted a Komsomol position in Stavropol. During the same year, he married Raisa Titorenko whom he had met several years earlier at the Moscow State University. The next year (1956), the young couple had their only child—a daughter, named Irina, who is a medical doctor today. She is married and has a young daughter—the Gorbachevs' only grandchild.

In 1956 and 1960, Gorbachev was promoted to be the head of the Komsomol organization in the city of Stavropol and in the Stavropol province, respectively.

In 1962, at 31, Gorbachev gave up his promising career in the Komsomol in favor of an entrance-level job in the local party machine with responsibility for agriculture. At the same time, he enrolled as a correspondence student in the Stavropol Agricultural Institute from which he received his second college diploma in 1967.

His rise in the party hierarchy was swift: In 1966, he became the First Secretary of the Stovropol city committee; in 1968 came his promotion to the Second Secretary of the province; and in 1970, Gorbachev reached the number one local position—the First Secretary of the Stavropol province. A year later (1971), he was made a full member of the CPSU Central Committee, skipping the intermediate status of candidate member.

But Gorbachev's real break came in 1978 when he was appointed a Secretary of the Central Committee in charge of agriculture for the entire country. The rank of a candidate member of the Politburo followed one year later (1979), and in October 1980, Gorbachev became the youngest full member of Brezhnev's Politburo. On the occasion of his fiftieth birthday in 1981, he was awarded the Order of Lenin. But in 1982, although there were no known disagreements between Brezhnev and Gorbachev, the latter's career seemed to be headed for an early demise, apparently because of a need for a scapegoat for poor harvests.

Under Andropov, who succeeded Brezhnev in November 1982, Gorbachev's star rose again. Still he was not seriously considered as a candidate for the top position at the time of the Kremlin's next change of guard in 1984. But during the short tenure of Chernenko (February 1984 to March 1985), Gorbachev began to act as his heir apparent.

Gorbachev became General Secretary on March 11, 1985. Since December 1988, he has also occupied the position of the chief of state. In 1990, his two titles were changed to "Chairman" and "President." Presumably, his tenure in either of these offices may not exceed two five-year terms.

Gorbachev is the author of several books, the best known of which, *Perestroika and New Thinking*, has been translated into many languages.

# Index